T0366906

A MIGHTY
FINE ROAD

RAILROADS PAST AND PRESENT

H. ROGER GRANT AND THOMAS HOBACK, *EDITORS*

A MIGHTY FINE ROAD

A HISTORY OF THE CHICAGO, ROCK ISLAND & PACIFIC RAILROAD COMPANY

H. Roger Grant

INDIANA UNIVERSITY PRESS

This book is a publication of

Indiana University Press
Office of Scholarly Publishing
Herman B Wells Library 350
1320 East 10th Street
Bloomington, Indiana 47405 USA

iupress.indiana.edu

Manufactured in the United
States of America

Library of Congress Cataloging-
in-Publication Data

Names: Grant, H. Roger, [date] author.
Title: A mighty fine road : a history of
    the Chicago, Rock Island & Pacific
    Railroad Company / H. Roger Grant.
Description: Bloomington, Indiana :
    Indiana University Press, [2020] |
    Series: Railroads past and present |
    Includes index. | Summary: "The
Chicago, Rock Island & Pacific Railroad's
history is one of big booms
and bigger busts. When it became
the first railroad to reach and then
cross the Mississippi River in 1856,
it emerged as a leading American
railroad company. But after aggressive
expansion and a subsequent change
in management, the company struggled
and eventually declared bankruptcy
in 1915. What followed was a cycle of
resurrections and bankruptcies; a
grueling, ten-year, ultimately
unsuccessful battle to merge with the
Union Pacific; and the Rock Island's
final liquidation in 1981. But
today, long after its glory days and
eventual demise, the "Mighty Fine
Road" has left behind a living
legacy of major and feeder lines
throughout the country. In his latest
work, railroad historian H. Roger
Grant offers an accessible, gorgeously
illustrated, and comprehensive
history of this iconic American
Railroad"—Provided by publisher.
Identifiers: LCCN 2019050592 (print) |
    LCCN 2019050593 (ebook) | ISBN
    9780253049889 (hardback) | ISBN
    9780253049896 (ebook)
Subjects: LCSH: Chicago, Rock Island,
    and Pacific Railroad Company (1948-)
Classification: LCC TF25.C53 G73 2020
    (print) | LCC TF25.C53 (ebook) |
    DDC 385.0973—dc23
LC record available at https://
    lccn.loc.gov/2019050592
LC ebook record available at https://
    lccn.loc.gov/2019050593

1 2 3 4 5   25 24 23 22 21 20

FOR MY RETIRED CLEMSON UNIVERSITY COLLEAGUE, RICHARD SAUNDERS JR. RICH, A DISTINGUISHED RAILROAD SCHOLAR, UNDERSTANDS AND APPRECIATES THE ROCK ISLAND EXPERIENCE.

CONTENTS

PREFACE

I HAVE LONG BEEN FAMILIAR WITH THE CHICAGO, ROCK ISLAND & Pacific Railroad, more commonly known as the Rock Island or the Rock. I knew it from personal experience, as well as from writing company histories of the Chicago & North Western, Chicago Great Western, and Wabash and biographies of two individuals who held executive positions with the road.

Although the Rock Island did not serve my hometown of Albia, Iowa, I saw its trains in the neighboring communities of Centerville and Chariton. I still recall happenings at the Chariton station. In September 1948 family friends took my mother and me to watch the Harry Truman campaign special make a whistle stop during his successful bid for the presidency. Four years later my brother Richard (Dick), a marine, arrived there on the *Twin Star Rocket*, coming home on leave from Camp Pendleton, California. That was a joyous event. The following week that happiness evaporated when Dick boarded the *Rocket* to return to California and deployment to Korea. Much later, as a student at Simpson College in Indianola, Iowa, I frequently heard and sometimes watched a Rock Island crew switch the Laverty grain elevators and Honegger's feed mill. Much to my delight, the railroad often assigned one of its odd-looking BL2 locomotives to this branch line.

Then there were my Rock Island–related biographies. In 2008 *Visionary Railroader: Jervis Langdon Jr. and the Transportation Revolution* appeared, and a decade later *John W. Barriger III: Railroad Legend* was published. As president of the Rock Island in the 1960s, Langdon valiantly attempted to save the company through upgrades and a merger with the Union Pacific. A decade earlier Barriger, as a vice president, served as the right-hand man to President John Dow Farrington, focusing on bolstering freight traffic and the corporate image. I also explored an episode in the aftermath of the Rock Island liquidation in *Railroaders without Borders: History of the Railroad*

Development Corporation, published in 2015. This book examines the troubled years of the Iowa Railroad and the successor Iowa Interstate Railroad. After a rocky start, the IAIS, which became a Railroad Development Corporation property, made the former Rock Island main line between greater Chicago and Council Bluffs and the Peoria branch into a progressive and profitable regional railroad.

Why study the Rock Island? My interest involved more than personal memories and specialized Rock Island–related professional interests; I realized that the company lacked a *comprehensive* modern history. The only non-pictorial book is flawed and badly outdated. This is *Iron Road to Empire: The History of 100 Years of the Progress and Achievements of the Rock Island Lines*, which appeared in 1953 from Simmons-Boardman Corporation, a New York City–based railroad publisher. Its author, William Edward Hayes, an experienced journalist and an accomplished short-story writer, served as the Rock Island's public relations person. Although his breezy and undocumented work is slanted favorably toward the Farrington regime, it contains insider information, especially about personalities. In this way the Hayes book has elements of a primary source document. Much, of course, has occurred since the appearance of this centennial publication. Most notably, the Rock Island received the dubious distinction of being the largest American railroad to have been liquidated. This chapter of the Rock Island has been told by Gregory Schneider in *Rock Island Requiem: The Collapse of a Mighty Fine Line*.

While the final years of the Rock Island story are fascinating, its history from gestation in the mid-nineteenth century to the last quarter of the twentieth century is one of boom-or-bust cycles, interregional development, "real" robber barons, dedicated leaders and employees, and technological and operational innovations and advancements. If the company had extended its Golden State Line beyond New Mexico to California or acquired an existing connection to the Pacific, it might have become a stronger and more enduring property. In reality, the Rock Island never became much more than a sprawling agriculturally dependent granger road with its heaviest concentration of lines in Iowa, Kansas, and Oklahoma. Although a well-known folk song called the Rock Island a "mighty fine road," such an assessment contains glaring flaws. Yet its catchy tune and varied lyrics, which date from the 1930s, have helped to give the Rock Island recognition and a degree of immortality.

Since the Rock Island Railroad experienced a lengthy history, dating back to the late 1840s, and operated thousands of miles of lines in multiple states and territories by the early twentieth century, it might seem wise to write a longer account. Some comparable railroads have had books that far exceed the word count in this work. Maury Klein's three-volume history of the Union Pacific and Richard Overton's detailed one-volume study of the Chicago, Burlington & Quincy are examples. Word limitations are the norm in present-day academic publishing, and so this Rock Island story has been limited to the more acceptable range of one hundred thousand words. This "short history," nevertheless, provides space to reveal the whats, whys, and so-whats of this "mighty fine road."

ACKNOWLEDGMENTS

ALL ACADEMIC BOOKS ARE THE RESULT OF OUTSIDE ASSISTANCE. THIS history of the Chicago, Rock & Pacific Railroad is no exception. Help came from the John W. Barriger III National Railroad Library, Chicago History Center, Cooper Library Interlibrary Loan Department at Clemson University, Library of Congress, National Archives, Rock Island County Historical Society, Windsor Chamber of Commerce, and from these individuals: Judith Anderson, F. D. Brosnan, Tom Brugman, Keith Bryant, Josh Catalano, Stephen Dock, Jim Farrell, Henry Frick, Nick Fry, Michael Hibblen, Bill Hoenig, Don Hofsommer, Tom Koglin, Bob Lipka, Scott Lothes, Ron Lundstrum, Louis Marre, Craig Myers, Dennis Opforman, David Pfeiffer, William Pollard, Henry Posner III, Eric Rasmussen, Rich Saunders, Ben Safourek, and George Werner. Dan Sabin deserves special recognition, having most of all taken time to supply a large number of illustrations from his vast Rock Island photographic collection.

A portion of the research stemmed from my earlier publications. These include studies on the Chicago & North Western, Chicago Great Western, Eire Lackawanna, and Wabash Railroads, Railroad Development Corporation, and biographies of John W. Barriger III and Jervis Langdon Jr.

With my previous books with Indiana University Press, staff members have been professional and supportive through the stages of publication. A generous William D. Middleton Fellowship from the Railway & Locomotive Historical Society aided my research. I also thank the Lemon family who created my Kathryn and Calhoun Lemon Professorship. This financial assistance has continued to advance my scholarly activities.

H. Roger Grant
Clemson University
Clemson, South Carolina

A MIGHTY FINE ROAD

PIONEER RAILROAD

IN THE EARLY 1830S THE RAILWAY AGE HAD ITS PRACTICAL BEGINNINGS. The Baltimore & Ohio Railroad, South Carolina Canal & Rail Road, Camden & Amboy Railroad, and several other companies blazed the way for what by mid-century had developed into a network of nearly nine thousand miles of iron ribbons. In the coming decades iron and then steel rails spidered their way across the landscape. The 1830s and 1840s especially became an exciting time for the evolving railroad industry, an era best described as the demonstration period.

Before prototypes of locomotives and other rolling stock, metal rails, roadbed, and track gauges had been introduced or standardized, transportation enthusiasts contemplated better ways to ship and travel. Toward the end of the eighteenth century and the beginning of the nineteenth century, hundreds of miles of improved roads were being built, usually in association with the short-lived turnpike craze. Still, travel by cart, wagon, or stagecoach was frequently an ordeal. Most roads and trails were miserable and often impassible during the "mud season" and at other times throughout the year. Bad roads remained a persistent problem for much of the nation, including the Midwest. Then there were the possibilities of enhanced water transport. Americans hoped that this alternative could improve their connectedness. The introduction of steam-powered vessels on coastal waters, lakes, and rivers did much to improve speed, dependability, and travel pleasures. Yet these natural waterways did not always serve well the needs of the Republic. "Bountiful as Providence has been in supplying our country with great lakes and mighty rivers, they are found inadequate to the wants of society," opined a nineteenth-century observer. They often failed to provide the most desirable routes. But by using a time-tested, low-level technology—canals—Americans found a way to improve their transportation network. As the 363-mile New York State–funded Erie Canal took shape, opening in 1825 between the Hudson

River at Albany and Lake Erie at Buffalo, it sparked a domestic ditch-digging boom. During this golden age of canals, more than four thousand miles of these artificial rivers linked hundreds of communities. Residents in sections of the Old Northwest and the Middle Atlantic region benefited the most from these slow, albeit safe and smooth, travel ways. Admittedly, natural and artificial water options had their shortcomings: rivers flooded and fell, and in cooler climes freezing temperatures halted river, lake, and canal movements. Additional problems plagued this transport form.[1]

Canals, however, provided an unintended benefit. Since communities and businesses sprang up or expanded at canal side, these waterways blazed the way for numerous railroad corridors. By the Civil War era, the New York Central & Hudson River Railroad paralleled the Erie Canal, the Pennsylvania Railroad followed much of the Pennsylvania State Works canals, and the Wabash Railroad (née Toledo, Wabash & Western Railroad) adjoined the northern portion of the Wabash & Erie Canal. There were more examples, including what became the Chicago, Rock Island & Pacific Railroad (Rock Island), which followed the Illinois & Michigan Canal (I&M).

Compared to neighboring Indiana and Ohio, Illinois claimed fewer canal miles, and it had only a single artery, the Illinois & Michigan. Just as canal fever developed elsewhere in the 1820s, internal improvement proponents appeared in the Prairie State. In 1823 lawmakers created a canal commission, and two years later they chartered a company for such a project. It was obvious where this waterway would be located. For generations the belief had existed that Lake Michigan and the Illinois River could be readily connected, and that assessment was correct. What became the I&M Canal would begin on the southwestern corner of Lake Michigan (site of Fort Dearborn and what is now Chicago) and terminate near La Salle, traversing a distance of slightly less than a hundred miles. In the process it would pass from the Chicago River, cross the summit to the valley of the Des Plaines River, and follow that stream to its confluence with the Kankakee River, where the Illinois River began. From that point the canal would continue to near the mouth of the Little Vermilion River and the rapids of the Illinois. Below that obstruction the Illinois was navigable by steamboat to where it emptied into the Mississippi River in Greater Saint Louis near Alton, Illinois.[2]

Although the topography for the proposed I&M Canal was conducive for construction, the actual building took time, resembling scores of antebellum canal and railroad projects. Various factors explain why this canal took a dozen years to build. They include the impact of the Panic of 1837, which crippled state finances; internal mismanagement at the I&M; chronic labor shortages; and disease. Yet canal boosters remained undeterred. They heartily endorsed the logic of this statement made in 1835: "What would be the value of even the fertile Prairies of Illinois removed from her large rivers?" Finally, the I&M officially opened on April 16, 1848, at a cost of $6.4 million ($180.2 million in current dollars). It became one of America's last great canals. Backers took pride in their accomplishment; they had created a modern waterway with its fifteen locks and four aqueducts. "Yesterday was an eventful period in the history of our city, of the state, and of the West," proclaimed the *Chicago Weekly Journal*. "It was the wedding of the Father of Rivers to our inland seas—a union of the Mississippi with Lake Michigan." Freight and passenger traffic boomed on this state-owned artery, making the northern and central sections of Illinois more attractive for settlement and economic development. Undeniably, the I&M Canal had a positive impact on its service territory, most of all on a rapidly growing Chicago. The Lakeside City captured much of the Illinois River valley grain trade and other traffic that previously had gone to its greatest rival, Saint Louis. It also became "the ordinary route for passengers from St. Louis to Chicago." The canal, in fact, became the city's first major commercial feeder.[3]

COMING OF THE IRON HORSE

Eighteen forty-eight was also the year when the first railroad to serve the future rail mecca Chicago began operations. The honor went to the Galena & Chicago Union Railroad (Galena), a component of the future Chicago & North Western Railway System. About the time work started on the I&M Canal, lawmakers approved incorporation of this hoped-for railroad. The Galena was intended to link the settlement around Fort Dearborn to the transportation-starved area to the northwest, reaching Galena and the surrounding lead district in Jo Daviess County, which adjoined the Mississippi River. (Galena was the larger community, and so it received top corporate-name billing.) Farmers and townspeople alike along this projected route considered the I&M Canal to be either inconvenient or impractical, and so they embraced the iron horse for this lake to river artery. Like the emerging canal, the Galena encountered setbacks, being especially hard-hit by the Panic of 1837. Rails never reached the announced destination, extending ultimately only to Freeport, 121 miles from Chicago.[4]

Other contemporary railroad projects in Illinois similarly experienced difficulties. Only one of several grand railroad schemes, which totaled 1,341 miles and which were instigated by the state's ambitious and financially disastrous 1837 "Act to Establish and Maintain a General System of Internal Improvements," ever became operable. This was the Northern Cross Railroad, designed to stretch from the Mississippi River at Quincy through Meredosia, Jacksonville, Springfield, Decatur, and Danville to the Wabash & Erie Canal in nearby Indiana. By 1841 only fifty-seven miles of rickety strap-iron track had opened, connecting Meredosia on the Illinois River with Springfield on the Sangamon River. The strategy was to build cheaply; future profits would permit rebuilding and modernization. Completion of the Northern Cross as a trans-Illinois artery became another victim of the strained financial circumstances of the state. Later in the decade, private investors bought this decrepit property at a bargain-basement price and eventually lengthened it and brought it into the orbit of the Wabash Railroad.[5]

Notwithstanding the failures to expand the presence of the iron horse in the Prairie State, in time a renewed spirit of optimism swept the region. By the mid-1840s the economic turmoil caused by the recent panic had mostly subsided, and Illinoisans concocted plans to exploit the best replacement transport—railroads. Advocates realized their unmatched speed, year-round dependability, and routing flexibility. Railroad fever, which had showed signs of developing in the 1830s, had blossomed forth by the mid-1840s. Yet early on most residents likely considered this statement, made by Abraham Lincoln in 1832 during his initial campaign for the state legislature, to be farfetched if not insane: "No other improvement that reason will justify as in hoping for can equal in utility the rail road. It is a never failing source of communication, between places of business remotely situated from each other." The future American president continued: "Upon the rail road the regular progress of commercial intercourse is not interrupted by either high or low water, or freezing weather, which are the principal difficulties that render our future hopes of water communication precarious and uncertain." Eventually virtually no one questioned the veracity of Lincoln's youthful remarks. After all, this was a time when most people longed for better transportation.[6]

ROCK ISLAND & LA SALLE RAILROAD

It is unclear exactly when the first segment of the Rock Island Railroad was contemplated, but by the mid-1840s, serious discussions were occurring. Although this scheme had strong backers in Illinois, some in neighboring Iowa also expressed a keen interest. Residents of the Hawkeye State who lived in Davenport, the bustling seat of Scott County situated on the Mississippi River across from Rock Island (known then as Rock Island City), caught the railroad bug. Several of its civic leaders spearheaded talk about having a rail-road link Rock Island to the projected terminus of the Illinois & Michigan Canal. These individuals included James Grant, a North Carolina–born law-yer, jurist, politician, and later first president of what became the Rock Island & La Salle Railroad (RI&LS). Grant had been an iron horse zealot for some time, having participated in the organization of the Davenport & Iowa City Rail Road, Iowa's first railroad, in 1850. Another advocate was Colonel George Davenport, prominent American Indian agent, respected businessman, and real-estate developer who lived on Rock Island (today's Arsenal Island).[7]

Citizens on both banks of the Mississippi River saw the great economic advantages of a railroad that would connect their communities to the East. Although they had access to water transport for such downstream destina-tions as Saint Louis, Memphis, and New Orleans, along with points on the Ohio River and the other navigable streams that made up this vast drainage system, there were disadvantages. From the perspective of those who shipped and traveled on the Upper Mississippi, recurring low water levels during the late summer and early fall caused problems. Moreover, the river often froze during the winter, remaining in that state for perhaps several months. And ice floes and flooding became a detriment to travel after spring thaws and heavy rains. Then the Lower Rapids, or Des Moines Rapids, which extended between the Iowa communities of Montrose and Keokuk, posed another inconvenience. When water was too low, freight needed to be reloaded into small shallow-draft lighters or be transported by wagons over twelve miles of rutted and dusty roads around this obstacle, and passengers needed to take the lighters or roadway vehicles as well. The delay took hours and increased trans-portation costs. A further impediment, albeit somewhat less severe, existed with the Upper Rapids, or Rock Island Rapids, located about fifteen miles north of Rock Island. Although the federal government improved river trans-port through the Lower Rapids in 1838–1839, the Mississippi River continued to have choke points. It was no misstatement that people and commerce faced "the tedious and uncertain route of the river to New Orleans."[8]

The plans for this Rock Island City to La Salle railroad reflected the widely accepted strategy for the use of the iron horse. During the demonstration period the common thinking was to extend iron rails from one form of water transportation to another. Generally speaking, the concept of a railroad oper-ating independently of water routes was only slowly evolving.

Railroad talk turned to action. Energetic men, including James Grant and others from along the anticipated route through this lightly populated and gentle prairie terrain, persevered in their quest. Early in January 1847 at a well-attended meeting of railroad enthusiasts in Rock Island City, the discussion focused on "taking into consideration the propriety of petitioning the Legislature of Illinois, now in session, for the grant of a charter authorizing a company to construct a railroad from [Rock Island] to intersect with the Illinois and Michigan canal." More meetings followed, and lawmakers responded. On February 27, 1847, the Illinois General Assembly granted a charter to the Rock Island & La Salle Railroad Company. It permitted formation of a corporation that could construct a rail line from Rock Island to "the Illinois River, at the termination of the Illinois & Michigan Canal." The capital stock would be issued in $100 shares for a total of $300,000, an amount that could be increased to exceed $1 million. Commissioners would receive subscriptions, and the books would be opened within twelve months. After the requisite amount of stock had been subscribed, the commissioners would oversee election of nine directors. The railroad could then take shape.[9]

The creation of a state charter did not mean that construction crews would soon go to work. There was, of course, the determination to make the paper Rock Island & La Salle Railroad a reality. "Let our Motto be agitate, agitate, agitate, until the object is accomplished," the *Davenport Gazette* editorialized in early March 1847. A preliminary survey took place, but unfortunately investors along the route did not rush to subscribe to company stock. In February 1848 books had opened, but fourteen months later the number of shares taken totaled 2,263, falling short of the 3,000 required to reach the $300,000 that would trigger an election of directors. At last good news came: the requisite number had been achieved by November 1850.[10]

The paper RI&LS project then stalled. It was not topography or matters of technology that stopped the railroad, but rather the overall lack of capital needed to construct and equip this eighty-two-mile line. Davenport and Rock Island remained frontier communities, and there were only modest settlements between the Rock Island area and the terminus of the I&M Canal. Major investors with a grander view of railroading became essential.

The year 1851 saw the appearance of outsiders with vision and money-raising skills. It would be Henry Farnam and Joseph Sheffield who did much to breathe life into the RI&LS. Both men made their own special contributions, although Farnam played the more active role.

Who was Henry Farnam? Typical of so many self-made railroad entrepreneurs of the nineteenth century, he came from old Yankee stock and grew up in a large farm family. Born in the west-central New York village of Scipio in 1803, Farnam received only a limited formal education. But this bright, ambitious lad loved mathematics and poetry, which one writer believed to be "strangely unrelated." He studied on his own and was mostly self-taught. In what was a Horatio Alger–style rags-to-riches story, Farnam, who despised farming, initially taught in a country school as a teenager but subsequently joined on with a contractor who was building a section of the Erie Canal. Here Farnam learned the art of surveying and civil engineering and advanced from rodman to assistant engineer. While working on canal projects in New York State, Farnam contracted malaria, prompting him to move to his parents' home state of Connecticut to find a healthier environment. Fortunately, he fully recovered. While there, Farnam became associated with Davis Hurd, a relative who was the chief engineer engaged in building the Farmington Canal. This involved constructing a waterway from New Haven north to the Connecticut border at Southwick, where it would connect with the projected Hampshire & Hamden Canal to Northampton, Massachusetts, on the Connecticut River. In 1828, following three years of construction, this fifty-eight-mile undertaking opened, although the twenty-mile Massachusetts connector would not be completed until 1833.[11]

When Davis Hurd resigned in 1827, Henry Farnam assumed his duties and struggled to make the waterway a success. The job proved challenging, facing problems ranging from damages caused by flash floods to endless financial headaches. In the mid-1830s the canal underwent a forced reorganization, becoming the New Haven & Northampton Canal Company. With this corporate change, the thrifty Farnam found his stock investments in the predecessor firm wiped out, but he stayed on with its successor.[12]

While Farnam served as chief engineer and superintendent in the employ of the New Haven & Northampton Canal Company, he met Joseph Sheffield, a Connecticut-born businessman with a fortune made in merchandising and the cotton trade. Sheffield, who had purchased a large block of canal stock, became president and paid close attention to his investment. Farnam caught his eye. Sheffield admired his new acquaintance for his honesty, loyalty, and singleness of purpose. It did not take long for Farnam and Sheffield to become good friends and business associates. "No disagreement ever seems to have arisen between the partners, and to their commercial relations were added an intimacy and friendship which nothing ever marred," remembered Farnam's son, Henry W. Farnam.[13]

Notwithstanding the hard work of Henry Farnam, by the mid-1840s the canal could not cope with growing operational problems and railroad competition. "Twenty years of experience had demonstrated that a canal would not pay," recalled his son. Transportation historian George Rogers Taylor agreed, calling this waterway "the longest, most costly, and least successful of

New England canals." It is easy to understand why Joseph Sheffield, who had become virtually the sole owner, sold most of his shares in 1845, following an unprecedented drought that badly disrupted traffic and decimated revenues.[14]

But the New Haven & Northampton Canal did not fade totally from the transportation picture. Farnam had an idea. Why not convert the canal into a railroad? "This measure would evidently save the expense of acquiring the right-of-way and of doing a great deal of the grading and would, at the same time, substitute for the antiquated canal a more efficient means of communication." Sheffield agreed. This was hardly a startling response; after all, in the early 1840s Sheffield had begun to acquire stock in the gestating Hartford & New Haven Rail Road, and he had become intrigued with the possibility of constructing a rail line from New Haven to New York City. Farnam likewise endorsed that scheme. Not only did work start on the Connecticut-chartered New York & New Haven, but in 1846 state lawmakers granted permission for the failing canal company to morph into a railroad, the New York & Northampton (Canal Railroad). Sheffield became president, and Farnam took charge of survey and construction work. By early 1848, rails extended from New Haven to Plainville, Connecticut, and two years later they reached the Connecticut town of Collinsville.[15]

The visionary Sheffield wanted to consolidate his railroad interests. He planned for the New York & New Haven to lease the Canal Railroad. When these roads became operational, it would be possible to create a through route from New York City to Boston via the Western Rail Road of Massachusetts. This plan fizzled. The problem became the Hartford & New Haven Rail Road (H&NH), a company that was extending its line toward Springfield, and "the canal railroad threatened unpleasant competition." Representatives of the H&NH somehow convinced directors of the New York & Hartford to halt work on the New York & Northampton. To worsen matters, the politically powerful Western Rail Road sought to prevent the canal road from obtaining a Massachusetts charter, "a move which some folk believed was instigated by the Hartford & New Haven." So what to do? In 1850 Sheffield and Farman decided to liquidate their holdings in the New York & New Haven and the New York & Northampton properties and to seek railroad investment opportunities elsewhere.[16]

Where would Sheffield and Farnam find projects that would strike their fancy? By mid-century much of the railroad frontier existed in the states of the Old Northwest, and shortly the two men entered the region. The 1850s, mostly before the Panic of 1857, saw the greatest wave of track mileage constructed prior to the Civil War. During this decade railroad builders moved beyond an emphasis on short-haul transportation to ambitious projects that connected more distant places.

It would be William B. Ogden, father of the Galena & Chicago Union Railroad, who piqued the interest of Joseph Sheffield and Henry Farnam in midwestern rails. In fall 1850 Ogden invited Farnam to visit a vibrant Chicago and its environs, hoping to involve these men with his Galena. By then this pioneer road had opened to Elgin, Illinois, a distance of forty-two miles. Farnam accepted. "My father was much impressed with the possibilities of the country that he saw," remembered his son. "Before committing himself to any project, however, he made a second visit in the same year, this time in company with Mr. Sheffield, and now pushed as far as Rock Island, on the Mississippi River." It was on this trip to Rock Island that the men became familiar with the proposed Rock Island & La Salle.[17]

Farnam and Sheffield did not get involved with the Galena or, at first, with the RI&LS. In late 1850 John B. Jervis, an experienced canal and railroad civil engineer, contacted Farnam about joining the developing Michigan Southern and Northern Indiana Railroads. Only recently had Jervis become chief engineer for these properties, designed to link Lake Erie with Lake Michigan. He wanted Farnam to become superintendent of the completed portion of the Michigan Southern, initially a state-sponsored railroad that had stalled at Hillsdale, Michigan, a casualty of the Panic of 1837. But in 1846 Michigan Southern came into the hands of a group of private investors, and its future looked promising. Yet only sixty-eight miles had been opened westward from Monroe, Michigan, a Lake Erie port community south of Detroit, and its primitive track structure could barely sustain train movements. Its obsolete rolling stock also needed replacement. Although Farnam declined that offer, he suggested to Jervis that he complete the road and help with acquiring the necessary capital. Jervis agreed, and a contract followed with Farnam and financial partner Sheffield.[18]

Once the details had been finalized, Henry Farnam charged ahead. In spring 1851, work began with construction crews pushing toward northwestern Indiana and ultimately Chicago. On August 22, rails reached the Indiana border, and they rapidly spread westward over a favorable building terrain. In a remarkable track-laying feat, gangs installed thirty miles in forty-two days. In early October the iron reached South Bend amid a gala celebration. This accomplishment astonished a local newspaper editor, who believed it "to be almost, it not entirely, without parallel in the annals of our country." Building farther on was made easier by using portions of the recently acquired and moribund Northern Indiana,[19] and finally the rails reached Chicago on

February 20, 1852. The Michigan Southern claimed to be the first railroad to enter that city from the east, edging out by three months the Michigan Central Railroad, a Detroit-based carrier, which had had a considerable head start with its line to Chicago. The Michigan Southern also had leased and rebuilt the pioneer thirty-three-mile Erie & Kalamazoo Railroad, connecting Adrian, Michigan, to Toledo and providing linkages to the East Coast. These rail connections contributed to the phenomenal growth of Chicago.[20]

The firm of Sheffield and Farnam was not finished with midwestern railroading. This was surely the best location in the nation to introduce the iron horse. By the early 1850s railroad mania had developed into a virulent fever throughout much of the Old Northwest. What should be the course of action? Farnam's son put it succinctly: "The task that now confronted him was first to build a road from Chicago to the Mississippi and then to carry it further, and open the way for the first railroad across the continent."[21]

The focus turned to the paper Rock Island & La Salle Railroad. The project had not turned a wheel, but it held a valuable corporate charter, faced no geographical barriers, possessed line surveys, and had determined backers. Its principal challenge remained a shortage of investment capital. Yet neither Farnam nor Sheffield wanted to become involved with a railroad that served as a canal feeder. They sought a carrier between the Mississippi River and Lake Michigan–Chicago, and one that connected directly to eastern points. Their wish for a trans-Illinois artery would be granted.[22]

Events unfolded rapidly. In late 1850 trustees of the Rock Island & La Salle petitioned Illinois lawmakers for a charter revision. But before a final decision was made, on January 22, 1851, Henry Farnam had told James Grant that the legislative document needed to be crafted in this manner: "Be sure to get the charter to make the road on the shortest route from La Salle to Chicago, even if they insist on your paying tolls on freights taken from points along the canal."[23]

A pivotal event took place on February 7, 1851, when the Illinois General Assembly permitted the Rock Island & La Salle to become the Chicago & Rock Island (C&RI). But there were stipulations, most notably this provision: the railroad must pay the canal trustees "upon all freight transported upon said railroad, the same rates of toll that are now or hereafter shall be fixed upon like articles of freight carried through the canal." The legislature was not about to damage the heavy investment of public funds in the waterway. Yet lawmakers were not wholly unreasonable. The C&RI would not have to pay on shipments of livestock; fees were due only when the canal was open; freight shipments were exempt from tolls if they came from or were destined for points twenty miles beyond La Salle; tolls would stop when the canal indebtedness had been retired; and taxes on railroad property could be deducted from all tolls paid.[24]

The railroad charter contained a loophole. Since trackage was to parallel the canal, its trustees needed to grant the right-of-way through canal lands. "If the trustees refused to comply before the first Monday in June after passage of the act," noted a student of the formative years of the Rock Island, "the railroad company could build without any restrictions in relation to tolls." Canal officials, however, received bad advice about their legal obligations, and they failed to act by the stipulated deadline. "The canal's refusal to grant a right of way annulled the toll provisions of the act, and the railroad company was thus relieved of conditions which might well have strangled it in infancy."[25]

Excitement filled the air; the future looked bright for the Chicago to Rock Island project. Already the Michigan Southern road had used the charter of the unbuilt C&RI to enter Chicago from the Indiana border, and it stood ready to be both investor and interchange partner. Another indication of this optimism involved the brisk sale of stock along the projected route. "Public opinion is becoming more and more inlisted [sic] in favor of the Rock Island and Chicago Railroad," reported the *Joliet Signal* in mid-June 1851. "Capitalists in the East are aware of the importance of this road, there is no question that the means will be forthcoming to speed its early completion." The newspaper would be proved correct; the wedding of local and outside financial support ended any doubt as to what was about to transpire.[26]

On August 25, 1851, another landmark event occurred when representatives from the Chicago & Rock Island met with Farnam and Sheffield in New York City to discuss contractual terms. Already surveys and cost estimates had been made. The parties agreed upon a remarkable document, unusual if not unique for any time during the railway age. For one lump sum, the firm of Sheffield, Farnam & Company would acquire the right-of-way for this 181-mile standard-gauge line, construct track and bridges, and equip the road with rolling stock, depots, and other betterments. The precise amount would be $3,987,688 ($116.7 million in current dollars). For their work the partners agreed to accept 7 percent first mortgage bonds at par in the amount of $2 million, cash at the rate of $25,000 per month up to $500,000, and stock certificates at par that bore interest at 10 percent payable in railroad stock when the road was finished. The Sheffield and Farnam firm could operate completed sections and receive all earnings until the completed project was transferred to the directors. Assuming construction could begin in spring 1852, Farnam promised to convey the railroad by January 1, 1856. Official approval of the contract came in September, and the Sheffield and Farnam partnership promptly ordered fifty-eight-pound iron rails from an English manufacturer.[27]

The energized Chicago & Rock Island found new leadership. Because of pressing political commitments, James Grant stepped down as president. John Jervis, who headed the Michigan Southern, took his place but continued to serve as the Michigan Central's chief executive. He retained both positions until 1858, revealing the close relationship between the two companies. Most of the officers and directors of the C&RI hailed from along its developing route.[28]

Construction soon grabbed the public's attention. Joseph Sheffield predictably remained behind the scenes. He assumed the financial responsibilities, focusing on purchases of materials and rolling stock and on sales of securities. Henry Farnam, on the other hand, oversaw engineering and actual building, and he became well known in Illinois.

By the 1850s the railroad-building process had become mostly regularized. Contractors sublet sections of the road for grading, and local parties generally handled these assignments. Farnam followed this practice. Construction began in Chicago, and in September 1852 the Chicago & Rock Island proudly reported on its progress. "The bridge over Rock River, the heaviest work on the whole line, has been let to subcontractors. Engagements have also been made for the iron for the entire road; ten thousand tons, sufficient to finish it to Peru, to be delivered in 1851, and the balance the year following. The track is already laid as far as the junction with the Indiana road, six miles from our depot in Chicago, and about eight hundred men are laboring on the line between that point and Ottawa." Early in October the C&RI officially opened between Chicago and Joliet. Impressive progress indeed.[29]

With rails to Joliet, forty miles from Chicago, it was time to rejoice. At ten o'clock in the morning on Sunday, October 10, 1852, an American Standard 4-4-0 wood burner called the *Rocket*—a name likely inspired by George Stephenson's experimental *Rocket*, which had reigned supreme at the famed British Rainhill Trials in 1829—became the star attraction. This Rogers Locomotive Works built product, which sported a bulge smokestack and 4′6″ drivers and was described by a witness as an "unbelievable thing," departed Chicago with a train of "six new and beautifully-painted coaches" that were crammed with "living freight." Celebrations by well-wishers occurred en route and in Joliet. "For a new road we may say it is remarkable for its smoothness and solidity," reported the *Chicago Daily Democrat*. "Those portions of it which are already ballasted are equal in these respects to the best constructed Eastern roads."[30]

Hundreds of graders and track layers continued westward. As with most of the trans-Illinois construction, workers benefited from the relatively level land. On January 5, 1853, the road opened to Morris, sixty-one miles from Chicago, and this joyous occasion prompted the *Morris Yeoman* to declare: "One would imagine that our town was the terminus of all creation instead of the Rock Island and Chicago Railroad." By the following December, track had reached within twenty miles of its destination. Freight and passenger traffic rapidly increased on the opened sections; in fact, the company found itself hard pressed to meet customer demands. Rails would have reached Rock Island sooner, but the hard winter of 1853–1854 delayed construction.[31]

Throughout the building process, Farnam and Sheffield toiled at their respective jobs. They had experienced financial headaches but had met these challenges with aplomb. Farnam also succeeded in creating an efficient workforce. It was a remarkable accomplishment since a labor shortage had arisen because of the "rapidity with which Roads were constructed in the West from 1851 to 1857." Of the workers available, a high proportion lacked experience and skills.[32]

On Washington's birthday in 1854, the Chicago & Rock Island completed its line, and celebration was the order of the day. For some time area residents had been dizzy with railroad fever, and their enthusiasm for the iron horse never flagged. The recognition of the arrival of the inaugural train from Chicago was most festive, but it had not been the only observance. Earlier celebrations had occurred, including that joyous one at Joliet when the first train of well-wishers arrived from the Lakeside City. The final event, however, held greater significance and was much grander. "On Wednesday morning, the 22d inst., at half past eight o'clock, the Mayor and Common Council of the City of Chicago, a number of citizens, in all about two hundred and fifty, left the depot of the Rock Island road, in a train of six splendid passenger cars from the manufactory of A. B. Stone & Co., of this city, for an excursion to Rock Island, in honor of the completion of the road," reported the *Chicago Daily Democratic Press*. "The train was tastefully ornamented with flags and evergreens, and its arrival at the different towns along the line was greeted with the shouts of the people, and the firing of cannons. At Joliet, Morris, Ottawa, Lasalle [*sic*], Peru, Tiskilwa, Geneseo, Moline, and other places, accessions were made to our numbers, and when the train arrived at Rock Island there could not have been less than three hundred and fifty persons on it." There was much more to tell readers. "The reception at Rock Island was a magnificent spectacle. Thousands of people lined the streets, and crowded the doors and windows. Fair ladies waved their kerchiefs, and stout men and youths shouted exultingly, while ever and anon the thunder of Col. Swift's gun went booming across the Mississippi, arousing the echoes from the majestic bluffs." The *Press* continued: "It was a glorious day for Rock Island, and for her neighboring city [Davenport]. The citizens of those places had looked forward to it for years, some of them with fear and trembling, lest their eyes should not behold it. We think we are not above the mark in estimating the number present, on the arrival of the train at from five to six thousand persons." Henry Farnam, who did not relish public speaking but who realized the necessity of making a presentation, said: "Today we witness the nuptials of the Atlantic with the Father of Waters. Tomorrow the people of Rock Island can go to New York, the entire distance by railroad, and within the space of 42 hours." In relation to travel time, the map of the United States had shrunk markedly. Journalists and others heaped praise on this historic lake-to-river route. "One could scarcely believe that a railroad, 181 miles long, could be built, and well built, too, in the short space of one year ten months and twelve days," wrote *Hunt's Merchants' Magazine*. Commented the *American Railroad Journal*, "it has been built with extra ordinary dispatch and bids fair to be a most wonderful work for both to its owners and the public."[33]

Commemoration of the first railroad to connect the Mississippi River with the Atlantic Seaboard also involved a memorable Rock Island to Saint Paul, Minnesota, steamboat trip, billed as the "Great Excursion to the Falls of St. Anthony" and the "Fashionable Tour." Sponsored by Farnam, Sheffield, and others associated with the C&RI, this river event began on June 5, 1854. Scores of dignitaries received invitations for the twenty-day journey, and the acceptance rate was high. Joining the party at the swanky Tremont Hotel in Chicago were former president Millard Fillmore, national politicians, academics, and journalists. Among the latter were Samuel Bowles of the *Springfield Republican*, Charles Dana of the *New York Tribune*, Cather Flint of the *Chicago Tribune*, and Thurlow Weed of the *Albany Evening Journal*. This core group of excursionists departed Chicago in two gaily decorated trains of nine coaches each, and along the way the consists were greeted enthusiastically at stations. Docked in Rock Island to await the guests were five steamboats well-stocked with food and beverage, along with musicians and attendants. But the number of unexpected guests was so great that the railroad had to charter two additional vessels. Unfortunately sleeping space became dear, and "the lack of berths caused fully one-third of the guests to renounce the steamboat trip and return to Chicago." Still, an estimated 1,200 guests made the voyage. They took pleasure in the trip, ate and drank well, and enjoyed the attention of folks along the way and in Saint Paul. This event announced to the world that the iron way between Chicago and Rock Island had opened and enhanced economic opportunities in the "Free West."[34]

As for the newly commissioned Chicago & Rock Island Railroad, the Farnam and Sheffield organization had done splendid work. It had honored provisions of its contract and had done so honestly. The C&RI directors would receive a railroad that was ready to operate profitably. On July 10, 1854, they officially took possession, gaining twenty-eight wood-burning 4-4-0 type locomotives with such names as the *Joliet, Peoria,* and *Rock Island* and an assortment of freight and passenger equipment. The company's annual report of December 1854 stated: "Through the able financial management of Mr. Sheffield and the skill and perseverance of Mr. Farnam, the Chicago & Rock Island Railroad has gone steadily on from the commencement to its completion, every engagement of the contractors in an expenditure of four and a half millions of dollars having been met at maturity; and all the settlements having been made with the contractors without putting a note of the President and Treasurer into the market during the whole time; and when the road was surrendered to the Company in July last, there was not a floating debt of any description."[35]

Sheffield and Farnam had not ended their railroad building in Illinois. On July 4, 1853, Sheffield, Farman & Company signed a contract with a Chicago & Rock Island satellite, the Peoria & Bureau Valley Railroad (P&BV), or the Peoria Branch Rail Road, as it was commonly called. Farnam, whom one journalist dubbed the "Railroad King of the West," oversaw construction of this forty-seven-mile appendage from Bureau Junction, twelve miles west of La Salle, to Peoria, an active trading and budding manufacturing community located on the Illinois River. Surprisingly, not everyone along the projected route, which "ran through a large portion of the fertile valley of the Illinois River," wanted the iron horse. In a German settlement, surveyors had encountered women who at least symbolically sought to keep out the railroad, coming out of their homes with brooms "to sweep the party off the grounds." Farnam, though, welcomed the presence of Dr. Thomas C. Durant, a Massachusetts native and trained medical surgeon who at the age of twenty-three had become involved in a family-related New York City securities firm. This smart, hard-driving, and sometimes erratic young man had become interested in railroads; in fact, he had joined Farnam during construction of the Michigan Southern and likewise had assisted with the C&RI. Another railroad enthusiast, William Walcott, began his association with the enterprise by becoming an important investor. The P&BV took shape rapidly and opened in less than a year at an estimated cost of $1.25 million. On April 14,

1854, the C&RI leased the property, an agreement that continued into the mid-twentieth century with its successor, Chicago, Rock Island & Pacific. The Peoria line added to the boom in Illinois trackage: 45 miles in 1851, 390 miles in 1853, and 1,096 miles in 1854.[36]

Passenger and freight traffic on the first trans-Illinois rail artery developed nicely. A correspondent who lived in Peru wrote in a New York newspaper that as early as spring 1853 the company daily hauled eight hundred passengers and generated $2,000 in revenues. By the following year more lumber, grain, and other commodities that heretofore had either gone to or come from Saint Louis and beyond by steamboat now moved over C&RI rails. It became common for lumber and grain dealers to send their shipments by water from Minnesota and Wisconsin to Rock Island for transshipment to Chicago and other eastern destinations. "The opening of the Chicago & Rock Island rather bewildered me," related a Davenport grain dealer. "It revolutionized the mode of doing business." He continued, "When the railroad got into operation, produce men were as thick as potato-bugs. If a man could raise two hundred and fifty dollars, he could begin business. That amount would buy a car-load of wheat. In the morning he would engage a car, have it put where he could load it, and have the farmer put his wheat, barley, or oats, as the case might be, in the car. By three o'clock in the afternoon the car would be loaded and shipped." Although freight traffic did not vanish from the I&M Canal, high-rated shipments declined, and its passenger business collapsed. In employee timetable no. 6, which took effect on July 1, 1855, the railroad dispatched daily through freight trains between Chicago and Rock Island and Peoria, and it carded daily passenger trains between the same destinations. There was also a Peoria passenger train that connected with the main line at Bureau.[37]

MISSISSIPPI & MISSOURI RAILROAD

Officials of the Chicago & Rock Island realized that revenues would increase if the railroad reached west into Iowa and beyond. Bridging the Father of Waters would make this iron way more attractive to freight customers and travelers alike. "It falls to our lot," opined Henry Farnam, "to forge an important link in this great chain across the Continent, and we have every motive of pecuniary advantage, and obligation of duty to ourselves and our country, to stimulate us to the successful completion of a work which we have commenced under such favorable circumstances." It would be the Mississippi & Missouri Railroad (M&M), backed by those who energized the Chicago & Rock Island, that sought to make real the Farnam dream. In December 1852 this process began in earnest when the railroad was formed by "articles of association" and a document filed on January 26, 1853, with the Scott County recorder in Davenport. Capital stock was set at $6 million with individual shares at $100 each with the stipulation that 5 percent of the subscription price must be a down payment. Soon John Adams Dix (1798–1879), a prominent New York politician, became company president, and William Ogden assumed the vice presidency. It was believed Dix, who had served in the US Senate from 1845 to 1849, could help in obtaining a federal land grant and promoting a congressional Pacific construction bill. There would be additional legislative assignments. Others, including Farnam, Sheffield, and Grant, made up the directorship.[38]

What were the construction ambitions of this proposed Mississippi & Missouri Railroad? The corporate name, of course, indicated that the company planned to become a trans-Iowa carrier, but there were other objectives. The board of directors sought to extend the railroad in three directions. Rails would head west from Davenport to Iowa City, Iowa's capital until 1857, and onward through Fort Des Moines (Des Moines) to the Missouri River in the general vicinity of Council Bluffs (Kanesville until 1853), amounting to 256 miles and becoming a potential transcontinental pathway. A line would also be extended toward the southwest. There was debate about whether the M&M would leave from Davenport or the trackage would be built southward along the east bank of the Mississippi to a point opposite Muscatine, Iowa, and from there head toward the Hawkeye State county seat towns of Washington and Oskaloosa. But because of pressures coming from Davenport and Iowa City, especially from those individuals associated with the stillborn Davenport & Iowa City Rail Road, the M&M board decided to push west from Davenport, extending the southwest route from those rails toward Muscatine. Eventually it was anticipated that the line would reach the Missouri River at Saint Joseph, Missouri, along roughly the route of future Rock Island affiliate Chicago & South Western Railway. The M&M also considered building northwestward, aiming toward Minnesota Territory through Cedar Rapids, Iowa.[39]

With the M&M gestating, a celebration seemed appropriate. Such a popular event always energized a railroad project, albeit perhaps only briefly. On September 1, 1853, a "Railroad Jubilee" took place in Davenport, and more than two thousand well-wishers from the community, Rock Island, and environs assembled at the corner of Fifth and Rock Island Streets to mark the start of construction. "Many of the old citizens, who had for years been living on in hope and confidence," observed a local historian, "now began to feel all their most sanguine wishes gratified." The honor of turning the first shovel full of earth went to Antoine Le Claire, an "enterprising citizen," the owner of the Le Claire House hotel, and a physically memorable three-hundred-pound French Canadian. "Mr. Le Claire pulled off his coat amid the cheers of the crowd," reported the *Davenport Gazette*, "and proceeded in a workmanlike manner to give the first touch to the great iron thoroughfare west of the Mississippi River." A ceremonial tie was then laid. "The occasion was one of universal rejoicing," reflected a Scott County historian in the 1880s, "[and] a great and important object had been accomplished for our city, our county and our State."[40]

Backers of the M&M had reason to feel optimistic. Already the company's engineering staff was in place. Peter A. Dey (1825–1911), a college-educated veteran of earlier Farnam and Sheffield projects who was considered one of America's finest civil engineers, assumed the post of chief engineer. Dey appointed as his principal assistant the academically trained albeit youthful Grenville M. Dodge (1831–1916), who had worked with him on the C&RI. On September 1, 1853, Dey and his surveying party began to explore a route west of Iowa City. He led his men through the existing and future communities of Marengo, Grinnell, Newton, Des Moines, Earlham, and Atlantic. In late November they completed their work at Council Bluffs. Like so many others attempting to fix a right-of-way in a mostly wilderness environment, these men experienced discomforts and problems. "The long summer's work in the field and in the rank vegetation had given many of my party the fever and ague and I was short on hands," recalled Dodge. There would be several rivers to cross, including the Iowa, North and South Skunk, Des Moines, and Racoon, and scores of creeks that gouged the projected route. Some heavy grading would be required near Davenport and west of Des Moines, especially as the line reached the steep sandy hills along the Missouri River. "The State of Iowa is more rolling and more cut up by small streams than the State of Illinois," explained a participant.[41]

Surveyors often became involved in land speculation along what they believed would be the ultimate route of a railroad. Those associated with the M&M were no different from others. Take Grenville Dodge. At the Grinnell, Iowa, townsite he saw to it that the future station grounds would be placed on property that he and his investor partner John Baldwin owned. Dodge and several others who were closely connected with the company bought on speculation considerable acreage in Council Bluffs. They would do their best to see that this settlement—and not Florence, in Nebraska Territory, or some other Missouri River site in what became greater Omaha—would become the M&M terminal.[42]

A rival project spurred the Dey-led survey to occur quickly. The Lyons & Iowa Central Air Line Railroad competed for a largely parallel river-to-river line. Officially launched in February 1853, this company planned to build from the Mississippi River community of Lyons City, Iowa (later Lyons and eventually part of Clinton), through Iowa City, Des Moines, and onward to Council Bluffs. Backers believed that their 308-mile trans-Iowa route was "destined to be the most important link in the great chain which is to connect the Atlantic and Pacific Oceans." The Lyons road became more than a paper one. Local tax bonuses allowed workers to grade much of the right-of-way between Lyons, Tipton, and Iowa City before money ran out in June 1854. Misappropriation of bond funds apparently explained the financial crisis.[43]

Dramatically different from the building of the Chicago & Rock Island, the Mississippi & Missouri was painfully slow to take shape. Still construction occurred before the Panic of 1857 ravaged the nation, an economic downswing that severely affected the Midwest. By autumn 1853 a small army of workers had appeared between Davenport and Iowa City, a distance of fifty-five miles, but most of them toiled near Davenport where river bluffs necessitated extensive grading. Limited construction also occurred during 1854 and the first part of 1855. Several reasons explain this lack of substantial progress. The company, most of all, faced difficulty raising adequate funds. For one thing, the competing Lyons railroad project captured aid from several of the communities projected to be on the line, including Des Moines. There were labor problems, stemming from wage reductions, and internal management changes. Joseph Sheffield retired from the project, and he endorsed the wily Dr. Durant. Farnam expressed reservations about his new business partner, believing that he lacked Sheffield's business acumen and common sense.[44]

Although a general economic stagnation continued, rays of hope appeared. On May 2, 1855, the firm of Farnam & Durant signed a contract with the M&M directors to complete the lines from Davenport to Iowa City and to Muscatine. Not only would they finish grading and install track, but as in the earlier agreement with the Chicago & Rock Island, the Farnam and Durant organization would construct depots, engine houses, and other facilities. For these betterments the firm would be paid $31,000 per mile, and this compensation would consist of cash and bonds. The latter included securities from the railroad and municipal and county governments. It was also agreed that the road would be completed by January 1, 1856, and would be turned over to railroad directors on July 1, 1856. Another provision of the contract was that Farnam and Durant would have an option on construction contacts for anticipated line extensions: from Iowa City to Des Moines, from Muscatine to Oskaloosa, and from the main stem to Cedar Rapids.[45]

Finally the M&M began to materialize. By the end of June 1855, workers had started to lay rail, and on July 19 the first locomotive arrived. This classic wood burner, built by Rogers, claimed the honor of being the first locomotive in Iowa. And it bore an appropriate name: *Antoine Le Claire* (antebellum locomotives, like boats and ships, usually had names rather than numbers). Since there was not yet a railroad bridge across the Mississippi River, a specially rigged flatboat delivered to the Davenport river front the trim 4-4-0, decorated with bronze statues of its corpulent namesake mounted on each side of the sand dome. Residents cheered, and the editor of the *Gazette* bubbled over with excitement: "Who shall contemplate its destiny? Will Cedar river bound its westward labor? Will Iowa City stay its course? Will the great Missouri river say, here shall thy proud course be stayed? Shall the towering ramparts of the Rocky Mountains give limits to its onward course? No, the quiet shores of the mighty Pacific shall be awakened by the shrill whistle of its engine—the welcome tones of its alarm bell."[46]

The trans-Iowa railroad forged ahead. Although not without challenges, construction continued westward and also on the Muscatine branch. On August 25, 1855, the first passenger train to operate in the Hawkeye State slowly made its way from Davenport to the newly platted town of Walcott, a distance of a dozen miles. It was a joyous occasion for trackside observers to hear the "puff and snort of the iron horse." Made up of an American Standard locomotive, two coaches, and five flatcars with chairs and settees protected by temporary railings, the inaugural train carried "some five hundred people, including seventy-five ladies and a brass band." At the end of the track, a town-lot auction was in progress, and celebratory festivities continued.[47]

The place thirteen miles west of the Walcott station soon became Wilton Junction. The twelve-mile southwestern extension to Muscatine was taking shape there. On November 20, 1855, the greater Muscatine community welcomed the steam-car civilization. "At twelve o'clock, First street, in the vicinity of Ogilvie House, and that spacious edifice were thronged with strangers, together with almost the entire population of our city," wrote the elated editor of the *Muscatine Daily Journal*. During the ensuing celebrations, Henry Farnam offered this short toast: "Muscatine and Davenport: May their greatest rivalry consist in every effort to live above all petty jealousies and lead in the great railroad enterprises in the state."[48]

The next long-remembered event took place on New Year's Eve 1855 in Iowa City, whose 1,250 inhabitants were "wild on railroad projects." Earlier voters had approved a $50,000 bond enticement, provided that the first train reach their community by January 1, 1856. Arriving in time seemed problematic. Even though rails were just several miles east of the corporate limits by Christmas, building conditions were dreadful. Bitterly cold weather caused the weary workers to suffer and machinery to freeze. On December 31 the gap had been closed to only a few hundred feet. Fortunately Henry Farnam was there to direct construction forces, and these men were joined by scores of civic-minded residents of the capital city. As time was running out, the engine froze up, but workers and volunteers pushed the dead locomotive over hastily installed track to the final goal as church bells pealed in the new year. The "Battle for the Bonus" had been won; much-needed funds would be forthcoming. Farnam told Dr. Durant that if he had not been on-site during these last critical days, track would not have reached Iowa City before February, an assessment that was probably correct.[49]

Although the corporate coffers of the Mississippi & Missouri hardly overflowed, there was another bright spot in addition to Iowa City funding. The company was about to benefit from a federal land grant, something Washington had been awarding railroads since its massive land donation to the Illinois Central and Mobile & Ohio roads in 1850. After considerable lobbying efforts, the federal government on May 15, 1856, approved the Iowa Land Bill, which granted 4,394,400 acres to the state. Iowa received each odd-numbered section of land within six miles of a projected road. But if some sections had been sold, officials could choose other parcels within fifteen miles. In July state lawmakers assigned portions to several railroad projects. The M&M received 483,214,036 acres. It was not the largest grant awarded, ranking behind the Dubuque & Sioux City, Des Moines Valley, and Iowa Central Air Line companies. Also, more than 35,000 acres had to be deducted when the US Supreme Court ruled that the land rightfully belonged to the Des Moines Navigation & Railroad Company, a bequest that the legislature had made in the early 1850s.[50]

The land grant did not mean that construction crews would proceed rapidly to complete the Mississippi & Missouri. The railroad temporarily halted its main line at Iowa City, and by the eve of the Civil War, it had succeeded in laying rails only thirty miles farther west, to Marengo. During summer 1858 there had been about a dozen miles of grading up the Mosquito Creek valley in the vicinity of Council Bluffs. That same year the Muscatine branch had been lengthened thirty-eight miles southwestward to Washington, where it also stalled. What interrupted the building process? Money. Although the Panic of 1857 had not yet struck, sales of securities became difficult. The situation was especially acute for railroads attempting to build through sparsely populated or underdeveloped locales. The American economy had become highly dependent on foreign money and conditions overseas. Capital was being drained out of the country, and moneyed men globally turned to more attractive European investments, especially in Great Britain. Following the Crimean War, which ended in early 1856, Russian grain reappeared on the international market. This hurt domestic producers who generated the greatest amount of European trade income, an indication of the causal complexities for these hard times. Investors began to realize that too much financial speculation had taken place. "It was everywhere a time of vast expansion," explained railroad historian Edward Hungerford. "Of over-expansion. Of splurge. Of financial wildness. There was a grey hour of reckoning to come for all of it. Which, in after years, was to be known as the great panic of 1857." This economic crisis dried up commercial credit, and some railroads, including the Erie and Illinois Central, failed.[51]

Henry Farnam, who never had been a reckless plunger, reflected on the worsening financial conditions in a letter to Dr. Durant on August 29, 1857: "I thought a week ago that I was a rich man; I now find the concern so involved that we cannot go on, and the firm must make an assignment tonight or Monday. The loss of property is nothing, if I was only sure that I had enough for the support of my dear wife and family; to lose everything now is rather more than I can bear." Farnam had overstated his perceived financial woes. "He was able to avoid failure," his son happily reflected. Although Farnam and the M&M remained solvent, rails would not reach the Missouri River for more than a decade, and the Muscatine line would not achieve its intended destination until the early 1870s.[52]

THE BRIDGE

Railroad officials and their supporters considered the line built by the Chicago & Rock Island and the one surveyed and laid by the developing Mississippi & Missouri to make up the logical route for a transcontinental railroad. In fact, the organizational statement of the stillborn Davenport & Iowa City Rail Road of November 2, 1850, included this provision: "That said road when completed would be a prolongation of a railway track from New York, Boston & Philadelphia by the way of Cleaveland [sic] & Chicago into the heart of Iowa in the direction of Council Bluffs & South Pass & would thus form an important section of the Atlantic & Pacific Rail Road." There would be rivers, mountains, and deserts to conquer, but from the perspective of the CR&I and M&M, the most daunting task would be bridging the mighty Mississippi River.[53]

Railroads during the pre– and post–Civil War years might have used ferryboats to transport rolling stock across bodies of water. But rivers, especially those with strong currents, made such undertakings expensive, time consuming, and dangerous. There was another option: if a body of water froze solid before the spring thaw, temporary track could be laid on the ice. A bridge, of course, was the only practical solution to overcome such natural barriers.

A well-recalled event in Rock Island Railroad history involved the construction and legal defense of the first railroad bridge over the Father of Waters. Prospects for such a structure between Rock Island and Davenport initially looked good. Since the project involved both Illinois and Iowa, it required their legislative approval. On January 17, 1853, Illinois lawmakers passed an act that incorporated the Railroad Bridge Company "with power to build, maintain and use a railroad bridge over the Mississippi River [at Rock Island] in such manner as shall not materially obstruct or interfere with the free navigation of said river." On February 22, 1853, their Iowa counterparts incorporated a companion firm. The C&RI and M&M guaranteed the bridge bonds, and Henry Farnam became president.[54]

Bridge construction began on July 16, 1853, when earth was excavated for a pier on the Iowa side. Technically this was not a single structure but two separate ones, with no lengthy span exclusively crossing the waters. When completed, the first section, which measured 474 feet, crossed the "east channel," the water-filled Sylvan Slough that separated the Illinois mainland from Rock Island, and the second and much longer section crossed the navigable portion of the river. Both were wooden and featured the Howe trust design, giving them a spidery appearance. Rails for a single track were laid directly on the island between these two spans, a lucky quirk of nature that made for a less expensive undertaking. The longer portion consisted of six masonry piers, two 250-foot fixed spans on the Illinois side, and three 250-foot fixed ones on the Iowa side. A 285-foot swing draw span, placed on the Illinois side, stood directly over the steamboat channel. It rotated at right angles to the bridge on a center pier mounted on an iron turntable. Construction consumed more than a million feet of lumber and several hundred thousand pounds of iron. The total length of this remarkable engineering feat was 1,535 feet. Benjamin Brayton, an experienced canal and railroad civil engineer, took charge, and Henry Farnam provided technical assistance.[55]

Long before the Railroad Bridge Company completed its work, which took slightly more than two years and eight months, river and port interests vehemently objected to what they considered to be a threat to navigation and to their business. A bridge was unacceptable. The classic contest between old and new transportation occurred; it became steamboat men versus railroaders. Furthermore, the bridge did not set well with Southern sectionalists.

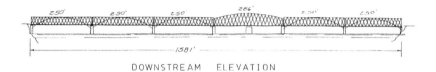

DOWNSTREAM ELEVATION

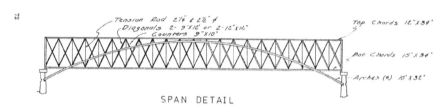

SPAN DETAIL

BRIDGE NO. 1   1853 - 1866

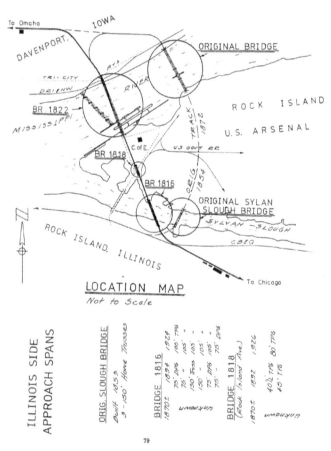

LOCATION MAP

Not to Scale

These sketches show the initial bridge complex and its location over the Mississippi River between Rock Island, Illinois, and Davenport, Iowa. The design featured the popular mid-nineteenth-century Howe truss, created by Massachusetts millwright William Howe in 1840.

National Archives, Courtesy of David Pfeiffer

Those in the future Confederate States of America believed that the structure would allow Northerners to settle the trans-Mississippi West faster and in greater numbers. Why this concern? The spread of slavery had become a burning issue following the 1854 passage of the Kansas-Nebraska Act. The measure provided popular sovereignty on the question of slavery for those white adult males who lived in these two territories. Slavery supporters, including Secretary of War Jefferson Davis, sought a southern transcontinental railroad, one stretching westward to California from New Orleans, Memphis, or possibly Saint Louis. Ultimately it would be a struggle in which river interests lost, and those with proslavery sentiments likewise failed.[56]

Before the bridge company reigned victorious, steamboat men and their allies, strongly backed by supporters in Saint Louis, took heed of the threat. As early as January 1853, a Saint Louis newspaper warned that a Rock Island bridge should "open the eyes of our citizens to what is going on elsewhere, to divert trade from us." City fathers showed a blind loyalty to waterway commerce. One contemporary source proclaimed that "commerce will flow from the equator in the direction of the poles, carrying the luxuries of the tropics to the inhabitants of colder climes, and returning with the more substantial products of the temperate zones." Pro-river forces would defend their views, instigating a series of legal challenges, and lawyers on both sides soon would be kept busy.[57]

Prior to the clash of river and railroad representatives in court, the federal government intervened. For nearly a decade the US Army post at Fort Armstrong, located on Rock Island, had been shuttered, and the bridge company believed that it had the right to a rail corridor on this island between the two designated bridge spans. And it was on sound grounds. Secretary of State William L. Marcy had announced in February 1848 that the property "is hereby relinquished, and placed at the disposal of the department which has charge of the public lands." An application was made to Jefferson Davis for such authority. The secretary said no and demanded that construction stop. Because sectional tensions were on the rise, proslavery people were not about to allow a potential Northern transcontinental project to race ahead over one that favored the South.[58]

The gutsy bridge company ignored the Washington mandate. Soon a US marshal appeared to enforce the Davis order, although by then graders had completed the right-of-way and workers had been quarrying "excellent rock" on the island for bridge piers. Surprisingly, the marshal did not evict the construction laborers. Davis was not pleased, and his next move was to seek an injunction in federal court to restrain further work. During the July 1855 term of the US Circuit Court for the Northern District of Illinois held in Chicago, Judge John McLean, an associate justice on the US Supreme Court, heard the case of *United States v. The Bridge Company, et al.* The bridge people rejoiced when the judge denied the injunction, arguing that the land in question had become public domain and could be used for other purposes, such as railroad and bridge building. The War Department had abandoned Rock Island, and therefore this property was no longer a military preserve. McLean concluded that "the state of Illinois has an undoubted right to authorize the construction of a bridge, provided that the same does not materially obstruct the free navigation of the river."[59]

Henry Farnam and his associates at the Chicago & Rock Island and the Mississippi & Missouri believed that the "mammoth" railroad bridge, which was rapidly taking shape, would usher in a new era for these two related properties; rails could bind the Prairie and Hawkeye States. A red-letter day came on April 1, 1856, when in a test run a C&RI locomotive cautiously crept over part of the structure. Farnam and C&RI superintendent John F. Tracy (1827–1878), who oversaw this event, were delighted. Twenty-one days later, the initial crossing took place when the locomotive *Des Moines* slowly made its way from Rock Island to Davenport. Next a "heavily-loaded" freight train rumbled over the bridge. The following day brought a local celebration when the first passenger train entered Davenport on its way to Iowa City from Chicago. "It consisted of an engine, baggage car, and one passenger car," reported the *Rock Island Daily Argus.* "Only a few gentlemen went over on that train, Mr. Farnam among the number." The newspaper did not fail to comment on the excitement associated with this landmark event. "The church bells of the twin-cities rang out their joyous notes in honor of the achievement, and cheer upon cheer went up from crowds along the line." Others celebrated, including businessmen in Chicago. A Philadelphia newspaper editor had these thoughts: "Now that civilization has got safely over the Mississippi by steam, we see no reason why we may not live to see her take a first class ticket in a lightning train for the shores of the Pacific." The way to the West looked promising.[60]

For railroad officials and their supporters, happiness soon turned to anguish. On the evening of May 6, 1856, disaster struck. The large and newly built steamboat *Effie Afton*, which was heading upstream from Saint Louis, hit the span next to the open draw. Although it had proceeded some two hundred feet above the bridge, one of its two powerful side wheels stopped, and a collision followed. The impact overturned a lighted galley stove, allowing flames to spread rapidly throughout the highly flammable wooden boat and reach bridge timbers. Soon much of the *Effie Afton* was incinerated, and the portion east of the swing span was destroyed, knocking the bridge out of service. It would take until early September before workers completed repairs and train movements resumed.[61]

Rivermen were overjoyed with the bridge fire, and, as expected, Captain Jacob Hurd, owner of the *Effie Alton*, brought suit against the bridge company to recover the financial loss of his vessel and cargo that amounted to at least $50,000. In September 1857 the trial of *Hurd et al. v. The Railroad Bridge Company* began in the Chicago courtroom of the US Circuit Court. Justice McLean again became involved, serving as the trial judge. The case was essentially one of water transport against land transport and of north-south traffic against east-west traffic. The jury needed to determine if the accident was due to the location of the bridge or was the fault of the *Effie Afton*. The plaintiff and the defense each hired capable attorneys: Hezekiah Wead of Peoria, Corydon Beckwith of Chicago, and T. D. Lincoln of Cincinnati for the former and Norman Judd of Chicago (lead attorney), Joseph Knox of Rock Island, and Abraham Lincoln of Springfield for the latter. These six litigants became proxies for sectional interests far greater than themselves.[62]

This legal contest attracted widespread attention, especially in Saint Louis and other river communities, and also in Chicago. The Wead-Beckwith-Lincoln team contended that the bridge was a major hazard to river navigation, and the Judd-Knox-Lincoln team argued that the bridge did not contribute to the accident but rather that the *Effie Afton* had been mishandled. Historian Brian McGinty has shown in detail that Abraham Lincoln, the forty-six-year-old trial lawyer, did an admirable job with the defense, revealing to judge and jury that he possessed intimate knowledge of the river, bridge, and steamboat pilots. Lincoln cogently pointed out the significance of commerce that the structure handled. "This particular railroad line has a great importance, and the statement of its business during little less than a year shows this importance. It is in evidence that from September 8, 1856, to August 8, 1857, 12,586 freight cars and 74,179 passengers passed over this bridge. Navigation was closed four days short of four months last year, and during this time while the river was of no use, this road and bridge were valuable." Bridge traffic represented the daily movement of two passenger trains, a mixed freight-passenger train, and one freight train. Lincoln's skill and honesty impressed jurors. "[Lincoln] conducted the case for the Bridge Company with such masterly ability," opined Rock Island journalist O. P. Wharton, "that the opposition had no show of any consequence for its contention against the right to bridge the Mississippi River at any point where the interests of the transportation east and west required such a structure." After two weeks of testimony, the case went to the jury, but its members could not render a unanimous decision. They voted nine to three in favor of the defense. The *Chicago Daily Democrat* editorialized that the verdict was "virtually a triumph for the bridge."[63]

The hung jury did not deter anti-bridge forces. In early 1859 Captain Hurd filed a second suit for damages caused by the loss of the *Effie Afton*. Rather than turning to a federal court, he sought relief in an Illinois state court. Hurd wanted the trial outside Chicago, that "friendly" railroad city. Initially, the suit was to be heard in Rock Island County, but railroads and their legal representatives forced several changes of venue. Before the case was dismissed, Captain Hurd died from a steamboat boiler explosion on the lower Mississippi River.[64]

While the Hurd suit moved slowly to its ultimate fate, other efforts, backed by river interests, took place to bring down the bridge. James Ward, a steamboat owner from Saint Louis, took action. He asked the US District Court for the Southern District of Iowa to declare the structure a nuisance to navigation and to order its removal. Victory followed. On April 3, 1860, Judge John Love upheld Ward's complaint, declaring the bridge "a common and public nuisance," and ordered the Mississippi & Missouri—that Iowa chartered railroad—to dismantle the three piers and the superstructure that stood within the borders of the Hawkeye State. Judge Love indicated that if this bridge remained, other Mississippi River bridges would follow. Hardly surprising, the railroad refused to remove any portion of the bridge, and it appealed the case to the US Supreme Court. M&M officials knew that they had a solid legal argument; the turntable pier was on the Illinois side, and steamboat traffic used those waters. It would not be until the December 1862 term that the high court heard arguments in *Mississippi and Missouri Railroad v. James Ward*. Although it was not a unanimous decision, on January 30, 1863, the court reversed the Iowa decision and permitted the bridge to remain. "According to this assumption [the need to have free navigation on the river], no lawful bridge could be built across the Mississippi anywhere," wrote Associate Justice John Catron in the majority opinion. "Nor could harbors or rivers be improved; nor could the great facilities to commerce, accomplished by the invention of the railroads, be made available where great rivers had to be crossed." He pointed out that the jurisdiction of the Iowa court extended only to the middle of the Mississippi. In an additional suit, decided on December 30, 1867, the US Supreme Court reaffirmed the Ward verdict in *The Galena, Dubuque, Dunleith, and Minnesota Packet Company v. The Rock Island Bridge*. This decision effectively ended the protracted battle between river and railroad interests. No longer would there be any legal question about the rights of railroads to bridge navigable rivers.[65]

The Government Bridge over the Mississippi River remains a valuable structure in the twenty-first century. In a March 2012 photograph, an Iowa Interstate Railroad eastbound train with a locomotive sporting the historic Rock Island shield and paint scheme crosses this major span. The second main line serves as a short siding that is used only for bridge maintenance.

Eric Rasmussen photograph

Although the legal system did not allow it, there was at least one effort to achieve the objective desired by river backers—destruction of the Rock Island bridge. This time it was not a steamboat but saboteurs. In June 1859 these individuals placed combustible materials on the structure, including "a quantity of powder and sulphur, oakum, saltpetre, camphene, brimstone, lath, etc.; in fact, all the paraphernalia of a professional incendiary." They expected that passing locomotives would set the wooden superstructure ablaze. Their scheme failed. A bridge watchman discovered the threat, and the railroad hired a detective agency to find the culprits. And it did. In their subsequent trial, however, these offenders won acquittal. What vandals failed to accomplish, Mother Nature succeeded at with two blows. In 1868 the bridge was heavily damaged first by ice and next by a windstorm. In both cases repairs followed, but there was no need to worry about the future of the Mississippi River span. The company (after 1866 the Chicago, Rock Island & Pacific) agreed to work with the federal government for a replacement bridge. Since the War Department wanted again to use the island for military purposes, Congress in 1867 appropriated $200,000 for a new structure. Predictably, Washington listed conditions. The site would be about 1,500 feet downstream from the original placement; the railroad must remove the original bridge and track leading to it; the span would be owned by the government but financed and maintained by it and the railroad; and tolls would be charged for train passage. The railroad complied. Known as the Government Bridge, the structure featured iron rather than wood construction, and it contained two decks, the lower one for vehicular traffic and the upper one supporting a single-track rail line. Included, too, were pedestrian walkways along the lower deck. Since a draw span was required for steamboats, to accommodate their usually tall chimneys, designers placed this signature component in the best place for river vessels, namely near the western side of the island. In 1873 workers completed the bridge.[66]

CHICAGO'S STATIONS

By the 1850s the affiliated Rock Island roads took pride in their Chicago passenger station. The initial structure, though, lacked both centrality and distinction. Opened in late 1852 and located on Twenty-Second Street on the city's pancake-flat landscape, this unadorned building with its board-and-batten walls measured sixty-five feet by twenty-five feet. It nevertheless served the needs of the recently opened Rock Island and Michigan Southern railroads. The Chicago, Alton & St. Louis Railroad (future Chicago & Alton) soon became a tenant for the remainder of the decade. Although this structure remained a passenger facility for several more years, railroad officials, pressured by Chicago civic boosters, agreed to relocate closer to the central business district. In 1853 a temporary depot appeared on Twelfth Street. Workers rapidly completed a nearby "permanent" facility, placed at the site of the city's long-enduring La Salle Street Station. Once again the latest building was a joint or "union" facility. On December 2, 1853, travelers gained access to a brick-and-frame structure that sprawled for 355 feet. The attached train shed was a distinguishing feature that caught the public's eye. "The span of the train-shed from the side-walls is 116 feet with but a single support for the entire roof, having been designed on the principle of the Howe Patent Truss which carried the weight of the roof unaided," reported the *Chicago Herald*. "Ventilators, to take care of the smoke from the engines, are installed in the roof. The height of the side walls are 22 feet from the floor line while the height to the center of the roof arch is 42 feet." The site was further enhanced when in 1859 Chicago's first street railway, a horse-car line, opened on State Street with Twelfth Street as its southern terminus.[67]

No different from scores of urban stations and terminals, the consolidated Chicago & Rock Island and Mississippi & Missouri Railroads decided that the

1853 facility had outlived its usefulness. By the Civil War era passenger business exploded, and another replacement structure was in order. In 1868 a larger, more efficient station opened on the corner of Van Buren (Twelfth Street) and La Salle Streets. This magnificent limestone building in the Franco-Italian style had three stories, full basement, multiple towers, and mansard copper roofs. It immediately became the pride of the Rock Island, Vanderbilt-controlled roads, and Chicagoans. The principal public spaces included waiting rooms, toilets, dining facilities, and other traveler services. There was also space for railroad operating and executive offices. A contemporary brochure extolled the structure, boasting that "from the towers an excellent view of the city may be obtained" and bragged that "there has been no lack of expenditure to secure for the traveling public every possible security, protection, and convenience." An observer commented: "[There is] one depot building which—architecturally, as well as in point of capacity and arrangement—[is] worthy of the city: that of the Rock Island and Lake Shore Roads." There was also a replacement train shed. It, too, was impressive, being 400 feet long and 186 feet wide and having limestone walls with ornamental cut pilasters. This structure featured wooden and iron trusses and covered twelve tracks. The station price tag: a whopping $554,000 for what some called the "wonder of the world." Yet Victorian-era terminals were more atmospheric if not thoroughly convenient. Unfortunately, this monument to the transportation boom did not last long. On October 9, 1871, the Great Chicago Fire destroyed the station, the nearby railroad-financed Pacific Hotel, and nearly twenty thousand other structures in the city. By summer 1872, and at a cost of more than $600,000, a replacement structure rose from the ashes. The overall design, except for minor architectural details, replicated the destroyed building and represented Chicago's heroic recovery from the worst urban conflagration in American history. A dynamic era had dawned for the railroad hub of America. "Not even the most sanguine of prophets, looking over the ruins of 1871," wrote city historian A. T. Andreas in 1886, "could have imagined that before two decades had passed, a new city would arise, in greater beauty and added wealth, to become like Rome, the point to which all roads should lead."[68]

Rock Island officials were not interested in promoting a bona fide union station. The fierce competition among independent railroads often precluded creation of joint terminals in the centers of American cities. By the Civil War era, five depots served Chicago, in a textbook example of the outgrowth of parochial railroad interests. Fortunately for travelers, the Parmalee Transfer Company, founded in 1853, efficiently transported passengers and their baggage between the city's downtown terminals.

The Rock Island and residents of Chicago took pride in the replacement station that rose phoenix-like following the conflagration of October 1871. This Victorian gem largely replicated the prefire structure, although with altered architectural details. The price tag exceeded $600,000, a tidy sum for the Gilded Age. The station announced entrance to a rapidly rebuilding city.

Chicago History Center

The series of Rock Island stations in the Lakeside City served an ever-increasing flow of passengers to and from Rock Island trains. After all, the railway age had matured after the Civil War, and Chicago had become a meeting place for travelers from the East and the West. Moreover, its population grew at a spectacular rate. Chicago claimed 29,963 residents at mid-century, 112,172 a decade later, and 298,977 in 1870. A local booster in 1870 noted how much the city had changed: "Chicago, which less than thirty years since imported grain and provisions of all sorts from the East is now in grain, lumber, live stock, and provisions, chief market of the world." The Rock Island contributed to this amazing development.[69]

The Great Chicago Fire provided a golden opportunity to establish a true union station that would serve all of the city's passenger business. That did not happen, and over time Chicago saw the appearance of seven separate facilities. For the Rock Island this meant a continuing relationship with the Vanderbilt

Lines and the Nickel Plate Road, a Buffalo-to-Chicago line controlled by the Vanderbilts' New York Central System. Station consolidation did not take place until 1971 with advent of the quasi-public National Railroad Passenger Corporation—Amtrak. At last the Windy City gained a single long-distance train station in what had been the misnamed Union Station, which was served by only four carriers, Alton, Burlington, Milwaukee, and Pennsylvania.

As with railroads nationwide, the Rock Island from its earliest years sought to attract passengers; their revenues constituted a major part of annual income. Long before rails reached the Missouri River, the company took advantage of the Colorado gold rush, which peaked in 1859. In February 1859 it advertised itself as the "Cheapest and most Expeditious Route to Cherry Creek, Pike's Peak, etc." Specifically, the company told perspective patrons: "This line is pre-pared to accommodate Emigrants to the Gold Region, to the fullest extent. Par-ties with teams, cattle, furniture, provisions, etc., can have them taken through to Iowa City on Passenger Trains, without charge, in twelve hours, for $50 per car." The copy continued: "This Line presents to the Emigrant a cheap expedi-tion and comfortable route through the most settled part of Iowa and Nebraska, with abundant facilities for procuring provisions, supplies, out-fits, etc. for a residence at the mines." There was more: "With extension of stage route from Fort Kearney [Nebraska], early in the spring, parties without teams can procure tickets through from Chicago to the mines, including fifty pounds baggage and meals, west of the Missouri River. Fare from Chicago will probably not exceed $125." The number of "fifty-niners" who boarded Rock Island trains for the greater Pike's Peak and Denver areas is not known, but surely some did.[70]

CONSOLIDATION

Before the Mississippi & Missouri Railroad reached its long-anticipated objec-tive of Council Bluffs and the Missouri River, a corporate union took place between the Chicago & Rock Island and its Iowa affiliate. By the early 1860s, these connecting carriers were two distinct companies. The C&RI was pros-perous; the M&M was not. The former not only served a thriving territory and controlled the interchange traffic of the latter but also tapped the Chicago market. The M&M, which had stalled in Kellogg, Iowa, forty-two miles east of Des Moines and nearly two hundred miles from its intended endpoint, had a much lighter freight and passenger business. The C&RI enjoyed a healthy gross income and beginning in 1865–1866 paid a ten-dollar annual dividend. That was not the case for the M&M, which was saddled with a burgeoning debt and was struggling to make interest payments.[71]

In an October 1865 circular to investors, M&M president John Dix revealed a troubling financial condition. He said, in part, "Your company is therefore driven to the necessity of selling the road or reorganizing on a basis which will furnish the means of constructing 40 miles of road and extending it to Des Moines, the Capital of Iowa, and deferring to a future time the payment of existing liabilities." Later that month security holders voted to sell the M&M to the CR&I for $5.5 million. On November 1, 1865, a formal agreement was inked. In order to forge a consolidation, the C&RI organized a new company—the Chicago, Rock Island & Pacific Railroad (Pacific No. 1)—under Iowa law. But it was not until July 9, 1866, that the entire M&M property was sold on courthouse steps in Davenport under a foreclosure decree to the recently formed CRI&P entity. Next the new company issued $9 million of 7 percent, twenty-five-year bonds to pay for the purchase price of the M&M, the existing mortgage of the C&RI, and the bonds of the Bridge Company. Fortunately, the subsequent corporate entities would acquire the Iowa land grant. As part of these financial arrangements, the official merger of the C&RI in Illinois and the CRI&P of Iowa took place on August 20, 1866, and the Chicago, Rock Island & Pacific Railroad Company (Pacific No. 2) came into being.[72]

The old M&M came to life. Under the generalship of John F. Tracy, who since 1854 had been associated with the now retired Henry Farnam, the main line advanced westward from the end of its track to Des Moines. On September 9, 1867, the first passenger train "made up of two express and mail cars, two passenger coaches and a splendid family stateroom coach" reached the capital city. Unlike those who had held earlier celebrations as rails linked communities with Chicago, local residents, while not indifferent to gaining a direct connection to the East, had waited impatiently for more than a dozen years to have this opportunity. In the interim, on August 29, 1866, the city had enthusiastically welcomed the arrival of the Des Moines Valley Rail Road (after 1874, the Keokuk & Des Moines Railroad) from the Mississippi River town of Keokuk, appropriately called the "Gate City." "Des Moines never saw a happier throng of citizens," recalled an eyewitness. "All Des Moines was there." A local newspaper proclaimed, "All doubts have fled! The great triumph has been achieved! The promised train is here today! The sun shines in a clear firmament! The day, yea, the hour of final victory has come!" The appearance of the first CRI&P train had been anticlimactic.[73]

What constituted the consolidated company? It controlled 452 miles, including the main line across Illinois and the leased Peoria & Bureau Valley Railroad. In Iowa the principal line linked Davenport with Des Moines, a distance of 173 miles, and a secondary route connected with the main stem at Wilton Junction and extended 50 miles via Muscatine to Washington. Its rolling stock adequately served customer's freight and passenger requirements. The Rock Island owned fifty-seven wood-burning and thirty-five coal-burning locomotives; 1,846 cars, including 1,109 freight cars; and 46 passenger coaches. Along the railroad corridor, it had appropriate support facilities, including combination-style frame depots, wood-supply and coal stations, water tanks, and strategically placed repair shops. There were also sidings, yards, and telegraph lines.[74]

Not radically different from other developing granger roads (so called from their original purpose as grain carriers), the Rock Island operated only a modest number of trains. A single daily-except-Sunday freight usually covered most of its network. Passenger service largely resembled freight-train frequency. The main line and the Peoria branch carded an express and an "accommodation," meaning a slower, local passenger train. The Muscatine–Washington line offered both a freight and an accommodation. During busy times the railroad dispatched extra freight and passenger movements, including holiday and excursion specials.[75]

At an early date the Rock Island also provided a skeleton suburban service. Other Chicago-centered roads did too, and like them the Rock Island carved out its own commuter territory. This expanding metropolis had a growing number of residents who wanted dependable transportation on a regular basis going to and from their places of employment at a reasonable price. Then there were the shoppers and others who sought similar transport to and from the heart of the city. It would be in the immediate post–Civil War years that fledgling operations began, concentrated on the sixteen miles of main line between downtown Chicago and Blue Island. By 1870 the company operated a suburban branch that left the main line at Ninety-Seventh Street and ran westward along Ninety-Ninth Street for about a mile and then turned southward for about four miles before reaching the main line at Blue Island. Real-estate developers, including the Rock Island itself, gave life to the bedroom communities of Washington Heights and Morgan Park. On this line service began with what locals called a "dummy train," which made two daily trips each way between Blue Island and Chicago. In subsequent years the Rock Island greatly expanded its suburban operations as area population soared.[76]

The consolidated company had a valuable asset in its real-estate holdings. By midyear 1865 it owned 481,774 acres. This expansive property included potentially some of the most productive farmland in the United States. Within less than a decade, much of it was sold profitably and came under cultivation.[77]

As with other land-grant railroads, including those in Iowa, the Rock Island aggressively marketed its real estate. Early on it included in its public timetables and elsewhere this type of promotional copy: "CHEAP FARMS. The Chicago, Rock Island & Pacific R.R. Co. is now offering for sale to ACTUAL SETTLERS a part of the magnificent land grant, containing more than a half million acres of the CHOICEST & MOST DESIRABLE LANDS IN THE STATE OF IOWA." The company's land commissioner, based in Davenport, explained that potential buyers had several payment options. They could pay cash. "A discount of ten per cent is allowed." Or they could choose short-term payments. "The purchaser pays *one-quarter* of the purchase money in cash, and the remainder in three equal annual payments, with interest at the rate of *six* per cent. Per annum, payable annually." They also had a long-term possibility. "This plan is suited for those who desire to earn the purchase money out of the land itself. On payment of two years' interest in advance at ten per cent., the Company gives a *contract* to convey the land by warranty deed, upon the completion of six annual payments, commencing *two years* after date, thus offering *seven years* to complete the purchase." Hundreds of individuals and families found these options to their liking.[78]

The successful sale of railroad lands and increased farm and community settlement throughout its service territory put smiles on the faces of Rock Island executives, board members, and investors. The growing agricultural riches flowed largely into company cars, and farm and nonfarm supplies, whether machinery, lumber, or merchandise, also increased tonnage. Officials did all that they could to bolster business, including the establishment of trackside lumber yards. "Wanting to increase traffic as well as help promote settlement along its line, the Chicago, Rock Island & Pacific Railroad induced Mr. [Henry] Getchell to establish branch yards along its line as fast as stations were laid out, as far west as the Missouri River, in which he was highly successful." Freight traffic for the fiscal year 1866–1867 was mostly evenly balanced between loaded cars going west and those going east. Not all of the Iowa shipments went to Chicago or through the Chicago gateway; the railroad transshipped mostly agricultural goods for river transport at sites located in Davenport, Rock Island, Muscatine, and Peoria.[79]

Everyone involved with the Rock Island must have had good feelings about the future of their conservatively managed railroad. Income increased, and operating expenses remained relatively stable. On a per-mile basis, the data for 1866–1867 showed earnings of $10,512 and expenses of $5,376, resulting in an amazingly low operating ratio of expenses divided by revenues of fifty-one. A good omen. More positive financial advances occurred during the Gilded Age, notwithstanding the disruptive Panic of 1873, which triggered a multiyear national depression.[80]

EXPANSION

2

THE CHICAGO, ROCK ISLAND & PACIFIC RAILROAD, SUCCESSOR TO THE
Mississippi & Missouri Railroad (M&M), continued its quest to reach the
Missouri River at Council Bluffs, Iowa, and to connect with the transconti-
nental Union Pacific–Central Pacific project. That goal was accomplished on
May 11, 1869, one day after the driving of ceremonial spikes at Promontory,
Utah Territory, yet it was somewhat anticlimactic for residents of the Bluffs.
Most railroad experts and other observers had expected the M&M to be the
first railroad to reach this community, but its progress had been slow and halting. An emerging Rock Island rival, the Chicago & North Western (North
Western), however, had already entered Council Bluffs under the banner of
its affiliate Cedar Rapids & Missouri River Railroad. That historic event took
place on January 22, 1867, and a euphoric celebration ensued. The local citizenry turned out en masse to give "a right royal reception" to those arriving
on the first train. "From that date a new era dawned on the city," opined one
commentator. "It ceased at that hour to be a mere frontier town." Ironically
Grenville Dodge, who had helped to survey the M&M, served as the principal
speaker to commemorate the North Western's masterful achievement.[1]

Arrival of the Rock Island in an aspiring Council Bluffs nevertheless
caused considerable buzz. This happening attracted a "dense crowd," even
though it was interrupted by an intense thunderstorm. Unlike the North
Western's earlier appearance, the occasion came with a razzle-dazzle flare. This
event had its customary celebratory music and flowery oratory, and the Rock
Island brought to town a remarkable locomotive. Not that this piece of motive
power featured an avant-garde design—it was an iconic 4-4-0 American Standard type—but its boiler jacket, smokestack, cylinders, and appurtenances
were finished and veneered in German silver, an alloy of copper, nickel, and

zinc. Moreover, the cab was made of the best hardwoods, being "a fine example of the cabinet maker's art."[2]

Why this eye-catching locomotive? The reason stemmed from its builder, Grant Locomotive Works of Patterson, New Jersey, recent successor to the New Jersey Locomotive and Machinery Company. The Grant firm sought to draw attention to its engineering prowess, having constructed a locomotive that employed a high percentage of standardized parts. The venue for its first public display was not a domestic event but the Paris Universal Exhibition, which was held between April 1 and November 3, 1867. Grant christened its silver engine the *America*, which became popular with exhibit attendees and won a coveted gold metal. After prolonged negotiations, the Rock Island purchased the *America*, which cost $35,000 to build and transport to and from France, for $10,000, the going price for an American Standard locomotive.[3]

Numbered the 109 by the Rock Island, the silver engine began its maiden run on June 4, 1869, from Chicago to Council Bluffs for the celebration. Coupled to four other locomotives and a string of crowded coaches, No. 109 grabbed attention throughout its westward journey. "When the silver engine passed Marseilles [Illinois] my father and three of us boys gave it a grand salute with a small cannon which we possessed," a resident remembered. "The Rock Island meant a great deal to us. It was the first railroad we ever saw." When No. 109 steamed to a stop near the Rock Island station on Pearl Street in Council Bluffs, it attracted considerable interest. Later, according to transportation historian John White Jr., "she proved herself more than a showy prima donna by winning a U.S. mail contract by merit of her speed and power." During the Centennial Exposition held in Philadelphia in 1876, No. 109 once again went on public display. Acquisition of this unusual locomotive worked out well for the company.[4]

Not long after the Rock Island established freight and passenger service between Chicago and Council Bluffs, speculation developed that the flamboyant Jay Gould, who headed the Erie Railroad between 1868 and 1872, might forge a transcontinental route between New York and California. It would be a complex undertaking, and one that presumably involved leasing the Rock Island. If this were to occur, it would be necessary to lay a third rail to accommodate Erie's broad-gauge rolling stock. In this instance Gould just dreamed, but he recognized the strategic value of the Rock Island.[5]

By 1870 Council Bluffs had emerged as an important node on the national railroad map. Although the North Western had won the race in 1867, arrival of the Rock Island two years later and the Burlington & Missouri River Railroad of Iowa, a Chicago, Burlington & Quincy Railroad (Burlington) affiliate, in

January 1870, meant that three east-west carriers served this transcontinental gateway.[6]

With the presence of multiple direct Chicago-to-Council Bluffs railroads, which forged a historic connection with the Union Pacific–Central Pacific route to California, the highly competitive situation created the potential to cause long-term financial harm to each Chicago-based company. Rate cutting became a growing concern among railroaders, and a pragmatic response followed. Spearheaded by Rock Island president John Tracy, during the summer of 1870 the three roads hammered out a traffic arrangement known as the "Iowa Pool." In order to cover operational costs, each carrier agreed to retain 50 percent of its freight revenues and 45 percent of its passenger revenues from business between the two terminals. The remaining money would be pooled and divided equally among the participants. Although it was not legally binding, for the next fourteen years this agreement functioned reasonably well, creating rate stability among the most direct Chicago-to-Union Pacific connections. If cutthroat rate cutting had erupted during the hard times of the 1870s, these railroads might have failed or become so weakened that they could not have readily expanded during the construction boom of the 1880s.[7]

The relationship between the Rock Island and the North Western involved more than the Iowa Pool. Contemporary rumors flew about a possible merger between the two companies. Not only did John Tracy play a pivotal role with launching the Iowa Pool, he also served as a guiding force that sought to make these twin granger roads a dominant force in midwestern railroading. A somewhat mysterious figure, Tracy had joined the Rock Island as superintendent in the mid-1850s after a stint with the New York & Erie Railroad. In August 1866 he won the presidency following the departure of Dr. Charles Durant, who went to join the Union Pacific and who in turn had replaced Henry Farnam in June 1863.[8]

Unlike other Rock Island chief executives during the latter half of the nineteenth century John Tracy exhibited a personal speculative bent. Throughout this period he invested heavily in securities and traded them both long and short. Tracy became associated with a financial group linked to the Pennsylvania Railroad. This "Tracy Crowd" acquired a large block of North Western shares with borrowed money, and this leveraged stock served as collateral. The goal was clear. They wanted the two properties to deter the Burlington's growth in the lucrative traffic regions of Illinois and Iowa. Burlington president James Joy made his road's position clear. "Our expenditures are the result of our policy, and we must enlarge our accommodations and equipment and power and all our appointments to suit our enlarged business. This is unavoidable if we mean to maintain ourselves and command the business of the country and keep it from rival projects." Tracy and his business partners did more than take seats on the North Western board of directors. About the time the Iowa Pool agreement was inked, Tracy became the fourth president of the North Western and served in that capacity from June 1870 to June 1873. Still, he continued to head the Rock Island. Tracy could boast that he controlled more miles of railroad than any other contemporary chief executive.[9]

As North Western president, John Tracy was not especially successful. Most of all, his company did not prevent the Burlington from making incursions into what the North Western and Rock Island considered to be their rightful territories. Furthermore, the two roads failed to merge, notwithstanding the belief of Tracy and his associates that such a consolidation would produce an exceptionally robust company. Tracy eventually lessened his grip on the North Western and resigned from the presidency, publicly indicating that he sought to "participate more actively in the field of [Rock Island] corporate expansion." Yet Tracy remained on the North Western board and its influential executive committee until shortly before his death in 1878.[10]

SOUTHWEST EXPANSION

As the decade of the 1870s began, the energetic John Tracy oversaw a major addition to the Rock Island, namely a second route to the Missouri River. Company executives, directors, and principal investors had their eyes on the growing Southwest. The central and southern Great Plains were becoming a productive part of the nation's breadbasket. Wheat, cattle, and other farm and ranch products needed to be sent eastbound to processors and markets, and these agriculturalists required a wide range of manufactured goods and other materials. From multiple corporate paper entities, the Chicago & South Western Railway (C&SW) emerged in August 1871. A $5 million bond sale, secured by a first mortgage that the Rock Island guaranteed, did much to finance this grand undertaking. The expected support from local units of government and adjoining property owners along the line likewise helped to complete this 271-mile extension.[11]

Construction of the C&SW proceeded with rapidity, hardly duplicating the story of the extension of the Mississippi & Missouri across Iowa. The immediate destination would be Leavenworth, Kansas, with its connection with the Kansas Pacific and the anticipated interchange with the gestating Atchison, Topeka & Santa Fe Railway (Santa Fe). Work gangs began their labors at both ends of the projected line. They built northeastward from Stillings Junction, located on the Missouri River opposite Leavenworth, and southwestward from Washington, Iowa, the end of Rock Island tracks from Wilton Junction and Muscatine. When the last spikes were driven in late summer 1871, this "Southwest Division" served more than a half dozen agriculturally dependent county-seat towns, including Fairfield and Centerville, Iowa, and Princeton, Trenton, Gallatin, Plattsburg, and Platte City, Missouri. In order to reach the Kansas side, the company leased the Fort Leavenworth Railroad and its span over the Missouri River. That same year the C&SW installed the twenty-nine-mile Atchison branch, between Edgerton Junction (Atchison Junction) and Winthrop, Missouri, work financed by a $1 million bond mortgage. Unfortunately, the C&SW soon defaulted on its interest payments for both the main line and the Atchison branch. The Rock Island paid the interest on the mainline bonds and continued to operate the line for the C&SW. It foreclosed on the property in 1874 and acquired it outright two years later. The Rock Island, however, had not guaranteed the Atchison branch bonds, and extensive litigation ensued with its bondholders. The US Supreme Court ultimately backed the Rock Island, allowing its purchase at a foreclosure sale.[12]

The predictable celebrations took place with completion of the Leavenworth project. The festivities began on September 26, 1871, with departure of a special Rock Island train from Chicago. On board were railroad officials, investors, and other notables and their spouses, including President Ulysses S. Grant and his wife, Julia, and former Confederate general P. G. T. Beauregard. These two former Civil War adversaries, who enjoyed each other's company, inspired newspaper stories about sectional reunification. It is not surprising that the company polished up No. 109 for this trip "around the loop." The itinerary included travel to Leavenworth for the principal activities, which featured an elaborate banquet at the imposing Planters Hotel. After the hoopla the train proceeded to Council Bluffs and finally back to Chicago, reaching the city early on September 30 after having journeyed more than 1,500 miles. That was good timing; the Great Chicago Fire erupted a week later, costing the company an estimated $300,000 in property damages, of which insurance covered only about $45,000. Yet this sizable loss never threatened the Rock Island's financial health.[13]

The Chicago conflagration, which garnered national attention and regional aid and assistance, did not stop the Rock Island from promoting its nearly thousand-mile system as the "Great Omaha and Leavenworth Lines." The "Great" did not refer just to mileage and connections but also to the company's modern motive power and freight and passenger equipment. Its good track structure made for dependable service.[14]

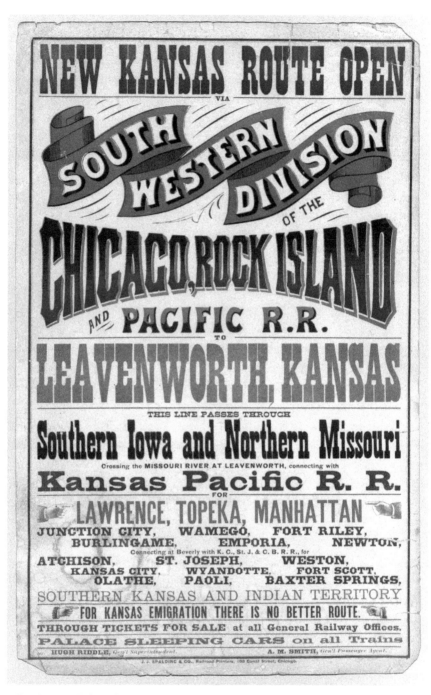

Following completion of the Leavenworth extension, the Rock Island distributed this broadside to announce proudly the opening of this strategic line. Major expansion had begun.

John W. Barriger III National Railroad Library Coll., University of Missouri, Saint Louis

By the 1870s the Rock Island had established itself in domestic and international money circles as a road with a bright future. Gross earnings for 1866 stood at $3,254,236, and four years later they amounted to $5,995,226. Then in 1879 the figure reached $9,409,833. Net earnings for that year were an impressive $4,548,117, or 48 percent of gross receipts. Capitalization remained moderate, due largely to a friendly building and operating terrain and honest construction practices.[15]

During the Tracy presidency, the Rock Island did not become overexuberant with new line construction. In fact, its expansion policies could be considered as conservative. Admittedly building challenges existed. The coming of hard times, which ravaged the nation following the severe Wall Street Panic of 1873, reduced railroad construction nationally, and the Midwest was no exception. Adding to the negativity, the states in the Upper Mississippi River valley, including Illinois and Iowa, became actively involved in railroad regulation, causing great consternation among affected carriers. "Do the people of Iowa really wish to confiscate the property of companies owning railways in that State?" asked a Rock Island official. The agriculturally oriented Patrons of Husbandry, better known as the Grange, instigated stringent laws designed to reduce freight and passenger charges and to end long- and short-haul rate discriminations. They also launched state regulatory commissions to ensure enforcement. The Hawkeye State, which claimed the largest Grange membership in the nation, gained fame in 1874 for its Granger-inspired antirailroad code, but four years later lawmakers under industry pressure toned it down.[16]

One aspect of Granger agitation caused the financially and political cautious Rock Island board to react proactively. Lobbying activities in the Illinois and Iowa capitols targeted the Granger "menace," but there was also a determination to dispose of "excess" earnings. Reformers showed hostility toward corporations that were perceived to be unduly wealthy. Between 1866 and 1876, the Rock Island distributed multiple cash payments to stockholders. Four of these amounted to 10 percent, five 8 percent, one 8.5 percent, and another 7.5 percent. As the political activities of the Grange waned, the dividend for 1879 again totaled 10 percent.[17]

Before the advent of the Granger movement, the Rock Island, which owned two core thoroughfares and the link to Peoria, constructed several branches in Iowa. The company designed them to tap inland communities, strengthen interchange connections, and protect its territory from "invaders." Its corporate objective was "Good sound branch lines."[18]

By the latter part of 1870s, the Rock Island map revealed several modest additions in Iowa. This trackage included two that funneled traffic through

Des Moines, one that extended from the Leavenworth stem at Washington, and another that connected with the main line at Newton, thirty-five miles east of Des Moines. In November 1871, a twenty-two-mile branch, built under the Des Moines, Indianola & Missouri Railroad banner, opened between the capital city and Indianola, seat of Warren County and home to a small Methodist institution of higher education, Simpson Centenary College (later Simpson College). "The railroad connection with Des Moines betokened good times for the school just as it did for Indianola," observed college historian Joseph Walt. "Students noticed that the Rock Island depot was located a short block east of the campus, and they concluded that it was located there for their convenience." Rock Island officials, who had ties with local organizers, quickly took control and contemplated building south from Indianola to a connection with the Leavenworth line. However, that never occurred. In the fall of 1872, several miles north of Indianola, an extension opened that stretched westward from Summerset Junction, about a mile from the village of Summerset, through the Middle River valley, to another central Iowa county-seat community, Winterset. This twenty-six-mile addition was constructed as the Des Moines, Winterset & Southwestern Railway. As the name suggests, it planned to expand, likely paralleling the main line and terminating somewhere south of Council Bluffs. Decades later there would be an attempt to build west from Winterset to Greenfield. In 1903 the Rock Island acquired the stock of the Des Moines & Southern Railroad, a company launched by local interests. Some grading occurred between these two county seats before the project collapsed.[19]

The Rock Island found that the Indianola and Winterset branches held another advantage. They did more than serve a prosperous agricultural and growing population area; they offered corporate protection from building incursions by the Burlington. In 1878 that company embarked upon an aggressive program of feeder-line construction in the Hawkeye State that peaked two years later. These additions radiated both north and south from its main stem across southern Iowa. Included in that northward picket fence were branches from Chariton to Indianola, Creston to Fontanelle via Winterset and later farther west to Cumberland, and Red Oak to Griswold. Yet Burlington historian Richard Overton contended that "throughout its building program in Iowa, the C.B. & Q. sought to maintain harmonious relations with the Rock Island." Perhaps so, but the Rock Island still saw need for territorial protection.[20]

The final construction undertakings that occurred during the Tracy years involved two additional projects. The first was the longest, namely the seventy-eight-mile Washington to Knoxville branch. This east-west line roughly shadowed the main stem to the south and appeared piecemeal. The initial building linked Washington with Signourney, covering twenty-eight miles, and opened in 1872. Next came the extension from Signourney to Oskaloosa, twenty-five miles, completed in 1876, and later that year the twenty-five-mile line to Knoxville opened. Residents of the latter community had long sought an east-west rail artery, having done so in the mid-1850s and again in the late 1860s. They showed interest in two projects: the Philadelphia, Fort Wayne & Platte River Railroad and the Muscatine, Washington, Oskaloosa & Council Bluffs Railroad. The latter one had aroused greater enthusiasm, "but not to the extent of raising money with which to build the road." As with the vast majority of paper projects, talk was cheap, but capital was not. Once more these additions meant that the Rock Island served three more county capitals and productive farming areas. It expected to close the twenty-five-mile gap between Knoxville and Indianola, but that never happened. Still, a "completed" line between these two county seats appeared on contemporary company maps.

Near Oskaloosa, an emerging soft-coal mining and trading center, the Rock Island forged an interchange with the Keokuk & Des Moines Railroad (K&D). As with previous lines, community support was strong. Take Oskaloosa. The company asked its citizenry to raise $20,000 and to furnish land for the right-of-way and station facilities, and they readily complied. During this age of railroads, urban residents and farmers consistently sought to improve their connectedness to business centers and distant markets. They also expected that these iron links would attract new residents and raise real-estate values. In the case of Oskaloosa (and many other communities), it was hoped that a railroad would increase its local investments. "The crossing of the two branches of this company [K&D and Rock Island] near Oskaloosa may be of very material benefit to the town, which it will be if the company decides to locate shops here, which there are strong reasons for doing."[21]

Another addition was the seventeen-mile Newton & Monroe Railroad. Opened in 1877, it connected Newton, the Jasper County capital on the Rock Island main line, with Monroe to the south. It launched in 1871 with the ambitious corporate name of the Iowa, Minnesota & North Pacific Railway, but local backers reorganized with a more realistic moniker. Although the line crossed an agricultural area, this property was principally a coal hauler. Although the Rock Island already served several coal-producing locales, this trackage at Monroe interchanged with the Keokuk & Des Moines, another coal carrier, and collectively supplied fuel for the railroad and other customers.

In 1875 the popular American type (4-4-0), No. 17, waits in Morris, Illinois, accompanied by crew and onlookers. Leaning out of the locomotive cab is engineer H. Knickerbocker, who later took the throttle of No. 109, the famed silver *America* 4-4-0. The 4-4-0 type became, as one commentator noted, "as American as the Stars and Stripes and the Colt Peacemaker."

Don L. Hofsommer coll.

The Rock Island, though, failed to construct the long branches that potentially would have generated large volumes of traffic to and from its main stems.[22]

The Rock Island strengthened its freight presence in greater Chicago with industrial or terminal trackage. In 1874 it acquired the graded 6.5-mile right-of-way of the Calumet & Chicago Canal Company and installed the track. Subsequently this appendage was lengthened about three miles to reach the Joseph B. Brown ironworks. Known as the South Chicago Branch, this addition extended from South Englewood to the South Chicago docks on Lake Michigan. "Freight can be transferred to all of the Eastern links of railway leaving Chicago, and to the Illinois Central Railroad, outside the city limits, and also to vessels in the South Chicago harbor," said the company. About that time the Rock Island added another industrial appendage, the six miles between two Hawkeye State locations, Wilton and Lime Kiln.[23]

In 1878, the existence of several affiliated companies prompted the Tracy administration to launch the Iowa Southern & Missouri Northern Railroad Company (IS&MN). It became a holding structure for control of the Chicago & Southwestern and the Iowa branch roads. On June 4, 1880, these properties were fused together to form a more streamlined Chicago, Rock Island & Pacific *Railway* Company. Indebtedness increased when the new company assumed $5 million of IS&MN bonds, and shareholders of the old Chicago, Rock Island & Pacific Rail*road* received for one share of stock two shares in the consolidated firm. Modernization of the corporate structure was not the only motivation. Since large cash dividends sparked political resentment, a good tactic was to water stock. Although the price and dividends per share dropped, investors did not suffer. Furthermore, the new bond obligations failed to make much of a financial drain, and the replacement stock produced no increase in fixed charges. "Instead of being occasioned by too little prosperity," noted a railroad economist, "it was caused by too much."[24]

THE JAMES GANG

Expansion of the Rock Island during the Tracy years gained long-lasting corporate significance, yet what is remembered (and romanticized) involves a daring train robbery that took place on the evening of July 21, 1873, near Adair, Iowa, about eighty miles east of Council Bluffs. The perpetrators were Jesse James and five members of his infamous gang. This brigandage involved robbing eastbound train No. 2, which the outlaws believed carried a large Wells Fargo Express Company shipment of western gold bullion destined for the New York precious metals market.[25]

The cunning gang selected a remote location in hilly terrain with a deep cut near a sharp curve. Before No. 2 (which contained baggage and express cars, coaches, sleepers, a smoker, and a ladies' car) reached the crime scene, gang members unbolted a section of rail, attached it to a length of rope, and waited in nearby brush. As the train slowly approached, several gang members yanked the rail from the track. When the locomotive was about to derail, they spattered it with bullets. Although engineer John Rafferty saw the impending danger, he could not stop in time; the train lacked air brakes, having only hand brakes and the throttle reversing lever, or "Johnson bar." Tragically, Rafferty died when the locomotive overturned, and his fireman sustained serious injuries. Unfortunately for James and his compatriots, the expected $75,000 in gold was not in the express car; it had been sent on an earlier train. Still there was about $2,500 in cash in the express car, and once they robbed the frightened passengers, the amount totaled more than $6,000, including watches and jewelry. Still, that was a lucrative take for a ten-minute heist, and the masked and mounted robbers slipped away into the darkness. The Rock Island offered $5,000 for the capture of the James gang, but that enticing reward went uncollected.[26]

In the minds of antirailroad and anticorporation citizens, the Adair train robbery appeared to possess Robin Hood qualities, taking from the rich to help the poor. In his assessment of the event, historical writer T. J. Stiles explained the motivation of these culprits. They expected a greater financial windfall from train robberies than from other types of plunderage, such as banks or the offices of county treasurers. And to their way of thinking, the robberies represented a personal attack on the most despised corporation of the Gilded Age—the railroad. The success of the James gang on the Rock Island led to its committing six more train holdups, including one on a Rock Island express in July 1881 near Winston in Daviess County, Missouri, about sixty-five miles from Kansas City. That event resulted in the shooting deaths of a passenger and the conductor.[27]

Soon, the Adair event, which became the first train holdup in the West,[28] became a part of American folklore. A contemporary ballad contained these factually garbled words:

Jesse James all alone in the rain
Stopped an' stuck up the Eas'-boun' train;
Swayed through the coaches with horns an' a tail,
Lit out with the bullion and the registered mail.[29]

The James gang inspired no love among Rock Island brass and rank-and-file employees. Management saw truth in the old adage that an ounce of prevention is worth a pound of cure. It soon placed armed guards on selected trains to protect vulnerable shipments and took other precautions.[30]

MORE EXPANSION

On April 14, 1877, John Tracy stepped down from the Rock Island presidency because of failing health. On that date Hugh Riddle (1822–1892), who served as general superintendent, took charge. This New Hampshire native, who was raised in humble circumstances, first worked as a schoolteacher but abandoned that vocation to study civil engineering. From 1846 to 1851, Riddle joined construction crews on the New York & Erie Railroad, and after a brief stint with future New York Central properties Buffalo & State Line and Canandaigua & Niagara Falls Railroads, he rejoined the Erie as its chief engineer. Riddle subsequently became a division superintendent and a general superintendent. In 1869 he left a troubled Erie for the general superintendency of the financially secure Rock Island. Although Riddle retained that critical position, the board of directors in 1871 elected him vice president, and subsequently he became president. He oversaw a robust carrier and helped to orchestrate the well-conceived 1880 reorganization. But on June 6, 1883, this fiscally careful executive resigned, apparently for health reasons. Riddle, though, did not sever his connection with the Rock Island; he chaired the executive committee of the board of directors until his death. "He died honored and full of honors," remarked a contemporary chronicler.[31]

The 1880s proved to be an exciting time for railroad builders. These years witnessed the tremendous expansion of the national rail network; more than 71,000 miles of lines appeared, bringing the total in 1890 to an impressive 163,597 miles. Most of this construction took place in the Midwest and Great Plains—Rock Island country. By the last decade of the nineteenth century, Americans claimed about half of all railroad mileage in the world.

The Riddle administration continued the process of modest expansion. By the time Hugh Riddle left the presidency, the Rock Island had become a 1,365-mile carrier. A major addition came on May 14, 1878, when it leased the 162-mile Keokuk & Des Moines Railway. This forty-five-year agreement helped to make Des Moines a "Rock Island town" and guaranteed the company's dominance. The K&D gave the railroad access to a third Iowa Mississippi River community, Keokuk, and to Ottumwa, the Wapello County capital and an emerging manufacturing and meat-packing center on the Burlington main line. The lease also allowed for an interchange south of Ottumwa at Eldon with the Leavenworth line. Another attraction was the end to the K&D as a rate disrupter. It had offered "through rates to Eastern and Southern markets, thus forcing at times a spirited and damaging competition at several points." The Rock Island, however, found the K&D to be in poor physical condition, and its rolling stock, especially motive power, lacked stellar qualities. But with company financing, heavier steel replaced antiquated iron rails, and obsolete equipment was retired. To further enhance the K&D, the Rock Island organized the Keosauqua & Southwestern Railroad to build a 4.5-mile extension from Mount Zion (formerly Summit) on the K&D to Keosauqua, a town on the Des Moines River and the seat of Van Buren County. The Rock Island was fortunate that a short-lived narrow-gauge pike, the St. Louis, Keosauqua & St. Paul Railroad, had recently been abandoned, and so rails were laid on that naked right-of-way. In 1880 service began on this twisty stub.[32]

The Rock Island did not ignore the territory west of Des Moines. While much of this agricultural land lacked the fertility of the best soil in the state, it was ideally suited for livestock raising; in fact, it became known as "Iowa's Blue Grass Country." Just as the company had penetrated south of its east-west line, it soon threw down a gaggle of laterals to both the north and south to "generate and protect traffic." The Rock Island considered construction costs to be reasonable. "These lines are located mostly in valleys, are not expensive to build and can be cheaply maintained and operated." North of the main stem came completion in 1878 of the twenty-five-mile Atlantic & Audubon Railroad (Audubon branch), which reached still another county seat and the thirteen-mile Avoca, Harlan & Northern Railroad (Harlan branch), which extended to yet another county capital. The following year the fifteen-mile Guthrie Center & North-Western Railroad (Guthrie Center branch) opened between Menlo and the Guthrie County seat. To the south, the year 1880 saw the appearance of the fifteen-mile Atlantic Southern Railroad (Griswold branch) connecting Atlantic with Griswold. Finally another short branch, but one with an imposing name, the eighteen-mile Carson, Avoca, Macedonia & South-Western Railroad (Carson branch), opened between Avoca and Carson. As with earlier feeders, the Rock Island embraced the policy of incorporating or taking control of separate companies. If one of these entities failed financially, its negative impact on the larger corporation would be negligible. Importantly, none of these branches encroached on either the North Western to the north or the Burlington to the south, being wholly within what the Rock Island considered its "natural territory." Yet the Rock Island did not show much of an adversarial relationship with the Burlington. The company did not fuss much when the Burlington extended its Albia-to-Knoxville branch to Des Moines between 1879 and 1880. In fact, the Burlington seriously considered purchasing the Rock Island in 1879 but concluded that its stock was too expensive.[33]

Obtaining a lease or trackage-rights agreement became a Rock Island hallmark and often the practical, less costly way to expand. That 1854 lease of the Peoria & Bureau Valley and the later one of the K&D would not be exceptional. In December 1879 the Rock Island signed a twenty-five-year agreement with the Hannibal & St. Joseph Railroad (H&StJ), the first road to cross Missouri, to operate freight and passenger trains over its fifty-four-mile line between Cameron, on the Leavenworth stem, and Kansas City. The Rock Island also could use its freight house and other facilities in the latter place. These were desirable arrangements. The Leavenworth interchange had generated less traffic than expected, and the Santa Fe failed to build its proposed link between Topeka and Leavenworth. Since the Rock Island would probably enter on its own rails into this competitive urban hub, H&StJ directors granted the concession for joint use. At this time the Burlington had lost the H&StJ to financier Jay Gould, but in 1883 it reacquired control. Still, the twenty-five-year lease remained in effect and continued for decades. The Rock Island also arranged with the Union Passenger Depot Company in Kansas City to have the same privileges as the other eight roads that served the busy station. Kansas Citians, especially business leaders, welcomed the Rock Island, having had continued problems with several other carriers. In early 1880 Rock Island inaugurated direct passenger service between Chicago and Kansas City, seven years before rival Milwaukee Road extended its line from eastern Iowa to the Missouri metropolis. In order to shorten the distance (and time) for its southwestern trains and avoid the original route via Wilton Junction, the Rock Island built along the west bank of the Mississippi River between Davenport and Muscatine. This twenty-six-mile cutoff opened in 1881.[34]

RIDING THE ROCK ISLAND

Since the Rock Island prospered, it offered passengers attractive transportation experiences. Business became heavy; this was also true for freight, mail, and express shipments. In 1880 the company carried 1,005,418 passengers, and volume remained on an upward trend. Earnings generated from ticket sales that year stood at $2,318,452, while net earnings generated an impressive $5,326,116.[35]

The number of dispatched trains had not changed dramatically since the early 1870s. Usually two daily passengers plied the main lines, although three daily-except-Sunday ones served stations between Chicago and Peoria. Branch lines had at least one but sometimes two daily accommodations, but Sunday service was rare. Company scheduling, though, did not trouble this public face of railroading.

Equipment was modern and well maintained, and reliability was prized. By the late 1870s the Rock Island immodestly advertised itself as the "Great Overland Route" and the "Best Equipped Road with the Smoothest Track." Few, if any, publicly disagreed. There were complaints, however, about the availability of convenient, satisfying meals. Passengers either brought their own food or purchased it at designated meal stops, where they usually had only twenty minutes to eat. These places existed only on the main line, though. One such trackside facility appeared east of Council Bluffs in Avoca. Not long after rails had reached the town in 1869, the company erected a large frame hotel and dining hall near the depot. Soon the company leased it to a former Council Bluffs hotel proprietor, and apparently the food and service satisfied travelers. This facility remained busy until dining cars appeared. Yet for decades there would be other meal stops at eating houses that became part of the Rock Island travel experience.[36]

In May 1877 a sea change in food service began when the Rock Island made a major commitment to pleasing passengers, especially those who traveled long distances. The company introduced "restaurant cars" on its principal trains, a convenience that at the time competitor North Western lacked but that the Burlington had already introduced. When this service began, the Rock Island owned four cars, built in its south Chicago shops and painted an attractive wine color. They had memorable names: *Australia, Occidental, Oriental,* and *Overland.* The passenger department assigned the *Occidental* and *Overland* to trains No. 1 and No. 2 between Chicago and Wilton Junction, Iowa, serving dinner on No. 1 and breakfast on No. 2. The *Oriental* operated both ways between Council Bluffs and Atlantic, Iowa, offering breakfast on No. 1 and dinner on No. 2. The railroad used the fourth car as a spare. Each diner seated sixteen patrons at four tables and provided a small lunch counter. Included was an "elegant smoking saloon" (or bar) for adult males. As more long-distance trains appeared on the expanding system, additional dining equipment joined the fleet. The company initially established support commissaries in Chicago and Davenport and later added other locations.[37]

When patronizing a Rock Island diner, passengers found attractive food choices. The dinner bill of fare offered traditional meat dishes and seasonal wild game, including venison, duck, and pigeon, along with an assortment of appetizers, vegetables, breads, and desserts. Meals were priced at seventy-five cents, and at the discretion of the steward, children paid half price. Trainmen might partake of a meal for thirty-five cents. Except for employees, adult passengers could acquire a small bottle of wine for an additional fifteen cents. There was a good chance that travelers agreed with company hype that "Rock Island Meals Are the Best on Wheels." Diners ate in pleasant surroundings, featuring hardwood paneling, polished brass fixtures, and gas lighting. Royal Dresden china, heavy flatware, linen tablecloths, and starched napkins graced the tables.[38]

The better long-distance trains also provided sleeping cars. Initially the Rock Island operated its own equipment. The first company sleeper dated back to the dawn of this specialized rolling stock; the *City of Chicago* entered service in March 1863. More and improved equipment followed, and by the mid-1870s the company boasted that it operated a fleet of "Magnificent Palace Sleeping Cars." They ran between Chicago and Peoria, Des Moines, Council Bluffs, and Atchison. In January 1880 the railroad contracted with the Pullman Palace Car Company to have it assume these operations. Pullman agreed

Walter No. 1 2 3 4

Chicago, Rock Island & Pacific Railway.

DINING CAR SERVICE.

COOK'S CHECK.

This Check must be taken to Kitchen with First Order.

WINE LIST.

—o—

CHAMPAGNE			Qts.	Pts.
Pommery & Greno (Sec),	. . . . . .		$3.50	$2.00
Veuve Cliquot, Yellow Label,	. . .		3.50	2.00
CLARET				
St. Julien, (Cruse & Fils Freres),	. .		1.00	.60
Zinfandel,	.			.50
WHITE WINES				
Haut Sauterne (Cruse & Fils Freres),	.		1.75	1.00
WINES, LIQUORS, ETC.				
Canadian Club Whisky	.	Individuals,		.20
Scotch Whisky, James Buchanan & Co., (Half Pints),	.			.50
Rye Whisky, (Half Pints),				.50
Fine Old Rye Whisky (Quarter Pints)	.			.30
Old Crow Bourbon Whisky,	. .	Individuals,		.20
Cognac Brandy, 1854, (Half Pints),	.			1.00
Bass & Co. Pale Ale, per bottle,	.			.30
Guinness' Dublin Stout, " "	.			30
Belfast Ginger Ale, " "	.			.25
Congress Water, " "	.			25
Apollinaris Water, " "	.			.25
Budweiser Beer, per pint,	. . .			.15
Lemp's St. Louis Beer, per pint,	. .			.15
Milwaukee Lager Beer, per pint,	.			.15
Hunyadi Water, per glass, 10 cents, per bottle,				.35
Manitou Water,	.			.15
Creme de Menthe,	. . . .	Individuals,		.25

CIGARS, 10c.; TWO FOR 25c.; 15c.; AND 20c.

Manhattan, Martini, or Whisky Cocktail, (Individuals), 20c.

Bromo Soda for headache and car sickness, per bottle, 35c.

Chicago, Rock Island & Pacific Railway.

DINING CAR SERVICE.

GUEST'S BREAKFAST CHECK.

This Check must be Detached and
Canceled by Conductor.

F. Stewart

SUPT. DINING CARS.

PATENTED SEPT. 20, 1892.

The reverse side of this 1890s Rock Island dining car menu contains breakfast offerings, but this side presents a comprehensive drink list, including alcoholic beverages. Perhaps this is surprising, yet the warning is not: "No Wines or Liquors sold in Prohibition States." By the late nineteenth century, drys had scored legislative victories in several Rock Island states, including Iowa and Kansas.

Author's coll.

During the late nineteenth century, the Rock Island issued oversized black-and-white public timetables. Noteworthy are the horseshoe logo and the slogan: "Good Luck to All Who Travel via the Chicago, Rock Island and Pacific Ry." But did they need good luck?

Author's coll.

to purchase a half interest in the existing fleet of fifteen Rock Island cars and eventually gained full ownership. It would be Pullman, not Rock Island, that staffed these sleepers with conductors and porter-attendants and provided onboard supplies and conducted maintenance and repairs.[39]

Much less elegant were trains that operated in commuter service in greater Chicago. After all, these trips were of short duration. The city and suburban areas boomed following the hard times of the 1870s; Chicago experienced a population explosion from 298,977 in 1870 to 508,185 a decade later, a far cry from its mid-century total of about 30,000 residents. Predictably, more riders flocked to these workday trains; weekends, however, offered fewer movements. Although the Vanderbilt-controlled Pittsburgh, Fort Wayne & Chicago Railroad, and later the Chicago & Eastern Illinois, offered competition between Englewood and the central business district, the Rock Island met these challenges, upgrading its commuter runs with better motive power and coaches. During this period the company installed a second track between Twenty-Second Street and Englewood. By 1886 multiple runs operated in each direction between Chicago and Joliet, the terminus of what developed into a busy commuter zone. Most of the Joliet trains, though, served western destinations. At the end of the decade, the railroad lengthened a connecting stub known as the "Washington Heights Suburban Line," providing greater patron convenience.[40]

RANSOM CABLE AND THE GREAT ROCK ISLAND ROUTE

On June 6, 1883, Ransom Reed Cable (1834–1909) became the seventh president of the Chicago, Rock Island & Pacific Railway. When compared to other railroad executives of the Gilded Age, he stands out as one of the most dynamic. Under his leadership the Rock Island became an interregional giant. An ardent expansionist, Cable oversaw his company's rail network spreading from 1,365 miles in 1883 to 7,123 miles in 1903, the year he retired as chairman of the board of directors, having relinquished the presidency five years earlier.[41]

Ransom Cable, or as he called himself, R. R. Cable, lived an active life. Early in his career this Athens County, Ohio, native, who possessed solid business training from his entrepreneurial father, entered coal-mining and railroad enterprises with his uncle Philander L. Cable in Rock Island and the nearby Coal Valley area. During this time he became involved with the Peoria & Rock Island Railway, a largely coal-hauling shortline, spearheaded by his uncle, that in 1903 officially entered the Rock Island fold. Then in 1870 Cable became president of the Rockford, Rock Island & St. Louis Railroad, a future component of the Burlington. Because of his prominence in business circles and public affairs, and most of all in his railroad and banking connections, he won a seat on the Rock Island's board of directors in 1877. Two years later Cable became the principal assistant to Hugh Riddle. In 1880 Cable rose to the position of vice president and general manager before assuming the leadership role. At his election, Cable took as his official title president *and* general manager, indicating that he reigned supreme at the Rock Island. Because of the demanding nature of the presidency, he relinquished the general managership in 1887. "His manner was always bluff," opined an obituary writer, "but seldom harsh."[42]

As Cable assumed his duties, the Iowa Pool was collapsing. For some time Jay Gould, who headed the Union Pacific (UP), had strongly opposed this traffic arrangement. The audacious railroad executive, more celebrated and feared than respected, repeatedly sought to exploit additional, albeit usually longer, routes to Chicago and other gateways. Then in 1882, with the Burlington's Denver extension penetrating deep into Union Pacific country, the door opened for other granger roads aggressively to cross the Missouri River. Only a durable traffic agreement between the Chicago-based carriers might prevent a spree of tracklaying.

During this time, competitive rate wars—called "unfettered competition" by industry personnel—intensified among trunk roads. Still, the Iowa Pool struggled on until the waning months of 1883, when the Tripartite Agreement served as its brief replacement. This pooling arrangement, designed "to establish and maintain a closer alliance between said systems," initially consisted of the Rock Island, Chicago, Milwaukee & St. Paul (Milwaukee) and the Union Pacific, but it quickly expanded to the Wabash, St. Louis & Pacific (Wabash) and the North Western. The Burlington was not pleased. With railroads suspicious of one another, the North Western withdrew from the Tripartite Agreement, and other internal problems developed. Not to be ignored was the changing railroad map of the West. It revealed more than a Burlington line to Denver; the Texas Pacific and Southern Pacific established a southern transcontinental route to California, and the upstart Denver & Rio Grande connected with the Central Pacific. The monopoly that the Union Pacific had once enjoyed on transcontinental traffic evaporated, and it no longer owned even the middle of the continent. Moreover, the UP experienced worsening financial conditions. Because railroad managers sought order and predictability, they made another attempt to establish stable freight rates. As the Tripartite Agreement dissolved, what turned out to be a longer-lasting organization, the Western Freight Association, emerged, bringing a degree of rate stability among these trunk roads, including the Burlington. Nevertheless, this arrangement did not cause Ransom Cable and his board of directors to ignore the advantages of building beyond the Missouri River. They had no idea how individual railroad strategies might change. Since there was nothing legally binding about the Western Freight Association, any traffic alliance could dissolve quickly. Soon the Rock Island decided to take the plunge into new territories during what became the golden age of railroad construction. Cable felt confident of the ability of the Rock Island to expand. "The road has never been in higher favor than now, and this confidence is warranted not only by the financial but the physical condition of the property."[43]

Before Cable's company dispatched surveyors and construction crews into the Great Plains, it attended to a strategic investment in its own backyard. This involved bringing the Burlington, Cedar Rapids & Northern Railway (BCR&N)—"The Iowa Route"—into its orbit. A long-held dream of those associated with the development of the Rock Island had involved tapping the traffic potential of the eastern and northern sections of the Hawkeye State and likely southern Minnesota. When the Mississippi & Missouri Railroad was in its gestation stage, backers considered building from some point west of Davenport in a northwesterly direction through the agriculturally rich Cedar River valley to the Minnesota border and perhaps beyond to the navigable Minnesota River or some other point. That plan came to naught.

After the Civil War, railroad promoters renewed their efforts to create a north-south route through Iowa. Heretofore, companies, including the Burlington, North Western, and Rock Island, had laid their rails mostly westward from Lake Michigan. The belief grew among regional shippers, businessmen, and others that Chicago—"Nature's Metropolis"—benefited unduly from such construction. This thriving metropolis, it was thought, was becoming too powerful as a commercial, financial, and railroad center. Yet this dominance might be mitigated if Saint Louis, whose leaders had long been wedded to river transport, played a more active role in railroad building. If lines radiated out of Saint Louis into Iowa and the Upper Mississippi River valley, outbound traffic from the north—most importantly grain, livestock, and lumber—could move to and through this Missouri gateway, and hopefully these commercial avenues would produce competitive rates, better service, and additional benefits. Similar advantages would be realized for an array of inbound merchandise. Direct connections to Saint Louis would lessen the increasing antipathy toward Chicago and the effects of its powerful urban mercantilism.

What would become the Burlington, Cedar Rapids & Northern originated shortly after the Civil War. As commonly occurred, this future road had paper predecessors: the Cedar Rapids & St. Paul Railway and the Cedar Rapids & Burlington Railroad. Since these entities shared similar interests, their largely local backers pooled resources in 1868 to launch the Burlington, Cedar Rapids & Minnesota Railway (BCR&M), a road that would link Burlington, Iowa, a Mississippi River and Burlington Railroad town, with the emerging milling and retailing center of the Twin Cities through Cedar Rapids. Construction commenced a year later.[44]

Although the Burlington, Cedar Rapids & Minnesota did not connect Burlington with Saint Paul with its own rails, the company made considerable progress in that direction. By the close of 1873 this Cedar Rapids–based carrier operated a 368-mile road. Its main stem linked Burlington with Plymouth Junction, Iowa (located near the Minnesota border), where it interchanged with a Milwaukee Road predecessor. This arrangement permitted access via trackage rights to Austin, Minnesota, and connection with still another Milwaukee Road property to Saint Paul. The BCR&M also spiked down a ninety-four-mile branch from Linn near Cedar Rapids to Postville, via the county-seat town of Independence—a thirty-one-mile line between Muscatine and Riverside, Iowa, south of West Liberty, and a twenty-mile extension from Vinton to Traer, Iowa. The company optimistically dubbed the latter line its "Pacific Division," although eventually it would be extended northwestward into Dakota Territory. At this time the Postville line held the greatest value; it connected at Postville with the Milwaukee Road and provided a route via Prairie du Chien, Wisconsin, to Milwaukee, Chicago's junior urban rival. BCR&M rails interchanged with the Rock Island in the Hawkeye State towns of Columbus Junction, Nichols, and West Liberty. The dream of that north-south Iowa artery had been achieved. Yet the BCR&M might have improved its main-line freight and passenger business had it passed through Iowa City rather than West Liberty, fifteen miles to the east.[45]

Replicating what happened to scores of railroads, the hard times, spawned by the Panic of 1873, forced the BCR&M into receivership. A shake-up in management and a reorganization followed. On June 27, 1876, the successor company, Burlington, Cedar Rapids & Northern Railway, made its debut.[46]

It did not take long for the newly constituted BCR&N to add trackage. In 1877 the company extended its main line five miles from Plymouth Junction to Manly Junction, Iowa, in order to gain trackage rights over the Iowa Central Railway to Northwood, Iowa. From that community the BCR&N built the few miles to the Minnesota border, where it connected with the Minneapolis & St. Louis Railroad (M&StL) for Albert Lea, Minnesota, a developing rail hub, and the Twin Cities. Then in 1879 the BCR&N took control of the tiny

Chicago, Clinton & Western Railroad, which extended from its main line at Elmira to Iowa City, a distance of about ten miles. That same year, puppet company Iowa City & Western Railway installed a seventy-three-mile line from the Iowa City vicinity south and west to the Poweshiek County capital of Montezuma and a stub between Thornburg and the coal-mining camp of What Cheer.[47]

With the advent of better times, the independent Burlington, Cedar Rapids & Northern became the subject of intense interest by the dominant regional roads. It seemed a worthy addition to the Burlington, North Western, Rock Island, and perhaps Illinois Central. In what turned out to be a complex corporate dance, the North Western believed that it had added the property when in 1879 its board approved a tentative lease. This attempt at control, however, failed; the BCR&N refused to ratify the agreement. Nevertheless, management accepted a counteroffer from the Rock Island, but complications followed. BCR&N stockholders rejected the Rock Island proposal. Ultimately a joint traffic agreement among the BCR&N, Rock Island, and Burlington took effect. Each trunk road benefited. The Rock Island stretched out to the northwest, and the Burlington achieved a cobbled-together route from Saint Louis to the Twin Cities, using in part its recently acquired St. Louis, Keokuk & Northwestern property. Since the Rock Island and Burlington had made sizable investments in BCR&N securities, they had financial muscle with the Cedar Rapids company. The tripartite deal, moreover, meant enhanced rate stability and the unlikelihood of unfriendly forces capturing the BCR&N. Furthermore, the BCR&N remained a largely independent and proudly Iowan carrier.[48]

The BCR&N continued to extend its web of rails. After all, the 1880s became years of expansion, and the Cedar Rapids road participated with sustained construction. By mid-decade the company operated 990 miles, and by the early 1890s it reached 1,134 miles.

Although the Chicago, Clinton & Western had built between Elmira and Iowa City, it also had grander plans. In the latter part of the 1870s, the carrier had installed eighteen miles west from the Mississippi River county-seat town of Clinton and had added another five miles when construction stopped. With the BCR&N takeover, a through line from Elmira to Clinton finally opened in 1883. It would be surrogate Cedar Rapids & Clinton Railway that closed the forty-seven-mile gap between Elmira and Noels. The BCR&N also installed a three-mile spur from near Tipton to a limestone quarry, tapping ballast and building materials for company use. Yet this Clinton Division "had little economic importance," opined railroad historian Frank P. Donovan Jr., "[and] probably never earned its keep."[49]

Vastly more important than the Clinton line was the Pacific Division. Soon the name sounded less farfetched. In 1877 the BCR&N had extended its Vinton-to-Traer branch to Holland, a distance of twenty-five miles, to capture agricultural traffic from this fertile grain-producing locale. Within a few years this Grundy County town lost its end-of-track status. Under the corporate banner of the affiliated Cedar Rapids, Iowa Falls & Northwestern Railway (CRIF&NW), organized in 1880, trackage pushed rapidly in a northwesterly direction. Between 1880 and 1883, 329 miles were built, serving such growing Iowa towns as Clarion, Iowa Falls, and Emmetsburg. Construction ended in Watertown, Dakota Territory. The final objective was apparently Bismarck, the territorial capital situated on the recently completed Northern Pacific (NP) route to the Pacific Northwest. This would create a potentially lucrative connection, allowing the NP to funnel traffic away from the Twin Cities and directly to Chicago via the BCR&N and Rock Island. About this time rumors suggested that the Rock Island might take control of the NP and become a truly "& Pacific" road. Adding to the construction, the CRIF&NW in 1882 opened a seventeen-mile line to Worthington, Minnesota, diverging from the yet uncompleted Watertown line at Lake Park, Iowa. At Worthington the company interchanged freight and passengers with the Chicago, St. Paul, Minneapolis & Omaha Railroad (Omaha Road), providing direct access to the Twin Cities. A more important piece of trackage involved installation of the forty-two miles from Ellsworth, Minnesota, to Sioux Falls, Dakota Territory. Officials had their eyes on the developing meat-packing industry in that growing city and on the possibility of pushing westward across the prairies and badlands to Black Hills gold mines.[50]

By 1900 the CRIF&NW had spiked down three additional area branches, including the ten miles from Trosky, Minnesota, on the Watertown line, to Jasper, Minnesota, between 1891 and 1892; another ten miles from Hayfield Junction to Forest City, Iowa, an extension of a forty-one-mile BCR&N line between Dows and Hayfield, Iowa, which opened in 1884; and a thirty-six-mile connector between Worthington and Hardwick, Minnesota, on the Watertown line in 1900. Ultimately the CRIF&NW became a more than 400-mile affiliate.[51]

The BCR&N continued the impressive construction made by the CRIF&NW. This building became part of a wave of midwestern feeder and connecting lines that appeared toward the end of the nineteenth century and during the first part of the twentieth century. The company itself built from Armstrong to Esterville, Iowa, nineteen miles; from Germania, Iowa (renamed Lakota because of intense anti-German feelings during World War I), to Albert Lea, Minnesota, forty-four miles; from Albert Lea to Comus, Minnesota, fifty-four miles; and from Rosemont to Inver Grove Junction, Minnesota, eleven miles. These latter three additions provided direct access to Twin Cities traffic. Somewhat earlier, affiliated companies installed these lines: Davenport, Iowa & Dakota Railroad between Davenport and Bennett, Iowa, thirty miles; Chicago, Decorah & Minnesota Railway between Postville Junction and the county-seat and college town of Decorah, Iowa, twenty-three miles; and Cedar Rapids, Garner & Northwestern Railway between Hayfield and Titonka, Iowa, nineteen miles. Also adding to this maze of names, lines, and construction dates was the Waverly Short Line, which in 1886 opened a six-mile stub between Waverly, the Bremer County seat, and Waverly Junction on the Cedar Rapids to Albert Lea core. Later, in 1892–1893, the BCR&N opened the forty-seven-mile line from Forest City to Armstrong, Iowa. By the time the Rock Island took possession of the combined properties in 1902, with a 999-year lease, the Iowa Route operated 1,367 miles in Iowa, Minnesota, and South Dakota. "The Burlington, Cedar Rapids & Northern was in a class by itself," said Frank P. Donovan Jr. "In the Hawkeye State no road was held in higher esteem than the old BCR&N."[52]

Ransom Cable enthusiastically backed BCR&N expansion. The Watertown extension came about in part because of his close relationship with the Minneapolis & St. Louis Railway (M&StL), a road that he sought to include in the Rock Island's penetration of Dakota and Minnesota. Simply put, Cable wanted to make the M&StL a strong arm of his expanding rail network. Rock Island investments in the M&StL allowed Cable to become its president in 1883. This Minneapolis-based carrier was no giant, although it benefited from access to major flour mills situated along the banks of the Mississippi River at that cataract known as Saint Anthony Falls. The M&StL, which dated corporately from 1870, had by 1877 reached south to Albert Lea from Minneapolis. Two years later it took control of the Fort Dodge & Fort Ridgeley Railroad & Telegraph Company, which ran a short distance north from Fort Dodge, Iowa. Also in 1879, the company extended its Albert Lea stem to the Iowa border, and the following year it closed the gap to Fort Dodge. The M&StL next headed toward Des Moines, reaching the coal-mining camp of Angus, Iowa, in 1882 and using the Des Moines & Fort Dodge Railroad to access the capital city. That same year M&StL rails reached westward to Morton, Minnesota, from the main line at Hopkins. The firm also operated its Pacific Division, stretching from Hopkins to Winthrop, Minnesota. This trackage and the short White Bear Lake branch created a railroad that by 1884 claimed nearly four hundred miles of line.[53]

At the close of the nineteenth century, travelers might have picked up the summer 1899 edition of the Burlington, Cedar Rapids & Northern Railway public timetable. Although closely tied to Rock Island interests with Ransom Cable serving as its board chairman, the "Cedar Rapids Route" was considered to be an independent Hawkeye State road.

Author's coll.

Cable and his associates financed additional properties and assigned them to the M&StL to operate. These transactions involved two companies, the Minnesota Central Railroad, which in 1882 had built the 66 miles between the Minnesota towns of Red Wing, located on the Mississippi River, and Waterville, where it connected with the M&StL; and the Wisconsin, Minnesota & Pacific Railroad (WM&P), which two years later extended 121 miles from Morton, Minnesota, to Watertown, reaching that Dakota trading center and the CRIF&NW. It would be the WM&P that operated the Minnesota Central property, known as the Cannon Valley Division, but the line was separated from the WM&P's Pacific Division, or Wheat Line, by about fifty miles.[54]

Early on Cable and his associates showed a real bullishness with their M&StL involvement, and they aggressively promoted the "Albert Lea Route." This interline arrangement offered through passenger service between the Twin Cities, Chicago, and Saint Louis. But in 1887 Cable left the presidency of the Mill City road, allowing his trusted lieutenant William Truesdale to take charge. (In the late 1890s Truesdale became a vice-president and general manager of the Rock Island and subsequently the long-time president of the Delaware, Lackawanna & Western Railroad.) Cable soured on the M&StL for multiple reasons. The investments made in the railroad had not been that attractive. Furthermore, the use of controlled properties M&StL and BCR&N to extend beyond Watertown to Bismarck or some other destination did not appear promising. Rival railroads–North Western, Milwaukee, Northern Pacific, and James J. Hill's St. Paul, Minneapolis & Manitoba–opposed expansion, and surely they would challenge Rock Island territorial incursions. Also the regulatory environment in Minnesota and throughout the Great Plains was increasing anti-railroad, and the federal government in 1887 passed the Interstate Commerce Act that had unknown consequences for the Rock Island and the industry. Not to be overlooked, the Great Dakota Boom, which had started in 1878, had run its course. The awful winter of 1886–1887 and rapidly declining wheat prices discouraged farmers and other settlers from coming to the territory. There remained, nonetheless, that friendly relationship between the M&StL and the Cable company. Yet liquidation of M&StL-related investments ultimately followed. By the start of the twentieth century an independent M&StL had purchased the Pacific Division, and the Chicago Great Western had leased the Cannon Valley Division.[55]

While Ransom Cable became involved with the burgeoning BCR&N and M&StL, he did not neglect to add two more lines to his developing "Great Rock Island Route." The first and larger one came on January 1, 1887, with lease of the 144-mile Des Moines & Fort Dodge Railroad (DM&FD), a company that connected the 89 miles between Des Moines and Fort Dodge and Tara (near Fort Dodge) with Ruthven, Iowa, 55 miles to the northwest. This historic property dated back to the early 1870s, when the Des Moines Valley Railroad built north from the capital city. Trackage rights over the Illinois Central between Fort Dodge Junction and Tara connected the two DM&FD units. The second, and thought to be more important, line resulted in the Rock Island taking control of the St. Joseph & Iowa Railroad, a sixty-four-mile property that extended from the Leavenworth line at Altamont, Missouri, westward to Saint Joseph and from Saint Joseph south to Rushville, Missouri, opposite Atchison, Kansas. The purchase documents for the line, built between 1885 and 1886, were finalized in 1888. This shortline gave the Rock Island direct access to the Saint Joseph gateway and the third largest city in the Show-Me State. The railroad realized that its population had grown at an impressive rate, increasing from 32,431 in 1880 to 52,324 a decade later.[56]

BREAKOUT

With accomplishments made in the Midwest, the Rock Island was about to embark on building long-distance arteries and branches beyond the Missouri River. For several decades this stream had served as an unofficial corporate divide, forming what a Kansas railroad commissioner sarcastically called a "magic line of moving mud." Through construction and trackage rights, the trans-Missouri West would be where the company "broke out" in a dramatic fashion from its historic core. Ransom Cable and his associates apparently shared the philosophy of contemporary railroad executive William Barstow Strong. This head of the Santa Fe Railway contended that a railroad must expand or die. Whatever the corporate outlook, the Rock Island was not going to stand still. There would be potentially handsome rewards but also financial risks on the Great Plains and possibly beyond. Irrespective of profit or loss, the Cable company was about to make the national economy more continental in scope and contribute to a host of upstart towns.[57]

The Cable men's plans for expansion would create a sea change from former administrations. When compared to other granger roads, the Rock Island had been conservative with line construction. Admittedly this was not wholly bad. "The careful policy had this advantage that the road attained maturity at a very early date," argued investor and business writer S. F. Van Oss, "and not being burdened with heavy capitalization the company was able to distribute good and regular dividends while most of its rivals, who invested vast sums in young and unremunerative branch lines, were not in a position to offer the same returns upon capital." His expanded commentary: "In this respect, therefore, the Rock Island is in a situation similar to that of the Chicago and Alton, but there can be no doubt that in the long run no Northwestern system can exist without feeders. The necessity of extension has presumably been most forcibly impressed upon the managers of the Rock Island by the fact that in spite of the rapid development of the country tributary to their road, freight business showed a very small increase which offered no compensation for the decline in rates."[58]

The plunge onto the Great Plains came under the corporate banner of the Chicago, Kansas & Nebraska Rail*road* (CK&N), launched officially on December 30, 1885. Yet this Kansas company never laid a mile of track, providing instead the groundwork for future building with franchises, rights-of-way, and property acquisitions. The actual construction entity made its debut on March 19, 1886, with the formation of the Chicago, Kansas & Nebraska *Railway*, successor to the original company. (Companion corporations were launched in Nebraska.) Legally the CK&N could build multiple lines. One was projected to run diagonally from Saint Joseph, Missouri, to the southwestern section of Kansas near Liberal in Seward County, reaching Indian Territory. Another line would leave the trackage in mid-state at the Herington townsite and head south to Caldwell and close to the Indian Territory border. The final segment would go northwest into southeastern Nebraska, drop back into Kansas, and extend westward to Colorado. Saint Joseph, rather than Atchison or Kansas City, became the jumping-off point, in part because of the willingness of its business community to provide a large subsidy. Construction followed.[59]

The Cable administration had made a major gamble. Under the financial arrangements worked out in July 1884 with the United States Trust Company of New York, the Rock Island mortgaged itself to raise the $35 million to pay for this monumental building undertaking. Technically the Rock Island advanced funds to the CK&N and in return received its securities. If the projected construction of more than a thousand miles fizzled financially, investors would sustain major losses. At the least, dividends would plummet or evaporate entirely. The corporate future of the company was at risk.

Who would marshal expansion? Ransom Cable would be involved, but he selected Marcus "Mark" A. Low, a Rock Island lawyer with political connections and common sense, to oversee the ambitious projects. Low served as president of the CK&N and "had practically unlimited powers"; that helps to explain why construction progressed smoothly and rapidly. He also headed the Chicago, Kansas & Nebraska Town Company and its successor, the Kansas Town & Land Company. Railroad officials—those associated with the

Rock Island were no exception—seized opportunities to launch communities on the line and to benefit personally from the sale of town lots and other property.[60]

Mark Low wasted no time making the Chicago, Kansas & Nebraska a physical reality and attempting to establish Kansas as a major Rock Island state, saying, "I have hopes of being able to make the map of Kansas look like a spider's web with railroads." An arrangement with the St. Joseph & Grand Island Railroad for use of its Missouri River bridge at Saint Joseph gave access to Elwood, Kansas, on the west bank. Grading commenced there on July 1, 1886, and the first forty-three-mile segment opened on November 12, 1886, to the recently established town of Horton. This upstart community immediately took on optimistic airs; it became the site for the CK&N shops and division offices. Local boosters expected that Horton would become the "Prodigy of the West," "The Wonder of Kansas," "The Magic City." Their enthusiasm was not unfounded; the town soon became a busy rail center and the headquarters for the Eastern Division (Lines West of the Missouri).[61]

The CK&N laid a monumental amount of track in 1887 and 1888. Unlike that of so many Gilded Age lines in the trans-Missouri West, construction quality was remarkably high. Grades and curvatures were kept to a minimum, bridges were usually iron rather than wood, and steel rails and hardwood ties graced the roadbeds. Officials, rightly or wrongly, anticipated heavy freight and passenger traffic. Construction connected Horton northwest to Beatrice, Fairbury, and Nelson, Nebraska (possibly with the intention of pushing into Wyoming and onward to the Pacific or a Pacific connection); southwestward to Topeka, McFarland, Herington, and Liberal; south to Wichita and Caldwell, Kansas (constructed by the satellite Chicago, Caldwell & Southern Railway between Wellington and Caldwell), and Pond Creek, Indian Territory (with congressional approval to cross tribal lands, permitted by an 1871 act); westward from McFarland to Belleville and a connection with the Fairbury-to-Belleville trackage; and again westward to Phillipsburg and Roswell, Colorado, a few miles east of Colorado Springs. In 1887 the company obtained a long-term trackage-rights agreement with the Union Pacific (née Kansas Pacific) for use of its double-track line between Kansas City and North Topeka. In order to connect with Union Pacific rails, the Rock Island a year later formed the Kansas City & Topeka Railway Company to build the 2.5 miles from Wyoming Street in Kansas City, Missouri, to Armourdale, Kansas. As early as New Year's Day, 1888, the *Topeka Capital* lauded this expansion. "Within a twelvemonth, the Chicago, Kansas & Nebraska Ry. has opened nearly twelve hundred miles of road, an average of one hundred miles a month, a record never surpassed by any railway company for an equal period of time." The paper admired the quality of these lines. "The roadbed is of the very best, the track is of solid steel and the bridges are the most substantial stone and iron structures." High praise, indeed.[62]

Unlike Rock Island predecessor Mississippi & Missouri Railroad, Cable's Chicago, Kansas & Nebraska Railway affiliate failed to receive gifts of public lands. Yet other railroads in its future service area won land grants. Most notably the Santa Fe got considerable acreages in south central and southwestern Kansas. Since such federal largess was unavailable, obtaining financial assistance from county, township, and municipal governments and from private citizens became a priority. The company's own resources needed to be augmented. Great Plains residents wanted more railroads, especially ones that provided direct lines or good connections to Chicago ("Chicago Air Line" objective) and other railroad centers. That desire augured well for the Rock Island; voters and local citizens showed their generosity. By 1890 public authorities had awarded the CK&N $2,696,000 in construction support. Critics charged "corporate extortion," but rarely did residents protest.[63]

The response among residents of White City and Morris County represented the enthusiastic support that the CK&N received. The town already had a railroad, though. The Missouri, Kansas & Texas Railway (Katy) linked Junction City and the Union Pacific to the north with Texas to the south. And via Parsons, Kansas, Katy rails offered a circuitous route into Missouri but not a direct way to Chicago. Furthermore, the quality of service, rates, and maintenance on the Katy disappointed patrons. Boosters wanted a second carrier, one better positioned geographically and more customer friendly. White City druggist and *White City Whig* newspaper owner George Simpson led the charge to attract the CK&N's line that was headed southwest from Horton. He believed that its arrival would be a godsend for his community and anticipated a substantial population jump. Simpson foresaw another attraction, namely that much-needed lumber from the upper Midwest could be acquired conveniently and more cheaply.[64]

What about financial support? George Simpson argued that the financial health of his hometown was excellent and that every dollar given in construction aid "will come back ten-fold." Again he emphasized that savings from lumber charges would "save the farmer five times over the amount of taxes required to retire the bonds." Voters agreed. The affected townships in Morris County and White City endorsed generous assistance: Clarks Creek Township, $15,000; Highland Township, $10,000; Ohio Township, $18,000; Rolling Prairie Township, $20,000; and White City, $10,000. No voter in White City cast a ballot against the bond measure. Even the largest taxpayer in the county backed the ballot issue.[65]

The Chicago, Kansas & Nebraska benefitted from support provided by one of the largest landowners in central Kansas, Monroe Davis "M. D." Herington. This "Dickinson County land pirate," as his detractors called him, owned extensive properties in Dickinson and Morris Counties and real estate in and around the Dickinson County village that bore his name. Herington had contributed generously to the Missouri Pacific when it built through the area from Kansas City to Colorado, and he wanted to make certain that the CK&N did not miss Herington. He realized that initial line surveys were often altered, resulting in route changes. In talks with Mark Low held at Topeka in early 1887, Herington promised much *if* CK&N rails went through his community. Sizable land bequests sealed the deal; Herington, of course, never eschewed realizing personal gains through real-estate sales and appreciation. Low allegedly said, "That [offer] sounds like the best proposition of any I've heard." Herington quickly emerged as a developing railroad town and became home to the South-Western Division. This rapidly growing community claimed the diverging main lines to Wichita and Caldwell, 122 miles opened in 1887, and to Liberal, 269 miles completed the following year.[66]

Kansans saw the increasing impact of the Rock Island. Liberal developed into an important town located near "No Man's Land," an area that after 1890 became part of the newly established Oklahoma Territory. Later both the Caldwell and Liberal stems penetrated present-day Oklahoma and beyond. A forty-eight-mile branch constructed in 1888 stretched from Herington to Salina.[67]

Mark Low's goal to cover the Sunflower State like a morning dew saw another, albeit modest, addition. While M. D. Herington got CK&N rails, residents of Dodge City, the famed cattle town located on the Santa Fe, wanted inclusion on the projected Liberal line. Like most places, they sought to have at least two railroads, but in this case they had failed. Unwilling to accept defeat and wishing to have competition to the Santa Fe, local interests took matters into their own hands and in 1887 won incorporation of their hometown Arkansas, Kansas & Colorado Railway (AK&C). In October of the following year, this pike, which had no serious intention of reaching either Arkansas or Colorado, completed twenty-seven miles of track southeastward to a CK&N connection at the new town of Bucklin. The Cable company quickly acquired the AK&C.[68]

Dodge City interests backed another plan to increase their rail options. Incorporated the same month as the Arkansas, Kansas & Colorado, this company, the Dodge City, Montezuma & Trinidad Railway (DCM&T),

Railroad companies often boasted about a "first," and the Rock Island was no exception. On September 10, 1887, the company's initial stock train left Caldwell, Kansas, for some undisclosed stockyards, likely in either Kansas City or Chicago. The engine crew and brakemen pose for this historic photograph.

Dan Sabin coll.

planned an approximately two-hundred-mile line from Dodge City southwest to the Colorado border. Some construction followed. In autumn 1888 rails had reached Montezuma in Gray County, twenty-six miles from Dodge City, and there the project stalled. Since the shortline did not own any rolling stock, it arranged for the CK&N to provide train service for a daily payment of twenty-five dollars, producing minuscule operational earnings for the owners. Debts mounted, and in late 1893 the DCM&T was sold under foreclosure proceedings. Soon salvagers lifted a portion of the rails, an event that angered civic boosters. Their subsequent court action failed to prevent a complete dismemberment. Before the final chapter of the DCM&T was written, an offer to transfer the remaining assets to the CK&N went nowhere. So Dodge City did not keep its second feeder railroad, and in this case the CK&N seemed content not to have increased its branch-line mileage.[69]

The Chicago, Kansas & Nebraska did much to make the years between 1886 and 1888 a time of extraordinary railroad construction in Kansas. "Within three years the railroad mileage of Kansas has been more than doubled," the state railroad commission happily observed. Of the 8,000 miles in operation, the Cable road contributed 1,055 miles, although the Santa Fe, Missouri Pacific, and Union Pacific each claimed larger totals.[70]

The extensive building that occurred in Kansas developed much beyond the immediate needs of residents. The accomplishments of the CK&N and other trunk roads bolstered the state's sagging economy and created a network that performed splendidly during the boom years of the early twentieth century. By the mid-1880s agricultural prices, especially for wheat, were steadily declining, and farming communities felt that negative impact. A deepening drought exacerbated these troubling economic conditions. Railroad building fortuitously pumped needed money into local economies. "The low prices for almost all classes of agricultural products, together with the unfavorable seasons the past three years, and the depressed state of agriculture, would, but for the extraordinary stimulus and support to business afforded by construction in the state, have depressed real estate values both in towns and country, and have brought widespread bankruptcy to commercial business," explained the state railroad commission in 1887. "Instead, however, the past two years have seen Kansas expand and grow beyond all precedent. Real estate values have in all parts of the state rapidly advanced, improvements in cities and towns have been the most substantial character, and on every hand signs of accumulating wealth and enduring prosperity are visible." Alas, the early 1890s saw worsening economic conditions in Kansas and throughout the trans-Missouri countryside. Drought and depression largely ended railroad construction, and the Rock Island was no exception. Furthermore, a number of struggling communities platted by railroad-related or independent townsite companies either disappeared or failed to grow. One such place was Jasper in Meade County, which was created by the Kansas Town & Land Company in 1888. "It was never absolutely deserted, but has never attained any great proportions." During this time thousands of settlers left the region, proclaiming, "In God We Trusted. In Kansas We Busted." One memorable statement, painted on a wagon canvas of a departing family, had these defeated and angry words:

> I'm tired of Kansas and starvation.
> I'm going back to my wife's relations.
> Damn Cleveland's administration.[71]

The Cable administration took pride in its remarkable record of construction in Kansas. So did others. "The Great Rock Island Route in Kansas is what may be called a new creation," opined an observer in 1890. "It did not begin with a few miles, built between fear and hope from one county-seat to another, but sprang into existence prepared to do the transportation business of a great State, over which its branches radiate in every direction; with spacious depots, and with such equipment in the way of rolling stock as had never been seen before in the State, and all within the space of two years." An exaggerated point of view, but these comments are within the realm of credibility.[72]

Before the American economy collapsed following the Wall Street panic of May 1893, the Rock Island also became a larger interregional carrier when it gained access to Colorado Springs, Denver, and Pueblo, cities located along the escarpment of the Front Range of the Rocky Mountains. This extension took shape rapidly. Construction began at Belleville in early autumn 1887, and by November service was established to Phillipsburg, 94 miles to the west. Goodland, 139 miles beyond, was reached in July 1888, and building continued across the high plains. Track gangs installed ties and rails at an impressive rate of two miles or more a day. On November 5, 1888, the first train, pulled by a flag-decked 4-4-0 locomotive, traveled the 564 miles from Horton to Colorado Springs, the Pike's Peak mining center and resort and wellness community. Even before that landmark event, on February 15, 1888, Cable representatives had signed a perpetual lease with the Denver & Rio Grande Railroad (D&RG) to operate over 120 miles of its line between Pueblo and Denver, "securing full and equal use of, and joint right in, that part of the [D&RG's] road including all main line terminals." The D&RG was not thrilled about the Cable road reaching Denver. "The D&RG had to choose between cooperation and competition," explained company historian Robert Athearn. Cable could build his own connecting trackage. Although the D&RG had been constructed to narrow-gauge width, the company in 1881 had installed a third rail between Pueblo and Denver to accommodate standard-gauge equipment, and in 1902 the line became standardized. Already Pueblo had become a railroad town, having welcomed the Missouri Pacific in December 1887. (Rock Island passenger trains served Pueblo until 1918, and freight service ended a decade later.) Then in May 1889 Cable representatives signed a long-term agreement with the Union Pacific to forge a more direct route to Denver, covering the ninety miles from the CK&N at Limon, the recently established "Hub City" of eastern Colorado. Officials considered this arrangement the easiest and most economical way to enter the Mile High City. To manage operations in the region, the Springs became the operational center for the new Western Division. At nearby Roswell the Rock Island constructed a depot, a sixteen-stall roundhouse, repair shops, yards, and additional support facilities.[73]

As the 1890s began, speculation spread that Cable had his eyes on a direct Colorado-to-California linkage. Such a route would involve operating from Colorado Springs to Salt Lake City over the Colorado Midland and Rio Grande Western railroads. Some observers believed that the Rock Island would buy the struggling Midland property. Such possibilities were just musings.[74]

While pleased with its entries into Colorado Springs, Denver, and Pueblo—the Centennial State's three major urban centers—the Rock Island wanted a shorter, faster, and cheaper way to connect Chicago with its trans-Kansas trackage. The pioneer Leavenworth line had heavy grades and excessive curvatures, especially as it crossed the pot-and-kettle terrain of southern Iowa and northern Missouri. Although affiliate CK&N made possible that through route from Horton to Belleville via the Nebraska towns of Beatrice and Fairbury, which dated from 1887, the Cable people sought a direct linkage from the better engineered, more heavily traveled, and partially double-tracked Council Bluffs line to a Belleville connection. Union Pacific officials, however, were not cooperative. The source of contention involved the Rock Island's use of the UP bridge over the Missouri River to reach Omaha and beyond. A determined Cable was not about to take chances. In case the UP denied crossing rights, the Rock Island organized its own bridge company and early in 1890 won federal approval for construction. The Milwaukee Road agreed to share such a structure. The UP soon relented about bridge and connecting access and gave the Rock Island trackage rights between Lincoln and Beatrice. The Rock Island in return agreed to accommodate UP trains between the Kansas towns of Hutchinson and McPherson. Although the Rock Island also gained trackage rights over the UP between the Omaha gateway and Lincoln, it quickly installed its own line between South Omaha and the Nebraska capital. That trackage opened in December 1890. Then there was another headache: the Union Pacific, which Jay Gould led, considered the Omaha bridge contract to be invalid, and his obstinance triggered a legal battle. Ultimately the Rock Island and Milwaukee Road argued their case before the US Supreme Court, and in July 1891 they received a favorable verdict. Associate Justice David J. Brewer concluded that the bridge issue involved "a public interest deserving of protection." This decision allowed the Rock Island to establish through service between Chicago and its Colorado termini on August 10, 1891. In May 1893 the Rock Island map in the area again changed when the company completed a connection between Lincoln and Jansen, outside Fairbury. This development permitted termination of its less direct Lincoln-to-Beatrice trackage-rights agreement with the UP and saved rental charges.[75]

The Ransom Cable regime continued its tracklaying spree with Chicago, Kansas & Nebraska penetration into present-day Oklahoma. Cable believed that such an artery through Indian Territory (after 1890, Oklahoma Territory) into Texas held great promise. Yet not everyone agreed. "The directors were conservative and regarded this as a risky investment," as one writer later

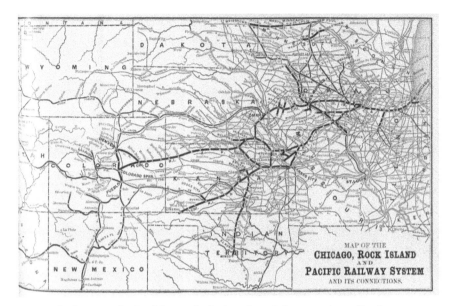

By 1891 the future Rock Island System had taken shape in large sections of its future fourteen-state network. But more building and acquisitions would occur. This map reveals the Rock Island's association with the Burlington, Cedar Rapids & Northern, Minneapolis & St. Louis, and Wisconsin, Minnesota & Pacific Railroads.

John W. Barriger III National Railroad Library coll., University of Missouri, Saint Louis

reported, "but Mr. Cable succeeded in getting the line built, and from time to time it has proved one of the most profitable parts of the system."[76]

By the late 1880s the company was also positioned to push tracks deep across the Panhandle to El Paso, Texas, or some junction point with the Southern Pacific to gain access to California. The major focus, however, was to march southward toward Fort Worth, Texas, along the ninety-eighth meridian, largely following the Chisholm Trail south of Caldwell, Kansas. Since the immediate post–Civil War years, cowboys had driven Texas longhorn cattle north along this route to railroad connections in Kansas in order to reach midwestern slaughterhouses. The Chisholm became the principal public artery north and south through Indian country. A March 1, 1887, congressional act granted the CK&N "the right to construct through Indian Territory from a point near Caldwell, Kansas, on the most practicable route to or near Fort Reno, and from thence in a southerly direction to the south line of Indian Territory." Building followed. Rails reached Pond Creek, located in what was known as the Cherokee Outlet, on July 15, 1888, and graders already were at work beyond that point. The following year the line opened to Hennessey, sixty-eight miles south of Caldwell, and surveys had been run south beyond the emerging El Reno, the speculative undertaking of the nonrailroad Oklahoma Homestead and Town Company, forty-one miles beyond Hennessey. It did not take much longer to extend the line to El Reno and from there to Minco, a distance of fifteen miles.[77]

For the immediate future, Minco became end of track. The ninety-eight miles of construction made by the Chicago, Kansas & Nebraska through Indian country had cost about $1.1 million, financed by funds advanced by the Rock Island. But financial problems encountered by its satellite made it impossible for it to manage these obligations. Since no collateral had been provided by the CK&N, the Rock Island took legal action in federal court in Kansas City. On June 3, 1890, the judge ordered the sale of all CK&N properties to settle the claim. This led to a $1 million settlement, finalized on June 17, 1891, that conveyed CK&N assets to the Rock Island. The Cable company now had nearly four thousand miles under its corporate ownership and trackage control. Yet those parties, particularly counties in Kansas, who had invested in CK&N stock found the court decision disturbing; their securities had become worthless. Nevertheless, citizens realized that they must have a railroad and that over time it would be a major, if not the largest, source of local tax revenues.[78]

Although the Chicago, Kansas & Nebraska had departed the corporate world, the Rock Island continued its expansion into north Texas. In order to adhere to the "colonial complex" sentiments of Texans, a mind-set that required out-of-state, or foreign, companies to incorporate under state laws, the Rock Island on July 15, 1892, received a charter for the Chicago, Rock Island & Texas Railway (after 1903, the Chicago, Rock Island & Gulf Railway). Using this corporate entity, the Oklahoma Territory trackage, which had been completed from Minco to Terral through Chickasha and Waurika, was ready to cross the Red River into the Lone Star State. On July 30, 1893, shortly after the national economy crashed, this ninety-three-mile Texas line opened via Bowie for traffic to Fort Worth, "America's Cow Town." Passenger service began in late August. The Texas affiliate owned no rolling stock; the Rock Island provided the equipment.[79]

Business along the Oklahoma Territory stem became brisk. This political unit encompassed much of the western half of Oklahoma after its admission to the union in 1907, when that territory united with Indian Territory to the east. Lands in the newly organized Oklahoma Territory opened for settlement in orchestrated phases. As the process developed, Rock Island freight trains hauled in carload after carload of merchandise and building supplies, most of all lumber, to recently established towns and farms. Passenger trains handled wave after wave of riders, who initially might have been positioning themselves for various land-opening runs.

The greatest single movement of passengers in the history of the Rock Island took place from Kansas into the Cherokee Outlet or Cherokee Strip on September 16, 1893. Some months earlier the federal government had agreed to pay the Cherokee Nation more than $8.5 million to allow public settlement on these lands. Popular interest ran high. Many of the estimated hundred thousand land seekers believed that it might be their last opportunity to acquire free government lands, and they wished to carve out their destinies on these virgin grounds. Caldwell, which straddled Rock Island rails, emerged as a principal jumping-off point for this memorable run. When the rush began, the Santa Fe, which marshaled its trains at nearby Arkansas City, experienced passenger chaos. As this description indicates, the Rock Island operated in a more orderly fashion: "As tickets were procured, the purchaser passed on from the east to the west side of the tracks, received successive numbers, were put into companies under captains, and placed in a position along the track ready, each company to board a car when the train came along." These rush participants encountered a strange Rock Island passenger consist. "The train was made up of Montgomery Palace Cattle cars—35 cars—and it was loaded with 5,200 persons who bought tickets and several hundred marshals and others, and officers of the road." Two locomotives supplied the power. In what was surely an uncomfortable albeit unforgettable travel experience, riders did not complain. "These cars proved to be just the thing," said a participant. "The tops allowed good seats for sight-seeing, and the side-doors gave easy egress to claim-takers." Rock Island personnel showed imagination when they used this rolling stock. Yet they had limited choices; regular passenger equipment was in short supply because of heavy passenger movements to and from the World's Columbian Exposition, which was then being held in Chicago. Using railroads might not have been the best land-staking strategy. The government forbade entering trains to travel faster than fifteen miles per hour, and they needed to stop at every station. Seekers on horses usually arrived at the choicest sites before those who took the Rock Island or another railroad.[80]

SERVING THE GREAT ROCK ISLAND ROUTE

As with any line construction, the Rock Island needed to erect support facilities along its tracks in Colorado, Kansas, Nebraska, Oklahoma Territory, and Texas, and it did so systematically, resulting in a range of structures, including a complex of roundhouse, car shops, and repair facilities at Horton. Freight and passenger patrons, however, became most familiar with their hometown depot. The Chicago, Kansas & Nebraska, paralleling other railroads that built in the trans-Chicago West, employed standard combination depots for its smaller communities. These single-story structures featured a baggage-freight room, center office with bay window, and passenger waiting room. Generally, the CK&N adopted four plans, believing that they would serve the needs of these stations. In a response to the absence of housing for its agents and their families in raw prairie settlements, the company built standardized two-story frame depots that provided a four-room upstairs apartment. If population and business growth exceeded expectations, a replacement depot usually appeared. When county-seat communities became permanently established and grew, a larger and more architecturally pleasing building emerged. It might be of brick construction. Take Liberal, Kansas, where initially a combination frame depot served patrons. In 1910 fire destroyed that building. Since Liberal had grown and had won a contested county-seat fight, the Rock Island erected a two-story mission-style depot that was clad in brick and stucco and had a red-tiled roof. It contained a waiting room, men's smoking room, agent's office, and baggage room, and the upper floor housed company offices. The most distinctive depot along these trans-Missouri lines was the broken-ashlar passenger and office building in Topeka. This three-story structure, built in the Romanesque style, featured an eye-catching clock dome and contained ample space for patrons and employees. This edifice cost $100,000 ($2.65 million in current dollars) and showed the Rock Island's commitment to the Kansas capital. Railroad management likely had state lawmakers and government officials in mind with this lavish expenditure.[81]

The Rock Island offered a reasonable number of passenger movements west of the Missouri River. There was usually twice-daily service. The *Official Railway Guide* for June 1892 revealed that the flagship trains operated between Chicago, Omaha, Lincoln, Denver, and intermediate points. This route provided three trains, two of which were solid vestibule limiteds, consisting of Pullman Palace sleepers, dining cars, and through coaches. Service on the lines into present-day Oklahoma were less frequent and less fancy. For stations south of Herington, the Rock Island dispatched only a local and in places supplemented it with a mixed train. Service was better on the line southwest from Herington. Two locals served communities between Herington, Pratt, Bucklin, and Dodge City, and there was a mixed train between Herington and Pratt. Places between Bucklin and Liberal had just a single train. Soon the Rock Island expanded its passenger operations south of Herington. Double daily service became established to Fort Worth, and a mixed train plied the rails between Herington and Caldwell. There was also mixed service between Chickasha and Terral. And the Rock Island provided a daily-except-Saturday sleeper between Kansas City and Hutchinson, and it sent one through to San Antonio, via the Gulf Coast & Santa Fe and International & Great Northern Railroads. Then there were a variety of special movements. When the National Education Association selected Denver for its annual convention in July 1895, it arranged travel by "personally conducted parties" from Boston to the Mile High City via the Boston & Albany, New York Central & Hudson River, Lake Shore & Michigan Southern, and Rock Island railroads. The organization pointed out that "the trains of the 'Rock Island Route' arrive in the same station as those of the 'Lake Shore Route'" and that "passengers will have the advantages of a splendid vestibuled limited train with dining-car service."[82]

The Cable company sought to increase its freight haulage in the trans-Missouri region. By the late 1880s regular freight and mixed trains served scores of communities, and the number of these places increased until the economic downswing in the early 1890s disrupted or halted town building. Agricultural commodities made up the principal outbound shipments; dependable rail transport stimulated greater production. According to Chicago Board of Trade annual reports, between 1872 and 1882 the Rock Island delivered 142,903,688 bushels of wheat to the Windy City. In the following ten-year period, that figure rose to 195,087,467, even though crop conditions deteriorated toward the end of the 1880s. Although the road had access to some coal traffic, most important were the wheat, cattle, and hogs. The town of Kingfisher in Oklahoma Territory, for one, became an important wheat-gathering center. "Kingfisher at that time was the world's largest primary wheat market," claimed a long-time resident, "serving as a shipping point for all the wheat raised west to the Texas panhandle." Livestock also took to the rails. As track approached Minco, cattle raisers eagerly awaited their railroad option. M. T. Johnson was the first shipper, having brought two hundred heads of his livestock to the station grounds and allowed them to graze around Minco until the first train left town. These animals then went to Kansas City. Hogs, too, soon left the new loading pens at Minco. Inbound traffic included the predictable commodities: building supplies, machinery, and a plethora of miscellaneous carload and less-than-carload (LCL) freight. All of this occurred at a time when railroads enjoyed a nearly virtual monopoly on intercity transportation.[83]

Throughout the service territory of the Chicago, Kansas & Nebraska and then the Rock Island, residents warmly received the coming of the iron horse. Place after place staged welcoming events. These citizens needed steel rails to shatter their isolation and to make town life and commercial agriculture profitable and comfortable. In various locales company trains brought in thousands of settlers. When the CK&N built through eastern Colorado, it employed a large number of German-Russian immigrants to assist in construction. Some of these men, joined by their families, remained in the little prairie communities that sprang up at trackside, helping to energize such Lincoln County places as Arriba, Bovina, Genoa, and Limon and to settle the surrounding countryside. They commonly sought local employment, even launching their own businesses, or they commenced farming operations. The large US Army post at Fort Reno, Oklahoma Territory, also welcomed a rail connection. "The long distance from railways had prevented the improvement of the fort beyond the demands of necessity heretofore to transfer troops and supplies overland," a contemporary chronicler of the territory noted, "but this is now done away with, and Reno will blossom as the rose, and additions to the buildings and other improvement are certain to follow."[84]

The image of the Cable company in Oklahoma Territory soared as crop conditions worsened about 1890. "The Rock Island proved a true friend to the pioneer farmers," recalled the *Kingfisher Free Press*. Because of drought, developing hard times, and a shortage of seed wheat, the railroad brought in from central Kansas 120,000 bushels of these seeds, describing them as "the best seed what that could be purchased" and made them available at El Reno, Hennessey, and Kingfisher. The company levied no transportation charges and sold the seeds by taking low-interest notes payable after the harvest of 1891. Farmers also got much-needed cash by selling cordwood to the railroad for locomotive fuel. Strangely, not all of the road's engines burned coal; these old-fashioned wood burners should have been retired. Yet some personnel argued that wood was less expensive and less corrosive for fireboxes than sulfur-laden soft coal. "Thousands of cords of wood were purchased which enabled many a farmer to buy his provisions and clothing while putting his farm under cultivation. Had it not been for the wood and seed wheat, many homesteaders would have been forced to go elsewhere to make a living."[85]

The presence of the Rock Island Lines, however, did not always please residents. Initially Native Americans, including members of the Five Civilized Tribes in Indian Territory, did not welcome the iron horse and "Little Houses on Wheels." They were agricultural peoples who rejected urbanization and industrialization. Some townspeople and agriculturalists fussed about rates and service matters. There were other complaints, including rude agents and crew members, cold and dirty depots, and poorly located stations. Then there was a well-publicized and long-remembered event: the "Enid Railroad War."

In what may be considered a textbook example of late nineteenth-century corporate arrogance, the Cable administration in 1893 and 1894 found itself embroiled in heated depot-location fights in Pond Creek (sometimes called Round Pond) and South Enid, Oklahoma Territory. When the Chicago, Kansas & Nebraska built from Caldwell south along the Chisholm Trail in 1888, it placed depots at Pond Creek Station and North Enid, about nineteen miles apart. Although the railroad expected that these stops would evolve into flourishing trade centers, rival communities Pond Creek and South Enid, each located about three miles south of the established stations, thought otherwise. These latter places became government-designated seats of Grant and Garfield counties, respectively (originally listed as counties L and O), and they reached a stable population of several thousand residents, with South Enid being somewhat larger. Understandably, civic leaders asked the railroad to establish an agency depot and telegraph connection in their hometowns. "It seemed a reasonable request," wrote company historian William Edward Hayes. "Weren't the people of these towns providing a lot of new traffic for the railroad? Weren't they depending on the railroad for service?" To bolster its request, each town offered to donate land for the station site and to pay for depot construction. Railroad officials refused.[86]

Tensions mounted. Activists in Pond Creek and South Enid attempted to stop trains by waving red garments and red lanterns in front of approaching passenger trains and placing such objects as dynamite caps, a wagon, and even a small frame building on the tracks. Others thought that a few "harmless" shotgun blasts at passing trains might prompt a corporate change of mind. Instead trains "hit these towns wide open, swirling the cinders and dust into a cloud with the speed of their passing." Freights, especially, which roared through at forty or more miles per hour, presented safety concerns. Both municipalities responded with ordinances that severely restricted train speeds within their corporate limits, allowing trains to pass at just four miles an hour, or about a person's walking speed. Once again the railroad ignored the public. When town marshals sought to enforce the law, they discovered that crews carried Winchester repeating rifles and were "willing to use them."[87]

What were these embittered residents to do? They circulated petitions to territorial and federal officials. One strategy involved asking the US Congress to require railroads that served county seats to maintain station facilities. Alas, no immediate legislation was forthcoming. In mid-June 1894, some Pond Creek residents tore up several hundred feet of track, arguing that they wished to stop a freight train to arrest its crews for violating the local speed ordinance. As a result, the train was wrecked, but no major injuries occurred, and a passenger train was delayed for nearly a day before the rails were replaced. Cable responded. In a telegram to US Attorney General Richard Olney, he sought federal assistance. "Parties at Round Pond and Enid, Oklahoma Territory, have been giving this company considerable trouble. The interference with interstate transportation and United States mails is serious." Cable continued: "Local authorities indifferent and something seems to be needed at the hands of the general government. Can you issue positive directions to the United States attorney that will lead to prompt and effective measures for the suppression of this violence and prosecution of offenders?"[88]

On July 13, 1894, a handful of citizens turned more violent; a spectacular act of consumer sabotage took place. These irate individuals sawed through the wooden bents on a trestle over Boggy Creek outside South Enid, wrecking a fourteen-car freight train. Although no crew members lost their lives, an unfortunate drifter did. After crawling out of the cab, the engineer allegedly said, tongue in cheek, "'A neat job, gentlemen,' and pointed to the sawed bridge timbers." Area residents flocked to the site to gawk at the wreckage. About the same time, dynamite blasts and fires destroyed track and bridges near Pond Creek Station. The Rock Island demanded that authorities crush this "insurrection" and placed armed guards at key points along twenty-five miles of right-of-way. "The situation is perilous and urgent," Cable wrote in another appeal to Attorney General Olney. "If we cannot have protection we must abandon operation of line south of Kansas." Federal officials intervened. The government declared martial law in both communities and arrested multiple insurgents, including several prominent individuals.[89]

Finally the "war" ended. Although arrests took place, the trial in neighboring Kingfisher led to a Rock Island defeat. A sympathetic judge dismissed the charges, and the troublemakers and saboteurs gained their freedom. When President Grover Cleveland signed a bill on August 8, 1894, that required that county-seat communities have railroad service, the Rock Island capitulated. The Santa Fe Railway may have played a role. If the struggle continued, its officials believed that the coming of statehood would prompt lawmakers to "pass railroad legislation that [would] be a yoke on the necks of railroads." Soon Pond Creek and South Enid got their depots with agents and team tracks, and these structures appeared in convenient locations. Why the Cable administration was so callous is unknown. A case can be made that the depots at Pond Creek Station and North Enid were better situated, being located on more level terrain. It probably was not wholly a matter of money; after all, both communities offered free land and buildings. It might have been just spite by Cable or Mark Low (who then served as corporate attorney), believing that the railroad had the right to select station sites. The Rock Island was not the only contemporary railroad that behaved poorly; other companies during this period committed arrogant acts.[90]

Although the Pond Creek and Enid conflicts stained the image of the Rock Island (at least in Oklahoma Territory), during the closing years of Cable's presidency the company made some popular community improvements. One that promoted public safety and improved operating efficiency involved track elevations in greater Chicago, which eliminated dangerous grade crossings. Carnage at the points where streets and rails intersected had become a growing urban concern; Chicago experienced more than two hundred crossing deaths in 1891 alone. In 1892 the Chicago City Council passed an ordinance that required the Illinois Central to elevate its tracks in the Hyde Park neighborhood, an undertaking that was completed the following year. Prompted by another city ordinance, one enacted in 1894, the Rock Island and Lake Shore & Michigan Southern jointly embarked on this costly betterment between Sixteenth Street in Chicago and Englewood. By spring 1895 the first portion, from Sixteenth Street to Twenty-Third Street, had been completed, and work advanced steadily, albeit slowly, southward until completion of this 6.61-mile project in 1899.[91]

EMPLOYEES

Paralleling other carriers, the Rock Island hired both native- and foreign-born workers. For many individuals, "goin' railroading" was their first wage-earning experience. Lads from farming backgrounds commonly migrated to train service, shop assignments, and track maintenance. Those who lived in towns and villages might hang out at the local depot and learn from a friendly agent, picking up Morse code, fundamentals of station bookkeeping, and other skills. These youngsters in turn performed odd jobs, sweeping floors; maintaining stoves, lanterns, and other equipment; and running errands. Recent immigrants more likely found employment as track laborers or in shop facilities. Upward mobility occurred. An agent, for example, might rise to the position of dispatcher, trainmaster, or auditor. Early on, the Rock Island became a white, Anglo-Saxon Protestant–dominated railroad; Roman Catholics were in a decided minority, especially among the ranks of the white-collar workers and train crews. These Protestants frequently belonged to the Masonic Order, a fraternal connection that often helped to advance their careers.[92]

Corporate attitudes toward labor were not to be overlooked. While no railroad established a workers' paradise, Cable's Rock Island did not take unduly harsh positions toward its employees. Officials recognized the increasing number of railroad brotherhoods, whether for operating or non-operating workers, the first being the Brotherhood of Locomotive Engineers. As with other carriers, management employed a book of rules, including the ubiquitous "Rule G," which prohibited the use of alcoholic beverages while on duty. If an employee violated this cardinal rule, it became justification for dismissal. The Rock Island's divisional structure created a chain of command that provided the enforcement mechanisms for any rule infraction. The brotherhoods themselves cooperated, seeking workplace order and temperance.

The Rock Island fortunately avoided the bitter strike that crippled the neighboring Burlington Railroad in 1888. A long list of grievances, including work-rule changes and low wages, precipitated this walkout by locomotive engineers, who were joined by firemen and switchmen. Management broke the strike, but not before scattered violence had occurred. For the Burlington, the legacy strained labor-management relations for years and also affected public sentiments toward the road in predominantly division and shop towns. The Rock Island, on the other hand, offered its engine crews more attractive work rules and wages, and these policies helped to prevent its engineers from "hitting the bricks." Throughout this strike, the Rock Island refused to handle Burlington interchange traffic, fearing that doing so would anger its union employees and cause them to leave their posts. Yet the company was not anti-Burlington. "You may be assured that the Rock Island is always glad to aid the C.B.& Q. when it can do so without getting itself into serious trouble," a Rock Island officer told the Burlington. But in this case it didn't, a policy that angered Burlington managers.[93]

The Rock Island was not so fortunate when it came to the Pullman strike of 1894, one of the nastiest conflicts in American labor history. Twelve people died, and tens of thousands of dollars in property damages resulted. Not long before workers at George Pullmans's Palace Car Company outside Chicago struck to protest drastic wage cuts, refusal to lower rents for company-owned housing, layoffs, and firings, Eugene V. Debs, the charismatic former official of the Brotherhood of Locomotive Firemen, had spearheaded creation of the American Railway Union (ARU). This industrial organization welcomed all white railroad workers below the rank of division superintendent and challenged the powers of the craft brotherhoods. The image of the ARU skyrocketed among railroaders when in spring 1894 it won an eighteen-day surprise strike over wages against James J. Hill's Great Northern Railway. A few months later the Debs union, claiming 150,000 members, joined the Pullman strikers, launching a nationwide boycott of any railroad that handled Pullman rolling stock. The appearance of the ARU angered Rock Island officials. "I think there is no necessity for an organization of that kind," observed general manager Everett St. John. "We have gotten along comfortably with the old orders [brotherhoods]."[94]

Before labor turbulence erupted at Pullman, all went smoothly at what Rock Island officials considered to be one of its finest facilities, the Blue Island shops and rail yards. They were modern and well designed. In 1892 this complex took shape: roundhouse, car shops and additional support buildings, and yards for freight and passenger cars. The property was strategically placed, and it covered an impressive acreage. When it was completed, nearly a thousand employees toiled in these facilities, and most lived in this former farming community that had morphed into a mixed industrial town of approximately four thousand residents.[95]

When the American Railway Union entered the Pullman strike, Blue Island became the epicenter for labor troubles on the Rock Island. Other Chicago railroads also felt the sting of worker discontent; the Pennsylvania and Illinois Central most notably saw strikers torch hundreds of freight cars. Perhaps the Rock Island unrest was expected; its shops were located only a mile or so from the company town of Pullman. And there were grievances among operatives throughout the system; a leading one involved promotion practices. Furthermore, the deepening national economic slump, a "withering depression," sharpened friction between workers and managers. As soon as events began to unfold, firemen and switchmen at Blue Island voted to strike in sympathy for their "Pullman brothers." Engineers refused, but they agreed not to operate any locomotive that did not have a union fireman.[96]

Rock Island management was not pleased. General Manager St. John, who chaired the General Managers' Association, which represented more than a score of Chicago railroads, strongly opposed the Debs union. He thought that the employees on his road who had left their posts had done so under intimidation, an explanation that is questionable. As the strike progressed, Charles Dunlap, Rock Island general superintendent, warned the Blue Island community: "Unless the people manifested more interest on the side of the right and justice and ceased to support the boycott movement [the railroad] would be obliged to retaliate by removing the shops and yards from the town, canceling all suburban trains to that point, and having nothing whatever to do with the town."[97]

Hundreds of Blue Island operatives and residents ignored Dunlap's not-so-veiled threats. Unrest led to violence. A striking switchman threw a switch that derailed a locomotive, a mob set seven freight cars ablaze, and "scabs" hired by the company to keep priority trains running were roughed up. No lives were lost, however. Legal injunctions and the presence of outside police and special deputies did not deter strong citizen support for the strikers. What turned the tide was the arrival of federal troops from Fort Sheridan, a military post outside Chicago, and their presence kept disturbances to a minimum. By mid-July the ARU had capitulated. Union leaders, including Debs, were arrested and prosecuted, the ARU collapsed, and the Rock Island resumed normal operations.[98]

The Pullman strike affected the Rock Island System to varying degrees. The financial losses were considerable. Although property damages amounted to less than $15,000, lost earnings totaled $460,000. Yet the financial impact was less than what several other carriers suffered. Notwithstanding the monetary setbacks, Rock Island management showed compassion toward its employees. The company rehired more than 4,000 of its approximately 4,500 strikers, something that most railroads linked to the General Managers' Association refused to do. Thousands of former ARU members found themselves blacklisted. Their service letters were apparently encrypted with the watermark of a crane with a broken neck, indicating their involvement with the failed Debs union.[99]

THE CABLE LEGACY

Ransom Cable proved to be the builder of the Great Rock Island Route. When he stepped down from the presidency in 1898, the company owned or leased 3,568 miles of line and had avoided bankruptcy during the depression of the 1890s, when scores of carriers, large and small, failed. Yet Cable cannot be placed on the same plane as an Alexander Cassatt, James Hill, or Charles Perkins. He had greater failings than these contemporaries, and several stand out. The Rock Island had too much leased or trackage-rights mileage, resulting from Cable's policy to reduce construction costs. Where these arrangements existed, the Rock Island could not perform any local service and therefore could not earn income from traffic that originated from or was destined to locations on these lines. Rental costs alone were hefty. For the 1897–1898 fiscal year, the outlay amounted to $789,562, out of gross earnings of $19,548,583. Moreover, Cable seemed slow to modernize motive power and to make additional betterments, including creating state-of-the-art terminal facilities. Such capital expenditures would have improved efficiency and reduced expenses. Cable also had a flawed business outlook. William Edward Hayes said it well: "He insisted that his railroad should emphasize more and more 'through freight'—loads from and to connections with the Rock Island serving merely

Ransom Cable's association with the Rock Island was personally rewarding. In the 1880s, he could afford to employ the services of the architectural firm of Cobb & Frost to design and supervise construction of his massive Romanesque revival–style mansion situated in a fashionable north Chicago neighborhood.

Author's coll.

as a bridge line over which the traffic could move fast. The railroad should own only such real estate as might be necessary to accommodate shops and yards. Nothing at all for lease to industrial projects or to sell to businesses that might want to build factories or warehouses."[100]

Although he was much more willing to take risks than his predecessors were, Ransom Cable was no robber baron; he was a builder and not a wrecker. However, as a captain of industry, he did well financially. As a symbol of his personal wealth, he owned a large house in Rock Island and an opulent fifteen-thousand-square-foot mansion in the elite residential section of north Chicago. Located at 25 East Erie Street, it was designed in the Richardsonian Romanesque revival style by the prominent Chicago architectural firm of Cobb & Frost.

Soon a new era dawned in the saga of the Chicago, Rock Island & Pacific Railway. There would be more expansion and consolidation, but after 1901 the management became reckless. The railroad would feel the negative impact of having bona fide robber barons at the throttle. After more than a decade in power, these men propelled the once financially stellar railroad into bankruptcy.

ROBBER BARONS

3

WHEN RANSOM CABLE RELINQUISHED THE PRESIDENCY OF THE Chicago, Rock Island & Pacific Railway in 1898, observers assumed that the company would remain profitable and would not overextend its route structure. Likely, though, the railroad would build from Liberal, Kansas, through the Oklahoma Panhandle, to a connection with the transcontinental Southern Pacific in Texas or New Mexico Territory. Modest expansion of feeder lines would also undoubtedly occur. Cable, however, was not out of the picture; he retained his positions as chairman of the board of directors and chairman of its executive committee.

The next individual to take the presidential post was Warren G. Purdy (1843–1910). This native Baltimorean possessed a solid formal education for a white male of his generation, earning a high school diploma. Following graduation at age sixteen, Purdy launched his railroad career. Initially he clerked for the Illinois Central Railroad in its Chicago shops, but several years later he took a similar position with the Ohio & Mississippi Railway in Saint Louis. In December 1863 Purdy resigned to join the US Army and became chief clerk for the quartermaster's department at Camp Douglas in Chicago and then served in Brownsville, Texas. At the end of 1866, he left the military and returned to Chicago, where he found employment with the Rock Island. His first position was that of a bookkeeper in the cashier's office, but he rapidly rose through the ranks. By 1877 Purdy had become secretary and treasurer, in 1885 second vice president, 1887 first vice president, and on June 1, 1898, president, a position that he would hold until December 31, 1901.[1]

How would Warren Purdy lead the Rock Island? Without doubt, he was a dedicated employee. His actions during the Great Chicago Fire displayed his loyalty. Assigned to the finance department, he protected valuable corporate records by securing them in the vault before flames engulfed the building. During his employment, Purdy had been influenced more by the conservative

Hugh Riddle than by the expansionist Ransom Cable. Unlike his predecessor, Purdy showed enthusiasm for modernizing and expanding the traffic base. This meant adding the latest motive power, fast Atlantic-type (4-4-2) passenger locomotives and husky Consolidation-type freight engines (2-8-0), as well as upgrading freight and passenger rolling stock. These betterments also included heavier steel rails, more rock and burnt-clay ballast, new and expanded terminals, and aggressive industrial development. "The new president resolved to make the Rock Island second to none in *every* [sic] department," company historian William Edward Hayes explained.[2]

When Purdy assumed the Rock Island presidency, the nation and the service territory had largely recovered from those five troubled years sparked by the Panic of May 1893. Notably, too, weather conditions, agricultural production, and market prices had improved markedly. Optimism reigned as Americans welcomed the twentieth century. The Rock Island was well positioned financially to achieve Purdy's improvement objectives. Its stock commonly traded at more than $200 per share, and it paid good, regular dividends. Simply put, it was a well-managed, blue-chip granger railroad.

Rock Island officialdom realized that the Liberal line served merely as a traffic feeder. Its end of track lay outside of town and was designed as a gathering point for Texas cattle; little additional business existed south of Bucklin, Kansas. If this trackage had been extended into the coalfields of the Raton Basin near Trinidad, Colorado, freight tonnage would have been much greater. In fact, the Cable administration had considered this as the original endpoint. If the Liberal line were to bolster revenues, it needed to be lengthened to some promising rail interchange or traffic-generating destination.[3]

An extension opportunity developed. El Paso entrepreneur Colonel Charles Eddy, a man with coal, lumber, and railroad interests, including the 318-mile El Paso & Northeastern Railway (EP&NE), encouraged the Rock Island to reach his rails at Santa Rosa, New Mexico Territory, a lively community on the Pecos River. Such a connection would forge a new transcontinental option, later styled as the "El Paso Short Line" and the "Golden State Route." In late 1900 Purdy received board approval to enter the territory, and two subsidiary companies soon won incorporation to advance the project. By the end of March 1902, three months after Purdy left the presidency, the Liberal extension officially opened. It consisted of several construction components: Liberal to Texhoma, Oklahoma Territory, a distance of 56 miles, built by the parent Rock Island; Texhoma via Dalhart to the Texas-New Mexico Territory border, 90 miles, completed by the Rock Island's Chicago, Rock Island & Mexico Railway, a Texas-chartered company; and 113 miles from

Even though the location and date of this construction photograph are unknown, it is possible that these workers are toiling in the greater Dalhart, Texas, region.

Dan Sabin coll.

the New Mexico border through Tucumcari to Santa Rosa, installed by New Mexico–chartered satellite Chicago, Rock Island & El Paso Railway. A connection with the EP&NE provided access to El Paso. The Rock Island achieved both an El Paso strategic connection with the "Sunset Route" of the Southern Pacific and access to the coalfields served by Eddy's properties.[4]

The 263-mile line between Liberal and Santa Rosa ranked as the most difficult piece of construction that the Rock Island encountered. A host of problems confronted this undertaking. The route traversed a virtually unsettled region; human habitation was localized to only a few places, including headquarters of the sprawling XIT Ranch. The desolation was made worse when workers almost immediately experienced the ravages of smallpox. "It soon spread to every camp, and we battled it all the way to Santa Rosa," remembered Otto Byers, a firsthand observer. "I believe I can safely say there is a man buried in an unmarked grave on every mile of the entire extension." The high death rate prompted these responses: "At first they were buried in graves, but as construction progressed it was found this consumed too much time, and they were thereafter loaded in carts, deposited on unfinished embankments and covered over with earth from scrappers." Those laborers who did not contract the smallpox virus or who survived encountered a raucous environment in

Not long after the Rock Island, in conjunction with the Southern Pacific, introduced the *Golden State Limited*, the five-car train speeds along the southwestern Kansas countryside.

Keith L. Bryant coll.

their tent encampments. "Every known vice was rampant, and camps were 'shot up' every night." Moreover, isolation meant no legal protection. "Highway robbers, gamblers and thugs abounded everywhere and plied their trade without fear of molestation." Nature added to the men's woes. "Gila monsters, scorpions, tarantulas, centipedes and snakes of many kinds beset the path of the builders; and men sleeping on the ground were frequently bitten." Then there were the construction challenges. These involved not so much making cuts and fills and building bridges but lacking water for locomotives. "We were in high, dry climate where running streams were almost unknown." Water had to be brought in before wells could be dug. "The town of Goodwell, Okla.," recalled Byers, "was given its name because after many weeks of search a well of sufficient volume was found there for our requirements." A notable characteristic of this extension was that it had the second longest stretch of straight track in the country, specifically a nearly seventy-two-mile tangent between Guymon, Oklahoma Territory, and Dalhart, Texas.[5]

Once it was completed, the Rock Island ballyhooed its El Paso route. By August 1902 the company carded a daily round-trip local passenger between Bucklin and Dalhart and dispatched the *Golden State Limited* between Chicago

A 4-4-0 workhorse locomotive brought the first passenger train to Mangum, Oklahoma Territory, on September 2, 1900. It was a proud day for residents of this southwestern town.

Old Greer County Museum & Hall of Fame

and California destinations via Kansas City. This varnish afforded standard and tourist sleepers and dining-car service. The train departed La Salle Street Station, for example, at 8:32 a.m. central time on Monday and arrived in El Paso at 7:20 a.m. mountain time on Wednesday. Los Angeles was reached at 11:00 a.m. Pacific time the following day, and from there connections were made to Santa Barbara, San Jose, and San Francisco. At this time the Rock Island promoted the Lodge at Cloudcroft, New Mexico Territory, which was convenient to its rails. "A new summer resort, 9,000 feet above sea level, on the crest of the Sacramento mountains, with a temperature of from 60 to 72 degrees during the months of June, July, August and September," announced the company. This delightful seasonal place was situated on the twenty-six-mile Alamogordo & Sacramento Mountain Railway, controlled by Charles Eddy. Alamogordo, located 186 miles south of Santa Rosa and 85 miles north of El Paso, was the access point. "The trip is made from the base of the mountains in observations cars," the Rock Island noted, "thus affording an unrestricted and comprehensive view in every direction." Railroad historian David Myrick offered this assessment: "The line of the Alamogordo and Sacramento Mountain Railway was probably one of the most spectacular among western railroads."[6]

Warren Purdy also saw advantages in increasing mileage in Oklahoma Territory. However, he would construct no exceptionally long lines; only small to modest feeders appeared prior to 1902. In 1899–1900 the company completed a seventy-nine-mile branch from Chickasha westward through Anadarko to Mangum. That same year it financed the Enid & Anadarko Railway. Opened in segments, this road by early 1902 stretched sixty-five miles in a largely southward direction between its namesake towns. Then there was a thirty-six-mile line that extended south from Anadarko to Fort Sill and Lawton. Smaller projects increased penetration east of the main north-south artery, including twenty-seven miles from Enid (North Enid) to Billings (later extended to Tonkawa and Ponca City) and sixteen miles from Kingfisher to Cashion. From Cashion, the Rock Island obtained trackage rights over the Atchison, Topeka & Santa Fe (Santa Fe) to Guthrie, the territorial capital.[7]

More building occurred on the southern Great Plains. In order to strengthen the Fort Worth line, the Chicago, Rock Island & Texas Railway, the company's Lone Star affiliate, installed a twenty-eight-mile branch from Bridgeport west to Jacksboro in 1898. Later this feeder reached Graham, fifty-five miles from Bridgeport. As with line construction in Indian Territory, trains handled outbound agricultural products, mostly livestock and wheat, and brought in building supplies, merchandise, and other goods. During the Purdy years, only a daily-except-Sunday mixed train provided connecting passenger service at Bridgeport for Fort Worth and other destinations.[8]

The Rock Island also laid track in Iowa. In 1900 the company built between Gowrie and Sibley, a distance of 109 miles. At Gowrie rails connected with the Des Moines & Fort Dodge Railroad (DM&FD), a property under lease to the Rock Island since 1887, and at Sibley they connected with the Watertown line of the Burlington, Cedar Rapids & Northern Railway (BCR&N). Purdy expected that his company would purchase the DM&FD; the lease was set to expire on December 31, 1904. Since the railroad paid handsomely for that right, purchase would become cost effective. Whether it acquired the DM&FD or not, this construction tapped some of the best farmland in America, which had become a center for hog-corn production.[9]

Company betterments, including either new or replacement depots, had been ongoing. In March 1900 Purdy and his associates took pride in the opening of a handsome brick depot in Peoria. This structure, which cost $75,000 ($2.25 million in current dollars) and was designed by the Chicago architectural firm of Frost & Granger, featured a clock tower that stood

The expanding Rock Island system served hundreds of small towns and villages. Shortly after the turn of the twentieth century, the agent and two other men pose outside a standard combination depot in the Keokuk County, Iowa, community of Delta, located on the fifty-eight-mile Washington-Oskaloosa-Evans branch.

Author's coll.

118 feet above ground level and "[added] much to the architectural beauty of the edifice."[10]

BIG FOUR OF THE PRAIRIES

Warren Purdy may have slept soundly during most of his tenure as Rock Island president. By the dawn of the twentieth century, the railroad was reasonably well situated. It operated 3,415 miles of line, of which 2,506 miles consisted of main line that extended from Chicago to five important gateways: Omaha, Colorado Springs, Tucumcari (El Paso), Fort Worth, and Kansas City. And improvements to its rolling stock and physical plant had made it into a premier road. The public also benefited from the passenger trains that handled US mail and express. For decades the latter was provided under contract with the United States Express Company (1854–1914), controlled by American Express Company.[11] Income for the Rock Island looked solid and was increasing; dividends remained good and steady. Gross revenues soared from $17,359,653 in the depression year of 1896 to $25,364,695 in 1901, and net revenues, which stood at $6,382,332 in 1896, reached $9,140,631 in 1901. By the close of Pur-dy's tenure, the Rock Island's operating ratio stood at an impressive 61.6, or about ten points below the ratio for the late 1880s and early 1890s. Under his management the company had developed good bridge and improved local traffic. "[The Rock Island] had become a very steady railway corporation, earning and paying good dividends under all circumstances, enjoying a repu-tation for excellent credit and for solid wealth," said *Wall Street Journal* writer C. M. Keys. No New York banking or investment group controlled the com-pany; it remained independent. There were critics, however. The consensus among these individuals was that the Purdy management team "lacked daring and imagination." Another writer put it this way: "There was not quite enough enterprise in extending its lines."[12]

By 1900 the maturing railroad industry in the American West had been largely partitioned into four great empires. These included properties con-trolled by George Gould, E. H. Harriman, James J. Hill, and J. P. Morgan. This division was hardly surprising. The history of railway development revealed a strong tendency toward consolidation in some form. None of the largest rail-way systems had been shaped by a single corporation, individuals working in a common interest, or a single plan. In 1901 there still existed several important carriers in the trans-Chicago West that could be classified as major indepen-dents: Santa Fe (7,481 miles); Chicago, Milwaukee & St. Paul (6,340 miles); Rock Island (3,415 miles); and St. Louis & San Francisco (2,887 miles). The latter two roads became the focus of a group of investors who became known variously as the "Moore crowd," "Moore gang," "Moore interests," "Tin Plate crowd," "Reid-Moore syndicate," "Rock Island crowd," or "Big Four of the Prairies." Whatever these men were called, they resembled a plague of locusts sweeping down upon a well-run railroad.[13]

The sparkplug for the four men who won control of the Rock Island and then the St. Louis & San Francisco (Frisco) was attorney and financier William Henry Moore (1848–1923), later in life referred to as Judge Moore. Throughout his business career, he was never afraid to make momentous deci-sions. Who was this dynamic person? Born in Utica in 1848, Moore came from a well-respected upstate New York family. His father was a banker and his mother the daughter of a banker. Unlike earlier Rock Island executives, Moore had a distinguished formal education: Cortland Academy in Homer, New York, and Amherst College in Amherst, Massachusetts. But because of an illness, he left Amherst before graduation. Rather than returning to his home state, Moore moved west to seek his fortune. As a resident of Eau Claire, Wisconsin, he studied law, and in 1872 he gained admission to the bar.

That same year Moore relocated to Chicago and became a clerk for Edward Small, a prominent corporation lawyer and his future father-in-law. After a year and a half, he became a partner in what became the firm of Small, Burke, and Moore. It did not take long for Moore to establish himself as an expert in the intricacies of corporate law. Following the death of Small, William and his younger brother, James Hobart Moore (1852–1916), also an attorney, launched the firm of W. H. & J. H. Moore. James, too, possessed high intelligence and a good education, but he had a "jollier outlook on life." The brothers' partnership prospered, enjoying an array of important clients that included Adams Express, American Express, and Vanderbilt Fast Freight Line. At the end of the 1880s, the Moore brothers went in a new direction; they entered the rough-and-tumble world of business.[14]

The industrial and railroad careers of William and James Moore began with their first important venture, reorganization of the Diamond Match Company. This firm, launched in 1881, consisted of a dozen smaller production units. The brothers succeeded in increasing its capitalization to $7.5 million in 1889 and later to $11 million, being rewarded handsomely for their promotional efforts. Soon they reorganized much of the strawboard (cardboard) industry, components that produced matchboxes as part of their product line. Once more the brothers invested little of their own money, relying on the profitability of generating watered stock, securities that represented anticipated profits rather than actual assets. Next the Moores took control of several East Coast cracker factories and united them as the New York Biscuit Company with a capitalization of $9 million. As the worst years of the depression of the 1890s passed, they returned to Diamond Match and formed a pool to boost and sustain its share price. When an acceptable dollar per share amount was reached, the Moores and fellow pool members planned to unload their investments. Although the stock price increased from $120 in January 1896 to $248 that May, investors by August worried that William Jennings Bryan might win the presidential election of 1896, as he was backed by anti–Wall Street and "soft-money" Democrats and Populists. "The free silver campaign began to play bogy-man." This concern, coupled with other problems, placed the Moores in a difficult position. They sought desperately to bolster their position but failed. The financial consequences were not pleasant. They lost several million dollars with their Diamond Match dealings, and their image in the business world suffered. At the same time, the brothers' speculation in the stock of New York Biscuit Company also flopped. There were other ramifications. "They had failed in the crash of those stocks, which in that year [1896] closed the Chicago Stock Exchange for weeks and brought many of the city's banking houses to the brink of ruin."[15]

Neither William nor James Moore showed any noticeable despondency because of their stock market misfortunes. "Their hearty competent grip upon life were unimpaired, and they immediately addressed themselves to the reshaping of their fortunes." Permanent failure was unacceptable. William used his personality to his advantage. In addition to being an imposing figure—"more than six feet in height" and "powerfully built"—he possessed "the spirit of good nature in his eyes and in the smile that always rests about his mouth. He would be picked out everywhere as the genial man, the warm friend." In another assessment, the observer suggested that Moore "has that gift of power upon men which no one can quite analyze or define." Yet when it came to publicity, he kept himself out of the limelight and became known as the "sphinx of the Rock Island."[16]

The comeback of the Moores arrived swiftly and dramatically. Working with other Chicago investors, the group in early 1898 succeeded in forging a merger between the American Biscuit and Manufacturing Company and New York Biscuit, creating the National Biscuit Company. The Moores chose to incorporate in New Jersey, a friendly business venue that held the distinction of being the "mother of trusts." This highly capitalized firm enjoyed control of about 90 percent of the domestic biscuit makers. The brothers regained their wealth and paid off their debts, and the National Biscuit triumph restored their prestige. By 1900 it was said that William Moore was besieged with requests to organize companies "from the marshes of Maine to the Pacific coast." He had become "the foremost representative in America of what has developed into a new profession—that of 'promoter.'"[17]

The years 1898 and 1899 saw more speculative investments by the Moore brothers, and ones that produced enormous personal profits. Not only did the National Biscuit Company take shape in 1898, but the brothers organized the American Sheet Steel and American Tin Plate Company between 1898 and 1899. Soon the Moores engineered formation of the National Steel Company and the American Steel Hoop Company. Their dealings contributed to the wave of corporate mergers and acquisitions that highlighted American business between 1899 and 1901. This emergence of giant enterprises alarmed an increasing number of Americans, and the consolidations would have a profound impact on national politics.[18] It was during the American Tin Plate transactions that the Moore brothers became associated with two Indiana natives, William Bateman Leeds (1868–1908) and Daniel Gray Reid (1858–1925). Both men grew up in Richmond, and they were boyhood friends, aptly described as "Damon and Pythias since childhood." Leeds initially entered the nursery business but subsequently joined the engineering corps of the

Pennsylvania Railroad and later became its assistant superintendent in Richmond. Reid took a different career path. He chose banking, rising rapidly from a messenger boy to head teller of the Second National Bank of Richmond.[19] The enactment of the McKinley Tariff of 1890 triggered the formation of the American Tin Plate Company. One protectionist feature involved a substantial duty on imported tin, and Leeds, joined by Reid, saw an opportunity. Fortunately, Leeds had a large investment nest egg; his wife had inherited a sizable legacy from her father, a founder of threshing-machine and steam-traction builder Gaar-Scott & Company. "The two young men swooped down upon the feeble little tin-making plants that had been fighting bankruptcy for twenty years, and swept them all together into the Tin Plate Trust before they had time to find out what was happening." Although this contemporary assessment is overly simplistic, Leeds and Reid essentially did just that—creating in 1891 a trust by amalgamating a number of struggling firms that had experienced difficulty competing with the dominant Welsh manufacturers. The Moore brothers joined the quest by Leeds and Reid to bring about what developed into a lucrative enterprise. As with past and future ventures, the tin-plate combine had ample watered stock. The men remained wedded to their commitment to using other people's money.[20]

The good chemistry between the Moore brothers and Leeds and Reid led to the greatest business deal of their relationship before their Rock Island conquest. This deal involved Andrew Carnegie's iron and steel empire. In the early months of 1899, the four, backed by John W. "Bet-a-Million" Gates, a "Wall Street Plunger" and president of American Steel and Wire Company, sought to bring the Carnegie properties into the consolidation movement. A super-trust would result. Carnegie associates Henry Clay Frick and Henry Phipps convinced the steel czar to give them, on behalf of "unidentified clients," a ninety-day option to acquire his 58 percent ownership of Carnegie Steel. "They did not dare tell Carnegie that the Moores were in on the deal, for if he had known it he would never have consented," explained historical writer Frederick Lewis Allen. "He disliked everything that these speculators-promoters represented." Judge Moore reportedly had once mocked Carnegie by saying that he knew how to make steel but knew nothing about making securities. For the senior group, the option amounted to $1 million. Frick and Phipps would be handsomely rewarded—$5 million—for successfully arranging the deal, and they gladly ponied up $170,000 with the understanding that Carnegie would return their earnest money if the deal collapsed. Alas, the $100 million in bonds and $57 million in cash that Carnegie demanded could not be raised, and Carnegie pocketed the option money.[21]

The Big Four of the Prairies did not abandon their quest for the Carnegie empire. It would be J. P. Morgan, the "Napoleon of Wall Street," who succeeded in organizing a syndicate that created the United States Steel Corporation in March 1901, capitalized at $1.4 billion, the largest corporation in the world. Yet the Moore brothers, Leeds, and Reid were heavily involved. This Morgan enterprise included such components as their American Sheet Steel, American Steel Hoop, American Tin Plate, and National Steel companies. As a result these men made "profits far beyond the dreams of avarice," receiving from Morgan approximately $140 million in US Steel securities. Moore took a seat on the US Steel board, and Leeds joined the executive committee. Morgan, though, had no intention of allowing the Moore group to wield control. Also in early 1901, the Big Four organized what turned out to be the highly ruminative American Can Company. These windfalls gave them the financial wherewithal and prestige within investment circles to take control and restructure the Rock Island.[22]

Their success with US Steel and American Can did not cause the immensely wealthy and highly regarded "Moore crowd" to consider retirement. During that hectic year of 1901, these men eyed the Rock Island. According to testimony given by Daniel Reid before the Interstate Commerce Commission (ICC) in 1915, the origins of their involvement were explained this way: "After he [Reid] and Mr. Leeds had bought some Rock Island stock, they learned that the Moore brothers also had bought some. Thereupon they decided to get together in buying Rock Island." Indeed they did. By 1901 the four had acquired about one-third of the company's stock. "This huge deal was put through so simply, so expeditiously, so silently," observed a contemporary, "that it had almost an air of negligence—of something 'dashed off in an idle moment' like a spring poem." These "wheeler-dealers," according to business historian Albro Martin, were about to seize control of the Rock Island and Frisco Railroads, and they "debauched them, and tarred the entire industry with their brush."[23]

Warren Purdy and his associates knew of rumors that the Moore crowd was buying large blocks of Rock Island stock, but they failed to anticipate a sweeping change in governance that was about to occur. Then reality set in. At the June 5, 1901, annual stockholders meeting, Daniel Reid replaced Hilton Parker, vice president and general manager, on the board of directors, and Judge Moore took the seat of another board member. A month later William Leeds joined the Rock Island directorate; he succeeded W. A. Nash, who resigned. Soon the Reid-Moore syndicate achieved full stock control, announcing that on January 1, 1902, it would take over the management of the

It is unlikely that these Rock Island maintenance-of-way workers ever saw members of the syndicate. In 1905 these men stand near a repurposed company boxcar at Volland, Kansas, located between McFarland and Herrington.

Dan Sabin coll.

property. Purdy was out, and Leeds took his place. Purdy, though, received a golden parachute, two years' salary at $22,500 annually. Even with his limited background in the railroad world, Leeds would manage technical matters for an expanding Rock Island. With Purdy's departure, his seat on the board of directors went to James Moore. The Moores, Leeds, and Reid also claimed places on the powerful executive committee. Cable remained briefly as board chair, being no more than window dressing for the syndicate. He disliked the new regime and soon retired from that pivotal post. Cable did better than Purdy, receiving a settlement that included securities in excess of $150,000.[24]

Having taken the Rock Island, the Reid-Moore syndicate wasted no time in increasing the amount of its outstanding shares. "[They were] untrammeled by traditions of conservatism," according to an understatement made in 1908 by Harvard University economist Stuart Daggett. As he saw the situation, "It is probable to a man of Mr. Moore's speculative disposition the very low capitalization of the road opened up vistas of almost indefinite increase." The four sought a long-term involvement with the railroad, and not for only a few years; this would not be a New York Biscuit or an American Tin Plate. Yet there would be securities manipulation, and eventually the level of debt became unmanageable.[25]

Before the syndicate took command, members planned on making the Great Rock Island System considerably larger by acquiring the Choctaw, Oklahoma & Gulf Railroad (CO&G or Choctaw Route). This was no tea-kettle shortline; as of October 1901, it owned 636 miles and operated another 104 miles on a largely "straight as the crow flies" east-west axis from Memphis, Tennessee, through Little Rock, Arkansas, and Oklahoma City, Oklahoma Territory, to Weatherford, also in Oklahoma Territory. Then in early 1902 the company's Choctaw, Oklahoma & Texas Railroad affiliate reached Amarillo, Texas, and another line in Indian Territory linked Hartshorne (Ardmore Junction) to Ardmore.

Like most roads its size, the Choctaw Route had predecessors. The eastern section had been built in multiple units, with the oldest dating from the 1850s, when the Memphis & Little Rock Railroad completed part of the distance between the cities of its corporate name. At last, in April 1871 the 133-mile route was finished. A financial reorganization in 1887 led to a name change; the property became the Little Rock & Memphis Railroad. The Choctaw Coal & Railway constructed another portion of the core between 1888 and 1889, a carrier that planned to connect Little Rock with Albuquerque, New Mexico Territory, with a branch to Denison, Texas. Yet by 1894 it had only 101 miles of line, which extended from South McAlester to Wister Junction, Indian Territory, and from Fort Reno, Oklahoma Territory, to Oklahoma City. This company failed in the wake of the Panic of 1893, and following a foreclosure sale a year later, it became the reorganized Choctaw, Oklahoma & Gulf Railroad. Its western section, which stretched from the Arkansas-Oklahoma Territory border to Weatherford, took shape between 1898 and 1899. Owners may not have seriously considered trackage extending to the Gulf of Mexico, but they planned to expand. In 1900 the CO&G took control of the Choctaw & Memphis Railroad, the 1899 successor to the Little Rock & Memphis. The following year the Choctaw Route added forty-six miles from Weatherford to Elk City, Oklahoma Territory. It also pushed beyond Elk City for another eighteen miles to Sayre, Oklahoma Territory, the latter being constructed under the banner of the Western Oklahoma Railroad. The Choctaw Route appeared to be profitable, having net earnings of nearly $900,000 for 1899. Fortunately for the Rock Island, it crossed the Fort Worth line at El Reno, making that community a key point on the system map, and it served the growing capital cities of Little Rock and Oklahoma City.[26]

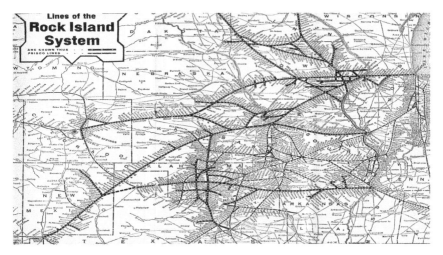

The Rock Island System public timetable for May–June 1905 reveals the railroad's expanding network of lines. The Reid-Moore syndicate continued aggressively to enlarge the property.

Author's coll.

In late spring 1902 the syndicate acquired from the Choctaw owners a potentially well-positioned railroad, which could become, if extended to the Southern Pacific or Santa Fe, a transcontinental rail link from the Memphis gateway. Yet the CO&G was no sparkling jewel. "It was essentially a coal-carrying road through sparsely settled territory," wrote William Edward Hayes. "Its roadbed was in none too good condition, its power was outmoded, [and] its rolling stock was in bad repair." It was expected that betterments could make a lengthened Choctaw Route into an attractive asset. "The property is a valuable one," an observer noted, "but will have to show great development to justify its purchase price." The syndicate had financed this acquisition largely with $23,520,000 in 4 percent collateral trust bonds.[27]

Just as the Choctaw Route held the possibility of becoming a strategic part of the Rock Island, the syndicate quickly took action to reach Saint Louis, a railroad gateway second only to Chicago. Resembling the complicated corporate genealogy of the Choctaw Route, what by 1904 had become the Rock Island's 298-mile Kansas City-Saint Louis line contained parts that predated syndicate involvement. The initial attempts to build from Saint Louis along this route, which began in 1870, got no further than on paper. Finally, in the late 1870s the Forest Park & Central Railroad Company completed a sixteen-mile commuter line west from Forsythe Junction in Saint Louis to Creve Coeur. Next to appear was the St. Louis, Kansas City & Colorado Railroad Company (StLKC&C), incorporated in 1884. Although this firm acquired the Forest

Park & Central, it failed for several years to expand. At last construction began, and the Santa Fe made this possible. The fifty-five miles from Creve Coeur to Union opened in 1888, yet the StLKC&C remained forty-five miles short of its announced objective of the mid-Missouri town of Belle. Tracks subsequently reached Bland, five miles east of Belle. But by the mid-1890s, the bankrupt Santa Fe had given up the road, which had become chronically unprofitable. The Santa Fe sold its assets at a "terrific loss" to a Saint Louis investor group led by David R. Francis and John Scullin. In 1902 the syndicate stepped in and took charge. Crews went to work, and the following year service had been extended to Eldon, 160 miles from Saint Louis, and subsequently pushed westward for another ninety-three miles. Construction also began from Kansas City. The forty-three miles between Kansas City and Hadsell was orchestrated by subsidiary Kansas City Rock Island Railway Company (KCRI). The entire length between Missouri's two largest cities opened officially on June 5, 1904, allowing more patrons to attend the popular Louisiana Purchase Exposition in Saint Louis. On January 1, 1905, the StLKC&C and KCRI became one, and the consolidated property was conveyed to the Rock Island.[28]

Passenger trains on the Saint Louis line were fewer and slower than what the Missouri Pacific and Wabash Railroads scheduled between Kansas City and Saint Louis; it was not the road of choice for most Kansas Citians, Saint Louisans, or those from connecting roads. The Rock Island offered basic accommodations much as it did on the Choctaw Route, dispatching a daily local and another passenger train that made somewhat fewer stops. Residents from on-line communities that lacked a direct route to the terminals or who had no prior rail outlet welcomed this service. Most everyone enjoyed the scenery east of Belle, with its curves, tunnels, and scenic vistas. This poorly engineered section became for the Rock Island a troubling legacy of the StLKC&C.

The Moore brothers, Leeds, and Reid surely burned the midnight oils during their first year in power. Not only did they orchestrate major line expansions in Indian and Oklahoma Territories and Missouri, but they assumed full sway over the Burlington, Cedar Rapids & Northern Railroad (BCR&N), a company for which the Rock Island wielded stock control. On June 1, 1902, the Rock Island obtained a 999-year lease of this 1,367-mile Cedar Rapids–based carrier. Operations of the BCR&N would be integrated into the Rock Island System. Yet as railroad historian Don Hofsommer pointed out, "Train crews [and others] had every reason to wonder what the 'Rock Island crowd' might mean to their employer and to themselves."[29]

By mid-1902 the Reid-Moore syndicate had developed its own plan to manage the financial structure of the Rock Island. The end goals meant inflating stock prices, permitting centralized control, and providing the four men with large profits. A contemporary financial writer believed that the syndicate engaged in "the most astounding piece of stock watering the world has ever seen." In fact, Wall Street men appeared bewildered by the intricacies of the scheme. This assessment rang true: "Moore was the most daring promoter in American business, just as Morgan was the foremost financier."[30]

In order to achieve these objectives, the syndicate organized not one but two holding companies, or what the financial community referred to as a "superimposed type" or "double-holding company" arrangement. The Chicago, Rock Island & Pacific *Railway* Company (Railway Company) continued to be the operating unit, and its structure remained untouched. Then there was the first holding or paper company, the Chicago, Rock Island & Pacific *Railroad* Company (Railroad Company), chartered under Iowa law and designed to hold the stock of the Railway Company. The second holding company was the Rock Island Company, launched in the friendly business confines of New Jersey. This paper firm controlled the stock of the *Railroad* Company and could be used for further acquisitions. The syndicate tapped the Central Trust Company of New York to work closely with this second corporate entity. About this time the Rock Island opened an office at 14 Wall Street in the heart of the New York City financial district.[31]

The Rock Island corporate structure resembled other holding companies in the utilities sector, reflecting an increasingly popular practice that dated back to the 1880s. As with other similar firms, these paper affairs issued common and preferred stock and bonds. Why have pyramid firms? For promoters and speculators they possessed several attractive features. Since a large part of the total capitalization was in nonvoting securities, control could be obtained without the support from a majority of stockholders. With two holding companies, power could be further concentrated; the holding firm on top had controlling interest. The money needed to buy the stock of one company could be borrowed, using the stock of another as collateral. Furthermore, the actual amount of investment required by the organizers was greatly reduced. Although the Reid-Moore syndicate stopped at two holding companies, the number of these entities between controlling interests and an operating property or properties could be multiplied.

Not long after the Reid-Moore syndicate took control of the Burlington, Cedar Rapids & Northern Railway (BCR&N), a Rock Island passenger train waits at the former BCR&N station in Montezuma, Iowa, seat of Poweshiek County and western terminus of a seventy-mile branch from Iowa City and a main-line connection. The depot represents the popular BCR&N two-story style.

Author's coll.

Although ten-wheeler No. 1254 sports "CRI&P" under the cab window, it has been recently acquired from the Burlington, Cedar Rapids & Northern. Workers have painted No. 1254 over the original number on the tender, but the first freight car has not been relettered. This photograph dates from ca. 1904 and was taken in Cedar Rapids.

Dan Sabin coll.

How did the syndicate construct its operating and pyramid firms? In 1908 economist Stuart Daggett explained the essentials: "The old Railway Company had a capital stock of $75,000,000; the new Railroad Company issued stock to the amount of $125,000,000 and 4 per cent bonds to the amount of $75,000,000. The Rock Island Company issued common stock to a total of $96,000,000 and preferred stock to a total of $54,000,000; and the aggregate, excluding the undisturbed bonds of the Railway Company, footed up to $425,000,000 instead of to $75,000,000 as before." He further elaborated: "From this total must be deducted $200,000,000, which represented issues of stock by one company to another, and $21,000,000 Rock Island Company stock and $1,500,000 Railroad Company bonds reserved for future extensions, leaving a net increase from $75,000,000 to $202,500,000." Daggett continued, "This involved some increase in fixed charges, since 4 per cent on $75,000,000 became obligatory; but the true significance lay in the inflation of principal rather than in the increase of interest charges, opening as it did an opportunity for great profit to the managers in the sale of the new securities." Although the exact dollar amount is not certain, the syndicate had invested about $20 million to win control of a railroad now capitalized in the hundreds of millions.[32]

Fortunately for the syndicate, the vast majority of shareholders in the Railway Company endorsed the syndicate's work, surrendering their common shares for a package of stocks and bonds in the Rock Island Company. They believed that "their holdings are actually worth considerably more than the present market price." An owner of each $100 face value share in the Railway Company received this package of securities: $100 common stock of the Rock Island Company, $70 preferred stock of the Rock Island Company, and $100 collateral trust bonds of the Railroad Company. The exchange meant that $100 face value of Railway Company shares yielded $270 face value in the two holding companies. "Those optimistic stockholders who participated in the syndicate's offering," opined William Edward Hayes, "bought nothing but a pig in a poke, and a pretty slippery pig at that." His analysis proved correct. Yet investor enthusiasm might be explained partially by financial advisers who believed that booms occurred every twenty years, followed by severe panics such as in 1873 and 1893. Since the last crash had already taken place, the next big downswing would not likely happen until 1913 or thereabouts. Yet the Panic of 1907 revealed that the twenty-year boom cycle had ended prematurely.[33]

With control and ample financial resources, the Reid-Moore syndicate could pursue creation of a vast railroad network. William Moore, most of all, reportedly dreamed of a transcontinental system. This meant some type of union between the Rock Island and an array of possible carriers, including the

Lehigh Valley; Delaware, Lackawanna & Western (Lackawanna); Lake Erie & Western; Wabash; Toledo, St. Louis & Western (Clover Leaf); Chicago & Alton (Alton); Missouri Pacific; St. Louis-San Francisco (Frisco); Denver & Rio Grande; and Southern Pacific. Depending on what companies fell under syndicate control, some construction might be necessary to connect from coast to coast. The Moore group not only invested heavily in the Lehigh Valley and the largely parallel Lackawanna, "old conservative railroad properties," but also took charge of the much larger Frisco.[34]

A glance at the railroad map of the greater Rock Island territory revealed that the St. Louis & San Francisco Railroad, known commonly as the Frisco—a corporate moniker that represented aspirations rather than eventualities—operated a web of lines. Its trackage, which exceeded five thousand miles, would provide the Rock Island System with a property that operated in eleven states and territories with good traffic opportunities, including access to productive agricultural, timber, and mineral regions. In what some contemporaries called an act of "system-perfecting," the syndicate coveted Frisco trackage in Arkansas, Kansas, Missouri, Oklahoma and Indian Territories, and Texas, as well as a developing direct route between Saint Louis and Memphis. This was the work of satellite St. Louis, Memphis & Southeastern Railroad, which opened in 1904. The satellite would give the Rock Island a convenient line to Memphis and allow it to compete directly with the Illinois Central. Since Frisco had taken control of the Kansas City, Memphis & Birmingham; Fort Worth & Rio Grande; and Red River, Texas & Southern railroads, more value had been added. Another attractive feature was that management had forged an alliance with the Southern Railway for an entrance into the port of New Orleans. Furthermore, the Frisco System offered a solid foundation for expansion.[35]

In May 1903 the Reid-Moore syndicate moved to control the Frisco. After prolonged negotiations the company agreed to be purchased. The offer that lured Frisco shareholders consisted of the following: "For every share of [Frisco] common stock of the par value of $100, so deposited, Chicago, Rock Island and Pacific Railway Company will deliver: Sixty dollars (par value) in five per cent. gold bonds of 1913 of said Chicago, Rock Island and Pacific Railway Company and sixty dollars (par value) in the common stock of the Rock Island Company (of New Jersey)." Frisco shares were to be deposited with Central Trust as collateral for the bonds of the Railroad Company. This transaction resulted in the acquisition of more than 90 percent of Frisco common stock.[36]

While the syndicate was in the midst of acquiring the Frisco, it sought a greater presence in Texas. This involved obtaining a half interest in the Texas lines of the Southern Pacific, properties that included the Houston & Texas Central (508 miles); Houston & East & West Texas (191 miles); and the Texas & New Orleans (374 miles). If implemented, this arrangement would expand traffic and "establish a line to the [Gulf] coast in a very satisfactory manner." The Texas Railroad Commission objected, claiming that the arrangement violated the state constitution and created an anticompetitive community of interest. Syndicate members considered challenging the decision but subsequently abandoned the Southern Pacific deal. Yet in late 1903 they did incorporate the Chicago, Rock Island & Gulf Railway, which not only took over the Texas affiliate of the Choctaw, Oklahoma & Gulf but opened a line between Fort Worth and Dallas.[37]

The creative minds of William Moore and his partners never rested. A new dimension of their expansion agenda involved the 1903 formation of another subsidiary, the Rock Island Improvement Company (RIIC). Once more the syndicate used New Jersey incorporation laws to advance its agenda. The main purpose of the RIIC was to take title to property and equipment that the Railway Company might require, "thereby [to] remove such property and equipment from falling under liens of the railway company's mortgages." In order to protect syndicate control, the Rock Island Company acquired the entire capital stock of the RIIC.[38]

During these halcyon years, the Reid-Moore syndicate became more heavily involved with Benjamin Franklin Yoakum (1859–1929), better known as B. F. Yoakum. As Frisco head he developed a both positive and negative reputation as either the "Empire Builder of the Southwest" or the "financial giant in railroad manipulation." The relationship between this native Texan and the Moore brothers, Leeds, and Reid was complex, and it extended beyond the Rock Island Company's quest to take control of the Frisco System. Who was this railroad executive? Yoakum came from a decidedly middle-class family. His father, a physician and Cumberland Presbyterian minister, once had been president of a struggling denominational college, a forerunner to Trinity University in San Antonio. Not surprisingly, the senior Yoakum wanted his son to enter the ministry. "But the smell of coal oil and the dream of empire was in the younger Yoakum's blood." Resembling so many railroad leaders of his generation, Yoakum lacked an extensive formal education, but he rose through the ranks, and he did so in meteoric fashion. He began his career at age eighteen as a freight clerk with the Southern Pacific. Soon thereafter Yoakum joined the International & Great Northern Railroad, filling several positions, including that of receiver, between 1890 and 1893. After a brief stint with the San Antonio & Aransas Pass Railway, he became an official with the

Gulf, Colorado & Santa Fe Railway. In 1896 Yoakum left that company for the Frisco; in four years promotions elevated him from vice president and general manger to president.[39]

Yoakum was an ideal fit for what observers called the "Rock Island gang." He was bright, focused, and forceful. He also thought big, being a proponent of a rail line between Texas and the emerging Panama Canal. The gang needed experienced executives, and the Yoakum connection would help, especially to fill top leadership positions. Although Leeds had been a minor official with the Pennsylvania, he faced daunting challenges as Rock Island president. Furthermore, his health was declining, constant stress being the likely factor.

A strong Frisco presence took place administratively. Immediately B. F. Yoakum joined the Rock Island board of directors. When Leeds stepped down from the Rock Island presidency on April 6, 1904, a trusted Yoakum lieutenant, B. L. Winchell, succeeded him. Leeds, however, remained a member of the executive committee and the board of directors until February 1906.[40]

Benjamin LaFon Winchell (1856–1942), the next president of the Rock Island, possessed a strong résumé. In 1873 at age fifteen, this Palmyra, New York, native began his professional career with the Hannibal & St. Joseph Railroad as a clerk for the superintendent of machinery, and he advanced through various departments. In 1880 Winchell resigned to become chief clerk in the passenger department of the Kansas City, Fort Scott & Gulf and Kansas City, Lawrence & Southern Kansas Railroads. After several additional assignments, he took charge of passenger operations for the Union Pacific, Denver & Gulf and Denver, Leadville & Gunnison Railroads. In 1898 Winchell again switched companies when he joined the Frisco, becoming its general passenger agent. But he left shortly afterward to assume the duties of vice president and traffic manager for the Colorado & Southern Railway. His tenure there lasted less than a year before he returned to his former employer Kansas City, Fort Scott & Gulf as president and general manager. His next position came in August 1902 as vice president and general manager of the Frisco System. As soon as Yoakum joined the Rock Island, the board made Winchell the third vice president. "Diligence in mastering details and that natural talent for organization account for Mr. Winchell's rapid rise," commented a contemporary magazine writer. Railroad authority Frank Spearman likewise lauded Winchell: "Outside of motive power it would be difficult to name a single department of the road of which he could not step and perform with ease the duties of the head."[41]

Benjamin Winchell was no armchair president; he was an energetic railroader. Within a short period, Winchell traveled in his office car over much of the Rock Island. He not only examined the physical plant but talked

More than two dozen locomotives, which are undergoing major repairs, reveal the massiveness of the Silvis Shops. This undated photograph dates from ca. 1915.

Dan Sabin coll.

with officials and employees. He intended to determine what was needed to enhance service and revenues. Apparently the Rock Island required large investments, ranging from better motive power and rolling stock to upgraded shops and terminal facilities. Some improvements followed, including the lengthy process of constructing a high-capacity shop complex in Silvis, Illinois, situated outside Moline. Winchell also promoted the Morris Terminal Railway in Morris, Illinois. This two-mile affiliate, opened in 1906, served manufacturing plants and other businesses that were "formerly compelled to haul freight by wagons at some inconvenience and considerable expense."[42]

Although syndicate members did not ignore reports made by Winchell and his staff, they expressed a greater interest in large-scale expansion. About the time B. F. Yoakum joined the leadership group, the Frisco used a leveraged buyout to take control of the largely bridge and coal-hauling Chicago & Eastern Illinois Railroad (C&EI). This 947-mile carrier, which claimed a bewildering array of predecessor companies, connected Chicago with both Saint Louis and Evansville, Indiana, and had a largely parallel line to the east of its north-south main stem that ran between the Indiana towns of La Crosse and Brazil. There were also a small number of connector and branch lines. The C&EI had a close relationship with the Evansville & Terre Haute Railroad, a 186-mile property that served the Evansville gateway with lines from both

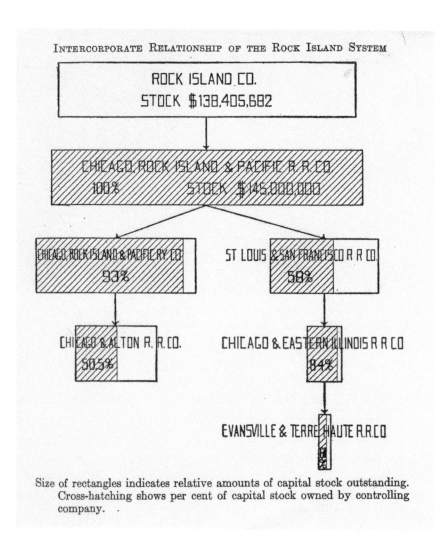

ROCK ISLAND CO.
STOCK $138,405,682

CHICAGO, ROCK ISLAND & PACIFIC R.R. CO.
100%   STOCK $145,000,000

CHICAGO, ROCK ISLAND & PACIFIC RY. CO.
93%

ST LOUIS & SAN FRANCISCO R R CO.
58%

CHICAGO & ALTON R. R. CO.
50.5%

CHICAGO & EASTERN ILLINOIS R R CO
84%

EVANSVILLE & TERRE HAUTE R.R. CO

Size of rectangles indicates relative amounts of capital stock outstanding. Cross-hatching shows per cent of capital stock owned by controlling company.

This chart suggests the complexities of the corporate structures created by the Reid-Moore syndicate. These four men creatively forged a highly leveraged railroad system.

Author's coll.

Brazil and Terre Haute. In May 1903 when the syndicate got possession of the Frisco, it established control over the C&EI.[43]

The quest to expand the Rock Island System continued unabated, and Arkansas remained a focus. The company already had a presence; its lines had come via the Choctaw Route, which ran on an east-west axis across the Diamond State. The syndicate sought more. After all, Arkansas had the potential for greater shipments of natural resources, especially lumber from its vast virgin forests of cypress, oak, and short-leaf pine. It also had coal to haul and agricultural products to tap, including fruit, rice, and most of all cotton. While lumber and cotton became the freight core, after World War I petroleum generated a traffic boom. In January 1921 oil was discovered near El Dorado, and the Rock Island handled more than 90 percent of the first year's production of 3.8 million barrels. The syndicate, too, saw the value of a possible direct route from Little Rock to New Orleans that would run through the state.

Arkansas trackage mounted. The syndicate eyed several of the state's numerous shortlines. With control of the Choctaw Route, the Rock Island readily assumed the eighty-year lease of the White & Black River Valley Railway. This added sixty-two miles, with fifty-six miles between Brinkley and Jacksonport and a six-mile stub from Wiville to Gregory. Two more feeders came in March 1904 when the Rock Island acquired the Searcy & Des Arc Railroad, which gave it a thirty-mile line between Des Arc, Searcy, and Kensett, and the fourteen-mile Hazen & Northern Railroad from Des Arc to Mesa. Later the Rock Island foolishly acquired the Dardanelle, Ola & Southern Railway, which ran northward for fifteen miles from Ola on the Choctaw to Dardanelle. Reorganized in 1911 as the Rock Island & Dardanelle Railway, it remained a financially feeble property.[44]

In an important strategic move, in 1905 the syndicate launched the Rock Island, Arkansas & Louisiana Railroad (RIA&L), designed as the corporate pathway to New Orleans. Into the RIA&L were folded these corporations: Little Rock & Southern (no track but some grading between Haskell and El Dorado and southeast from Tinsman to Crossett); Arkansas Southern (ninety-eight miles between El Dorado and Winnfield, Louisiana); and Arkansas Southern Extension (ten miles from Winnfield to Packton, Louisiana). This totaled 108 miles. But completing trackage to Eunice, Louisiana, where a connection could be made to the Crescent City with Frisco subsidiary Colorado Southern, New Orleans & Pacific Railroad (CSNO&P), which was then taking shape, would require more than 200 miles of construction. Fortuitously the Rock Island already controlled some trackage south of Little Rock. This mileage was the legacy of the former narrow-gauge Hot Springs Branch Railroad, the pet project of Mississippi River steamboat owner Joseph "Diamond Jo" Reynolds, and the Choctaw Route. The CO&G, which grasped the potential of passenger traffic generated by this resort community, gained access through a combination of connecting construction with the former Reynolds property and the lease of twenty-six miles of the Little Rock & Hot Springs Western Railway. Eventually, the Rock Island extension deep into Louisiana began a reality, although it would be a drawn-out process; service finally started between Little Rock and Eunice in January 1908. The syndicate

Shortly after the turn of the twentieth century, a handsome Ten-Wheeler heads a Rock Island passenger train at the Hot Springs, Arkansas, station. The community had become a popular destination for those who wished to "take the waters." Bathhouses and other support facilities made for relaxing and memorable experiences.

Dan Sabin coll.

rejected the idea of building from Eunice to New Orleans, relying on friendly connections at Alexandria and Eunice. Yet the favored interchange was with the CSNO&P at Eunice, which opened in August 1909, creating that desired through route.[45]

As the twentieth century progressed, the Rock Island expanded its Arkansas network. With the Hot Springs line in tow, the company built south from Malvern to Camden, increasing trackage by fifty-nine miles. This construction used a five-mile stub on the Hot Springs extension between Butterfield and Marvern. Part of this Diamond State penetration included a forty-three-mile branch between Tinsman, situated on what became the Eunice line ninety-five miles south of Little Rock, and Crossett, forty-three miles to the southeast. This Ashley County seat served a thriving lumber industry and connected with the Arkansas, Louisiana & Gulf Railway (AL&G). That independent sixty-five-mile shortline linked Crossett with Monroe, Louisiana, and there were plans to build to Pine Bluff, Arkansas, creating a 183-mile railroad. By 1915 part of that mileage had been completed, namely the forty-one miles from Crossett to Monticello (later the Crossett, Monticello & Northern Railroad). The syndicate probably expected that the AL&G would enter its orbit.[46]

This line construction south of Little Rock meant better transportation for residents. Arkansas and Louisiana suffered from miserable roads. And numerous river fords and ferries became treacherous during periods of high water; bridges were often absent even on the most heavily traveled routes. The arrival of the Rock Island changed the transport picture and brought about happier times. "New settlers moved in, more land was cleared, the spirit of the people seemed to rise phoenix-like from the aftermath of the Civil War and a more general prosperity perveded [sic] the whole country," an El Dorado resident said about Rock Island service. Such feelings about the coming of the iron horse really knew no geographical bounds.[47]

Early on, the Reid-Moore syndicate coveted the 902-mile Chicago & Alton Railway (C&A or Alton), and it sought another conquest. The Alton operated its principal route between Chicago and Saint Louis; a secondary line between Roodhouse, Illinois, and Kansas City; and a few scattered branches in Illinois and Missouri. This railroad was the popular passenger carrier between Chicago and Saint Louis; in fact, it had long advertised itself as "The Only Way." The Alton served a rich freight-producing territory and benefited from the haulage of agricultural products, livestock, coal, merchandise, and other products. The Alton offered an attractive way to move traffic between Chicago and Kansas City, superior to that of "the admittedly unsatisfactory line of the Rock Island," and if the Rock Island were to take it, it would end rental payments to the Burlington for entry into Kansas City. The Frisco property would be strengthened if it gained direct access from Saint Louis to Chicago.[48]

During the latter part of 1903, the Reid-Moore syndicate became focused on the Alton. Edward H. Harriman, who led both the Union Pacific and the Southern Pacific, and his business allies believed that they held a firm grip on the property. Starting in 1899, Harriman interests had done much to modernize the Alton, upgrading its old and uneconomical equipment and repair shops. However, they lacked stock control. It was B. F. Yoakum who served as point man for the Rock Island's takeover efforts. Previously he had worked with railroad executive and Wall Street financier Edwin Hawley, called by some the "Little Harriman," in gaining control of the Colorado & Southern Railway. Then in 1904 Yoakum asked the shadowy Hawley to acquire Alton stock for the syndicate. The financial house of Hawley & Davis worked its magic, aided by considerable market price swings that occurred that year. The price tag reached nearly $10 million. By late summer Harriman realized that he had been beaten. Business historian Albro Martin suggested another motivation for the syndicate's involvement: "The acquisition of the Chicago & Alton, which Edward H. Harriman lost to them in an unguarded moment, seems to have been not much more than a 'lark,' an attempt to 'put one over' on the seemingly omnipotent Harriman." Yet there were fundamental advantages of having the Alton's core lines and an upgraded property.[49]

Major involvement with the Alton did not last long. In 1907 the syndicate exchanged a substantial amount of its Alton securities for those of the Toledo, St. Louis & Western Railroad (Clover Leaf). This woebegone largely former narrow-gauge road linked Toledo with Saint Louis, creating a 450-mile carrier. It also had joint ownership of the forty-eight-mile Detroit & Toledo Shore Line Railroad. With Hawley on the Clover Leaf board since 1905, and with the road being a connector to the Toledo gateway and a possible component in a transcontinental system, this financial transaction was not too surprising.[50]

Although Edwin Hawley ably served syndicate members, he became an irritant because of one business transaction. These men made a costly misstep that involved the Des Moines & Fort Dodge Railroad (DM&FtD). The Rock Island had long leased this company, but the arrangement was set to expire on December 31, 1904. This 144-mile road connected Des Moines with the Rock Island's Gowrie-to-Sibley, Iowa, extension. In the months before the lease terminated, Hawley saw value in the property. He considered the DM&FtD to be a practical way to strengthen his Minneapolis & St. Louis (M&StL) and Iowa Central holdings, and so he quietly acquired its stock. With the railroad under Hawley's control, the Rock Island had no choice but to pay trackage rights to the DM&FtD (operated by the M&StL); it did not want the Gowrie-Sibley line to become an orphan. The Rock Island furthermore lost access to former and future on-line customers between Ruthven and Des Moines. Gross inattention explains why Hawley could seize the DM&FtD.[51]

The capture of the Des Moines & Fort Dodge hardly demoralized syndicate members; they continued their expansion, always striving for a stronger system. Because of his skills, Edwin Hawley was neither punished nor shunned. The next major involvement for Judge Moore and his compatriots involved the Trinity & Brazos Valley Railway (T&BV), known formally as the "Valley Road" and informally as the "Boll Weevil Line." This venture sparked a desire to serve Houston and Galveston and to tap the Gulf trade. With service established to Fort Worth for more than a decade and with a line stretching between that city and Dallas since December 12, 1903, the T&BV made strategic sense. The syndicate responded by partnering with the Colorado & Southern (C&S). Within two years, the T&BV, launched as an independent road in 1902, had a seventy-nine-mile line between the Texas towns of Cleburne and Mexia. By 1907 the railroad had been extended 157 miles from Mexia south to the Houston area and from Teague, near Mexia, north to Waxahachie. With trackage rights over Santa Fe subsidiaries, Cleburne was connected to Fort Worth and Houston with Galveston. By running over Missouri-Kansas-Texas (Katy) rails from Waxahachie, the road gained access to Dallas. These arrangements created a 302-mile railroad that also used an additional 106 miles of rental lines. Through service began between Fort Worth and Houston on January 28, 1907, between Dallas and Houston that July, and between Houston and Galveston the following year.[52]

The Trinity & Brazos Valley evolved, and the Colorado & Southern took control in 1905. On March 31, 1906, a contract, instigated by B. F. Yoakum, was signed between the C&S and the syndicate, amounting to an equal split of the Texas railroad. Even though the C&S had financed most of the T&BV, the agreement called for the Rock Island, on May 1, 1935, to pay the C&S one-half of the entire cost of the line, receiving in return one-half of its bonds and one-half of "other evidence of debt included in the total cost of the Brazos line." The contract further stipulated that the two parties share equally the profits and losses of the road. The poorly constructed T&BV, however, was a financial loser, draining funds from company coffers. As of 1911 the syndicate had invested more than $2.3 million. The road fell into receivership in 1914, but the oil traffic boom of the 1920s and a physical rebuilding freed it from court control in July 1930 as the reorganized Burlington-Rock Island Railroad. For decades the Rock Island then profitably used the original Valley Road to access Houston and Galveston and benefited from its interest in the Houston Belt & Terminal Company.[53]

The last major additions to the Rock Island System during the Reid-Moore era came between 1910 and 1913. First the Choctaw Route gained greater importance. Although the syndicate had succeeded in extending the line from Memphis to Amarillo, there remained a 113-mile gap between that Texas Panhandle trading center and Tucumcari, the connecting point with the Southern Pacific for West Coast destinations. Using Texas and New Mexico chartered satellites Chicago, Rock Island & Gulf Railroad and Chicago, Rock Island & El Paso Railway, the 874-mile line opened for through traffic between Memphis and Tucumcari on May 9, 1910. The company boasted that it was "the shortest line between Memphis, Tenn. and Southern California, via New Mexico and Arizona." Completion made trackage rights unnecessary over the Fort Worth & Denver City Railway between Amarillo and Dalhart, Texas, a distance of eighty-two miles. Next came the February 1911 incorporation of the St. Paul & Kansas City Short Line Railroad (Short Line). The syndicate sought a noble objective: the shortest rail line between Kansas City and the Twin Cities. The Rock Island already controlled a route between the Minnesota metropolises and Des Moines, having recently taken over the 115-mile St. Paul & Des Moines Railroad, which linked Clear Lake Junction, Iowa, with East Des Moines, and having acquired trackage rights over additional short stretches, including the Chicago Great Western Railroad in the Mason City area. South of the Iowa capital, the Indianola-Winterset branch provided a nine-mile segment to Carlisle. Now the Rock Island needed to build the sixty-five miles between Carlisle and Allerton, located on the Davenport-to-Kansas City main line. Fortunately, construction crews of this well-engineered "air line" did not encounter major streams, but the hilly landscape required considerable cut and fill work in places. On September 14, 1913, the first through trains steamed between the two urban terminals on what railroaders later called the "Spine Line." This trackage became the last major railroad-line construction in Iowa. The Rock Island advanced more than $11 million to finance this most useful undertaking and took a ninety-nine-year lease on the property.[54]

ALONG THE LINES

Virtually every railroad interacted with the general public, and the Rock Island was no exception. Although the company handled large volumes of through and local freight, most patrons knew it for its passenger trains, whether limiteds, locals, or mixed. Like other interregional carriers, the Rock Island dispatched its flagship named trains. By the early years of the twentieth century, the railroad claimed two widely recognized ones: *Rocky Mountain Limited* and *Golden State Limited*. The former dated from the late 1880s and traveled daily between Chicago, Des Moines, Omaha, Colorado Springs, Pueblo, and Denver. The latter made its debut in 1902, almost exactly fifty years after the first passenger train rolled over Rock Island rails, and operated mostly on a daily basis between Chicago, Kansas City, El Paso, and Los Angeles, with a Saint Louis connecting section.[55]

The Rock Island assigned to the *Rocky Mountain Limited* and *Golden State Limited* equipment that offered passengers what they expected in first-class travel. The public timetable for midyear 1905 revealed that the electric-lighted Colorado consist featured sleeping cars, chair cars, and a buffet-library-smoking car between Chicago and Denver, a double drawing-room sleeping car between Chicago and Pueblo via Colorado Springs, an observation sleeping car between Chicago and Omaha, a chair car between Limon and Pueblo via Colorado Springs, and a dining car between Chicago and Rock Island and Council Bluffs and Denver. The California train offered comparable rolling stock. Its equipment included a drawing-room sleeping car between

LET'S GO TO COLORADO

F IRST on the wings of fancy, and then—if you like the journey—on the Rocky Mountain Limited, which flies almost as fast, and which is every bit as luxurious.

During the early years of the twentieth century, the Rock Island advertised extensively its *Rocky Mountain Limited*. A beautifully produced illustrated booklet, which dates from ca. 1905, lauds features of this Chicago-to-Colorado Springs and Denver train. The railroad engaged the prestigious American Bank Note Company in New York City to do the printing.

Author's coll.

In July 1911 Rock Island No. 653 waits with its commuter train at the Englewood, Illinois, station. At this time the company-built 4-4-0 locomotive had served the railroad for seventeen years.

Keith L. Bryant coll.

Saint Louis and San Francisco (via Southern Pacific's *Owl*), a buffet-library car between Chicago and Los Angeles, an observation sleeping car between Chicago and Los Angeles, a drawing-room sleeping car between Chicago and Kansas City, "Pullman's latest pattern tourist sleeping car between Chicago and Los Angeles and annex tourist sleeping car between St. Louis and Kansas City," and a dining car between Chicago, Los Angeles, and San Francisco. Usually Atlantic-type locomotives pulled both limiteds.[56]

The Rock Island passenger department, led by John Sebastian, aggressively marketed its premier trains. It did so through public timetables, named-train brochures, and other company-sponsored tracts and through advertisements in newspapers and mass-circulation publications. In a 1905 timetable, these were the words to entice riders to the *Rocky Mountain Limited*: "Colorado? Yes! For one thing there's the fun to be had—for old, for young, for middle-aged—a great variety of it. Then there's the tonic mountain air that adds a zest to every pleasure—clear, cool and bracing. Then, too, the economical side—Colorado will house and entertain you at a most reasonable cost. *Good* board and lodging—$6 to $20 per week. Camp out and 'rough it' if you like, much cheaper." In February 1903 Sebastian's office offered this promotional message about California to *Literary Digest* readers, stressing that the state likewise provided a tonic for all of life's ills and discomforts: "Soon after a traveler steps off the *Golden State Limited* in Los Angeles, you can be on the shores of the Pacific, listening to the roar of the surf, drinking in the wine-like air; the bluest of blue skies above you and the most charming landscapes in America all about you." This surely appealed to midwesterners, who battled snow, ice, cold, and winter gloom. There was this attractive feature of a sixty-eight-hour West Coast trip on the *Golden State Limited*: "The Direct Route of Lowest Altitudes."[57]

The Rock Island dispatched less stellar passenger movements. Some were named, but most were not. A secondary or local line train commonly consisted of an American Standard–type locomotive pulling a baggage/mail car and one or more coaches. A mixed train meant just that: "hog and human." Passengers might ride in a vintage coach or perhaps a caboose behind a string of freight cars. With the advent of Jim Crow laws in the South toward the end of the nineteenth century, African Americans were relegated to "colored" sections in trains and depots—accommodations that usually ignored the US Supreme Court's doctrine of "separate but *equal*" as set forth in the 1895 landmark case of *Plessy v. Ferguson*. Yet no matter the nature of these trains, they served the needs of travelers and hundreds of communities. An arrival sparked a beehive of activity at the local station.

Under syndicate control, the Rock Island worked to replace its obsolete fleet of wooden passenger cars with ones of steel. It was a lengthy process; as late as 1914 the passenger car roster counted 1,163 pieces, of which only 346 were all steel. The Pullman Company had taken the lead with upgrades, and the Rock Island (and other roads, too) followed suit with modern consists for its mostly main-line trains. Before the replacement process could be completed, the company experienced its deadliest wreck. On March 21, 1910, an accident occurred near the central Iowa community of Green Mountain. Oddly the track was not that of the Rock Island but of the Chicago Great Western (CGW). The accident happened because of an earlier derailment on the former BCR&N between Vinton and Shellsburg. Freight and passenger traffic had to be detoured, explaining why two Rock Island passenger trains bound for the Twin Cities, one from Chicago and the other from Saint Louis, found themselves on foreign rails. Since these trains had been badly delayed, they were consolidated and sent on their way over the Chicago & North Western from Cedar Rapids to Marshalltown. There they were switched to the CGW so they could rejoin home rails in Waterloo. Unfortunately a tragic mistake was made in Marshalltown. It was decided *not* to turn the two locomotives, a 2-6-0 and a 4-4-0, and so they departed running in reverse, preceded by their tenders. Their speed, though, was not excessively fast. Near Green Mountain, eight miles into the final leg of the detour, the tender of the lead unit jumped the tracks, plunging it and the locomotive, along with the second tender and locomotive, into a deep cut. The derailment telescoped the steel Pullman of the Saint Louis train into the attached wooden coach, and everyone in that ill-fated car was either killed or seriously injured. The next car, a wooden smoker, was smashed at both ends, having been coupled to the steel coaches and sleepers of the Chicago train. Few of its occupants escaped death or major injury. Nearly forty passengers died immediately, and scores more sustained life-threatening injuries; the death count eventually reached fifty-one. Blame centered on both Rock Island and CGW personnel. Locomotives running backward, even at reduced speeds, were prone to derail.[58]

While the Rock Island could not claim to be in the vanguard of passenger rolling stock modernization, it nevertheless joined a number of carriers by trying experimental equipment. In 1904 management launched a study of passenger-train expenditures, focusing on lightly patronized branch lines. After examining the cost differential between a traditional steam-powered train and self-propelled equipment, it decided to purchase several of the latter. It was a sensible decision; after all, even a small train with a 4-4-0 locomotive, baggage car or "combine," and coach was nearly always required by state law to have a five-member crew.[59]

By the time the syndicate lost control, the Rock Island had experimented with eleven self-propelled cars. The first one arrived in January 1907. This tiny vehicle consisted of a Pullman-built car body and a Fairbanks Morse water-cooled gasoline engine. It had a motorman and could seat only twenty passengers. Its maximum speed on level track was just twenty miles per hour. This initial car, however, proved to be an operating disappointment, and a few years later it became scrap. Also in 1907, the company received from the Baldwin Locomotive Works an Americanized version of a Ganz Company (of Budapest) coal-burning steam car. In appearance this combination baggage-passenger unit resembled a contemporary electric interurban car. The following year the Rock Island acquired a similar steam car, albeit an oil burner from the American Locomotive Company (Alco). Of these two experimental steam vehicles, the latter one performed better, operating economically on the branch between Herrington and Salina, Kansas. After various and substantial modifications, these cars remained in service for decades, with the Baldwin being retired in 1943 and the Alco five years later. Still intrigued by small gasoline cars, the Rock Island purchased another twenty-passenger vehicle from the Stover Motor Car Company in 1909. Although it was cheap to operate, passenger revenues proved disappointing on its assigned run between Enid and Anadarko, Oklahoma. Within a year it was sold to the Missouri & North

Arkansas Railroad so the Searcy-Kensett Transportation Company could use it to transport logging-company employees between these two Arkansas towns.[60]

In 1909 and 1910 the Rock Island joined a range of railroads by purchasing five knife-nosed McKeen cars, what might be considered America's first streamliners. These gasoline rail cars came from the McKeen Motor Car Company in Omaha. The manufacturer made these claims: "Highly economical motor, self-starting reversible, exceedingly easy to control and above all dependable." These McKeens featured attractive interiors, including comfortable imitation-leather seats and tasteful electric lighting. This equipment, later converted to gasoline-electric, served the company well and survived into the 1930s. In 1912 the company acquired two General Electric gasoline-electrics, each featuring a roomy baggage compartment and seating seventy-nine passengers. When modernized with better power plants, they, too, lasted into the 1930s, with one sold to the El Dorado & Wesson in 1935 and the other dismantled in 1937. After World War I the company became more invested in self-propelled cars, or "doodlebugs." They would not have steam or gasoline engines but rather gasoline-electric and then diesel-electric propulsion.[61]

Reactions to self-propelled equipment were mixed. Passengers on the Rock Island probably appreciated the McKeen and General Electric cars, but they became upset when mechanical problems developed, especially beyond stations. Apparently some Indian passengers in Oklahoma thought McKeen cars were too luxurious. "I never saw them sit in the seat," a conductor recalled. "They weren't used to such luxury. They'd sit on the floor cross-legged in the aisles." Motormen had varied reactions. Some liked the cleanliness and the "modernity" of the cars, but others complained about engine noise or simply preferred traditional steam-powered trains.[62]

Rock Island stations became well-known places, whether residents of an on-line city, town, village, or somewhere else. If they lived in greater Chicago, they recognized the newest La Salle Street Station. Just as rolling stock changed over the decades, so did this iconic structure. As the Reid-Moore syndicate assumed power, workers toiled on what would be the last replacement facility situated at South La Salle and West Van Buren streets. During the construction phase, which began with site preparation in 1901, passengers temporarily used Grand Central Station, located nearby at Harrison Street and Fifth Avenue. On July 12, 1903, the grand day arrived for patrons of the Rock Island and two Vanderbilt properties, Lake Shore & Michigan Southern and New York, Chicago & St. Louis (Nickel Plate Road). Thousands—passengers and non-passengers alike—poured in to use or to tour this massive beaux arts monument to the railway age that was one of America's earliest high-rise station-office buildings.[63]

The excitement, and certainly the novelty, of a McKeen "windsplitter" motor car, with its porthole windows and heavy-gauge steel body, is seen in this August 23, 1909, photograph taken in Reinbeck, Iowa, on the Iowa Falls line. A large audience gathers to welcome this "most modern" piece of contemporary railroad rolling stock.

Don L. Hofsommer coll.

The Rock Island took pride in its last version of the La Salle Street Station. Construction began in 1901, and the grand opening occurred in July 1903. This photograph, taken in 1904, reveals the massive train shed and the high-rise station and office building.

Chicago History Museum

When this imposing twelve-story, steel-framed structure was completed, featuring the creative efforts of the Chicago architectural firm of Frost & Granger, there was much to admire. Although public spaces were similar to those found in the predecessor station, including a general waiting room, separate men's and women's areas, a newsstand, and lunch and dining rooms, important changes had occurred. To enhance efficiency, baggage and mail facilities were placed on the ground floor, and tracks were located on the second floor. A grand staircase and two elevators connected the street or main level with the trackside level and the spacious general waiting room. Eventually conventional platform canopies replaced the massive train shed. The Rock Island ballyhooed the convenient location, noting that its station "is only half a block from Board of Trade; two blocks from the Post Office; within easy walking distance of the principal theatres, hotels and stores." It added, "Trains of all Chicago's elevated railroads pass the doors and take you quickly."[64]

The new La Salle Street Station was not the only passenger facility that appeared during syndicate rule. Other replacement depots dotted the system. Take these three in Oklahoma: El Reno (1906), Chickasha (1910), and Anadarko (1912). Unlike the plain wooden combination depots, these stylish brick or brick-and-stucco structures featured attractive red-tiled roofs. Collectively they enhanced operational efficiency and fostered community pride.[65]

Throughout the railway age, companies—the Rock Island being no exception—provided special rates at the drop of a hat. Early in the twentieth century, the passenger department, for example, issued a *Bulletin of Excursion Rates*. Numerous enticements were advertised for the 1905 travel season, including reduced fares to the Methodist Epworth League Convention in Denver and general excursion rates to and from Chicago and Saint Louis: "Round-trip tickets, specially reduced, on sale at points at and west of Missouri River—daily June 1 to September 30. Return limit October 31, 1905."[66]

There were special movements. A good example involved agricultural demonstration trains, whose overall objectives were to promote science and modernity. In 1904 the Rock Island and the Burlington took the lead in Iowa in operating these "agricultural colleges on wheels." Perry Holden, an Iowa State College professor who spent much of his professional career fostering practical knowledge of corn production, served as the principal organizer. His quests centered on better seeds, proper planting, and effective crop care. Holden oversaw cars with lecture seating, educational displays, and free literature. On a later occasion the Rock Island dispatched in Missouri its "Cream and Egg Special," which consisted of four lecture cars and included representatives of the University of Missouri College of Agriculture. H. M. Cottrell, the Rock

Island agricultural commissioner, also played an active role. During one week in the winter of 1911–1912, the Missouri train made stops at thirty stations.[67]

An unusual piece of equipment graced Rock Island rails during this time: the chapel car. Several denominations—Baptists, Episcopalians, and Roman Catholics—operated missionary cars, which accommodated a minister and his wife or a priest and his assistant and provided space for services. "A chapel car is nothing more nor less than a church on wheels," explained a Kansas newspaper. The Northern Baptist chapel car, *Good Will*, toured company trackage in the Oklahoma and Texas Panhandles. Its deployment made sense; communities were mostly raw settlements that lacked proper religious facilities. Until permanent houses of worship could be erected, a railroad car became the practical solution. For these religious organizations and a range of groups, including town residents, farmers, ranchers, and railroad workers, the winning of souls for Christ became a priority.[68]

BIG TROUBLES

Dark clouds appeared on the financial horizon after the Wall Street panic of October 1907. The Reid-Moore syndicate constantly needed to juggle aspects of its Tinkertoy railroad empire. The recession that followed the panic damaged the critical revenue stream for the Railway Company when freight traffic, most of all, sagged. State governments, including those in Illinois and Iowa, also hurt the bottom line when they forced rollbacks of passenger rates. The Railway Company faced a big drop in gross income; the amount for 1908 was $17,289,089, down from nearly $20 million the previous year.[69]

Financial relations with B. F. Yoakum and the Frisco must have given Judge Moore and his associates pause. "Frisco troubles" served as the first major blow to the wealth and prestige of the syndicate. The absence of anticipated dividends from Frisco common stock triggered this crisis. There had been an earlier exchange of Frisco shares for Rock Island securities, and by 1909 this meant inadequate resources to pay the interest of these obligations. Moreover, the debt that the syndicate had amassed had already reached a potentially crushing level.

Yoakum was well aware of the growing money crisis that faced the syndicate, and he seized the opportunity for personal gain. What did this crafty railroader do? His plan was straightforward: he offered to buy *all* of the Frisco shares. Yoakum wanted once more to take control of his railroad and to fashion his own rail empire in the Great Southwest, and one that would include the Katy. Having obtained the necessary financial backing through his association

At the time of the financial collapse of the Reid-Moore syndicate, a dapper William Henry Moore attends an East Coast horse show, which was his passion outside business and finance.

Author's coll.

with Edwin Hawley, Yoakum made this proposal to board members: $37.50 a share for a total of $10,852,000. They had no choice but to accept, meaning that "this would leave the syndicate with a nice unhealthy loss." The cash amount was insufficient to redeem the Rock Island Railroad collateral trust bonds, which were necessary to make delivery of the Frisco stock. Since the holding company had no resources, the syndicate tapped the Railway Company, its cash cow, for the funds. The deal meant that the Railway Company sustained a loss estimated to be about $6.5 million, and the stock sale cost the syndicate nearly $20 million. The Reid-Moore "system" now had unraveled. No longer could it claim to control more than fourteen thousand miles of line serving seventeen states and New Mexico Territory.[70]

Once the stock sale was finalized, B. F. Yoakum severed his ties to the Rock Island, and Yoakum's associate Benjamin Winchell resigned from the presidency to take a similar position at the Frisco. (He completed his long business career as president of the Remington Typewriter Company.) With Winchell gone, the board needed to find his replacement, and on December 1, 1909, it tapped Henry Uri Mudge (1856–1920). The next chief executive was no newcomer to the Rock Island. Since May 1, 1905, he had been a top official, having been lured away from the Santa Fe by a substantial salary increase.[71]

When the syndicate picked Henry Mudge, it made a good choice. The new Rock Island president might be considered a "railroader's railroader," and he was undeniably a Horatio Alger–type self-made man. He was born on a hard-scrabble farm near Minden, Michigan. His mother died when he was small, and his father, a Civil War veteran, remarried and started a second family. "We were indeed very poor and all hands had to work," recalled Mudge. Hoping to find a better life for his wife and six children, the senior Mudge in 1872 moved the family to a farm in central Kansas. Detesting agricultural work, Henry Mudge at age sixteen landed a job with a Santa Fe construction crew. Being "ambitious, bright, and earnest" yet having a limited formal education, he worked his way up the ladder on the Santa Fe in an impressive fashion. This up-by-the-bootstraps railroader rose from water boy to telegrapher, trainman, dispatcher, roadmaster, trainmaster, superintendent, general superintendent, and finally general manager.[72]

Henry Mudge, who had worked closely with Benjamin Winchell in seeking to upgrade the Rock Island, continued that goal as president. It was a daunting task, requiring expensive betterments and generating constant pressure for strong revenues. The priority for Judge Moore and his associates was to divert money to the holding companies and to reward insiders. The result was predictable; the syndicate was starving the railroad.

Silvis July 18. 07
This train was going
about 7 miles an hour
when picture taken
B Cin

A real photo postcard captures a husky Consolidation-type locomotive (2-6-0) and its consist of freight cars moving through the yards at Silvis, Illinois. The date is July 18, 1907, and the train is traveling at only seven miles per hour. The locomotive's massive smoke plume would surely bother latter-day environmentalists. Soon after this image appeared, the Reid-Moore syndicate began to unravel.

Don L. Hofsommer coll.

Mudge, like Winchell, was a hands-on railroader. He worked out of his Chicago office rather than the one in New York City. His coworkers described him as "generous, gentle, courteous, and democratic" in the conduct of his daily duties, and he lacked a prickly ego. His personality paid dividends by encouraging the rank and file to do their best.

Mudge was apparently the ideal boss, and he remained popular throughout his six-year tenure. For one thing, he spearheaded a pension system that took effect on January 1, 1910. The Rock Island was not an innovator but an imitator; the first railroad to offer such a plan was the Pennsylvania (lines east of Pittsburgh) in 1900. The Rock Island pension, moreover, was not as generous as those of some other carriers, including the Pennsylvania, Illinois Central, and North Western. Its broad outlines were described in this manner: "[When] employees, who after long years of faithful service, have reached an age when they are unequal to the performance of their duties, will be retired and receive monthly incomes during the remainder of their lives, based on their salary for the last ten years next preceding retirement, and the entire length of continuous service with the company." By 1915, 225 retired employees had benefited from this plan administrated by the company's Pension Bureau. Also endearing to the rank and file was the Mudge administration's creation of the Safety Bureau in August 1912. By stressing a program of "safety first," the company reduced workplace accidents.[73]

Henry Mudge made other noteworthy decisions. He bought in a senior Santa Fe official, James E. Gorman, to be the first vice president. Gorman had been the freight traffic manager for his former employer, and his skills were desperately needed. Talented Rock Island veterans filled all additional executive openings. Yet Mudge could only accomplish so much as president; he simply lacked the power to make the Rock Island a first-class road. "Mudge's technical and operating skills were no match for the financial machinations of Judge Moore and his allies," concluded railroad historian Keith Bryant Jr.[74]

Still, the "looters" did not prevent improvements to the railroad. In the annual report for 1914, Henry Mudge indicated that major advances had occurred since the syndicate took control. Such betterments included installation of better steel rail. In 1902 only 938 miles sported the heaviest steel, which weighed eighty pounds per yard, but in 1914 there were 276 miles of 100-pound, 142 miles of ninety-pound, and 1,526 miles of eight-five-pound steel. The ballasted roadbed figures for 1902 revealed just 2,018 miles of rock, cinders, or burnt clay, and the rest were dirt. In 1914 rock ballast covered 1,466 miles; gravel 2,606 miles; cinders 686 miles; and burnt clay 681 miles. That left less than 3,000 miles with ties and rail on the ground. Also noteworthy

An unusual locomotive type found on the Rock Island was this center cab or "Mother Hubbard." In April 1910 this 2-8-0 stands near the water tank in the Davis County, Iowa, village of Drakesville. Critics of this design considered Mother Hubbards dangerous because the engineer was removed from the fireman, therefore preventing quick and effective communication.

Don L. Hofsommer coll.

was that during this twelve-year period the company went from owning 661 locomotives with an average tractive power of 18,015 pounds per unit to 1,678 locomotives with an average of 29,345 pounds each. Mudge rightly bragged about other gains. Two key line additions had opened: the Choctaw extension from Amarillo to Tucumcari and the Twin Cities connection between Carlisle and Allerton, Iowa. Another solid improvement involved automatic block signals. As of June 30, 1902, there were only 19.6 miles of these devices, but on June 30, 1915, coverage had increased to 1,257 miles of automatic and 1,087 miles of manual or other block signaling. The main lines from Chicago to Omaha and from Chicago via Kansas City to Herington, Kansas, had become entirely protected by the automatic equipment.[75]

Yet the realities of syndicate control meant that all was not well with the Rock Island's physical property. A contributing factor involved a provision of the general mortgage of 1902 that limited betterment expenditures to $3.5 million annually. As *Railway Age Gazette* later noted, "A bond issue of $3,500,000 annually even if the proceeds should be available without discount, is entirely too small to provide for the addition and betterment work necessary to keep a railway system of 8,330 miles abreast of the requirements made upon it." Deferred maintenance resulted, costing about $8 million to remedy.

For another example, as many as twenty thousand, or half, of its freight-car fleet required replacement, at an estimated cost of $15 million. Moreover, the railroad operated 273 miles of second track on March 31, 1902, and operated 282 miles, the addition of a scant 9 miles, on June 30, 1915. During that same thirteen-year period, the Burlington added 379 miles and the Milwaukee 742 miles, showing that the Rock Island had failed to keep up with two granger competitors. Furthermore, if the books were fairly evaluated, the company was grossly overcapitalized; there had been an excessive issue of securities in proportion to the physical assets.[76]

Although the Reid-Moore syndicate weathered the Frisco debacle, the revenue stream from the operating railroad never seemed adequate to meet its growing financial requirements. Admittedly, some matters were beyond the control of either the Mudge administration or the syndicate. Increased federal railroad regulation—which came with the Hepburn Act of 1906 and four years later with the Mann-Elkins Act, landmark laws of customer-driven progressive era reforms—permitted the Interstate Commerce Commission to become all powerful in terms of rate making. The Rock Island felt the sting of the ICC's 1910 decision to reject carriers' request for substantial rate hikes, although a second request in 1913 led to a modest 5 percent advance in freight charges. During this time the ICC also dealt with labor's growing wage demands. In 1907 the commission's chair, who mediated a dispute between the brotherhoods and western railroads under the terms of the Erdman Act of 1898, secured for them a 10 percent raise and convinced carriers to reduce the maximum day from twelve to ten hours with no reduction in pay. These actions occurred during a time of rising inflation and property taxes, greatly increasing the company's financial burden.[77]

The Rock Island was on a course toward bankruptcy and reorganization; its overall financial condition had become badly impaired. According to an ICC investigation conducted in 1915, the official reports to stockholders severely misrepresented assets. The conclusion read: "In view of the fact that the reported value of the 'securities' listed for the year 1914 was $18,000,000 in excess of their actual value, instead of a surplus of more than $6,000,000 claimed by the railway company, there should have been shown a deficit of over $11,600,000."[78]

Syndicate members knew that big troubles were brewing. First the Railroad Company, one of the two holding companies, faced foreclosure proceedings. Recognizing the financial weaknesses of the Railway Company, bondholders of the Railroad Company formed protective committees and took legal action. On December 21, 1914, the US District Court for the

It is unlikely that Rock Island employees knew much about the nefarious activities of the Reid-Moore syndicate. The appropriately attired station agent in Earlham, Iowa, stands by the ticket case and counter in this period photograph. The operator is seated by the telegraph key and sounder; another employee, likely the station helper, is using either a company or a local commercial telephone. The closed window shades indicate that this is a staged photograph, allowing the photographer to avoid the glare of outdoor sunlight.

James L. Rueber coll.

Southern District of New York ordered the sale of the collateral securities, the $71,353,000 par value of the railway's common stock. Soon a special master executed a sale to the president of the Central Trust Company of New York, who headed the protective groups. The bid amounted to just 10 percent of the stock's par value. Recognizing the need for defensive action, the syndicate responded by organizing its own bondholders' protective committee, the handiwork of Daniel Reid. This committee asked that Railroad Company bondholders deposit their securities in trust under its control, hoping to retain power over the threatened holding company. Yet after five months the syndicate got a disappointing response, receiving only about $23 million out of $75 million. On January 18, 1915, the Railroad Company entered formal receivership. More legal maneuvers followed, including calculated delays.[79]

Judge Moore was not about to permit his fortunes to sink; he was a scrappy, clever strategist. Interestingly, Daniel Reid, who saw defeat forthcoming, resigned from the Rock Island board, a public indication that the syndicate was dissolving. Moore planned to have the railroad's general counsel draw up a bill to place the Railway Company in receivership. A pivotal feature of this secret document was that the name of the complainant was omitted. The next step was to find a creditor to act in that capacity, and soon a friendly one was found. The American Steel Foundries Company was owed a modest $16,000 by the Railway Company. Later the ICC reported that "the board of directors of the railway company was not informed of the intention to file a bill for receivership and at no meeting of the board was any authority ever given for such action."[80]

The Railway Company appeared to be speeding toward bankruptcy. It needed about $6 million to meet immediate bond and interest obligations. Nathan Amster, a board member who represented a group of stockholders, believed that he had raised the necessary funds. But Moore struck before the necessary financial matters could be settled. The bill for receivership was filed on April 20, 1915. And approximately a month *prior* to this legal action, an amazing event occurred on Wall Street. Railway Company stock in brisk trading surged from between $21 and $26 to between $31 and $38 on the belief (or hope) that the property was economically sound. On March 31, 106,000 shares were traded at a price that fluctuated from $31 to $36 per share. There were other active trading days. The number of shares sold on March 22, however, had been only 406, and they traded between $20 and $21. When the railway was placed in receivership, the stock plummeted from $32 to $21 a share on a volume of 251,400 shares. What explains these happenings? The volatility and price fluctuations resulted when Moore and other insiders entered the market, and in the process they were able to unload their stock at the best prices in what William Edward Hayes called "a farewell grab at profits as the dream of empire broke and faded."[81]

It did not take long for the ICC to launch an investigation of the Reid-Moore syndicate and the resulting bankruptcy. Such a probe fit the character of the progressive movement as it matured at the federal level. Already Washington had examined the New York, New Haven & Hartford Railroad (New Haven) and its creation of a transportation empire in southern New England. Targets became Charles Mellon, a J. P. Morgan lieutenant and company president, and other top officers. The Department of Justice took antitrust action against the combine. Ultimately Mellon and twenty-one New Haven directors faced antitrust charges, and the railroad was forced to surrender its electric railway properties. The ICC also became involved, and it concluded that the Mellon affair had resulted in "one of the most glaring instances of misadministration revealed in all the history of American railroading."[82]

On the heels of the New Haven investigation, the ICC examined syndicate activities. Action started with hearings on October 16 and 17, 1914. The inquiry centered on financial transactions, and the findings revealed that the public interest was not being protected. After all, the Rock Island had been a thriving railroad prior to the syndicate. Once shares of the Railway Company had commanded more than $200 each, but in 1914 they had fallen to $20, leading to bankruptcy. Railway Company earnings, on the other hand, had steady increased, and in 1914 they were the largest in the company's history. This disconnect needed to be explained. A contributing factor involved excessively high salaries for officers and directors. Henry Mudge, for example, received an annual salary of $60,000, and Daniel Reid got $32,000 as chairman of the board of directors. But there had been multiple secret payments. Take James Gorman. He received an additional yearly payment of $18,750, making his total compensation $43,750, although the payroll showed $25,000. When an ICC examiner questioned Reid on the witness stand, he answered as follows:

> Question. Mr. Reid, do you think these men earned these high salaries?
> Answer. I do not think there is a man who did not earn more than he was getting.
> Question. In other words, you defend paying these high salaries?
> Answer. I defend nothing. Here is 8,000 miles of railway; a man who can run 8,000 miles of railroad is worth all he can get.[83]

When interrogated about his personal profits from various syndicate transactions, Daniel Reid explained that he always burned his books at the end of each month.

The ICC learned much more. A troubling revelation showed that the syndicate violated the federal anti-rebate law. Investigators discovered that the Railway Company had paid the *Denver Post* $44,066.05. The attached vouchers claimed that they covered "advertising in editorial and news columns." Not really. Most of this money comprised refunds made to the publisher on newsprint shipped from paper mills in Wisconsin.[84]

More dramatic than rebate abuse were the losses that came from syndicate investments. The list was disturbing: $6.5 million on Frisco stock, $6.37 million with the Alton deal, and $4.5 million from Trinity & Brazos Valley investments. Funds were wasted in two auxiliary coal mines: $1.3 million with Consolidated Indiana Coal Company and $1 million with Dering Coal Company. Other big splashes of red ink had occurred. The ICC estimated that the syndicate incurred losses of nearly $300,000 in housing the Iowa and New Jersey holding companies. The report said: "In addition thereto it is to be noted that prior to June 30, 1914, the Railway Company paid to financial institutions, in connection with the issuance of bonds, commissions aggregating more than $1,600,000, being money drained from its treasury." Betraying public interest, the Railway Company badly misrepresented assets in its annual reports to stockholders. It repeatedly claimed as assets worthless securities that had "no existence, except on paper." The ultimate findings: "These items show an aggregate loss to the railway company of more than $20,000,000." The commission made this interesting observation: "The amount of gains accruing to W. B. Leeds, D. G. Reid, W. H. Moore, and J. H. Moore through their control and manipulation of the railway company are probably not ascertainable." Forensic accounting had limitations. The ICC report ended this way: "The property of the railway company will be called upon for many years to make up the drain upon its resources resulting from transaction outside the proper sphere in which stockholders had a right to support how their moneys were invested." It believed that "by this case the need of some limitations on the issuance of stocks and bonds by common carriers, whether directly or through holding company devices or otherwise, is again demonstrated." The recently passed Clayton Antitrust Act, which took effect in October 1915, addressed some of the shortcomings associated with the Reid-Moore syndicate.[85]

In 1915 William Z. Ripley, a professor of economics at Harvard University and a recognized authority on railroad finance, offered his thoughts about the Reid-Moore control of the Rock Island. He emphasized that "personal greed rather than constructive impulses have been the leading features in its management." Several "financial vices" contributed to bankruptcy. Ripley wrote: "It was grossly overcapitalized. It was organized solely for the benefit of a few 'insiders.' The general investing public was rigidly denied all information as to the real status of affairs. Its securities at all times constituted a blind pool of a highly speculative sort." He further blasted the syndicate: "And there is little evidence of any real constructive transportation policy, which by upbuilding either the property or the territory served, might in the course of time overcome or counterbalance its financial weakness—little evidence, in other words, of the upbuilding genius which in a measure palliated some of the offences of the Harriman administration of the Union Pacific."[86]

A bankrupt Chicago, Rock Island & Pacific Railway meant a corporate reorganization. There existed the legal option of liquidation, but at this time that would not happen. A better day would dawn, and the hope emerged that this far-flung carrier could properly serve the needs of shippers, passengers, employees, and investors.[87]

ROUGH TRACKS

4

REORGANIZATION

The year 1915 offered high hopes for everyone who wanted a modernized and financially vibrant Chicago, Rock Island & Pacific Railway Company. The signs looked encouraging. There was widespread agreement that Judge George A. Carpenter of the US District Court for the Northern District of Illinois had appointed an excellent lead receiver, Jacob McGavock Dickinson. There was less enthusiasm for his co-receiver Henry U. Mudge, who some believed represented "the old gang."[1]

It would be Jacob Dickinson (1851–1928) who shaped the reorganization. This bright, honest, and dedicated lawyer understood the workings of large bureaucracies. A native Mississippian, Dickinson possessed a remarkable education, having earned bachelor's and master's degrees from the University of Nashville, studied at the Columbia Law School in New York City, and continued his legal work in Leipzig and Paris. Once he returned home, his career soared, and he served first as justice on the Tennessee Supreme Court and then as US assistant attorney general during the waning years of the Grover Cleveland administration. Between 1897 and 1899, Dickinson worked as a law professor at Vanderbilt University Law School and as an attorney for the Louisville & Nashville Railroad. In 1899 he moved to Chicago, becoming general solicitor for the Illinois Central Railroad (IC), and he remained in that position until 1909. While at the IC, Dickinson served a term as president of the American Bar Association. Although he was a lifelong Democrat, President William Howard Taft asked him to serve in his cabinet as secretary of war, a post he held with distinction for two years. Before Dickinson became involved with the Rock Island, he had been a special US attorney general, helping to prosecute the United States Steel Corporation antitrust case in 1913.[2]

On April 20, 1915, Jacob Dickinson tackled the Rock Island reorganization with determination, finesse, and confidence. It was a daunting assignment. The Moore brothers and Daniel Reid tried to protect their investments, stockholders demanded restitution of the money they had lost in the Frisco fiasco, and others made legal claims and challenges. Then Mother Nature posed immediate challenges. During May, June, and July, unprecedented rainfalls occurred over large portions of the system. The resulting high water and washouts caused roughly $1 million in damages, and this financial blow did not reflect revenues lost from disrupted service.[3]

Dickinson also no longer had the services of Henry Mudge. His co-receiver quickly tired of his role, and he resigned that November. "By the fall of 1915 [Mudge] remained a popular figure among employees, and company revenues continued to rise," noted railroad historian Keith Bryant Jr., "but his reputation was stained by the legal proceedings and the ICC investigation." Mudge worked briefly for Judge Carpenter and Dickinson as the company's chief executive officer but then left. Yet he remained a railroader. Mudge accepted the presidency of the Denver & Rio Grande Railroad, part of the financially embattled Gould System. But Mudge's tenure at the Rio Grande was of short duration. In October 1917, after he had served less than two years on the job, anti-Gould board members forced him out, and he retired from railroading.[4]

Restructuring the Rock Island's finances and undoing the holding firms, including the Rock Island Improvement Company, took time. Dickinson oversaw a plan that proved acceptable to the vast majority of the interested parties and also to Judge Carpenter. These men agreed that the 8,330-mile railroad could be financially rehabilitated. The Rock Island, it was thought, had the potential to become a strong trans-Chicago West carrier. No liquidation would occur, even though there were offers to buy the best lines.

The reorganization, which was not a foreclosure, consisted of several key components. Since the underlying bonds of the railway company went undisturbed, stockholders and creditors agreed overwhelmingly to two new classes of preferred stock, the larger one being a 7 percent preferred and the lesser a 6 percent preferred. Shareholders of common stock had the right to acquire four-tenths of a share of the 7 percent preferred if they paid forty dollars for each share that they held. The 6 percent preferred would be sold mostly on the market. The money generated from these two securities paid off loans, receiver's certificates, and other liabilities. As with typical railroad reorganizations, the Rock Island saw a number of its unprofitable financial obligations either modified or eliminated. Judge Carpenter decreed that those creditors who had not approved the final plan must accept the 6 percent preferred stock for their claims. This meant one less headache for the reorganized railroad.[5]

On June 21, 1917, Jacob Dickinson stepped down as receiver after what turned out to be a "markedly successful" reorganization. With his assignment completed, he gradually ended his distinguished legal and public service career. At last the Rock Island could chart its future course without court supervision.[6]

Although Judge Dickinson was sanguine about the fate of the reorganized Rock Island, not everyone agreed that it was poised for long-term financial bliss. It was believed that the terms of the final arrangements were not sufficiently crafted to ensure a sound capital structure and adequate physical development to meet future difficulties.[7]

While financial journalists covered the Rock Island reorganization, they had other railroad insolvencies to report. As late as December 1916, about one-seventh of all railroad mileage in the nation was under court protection. Geographically these bankruptcies were concentrated in America's heartland. Henry Mudge had not been far off the mark when he argued that outside forces had adversely affected the rail industry. Companies, including the Rock Island, felt the sting of inflation, a bankers' panic, higher wages, and most of all stifling progressive era regulation, making it difficult to raise rates and hence to support physical betterments and to earn reasonable returns on capital. Yet, in what seems to be a disconnect, America's gross domestic product (GDP) on the eve of World War I was already equal to that of all the European nation-states combined. "Generally speaking, the whole railroad net of the country was in a worse condition in 1911 than it had been in 1907," economist Stuart Daggett concluded in 1918, "and was still worse in 1914 than in 1911." Other distressed railroads, however, had not suffered from a "den of thieves."[8]

WORLD WAR

During the Rock Island reorganization, war raged in Europe. After August 1914 it became an entrenched struggle between the Central Powers of Germany, the Austro-Hungarian Empire, and the Ottoman Empire and the Allies of France, Great Britain, Italy, and Russia. Although during the presidential campaign of 1916 Woodrow Wilson had promised that he would avoid American involvement, soon after his reelection victory his position changed. On April 6, 1917, Congress approved Wilson's war message. Patriots rapidly mobilized for what became America's bloodiest conflict since the Civil War, committing themselves "to make the world safe for democracy."

Before Washington federalized much of America's railroads in late 1917, the Rock Island enjoyed renewed life following the Reid-Moore years and the receivership. Beginning July 1917, an experienced insider, James E. Gorman (1863–1942), occupied the president's office and joined the board of directors. The board, dominated by Charles Hayden, a prominent Boston and New York City banker, believed that Gorman knew the railroad and could handle this demanding job.[9]

As was common for contemporary railroad executives, James Gorman, a Chicago native, had obtained only a public school education and had gone railroading at a young age. Like Henry Mudge, he lived a Horatio Alger life, rising from "the humblest job on the railroad to become president." Gorman began his career in 1877 as a car checker for the Burlington. In the 1880s he held clerk positions with the Rock Island, a Chicago lumber company, and the Chicago & North Western (North Western). During this time he studied stenography and shorthand, providing himself with skills for advancement. In 1887 Gorman became chief clerk for the newly launched Chicago, Santa Fe & California Railway, the Kansas City-to-Chicago extension of the Atchison, Topeka & Santa Fe Railway (Santa Fe). But he left the Santa Fe to accept a clerking post with the Illinois Central, and for two years he worked as traffic manager for Joy Morton & Company of Chicago. In 1895 Gorman returned to the Santa Fe, where he advanced from chief clerk to freight traffic manager. In December 1909 he joined the Rock Island, serving as chief traffic officer and subsequently as chief executive officer for Jacob Dickerson, from November 1915 to July 1917.[10]

Gorman's principal attributes were his loyalty to authority, his tact and diplomacy, and his effervescent personality. And Gorman knew the ins and outs of traffic politics; after all, he had had extensive hands-on experience in this rough-and-tumble business. Throughout his professional life, Gorman readily followed the orders of his superiors, and now he listened to board chairman Hayden. "Whatever the boss asks for, that's what he gets," Gorman once said. "I never say no to the boss." Gorman obeyed Hayden and later his successor, Edward Brown, and that likely ensured his long tenure as president. He resembled the typical traffic man of his day, and contemporaries remarked about his outgoing nature. They said, "He is a big soul, as he is in stature," and called him "a big genial railroad president." They explained, "He knows men, because he never forgets that he once had to look to someone higher up." While "Big Jim" Gorman might have been the life of a gathering, his knowledge of the intricacies of modern railroading was not his strength. Fortunately the Rock Island board in 1918 hired as vice president and chief engineer Louis

C. Fritch, a civil engineering graduate of the University of Cincinnati who served as general manager of the Seaboard Air Line Railroad. Fritch did much to compensate for Gorman's weaknesses. Lamentably, these two men often sparred with each other.[11]

The Great War triggered an enormous spike in freight traffic. Shippers needed to send products of farm and factory to Atlantic and Gulf ports. These movements created a largely one-directional and badly snarled rail flow, over-whelming yards at dock facilities when they filled up with thousands of loaded freight cars. Although industry representatives in 1916 had launched the Rail-roads' War Board to rectify what was becoming a logistical nightmare, they struggled to untangle congestion and alleviate equipment shortages. Conditions worsened. Such factors as carrier rivalries, inadequate rates, and rising costs contributed to this national crisis. The Wilson administration, which had already expanded the federal bureaucracy, opted to approach the transportation sector in a similar fashion. Lawmakers and the president backed a plan to federalize most Class I railroads, strategic electric interurbans, and certain steamship lines. On December 28, 1917, the hastily organized US Railroad Administration (USRA) emerged with the able William Gibbs McAdoo as director general. A few months later Washington passed the Railroad Control Act. It promised railroad owners that their financial positions would be protected, making annual compensation based on their net operating income for the three years preceding June 30, 1917. There were two other important provisions. Twenty-one months following this wartime "emergency," all properties were to be returned "in substantially as good repair" as at the time of seizure. Carriers, however, would need to reimburse the federal treasury for all additions and improvements that could not be justly charged to the government.[12]

What did federalization mean for the Rock Island? Before the USRA took control, the company had experienced a noticeable spike in freight haulage. Although the burst of traffic was less than what the New York Central and Pennsylvania Railroads handled between the Chicago and Saint Louis gateways and Atlantic ports, freight-train miles grew steadily. The amount rose from 15,962,289 as of December 31, 1915, to 16,631,158 a year later, closing at 17,145,112 on the last day of 1917. The USRA quickly led a restructuring of railroad operations to move freight and military personal in a single giant system. Later it fostered locomotive and freight car standardization, seeking to improve rolling stock and maintenance. In mid-January 1918 McAdoo divided the country into three operating regions: Eastern (east of Chicago and the Mississippi River and north of the Ohio and Potomac Rivers), Southern (east of the Mississippi River and south of the Ohio and Potomac Rivers), and

Western (west of Chicago and the Mississippi River). Several months later USRA officials decided to subdivide these regions to improve efficiency. For the Rock Island these actions meant that all of its lines, except those in Texas, became part of the Central Western Region, and those in the Lone Star State joined the Southwestern Region. Regional federal directors and local federal managers were appointed for each railroad, in place of the railroad's president. When James Gorman became the Rock Island federal manager, Charles Hayden assumed some of Gorman's responsibilities.[13] Those railroads that came under the thumb of McAdoo and his successor, Walker D. Hines, had to accept forced cooperation and retrenchments. They underwent a multitude of changes, including the discontinuance of traffic solicitation, trimming of advertisements, cancellation and consolidation of passenger trains, and closing of "wasteful" stations. Examples abound. The Rock Island was prevented from handling cross-country movements; named trains, including the *Rocky Mountain Limited*, were obliged to serve local traffic; and some small-town stations were either closed or consolidated. An illustration of the later directive was the shuttered depot at University Place, Nebraska, which served Nebraska Wesleyan University outside Lincoln. The Rock Island also moved its New York City offices, located at 14 Wall Street, to the more economical Manhattan Life Building at 44 Broadway Avenue. The company did see its Silvis, Illinois, shops become busier; the USRA sent considerable outside work to this sprawling complex. Less obvious to the public was an increase in the number of employees and an enormous increase in monthly payroll. At the time of federalization, the Rock Island employed 40,326 workers, but at the end of USRA control, the number reached 45,950; annual payroll figures skyrocketed from $3.5 million to nearly $6 million.[14]

A bone of contention involving locomotives and freight cars developed between the Rock Island and the government. In 1917 the company had purchased thirty new locomotives, which were delivered the following May. But then the USRA allocated to the Rock Island twenty road and ten switching locomotives that cost approximately $1.4 million. Management protested, believing that these locomotives were unneeded. There was more. "At the date our objections were filed 23 Rock Island locomotives, including 15 of the 30 that had just been purchased, were being used on foreign lines," explained Charles Hayden, "so we felt that it was not fair to the Rock Island to buy new power for it when the power it already had was not being used on its own road. At this time there are approximately 90 idle locomotives on the system, so this protest is even more meritorious now than when it was first made." Additional freight cars added to the unhappiness. The USRA earmarked a thousand forty-ton doubled-sheathed boxcars and a thousand fifty-ton gondolas; the total cost reached approximately $5.6 million. "Your directors have protested against this allocation on the ground that the acquisition by the Receiver of 4,000 new box cars and the rebuilding of 3,000 old cars rendered the purchase of new equipment at this time unnecessary." But Washington overruled the Rock Island's protest. Yet as company historian William Edward Hayes observed, "The whole thing turned out to be a blessing in disguise, however. The new cars were found to be needed." The USRA locomotives likewise proved useful.[15]

Once Washington restored the Rock Island to private hands on March 1, 1920, the Gorman administration charged that the government had not honored its pledge to return the property in the same general condition in which it had been at the start of federalization. Some equipment, which had been pooled for efficiency, had been poorly maintained by the other roads, and many locomotives had been taxed to their limits or had worn out. Management also complained about the state of the physical plant. "The Railroad Administration failed to do the same amount of maintenance work on the lines as was done by the company and the receiver in the years before Federal control." The government demanded payment of $7.9 million to adjust the wartime accounts. After extended negotiations, the two parties reached an agreement whereby the maintenance claims would substantially reduce the final obligations. The settlement meant that the Rock Island paid Washington $2.5 million in a 6 percent collateral trust note due on March 1, 1930.[16]

TRANSPORTATION ACT OF 1920

The United States Railroad Administration accomplished what President Wilson and Congress had wanted; federalization had bolstered the war effort. The merits of industry consolidation that the USRA had demonstrated and the demands made in 1919 by railroad labor for nationalization under its proposed Plumb Plan influenced Washington policy makers. The result was the Transportation Act of 1920, or the Esch-Cummins Act, named after its progressive Republican sponsors Representative John J. Esch of Wisconsin and Senator Albert B. Cummins of Iowa. This legislation, which took effect on the eve of the official termination of the USRA, was the product of extensive debate, yet it won bipartisan congressional support. The statute, with its great complexities, mandated that the Interstate Commerce Commission (ICC) develop a comprehensive plan for the amalgamation of most steam railroads. During the immediate postwar period, the belief grew that increasing competition from private automobiles, commercial trucks, and water carriers meant struggling railroads could not survive. Scores of marginal roads would surely fail and perhaps be liquidated. The reasoning went that the weak should be combined with the strong, creating a limited number of investor-owned systems with approximately equal financial strength. The measure gave the ICC power to facilitate these consolidations; the body had the authority to approve any proposed merger, and it controlled the issuing of railroad securities. Still, the 1920 law contained a glaring flaw: groupings would be *voluntary*.[17]

The ICC commissioners and others worried about the practicability of the congressional mandate to bring about a private cartelization of America's railroads. Yet the consolidation of hundreds of companies into a handful of regional systems designed to reduce or end redundancies and to forge an efficient and solvent network had merit. The consensus among the knowledgeable was that the devil was in the details.

Even before the grouping task went forward, John Oldham, a Boston investment banker and authority on railway finance, offered his own plan. In his fourteen-system pairing, the Rock Island was consolidated with the Missouri Pacific, International & Great Northern, Denver & Rio Grande Western, Western Pacific, Texas & Pacific, and El Paso & Southwestern Railroads. This well-conceived Rock Island-Missouri Pacific System did not resemble the famous Ripley plan that soon appeared.[18]

The ICC hired transportation expert William Z. Ripley of Harvard University to develop this tentative unification plan. He was a logical choice, being respected within railroad industry and government circles alike.[19]

Professor Ripley plunged into preparing the unification plan. He checked data, including statistical materials generated by government agencies, especially the ICC and USRA, and he interviewed business, financial, and railroad executives. Early in 1921 Ripley submitted his proposal to the commission. He faithfully adhered to the law's mandate that existing routes and channels of commerce be maintained. Ripley avoided coast-to-coast systems that would create bona fide transcontinentals, as well as groupings that did not fit into geographic and rate-making divisions. He recommended six principal groupings and named them as follows:

1. Trunk Line Territory (Atlantic Seaboard to Chicago and Saint Louis)
2. New England
3. Chesapeake Region
4. Southeast

5. Western Transcontinental Region

6. Southwestern-Gulf Region

In these six pairings (or what Ripley called "divisions"), there were twenty-one systems. Specifically, there would be five eastern trunk lines, five western combinations, four southeastern systems, two Great Lakes–to–tidewater coal roads, and two southwest combinations. Three compact units would also be formed: Florida, Michigan, and New England. Ripley did not include short-lines and terminal companies, leaving them to survive on their own.[20]

Where did Ripley place the Rock Island? Its home would be System No. 17, Southern Pacific-Rock Island. In addition to these two major Class I carriers, the grouping included these roads: Arizona & New Mexico; Chicago, Peoria & St. Louis; Chicago, Rock Island & Gulf (Rock Island subsidiary); El Paso & Southwestern; Midland Valley; Nevada Northern, San Antonio & Aransas Pass; Trinity & Brazos Valley (Rock Island's semi-owned bankrupt affiliate); and Vicksburg, Shreveport & Pacific. There was debate about whether the Trinity & Brazos Valley should be placed in System No. 17 or in System No. 18, Frisco-Katy-Cotton Belt, but it was not a burning issue.[21]

The Ripley plan for System No. 17 made sense. The Rock Island and Southern Pacific created a direct Chicago-to-California traffic corridor and included several important feeder roads. As required by law, weak carriers were added, most notably the Chicago, Peoria & St. Louis. How Rock Island officials felt about these groupings is not clear. Senior management might have worried about which of the two largest corporate cultures would reign supreme. It would likely be the more powerful Southern Pacific. And surely Ripley's handiwork was not the system that Rock Island leaders had envisioned. They probably preferred coupling with the St. Louis-San Francisco (Frisco); in fact, that later became a possibility. Few if any executives wanted "weak sisters" to be part of any consolidation.

When the ICC released the completed plan, controversy erupted. At the core of the complaints, which were articulated at public hearings held between April and December 1923, were major carriers objecting to the anti-Darwinian notion of the strong aiding the weak. In an obvious outcome, railroad consolidation was a hot potato, becoming a seemingly impossible task.

It was not surprising that ICC officials wished to scrub a master consolidation plan. They wanted mergers to develop "in a more normal way." But Congress demanded the Ripley-based proposal. After several years of wrangling, the ICC reluctantly pushed ahead with what it called the "Final Plan," largely the handiwork of Commissioner Claude Porter. Announced in December

1929, the modified scheme identified nineteen systems, and again they would be clustered around one or two major railroads. And there were major changes within the earlier groupings.[22]

The Rock Island found itself in System No. 19, "Rock Island-Frisco." It would no longer be linked with the Southern Pacific but would join its former partner. A plethora of minor roads would be added. Differing from the original Ripley plan, this grouping contained some fragile (and soon to be abandoned) shortlines. For example, it included two tiny Iowa weaklings, Atlantic & Northern (née Atlantic Northern & Southern) and Burlington, Muscatine & Northwestern (née Muscatine, Burlington & Southern). This time the bankrupt Trinity & Brazos Valley came into the fold.[23]

Although Rock Island officials endorsed System No. 19, they would not see its implementation. The onslaught of severe economic dislocations, triggered by the stock market crash in October 1929, dampened serious discussions about unification. The Final Plan was essentially dead. Here was a textbook example of a well-meaning proposal that went nowhere.

THE ROARING TWENTIES

When Warren Harding took the oath of office on March 4, 1921, as the nation's twenty-ninth president, Americans overwhelmingly endorsed his philosophy of "normalcy." Yet the new decade did not mean universal prosperity and happiness. A postwar recession ravaged the country between 1920 and 1923, an event that has been described as the "Forgotten Depression." Most agriculturalists experienced financial troubles; commodity prices plunged, farm foreclosures increased, rural banks failed, and crop surpluses mounted. Moreover, tens of thousands of workers, especially those involved in coal mining, electric traction, and steam railroading, became either unemployed or underemployed.[24]

During this difficult period of the early 1920s, the nation experienced its worst railroad labor dispute in the twentieth century, the shopmen's strike of 1922–1923. Labor troubles on the Rock Island had never been a chronic problem. There had been unrest during the Pullman Strike of 1894, but it was neither particularly violent nor long lasting. The walkout by shop personnel became a stressful time for the Rock Island family and had a long-term impact.

Throughout much of the progressive era, railroad labor had made substantial gains. As reform efforts matured, a growing number of politicians, including many associated with the Woodrow Wilson administration, believed that trade unionism and collective bargaining would reduce class conflict. Not only did progressive forces back the Adamson Act in 1916, which gave operating personnel and telegraphers an eight-hour day, but they encouraged formation within the USRA of the Board of Railroad Wages and Working Conditions. This body endorsed the eight-hour day, time-and-a-half pay for overtime work, and stringent seniority rules. It also authorized a substantial pay hike. Once peace returned, shopmen overwhelmingly sought to continue government operations, backing railroad labor's Plumb Plan of 1919 for nationalization.[25]

Shopmen became uneasy with terms of the Transportation Act of 1920. From their perspective the Railroad Labor Board (RLB) and boards of adjustment seemed potentially threatening. Although decisions of the RLB were not legally binding, they had influence within corporate ranks. Furthermore, pro-business types dominated the board. Soon workers' fears were realized. In June 1921 the RLB recommended a cut in wages by an average of 12.5 percent. It further angered shopmen by endorsing the outsourcing of work, reducing overtime pay, and sanctioning piecework payouts rather than the more remunerative salaries. The RLB also abrogated the shop crafts' national agreement, ratified in 1919, which had standardized wages and industry-wide work rules that favored labor.[26]

Although they threatened to strike, shopmen remained at their jobs. Contributing factors were the drop in the cost of living, especially between May 1921 and January 1922, and the hope that wages would be adjusted upward. But by June 1922 the shop-craft membership became alarmed about their financial future. On June 6 the RLB recommended a wage reduction of seven cents per hour, to take effect on July 1. (The board had not suggested wage reductions for the more conservative operating brotherhoods.) Because the industry, including the Rock Island, planned to follow the RLB guidelines, a work stoppage appeared inevitable.

The stage was soon set for the shopmen's response. At its national convention held in late April, the Railway Employees' Department (RED), an umbrella organization of the American Federation of Labor shop-craft unions, decided to put the strike issue to a vote of its more than four hundred thousand members. Balloting began on June 8, and it did not take long for the RED rank and file to approve a walkout.

What developed into a hostile and lengthy strike began officially on July 1, 1922. Backed by the United Brotherhood of Maintenance-of-Way Employees and the United Mine Workers of America (also involved in their own strike), RED leaders, led by former Seaboard Air Line boilermaker Bert Jewell, believed that the work stoppage would "seriously hamper railroad operations."

They anticipated that bad-order rolling stock, especially locomotives, would limit or halt train movements and believed that the public would shy away from the potentially dangerous equipment that management continued to use. The industry understood. "This shop strike had for it its avowed purpose the crippling of the railroads to such an extent that, because the loss and inconvenience resulting to the shipping and traveling public, the latter would force the railroads to make an immediate settlement with the strikers by granting all their demands," opined William Truesdale, Delaware, Lackawanna & Western Railroad president and a former Minneapolis & St. Louis and Rock Island official.[27]

All shops along the Rock Island System were adversely affected, particularly major ones at Chicago and Silvis, Illinois, and Horton, Kansas. Lesser facilities were also struck, including those at Cedar Rapids, Iowa, Fairbury, Nebraska, Goodland, Kansas, Shawnee, Oklahoma, Trenton, Missouri, and Valley Junction (Des Moines), Iowa.[28]

Spirits ran high among the more than 11,500 Rock Island strikers. They expected that management would settle quickly. That did not happen. Officials, including President Gorman, showed determination to break the walkout and to reestablish normal freight and passenger operations. The company wasted no time in advertising for boilermakers, machinists, electricians, and other workers. In an official statement, which appeared on September 18 in newspapers throughout the system and was posted in shop communities, Gorman announced: "An association of Rock Island shop employes is being formed by those now in service with which all future negotiations will be conducted." A company union was organizing. He told strikers that they would face penalties for their "unwarranted" actions. "The men who were in the service July 10, 1922, will head the seniority list and those employed since July 10th will follow on that list in order of their employment." Gorman held out a carrot of sorts. "There are vacancies to be filled and our officers will give preference to former employes who apply for work and whose record is satisfactory to the employing officers, and while such former employes cannot be given their old places on the seniority list they will have restored full pass and pension privileges." He also added this incentive to return: "As to such former employes returning to service before October 1, 1922, pension continuity of service will be computed without regard to any breaks on account of strikes."[29]

Gorman and the Rock Island took a more accommodating stance toward the striking shopmen than did some railroads. The Pennsylvania vice president in charge of operations, William W. Atterbury, for one, sought outright destruction of the RED and punishment for its leaders and members.

Atterbury and his colleagues despised craft unions and those employees whom they perceived to be radicals or "Bolsheviks." They were to a degree correct; the small Communist Party of America backed the walkout. (The RED acronym, to Atterbury and other anti-union executives, seemed appropriate, especially in the aftermath of the Red Scare of 1919–1920.)[30]

Conditions on the Rock Island were mostly peaceful as hundreds of scabs and a few non-strikers assumed their duties. These replacement workers hailed from a variety of backgrounds, ranging from local farms to automotive repair shops. Some were recently arrived immigrants from Europe, Canada, and Mexico. It did not take long for management to launch the Rock Island Association of Mechanical and Power Plant Employees to accommodate its new hires. As the weeks and months passed, scores of strikers, who hated a company union, became impatient and at times financially desperate. They would be the ones prone to violence.[31]

Occurrences in the shop town of Horton represented happenings system-wide. Throughout the strike residents commonly supported those shopmen who left their posts. Horton was a small, somewhat remote place where almost everybody knew one another and realized that these strikers were good, hard-working men who could not be categorized as radicals. "It was the unanimous feeling," wrote a local journalist, "that the strikers have the moral support of the entire town." That was the prevailing attitude throughout the country in the smaller shop locales, supporting labor historian Herbert Gutman's findings that interpersonal relationships usually meant hometown backing for workers involved in labor-management disputes.[32]

When the railroad reopened the Horton facility with replacement workers on August 16, tensions mounted. At the request of management, the Kansas governor placed the town under martial law. That response appeared to be more extreme than it actually was; only a small contingent of National Guard troops patrolled the shops complex, apparently to protect non-strikers. "A part of the coach shop became the sleeping quarters and a dining area for new hires, to keep them from certain harassment if they left the property." In September a "mysterious explosion" inside the shops fence caused momentary alarm, although this "low-power bomb" or large firecracker did not cause damage. Relative calm prevailed. Some strikers returned, influenced by Gorman's circulated statement. The combination of new hires and former RED members resulted in the shops functioning rather well. Troops remained for a while, but in early December they departed.[33]

The shopmen's strike, however, continued in Horton and elsewhere on the Rock Island. By year's end those men who refused to return struggled financially, as did their families and most local businesses. In December the *Horton Headlight-Commercial* explained the state of affairs: "The striking shopmen have shown unusual courage and fortitude in standing firm for over five months. A lot of them have used up their savings, have cashed their [World War] Liberty bonds and in some cases even sold their homes to continue the struggle."[34]

Once the National Guard departed, the diehards became more aggressive. Rumors spread that these men and their supporters planned to drive the strikebreakers out of Horton. Taunting occurred, and scuffles broke out between the two groups. At one point objects—bolts and bottles—were hurled at non-RED workers. Local law enforcement personnel had their hands full, yet they succeeded in maintaining peace. They publicized this message: "No foolishness will be tolerated from any quarter."[35]

As 1923 progressed, the shopmen's work stoppage on the Rock Island had largely ended, and mostly with a whimper. That was generally the case throughout much of the industry. The aggressive actions of US Attorney General Harry Daugherty, supported by federal judge James Wilkerson of the Northern Illinois District Court, had aided the carriers. Wilkerson's anti-labor (and arguably anti-constitutional) injunction did much to break the strike. Officially the dispute continued, ending formally for most roads on March 28, 1924. Yet the RED did not call off its strike against the intensely anti-labor Pennsylvania and affiliate Long Island Railroad until September 10, 1928.[36]

There were aftereffects. Hard feelings often remained between strikers and non-strikers. The Horton newspaper said it well: "Homes have been sacrificed, savings lost, civic, fraternal and church organizations disrupted, business has suffered greatly, and bitter feeling has developed that only time and tact can eradicate." For years the legacy of the strike permeated life in Holton and other Rock Island shop towns. Even in the ranks of organized labor, tensions persisted; operating brotherhoods had shown little or no support for the craft unions. With multiple carriers, although to a lesser degree for the Rock Island, there were lost revenues, and some freight traffic shifted permanently to truck transport.[37]

CELEBRATIONS

Despite the shopmen's walkout, Rock Island officialdom decided to celebrate the seventieth anniversary of its first passenger-train operation. The reasons for "Our Septuagenary" were severalfold. Revenues were good, and company coffers could afford extra expenditures. Leadership likely saw "family festivities" as a way of counteracting the negative impact of the ongoing unrest among shopmen. There were also anticipated public relations benefits. The railroad sought to demonstrate, as did later corporate galas, that great advances had occurred since 1852—the move from primitive to modern rolling stock, increased speed and reliability, and other improvements. The Seventieth Anniversary Committee called this the "Spirit of Progress." There was an unusual aspect: no railroad had ever recognized a seventieth anniversary. Centennials, however, were widely observed, with the Baltimore & Ohio holding the first in 1927 and a rash of them taking place following World War II, including those sponsored by the Burlington, Erie, Illinois Central, Milwaukee, Monon, and North Western. William Edward Hayes, who wrote the centennial history of the Rock Island, commented: "Just why he [President Gorman] picked the 70th year instead of say the 75th, which would have been the Diamond Anniversary, has never been logically explained." Gorman said this about the event: "In the celebration of our Seventieth Anniversary, which commemorates the achievements of those who have passed on and marks our reconsecration to Public Service, we adopt as our motto—SERVICE—A Square Deal for Every Employee and Patron of the Company." He was surely mindful of the ongoing shopmen's strike and the desire to affirm the railroad's commitment to serve the public.[38]

The big day for celebration came on Tuesday, October 10, 1922. It was on this date seventy years earlier that the little wood-burning *Rocket* traveled the forty miles with four wooden coaches from Chicago to Joliet. The official Rock Island remembrance began at ten o'clock in the morning. "Another historic train rolled out of La Salle Station, Chicago, toward Joliet, drawn by a locomotive of many times the power of that 'first engine' and pulling a train of four modern steel cars," wrote W. E. Babb, associate editor of the *Rock Island Magazine*. "At the throttle of this 'Anniversary Special' was Charles Hayden, of New York, chairman of the Board of Directors of the Rock Island Railroad. Beside him, was his father, who in his boyhood days had witnessed the coming and going of those earlier pioneer trains." The trailing coach was Gorman's office car, and riding in it was a special guest, Mrs. W. W. Stevens of Hubbard Woods (Winnetka), Illinois, who as a teenager had ridden that inaugural train. "She was attended by six young women, dressed in the costumes of the period of the early fifties, and she smiled at them as if she found it hard to realize that she was not a girl once more in crinoline."

The flag-decked *Anniversary Special* did not travel unnoticed. The Rock Island made certain that its itinerary was well publicized, prompting crowds in greater Chicago to watch at the side of the tracks. "Rock Island employees at the Chicago offices and shops crowded the right of way within the city limits, waving flags, while the national colors were flown from every company building. School children and citizens at Hamilton Park, Blue Island, Midlothian, Oak Forest, Tinley Park and Mokena were at the stations to wave their greetings." Throughout the route thousands more observed the anniversary special. "In all the towns along the line, citizens crowded the station platforms and schools were dismissed that the children might witness the re-enactment of an historic event of their grandfathers' pioneer days."[39]

After the train reached Joliet, where onlookers jammed the station grounds and adjoining streets, speech making occurred, including brief addresses by various notables, such as President Gorman. Following their presentations, a memorial tree was planted nearby to honor Roswell Flower, a former company director. In some ways the ceremonies in this Illinois city resembled those earlier celebrations when the first iron horse steamed into a community. The seventieth-anniversary observance also included a luncheon for hundreds of company officials, veteran employees, and other invited guests at the Drake Hotel on Michigan Avenue in Chicago. Many arrived there from La Salle Street Station in a caravan of Parmalee Transfer Company motor cars.[40]

The celebratory events of October 10 were not confined to Chicago and Joliet. Throughout the system special happenings took place. In more than fifty Rock Island communities, large and small, public meetings were held "in which the progress of these various communities were reviewed since the coming of the railroad." There was almost always a tree planting with an accompanying bronze plaque that honored a deceased employee or someone associated with the company. There were parades, including one in Fort Worth.[41]

Take the celebration in Des Moines. "In addition to the tree-planting ceremonies, a meeting was held in the evening at the Savory Hotel under the auspices of the Des Moines Association of Commerce at which Vice-President S. H. Johnson of Chicago spoke," reported the company magazine. "Charles H. Davis, the veteran Rock Island locomotive engineer, was a guest of honor at this meeting, where he was presented with a bronze service metal as one of the 'Fifty-Year-Service' men." Events in the capital city delighted the anniversary committee. "This meeting was one of the most important held on the system and was attended by representative business men of Des Moines, as well as Rock Island employes at that division point."[42]

The following day, October 11, the company held its "First Anniversary Tournament" in Chicago. This event attracted employees from the eastern part of the system. It offered many competitions, including baseball, tennis, bowling, soccer, football, swimming, relay races, track and field events, tug-of-war, horseshoe pitching, and checker contests. Winners received gold, silver, and bronze medals together with other forms of recognition. The idea, of course, was to foster a sense of the "Rock Island family."[43]

The editor of *Railway Age* aptly explained the significance of the Rock Island celebration. "The conception and carrying out of the Rock Island's celebration undoubtedly has done much to make a very large part of its employees and patrons think and speak of it as 'our railroad' who had not shown the same interest in it or had the same feeling toward it for years before." The editor concluded that "the Rock Island hit upon and carried out one of the happiest and most effective methods of selling itself to its employees and the public that could have been adopted."[44]

A corporate response to the shopmen's strike involved more than the commemoration of the seventieth anniversary of the first Rock Island passenger train between Chicago and Joliet. Under the guidance of President Gorman, the company embraced the then popular tenets of welfare capitalism, such as a stock-purchase plan that sought to enhance employee loyalty. In fall 1923 management inaugurated a program whereby workers could acquire preferred stock on a monthly payment basis. "Any employee of the company of more than six month's service may invest." The Rock Island did more to create a harmonious workforce. Shortly before the stock-purchase offering, the railroad launched a department of personnel and public relations to help mitigate employee problems and to project a positive company image. Throughout the decade, management promoted additional athletic tournaments and sponsored citizenship courses for its non-naturalized employees. Much of the corporate attitudes toward the "Rock Island Family," white and blue collar, were summarized in a pamphlet written by Gorman, "On the Human Side of Railroading." It emphasized teamwork. "The cooperative effort of employes, sometimes widely scattered, who realize that their particular jobs, whether of great importance or humble, can only produce the best results when it fits into the whole scheme and when everybody is working in harmony and friendly cooperation." The Rock Island acted no differently with personnel matters than did many other contemporary Class I railroads and such industries as auto, rubber, and steel.[45]

EXPANSION AND BETTERMENTS

In the minds of many, the seventieth-anniversary festivities might have suggested that the Rock Island System had been fully completed. Except for oil workers and residents in the vicinity, few paid much attention to the May 1920 opening of a fifteen-mile extension of the Chattanooga branch to Grandfield, located in the "Big Pasture" region of southwestern Oklahoma. Its raison d'être included cattle, cotton, and grain but most of all oil. By 1919 large quantities of oil were being pumped in the region, and the boom made Grandfield a refinery town. This line came with limited costs to the railroad. The citizens of Grandfield (née Eschiti) provided the right-of-way from Chattanooga, gave forty-five areas for the station grounds, and paid a bonus of $5,000.[46]

Although main arteries were established, the Rock Island continued to add to its system. This construction would be concentrated in the Oklahoma and Texas Panhandles. This region experienced a surge of railroad building from the mid-1920s into the early 1930s and included some projects that exceeded one hundred miles.[47]

Why construction, when motorized vehicles and improved roads had already contributed to increasing line abandonments and liquidation of a growing number of shortlines? The principal answer is wheat. Such a crop was ideally suited for the Panhandle, which produced a variety of hard winter wheat called Turkey Red. Demand for food products boomed during World War I, and commodity prices soared. Furthermore, there were advances in agricultural machinery, especially gasoline-powered tractors and combines. This equipment allowed wheat growers to cultivate more acres of what formerly had been drought-tolerant bluestem and grama grasses, resulting in what residents called the "Great Plow Up." This optimism prompted producers to acquire more land in order to expand their operations. Mother Nature also smiled on the southern plains, providing adequate moisture at critical times. Some believed that the weather had changed permanently; perhaps rain did follow the plow. By 1920 the Panhandle had emerged as a banner supplier of high-protein winter wheat. For railroads, bountiful crops meant opportunities for enhanced revenues. Grain could be transported to milling centers like Chicago, Kansas City, and Minneapolis for mixing with more northerly grown wheat with a lesser protein content. Trucks, of course, could not transport the hundreds of thousands of bushels to their ultimate destinations. Railroads in the region, notably the Burlington, Rock Island, and Santa Fe, coveted long hauls to the principal milling locations and Gulf ports. New trackage likewise tapped livestock trade, a historic pursuit in the region. Oil, too, was being produced, especially in the Texas Panhandle, where the first gas well began production in 1919 and the first oil well two years later. Crude and refined petroleum products required rail transport before the availability of pipelines. There also existed possibilities for railroad insiders to profit from new townsites, repeating a time-tested practice.[48]

The last large addition to the Rock Island System involved construction of a 153-mile link between Amarillo on the Memphis-Tucumcari line and Liberal on the Golden State Route. This trackage crossed what the company called "the Panhandle of Opportunity." Building began north from Amarillo in 1926 under the banner of the Rock Island, Texas & Gulf Railway subsidiary in four construction stages and was officially completed on July 26, 1929. Several new communities took shape, including Hitchland, Morse, and Stinnett, Texas. Soon a sixty-two-mile connector, designed to tap additional agricultural traffic, opened between Morse Junction and Dalhart. Freight explains these two projects; passenger service was minimal. Beginning on January 15, 1931, a General Electric–built motor car made a daily round trip between Amarillo and Liberal, and a mixed train served the Morse Junction-to-Dalhart branch.[49]

In addition to the agricultural and petroleum business, the Amarillo-Liberal line offered further value. It afforded an alternative through route between Liberal and Tucumcari and the West, providing a detour to relieve any disruptions on that section of the Golden State Route. Although this construction was about fifty miles longer, it sported more attractive ruling grades than the trackage through Dalhart, at 0.5 percent northbound and 0.6 percent southbound. Yet the line had a nasty choke point. The railroad planned to install a long, high bridge over the Canadian River near Sanford, Texas. But that never happened because of financial woes caused by the onset of the Great Depression. Instead a "temporary" wooden deck bridge was built, resulting in horrendous grades up to 3.6 percent on the south side of the river and 2.35 percent on the north side. Moreover, curves approaching this bridge reached ten degrees.[50]

Stinnett became the shining community on the Amarillo-Liberal line. As plans for the expansion materialized, Rock Island officials joined local boosters, led by A. S. Stinnett, to launch the Stinnett Townsite Company. After a successful town-lot sale, the railroad used its share of the proceeds—$25,000—to build an imposing brick depot. The company did more. Once train service began in November 1927, it contributed to the infrastructure needed to handle wheat shipments by installing five portable loading devices. Soon thousands of bushels of grain left town. Although oil was being pumped in the area, Stinnett, which grew rapidly and became the seat of Hutchinson County, depended heavily on farming and livestock production: wheat, kafir corn (sorghum), maize, and cattle. During good times this Panhandle town became an active shipping point. And the community grew steadily, from nearly 400 residents in 1930 to 2,695 in 1960.[51]

The Rock Island proposed more trackage in the Lone Star State. As the decade of the Roaring Twenties closed, both the company and the Frisco, then contemplating a merger, wished to establish a greater presence in West Texas. The most likely undertaking involved building from the Memphis-Tucumcari line at Shamrock southward through Wellington and Quanah to a connection with a proposed Frisco line between Seymour and Vernon. By linking up with the Gulf, Texas & Western Railway (controlled by the Frisco after 1930), this trackage would forge a route between the Panhandle and Fort Worth, allowing the seamless flow of grain and livestock to a major market. With ICC approval, the Rock Island worked out an agreement with Burlington affiliate Fort Worth & Denver City (FW&DC) that called for that company to build from Shamrock to Wellington. Once it was completed, the Rock Island would have 120 days to buy a half interest in this twenty-seven-mile line. Although the FW&DC finished the trackage in 1932, the Rock Island failed to exercise its option. The Great Depression, drought, and bankruptcy killed off expansion.[52]

Operating a railroad requires regular maintenance and selected major improvements. As with a host of carriers, the US Railroad Administration had not returned the Rock Island in as good a state as when federalization occurred. Yet during the 1920s track and equipment generally had not received the attention that was needed.

The Rock Island excelled in one area during the mid-1920s, and it involved acquisition of modern locomotives. Yet perhaps it acquired too much replacement power. Charles Hayden, the acknowledged master at the railroad, pushed successfully for the purchase of sixty-five locomotives of various types from the American Locomotive Company (Alco). Why such a large number? Hayden served on the Alco board and chaired its finance committee. This New York City–based company, with its principal production facility in Schenectady, New York, was suffering financially, and Hayden knew that the Rock Island was in a position to bolster Alco's bottom line. William Edward Hayes considered such expenditures to be foolish in the extreme. "At that particular time, he [Gorman] needed [these locomotives] just about as much as he needed a cavernous hole blown through his right-of-way."[53]

Even after Charles Hayden lost influence at the Rock Island, the company remained a loyal Alco customer. In 1929 it ordered twenty-four 4-8-4 Northern-type locomotives designed to handle main-line freights on the El Paso-Kansas and Missouri divisions. This power could also be assigned to fast

This photograph captures a gang of construction workers installing steel rails near the Clay County, Missouri, community of Mosby on March 5, 1931. The Rock Island called this line relocation project the "Kansas City-Trenton Short Line," a joint project with the Milwaukee Road. This betterment was expensive, costing about $14 million.

Dan Sabin coll.

passenger runs. By 1931 the railroad owned fifty-four of these mighty locomotives. And additional Northerns appeared. In 1944 management purchased ten Alco-built 4-8-4s, and two years later it acquired from Alco its final ten 4-8-4s. This stable of Northerns provided the principal freight power over most core lines, serving faithfully until the complete dieselization of freight service took place in the early 1950s.[54]

The 4-8-4 fleet is noteworthy in that it revealed that the Rock Island embraced more of an evolutionary rather than a revolutionary approach to steam power. Freight locomotives followed the common development of 2-8-0 to 2-8-2 to 2-10-2 to 4-8-4. Passenger locomotives had progressed from 4-4-2 to 4-6-2 to 4-8-2.[55]

While the Rock Island could boast of replacement power, it could not claim stellar status in upgrading its physical plant. Chief Engineer Louis Fritch wanted to spend heavily on such improvements, including bridge-strengthening and replacement projects between El Reno and Fort Worth. His department also developed an extensive systemwide to-do list. Most of these betterments never materialized. Still, the company did commit to a major line relocation in Missouri. This "Kansas City-Trenton Short Line," which was designed to lower grades and reduce curvatures, involved eighty-two miles of new trackage between Trenton and Birmingham and a cooperative double-track line with the Milwaukee Road between Birmingham and Polo, a distance of thirty-seven miles. Work on this $14 million project began on July 8, 1929, and was completed with appropriate fanfare twenty-five months later. Traffic moved faster, and no longer did payments go to the Burlington for trackage rights to reach Kansas City.[56]

With the major exception of line relocation work in Missouri, why did Rock Island skimp on physical improvements? After all, competitors were hard at work bettering their properties. The Burlington is representative. During the 1920s that company made substantial upgrades. Investments in plant and rolling stock were sizable and featured heavier rail, line relocations, and a new joint passenger station in Chicago. The Rock Island response was to divert money from betterments to dividends. That was the Hayden objective, and he was the boss. He could accomplish it by increasing revenues and slashing expenditures. With Republican-era prosperity at hand, and with Washington fostering private enterprise and keeping government regulation to a minimum, the business environment looked bright. The Rock Island freight traffic was the heaviest on record. Unattractive ICC rate policies and declining passenger revenues caused by a sharp decline in short-haul ridership did not set off alarm bells. Net railway operating income was on the rise: $14,841,165 in 1923; $17,713,590 in 1924; and $17,926,385 in 1925. Good times seemed permanent. In November 1928 the Standard Statistics Company lauded management's generous dividend payments. "Since reorganization the company has paid out approximately half of its net income in dividends." This firm predicted that "if this policy is maintained, an increase in the common dividend rate to $7 is practically certain early in 1929."[57]

TAKING THE ROCK ISLAND

The golden age of intercity passenger train travel during the age of steam took place in the 1920s, when the nation rode the crest of prosperity. All major railroads had their marquee trains, and they were nearly always named. Americans knew about such posh "varnish" as the New York Central's *Twentieth Century Limited*, the Pennsylvania's *Broadway Limited*, and the Great Northern's *Empire Builder*. Even lesser roads had their premier trains, whether the *Bon Air Special* on the Georgia & Florida or the *North Star Limited* on the Minneapolis & St. Louis. The Rock Island was no different. Its *Golden State*

During the golden age of long-distance passenger service, the Rock Island staged in the La Salle Street Station this publicity photograph of three trains, including the *Iowa-Nebraska Limited* (Chicago-Omaha-Lincoln) and the *Golden State Limited* (Chicago-Los Angeles). The labor-intensive nature of staffing such trains is readily apparent.

Dan Sabin coll.

Limited (with the Southern Pacific) and *Rocky Mountain Limited* claimed the greatest recognition.

At times the La Salle Street Station teamed with travelers and well-wishers, especially when its premier trains arrived and departed. During the prime years of long-distance train service, this facility was second among Chicago terminals in total passenger volume. Equally impressive was that it ranked first in the number of intercity trains, those operated by the Rock Island, New York Central, and Nickel Plate.[58]

The pride of the Rock Island was its highly promoted *Golden State Limited*. This crack all-Pullman train was advertised as "extra fine, extra fare." It was a train of solid comforts. The *Limited* offered passengers the latest Pullman accommodations and featured such amenities for female patrons as "Ladies' Lounge," "Shower Bath," and "Maid-Manicure Service." Males were not overlooked, and they had access to a barbershop, valet service, and secretarial support. There was also a playroom for children. A tour through the train revealed heavily embossed stationery in the lounges and cut flowers and finger bowls in the diner. The train regularly carried ten Pullman sleepers from Chicago, Des Moines, Kansas City, Minneapolis, Memphis, and Saint Louis through to Los Angeles, Santa Barbara, and San Diego. A deluxe observation car was included in the consist. Every day six *Limiteds*, some operating in multiple sections, sprinted across nearly two-thirds of the nation—three westbound and three eastbound.[59]

The *Golden State Limited* delighted its famous clientele. "I had the pleasure of returning from Los Angeles yesterday on the Golden State Limited,"

Although the *Apache*, which operated between Chicago and Los Angeles, lacked all of the first-class amenities of the *Golden State Limited*, these trains offered comfortable travel experiences.

Dan Sabin coll.

observed chewing-gum magnate and Chicago Cubs baseball executive William Wrigley Jr. "Without exception it was the most comfortable and pleasing ride I have ever had from the Pacific Coast to Chicago." No wonder the body of the silent-screen idol Rudolph Valentino, who died in New York City on August 23, 1926, made its way on the *Golden State Limited*, his favorite train, from Chicago to Los Angeles for a second funeral and interment in the Hollywood Memorial Park Cemetery. The five-day trip on the New York Central and Golden State routes attracted thousands of trackside mourners.[60]

Somewhat less elegant than the *Golden State Limited* was the *Rocky Mountain Limited*. This Chicago-to-Denver train provided Pullman sleepers between Chicago, Denver, and Colorado Springs; an observation lounge car between Chicago and Denver; a parlor car between Chicago and Omaha; a diner "serving all meals"; and standard steel coaches. Barber and valet services were available.[61]

Others who lived along the Rock Island main stems had access to additional named trains; these were not poky locals. For those who did not want to spend extra for the *Golden State Limited*, there was the *Apache*, a secondary train between Chicago and Los Angeles that provided standard and tourist sleepers and coaches. There was the *Colorado Express*, with a through sleeper in conjunction with the Denver & Rio Grande Western and Southern Pacific

The emptiness of the western Oklahoma landscape is the locale for an eastbound passenger train, likely traveling on the Choctaw Route. Automobile usage on the parallel road likely had caused a decline in short-haul patronage.

Dan Sabin coll.

beyond Denver. Then there was the *Mid-Continent Special*, which carried sleepers between the Twin Cities and Dallas. Also part of the passenger picture of the 1920s were the *Choctaw Limited* between Memphis and Oklahoma City; the *Iowa-Nebraska Limited* between Chicago, Omaha, and Lincoln; and the *Oil Special* between Oklahoma City and Amarillo.[62]

The Rock Island tradition of serving the "best meals on wheels" pleased dining-car patrons. It operated well-equipped commissaries, with the principal one located in Chicago. This facility took pride in producing its own ice cream. Fortunately, the company employed two outstanding dining-car employees, German natives W. Heidenreich, who served as general dining-car supervisor and who had previously served in several premier American restaurants, and Herbert Bannwolf, trained in Cologne, who had worked in leading American hotels before becoming a traveling chef. A favorite among diners was the Colorado mountain trout that was served fresh on the *Rocky Mountain Rocket* and that became its signature menu item.[63]

The Rock Island operated its share of local, branch line, and mixed trains. They lacked any pretensions of elegance, offering only basic transportation. These trains contained older rolling stock and had leisurely schedules. An Iowan remembered taking a mixed train on the main line from Stuart to Menlo and then going up the branch to Guthrie Center as a young girl in the 1920s. The journey covered only twenty miles but consumed nearly two hours. "I found that these trips always exciting [*sic*]," recalled Mildred Middleton.

"The conductor watched over me and my mother knew that I was in good hands to visit my relatives. For a number of years I took this trip at least once every summer, and I remember smoke and cinders coming through the open windows of the coach. But I didn't really care much about the dirt." Such speed and travel conditions did bother others.[64]

ANOTHER JUDGE MOORE?

It would be Edward Norphlet Brown (1862–1956) who contributed to a second Rock Island bankruptcy. Unlike members of the Reid-Moore syndicate, Brown was a well-trained and experienced railroader. In 1882 this native Alabaman earned a civil engineering degree from the Agricultural and Mechanical College of Alabama (today's Auburn University). Before graduation, Brown found summer employment with the Northeastern Railroad of Georgia, where he did survey work. With diploma in hand, Brown joined the Central of Georgia Railroad, rising rapidly to the position of maintenance engineer. In 1887 this high-energy and adventurous young man went to Mexico to become assistant chief engineer in charge of construction for what became the National Railway of Mexico. He worked there until 1914 in various engineering and administrative capacities, including serving as company president. Because of the intensifying Mexican Revolution, Brown returned to the United States, moving to New York City to engage in banking and railroading. In 1919 he took over active management of the Frisco.[65]

Edward Brown, a shrewd money man, realized that the Frisco suffered from poor financial health and faced potential bankruptcy. He understood the Rock Island's historical relationship with the Frisco, and he knew that its stock paid an attractive dividend. But what to do? In 1926 Brown and his associates, with ICC approval, acquired 183,333 one-third shares of Rock Island common, or about 25 percent of its outstanding common stock, at a cost of $10,506,000. Quickly they took three seats on its board of directors, much to the consternation of Charles Hayden and his allies. The aggressive Brown pushed Hayden out as chair of the executive committee and proceeded to run the railroad. He realized that the Hayden-Gorman efforts to establish closer ties with the St. Louis-Southwestern Railway (Cotton Belt) through a minority stock interest could damage the Frisco. Brown responded. These Cotton Belt shares were sold profitably to the Kansas City Southern, providing "evidence of Brown's master hand." Not only did the dividend stream provide the Frisco with "a beautiful short in the arm," but disassociation of the Cotton Belt from the Rock Island helped rival Frisco.[66]

Although hardly luxury varnish, a Rock Island passenger train is being "worked" about 1920 at the Manly, Iowa, station, a joint agency also used by the Chicago Great Western and Minneapolis & St. Louis Railroads. Train time, no matter the carrier, was an important event in communities like Manly.

Dan Sabin coll.

Brown had more on his agenda than to enhance Frisco coffers and thwart the Cotton Belt; he sought a Rock Island-Frisco union. After all, the ICC Final Plan had called for such a grouping. Brown did what he could to improve the physical links between the two railroads. One example was the construction of a joint station in Oklahoma City. Its location away from downtown was ill suited from the Rock Island perspective, especially for passengers, but it benefited the Frisco.[67]

The dream of a Rock Island-Frisco corporate marriage went nowhere. In 1956 John W. Barriger III, then serving as a Rock Island vice president, offered this assessment of the multidecade longing of Rock Island brass to unite the two carriers. "The past corporate affiliations of Rock Island-Frisco (1903–1909 and 1925–1933) failed only because of the unsound fiscal policies and poor capital structures of both companies in those periods and not because of any inherent weaknesses in an actual integration of their properties and operations—such a step, however, was not consummated in either instance." As he further noted, "Had it occurred, the subsequent results would have proved beneficial for both companies even though these might not have been realized soon enough to avoid a subsequent financial reorganization."[68]

In late October 1929 financial disaster struck the nation when the stock market crashed. Neither Edward Brown nor the Rock Island would be spared the ensuing economic pain. Yet management believed, as did President Herbert Hoover and so many others, that what had occurred on Wall Street was a necessary market correction. "I see nothing in the situation that warrants pessimism," Secretary of the Treasury Andrew Mellon famously remarked. The optimists were wrong.

At this time the Brown regime made a disastrous decision; it would continue to declare regular dividends on common stock. It also wanted to increase the authorized capital stock from $140 million to $170 million, but the developing depression squashed that plan. The financials did not look good. As of the close of 1930, the funded debt stood at $389,064,235, and the annual interest payment amounted to more than $13.8 million. The latter became a staggering burden.[69]

American companies, large and small, encountered financial hardships, especially as the 1930s progressed. Railroads, including the Rock Island, being dependent upon a high level of business activity, often found themselves in difficult straits. Still clinging to the hope for an economic turnaround, the Rock Island board in 1931 decided to maintain stock dividends, albeit at a reduced level. Nevertheless, these payments drained nearly $3.4 million from corporate coffers. The following year, 1932, did not bode well for the company. Operating revenues tell the story: $139,470,580 in 1929; $116,384,319 in 1930; $93,050,288 in 1931; and $66,783,778 in 1932. The spectacular fall of passenger revenues—dropping from nearly $30 million in the early 1920s to less than $6 million in 1933—reveals the economic malaise.[70]

With a major financial crisis brewing, retrenchments became mandatory. Maintenance was slashed, equipment stored, and workers faced furloughs or reduced hours. Employee morale slipped badly. "They couldn't understand the layoffs, the talk of salary reductions and wage cuts—and the lust for dividends." Soon those salary reductions occurred, and they amounted to a 10 percent cut. In a further indication of the pullback, after the May–June 1932 issue the company discontinued the *Rock Island Magazine*, which dated back to 1907, and this popular employee publication would not be resumed until 1940.[71]

The developing Great Depression forced the Rock Island leadership to seek financial aid. The hoped-for cash infusions would not come from commercial banks but rather from the Reconstruction Finance Corporation (RFC). For scores of troubled carriers, the RFC became a godsend, although its loans failed to prevent multiple bankruptcies.

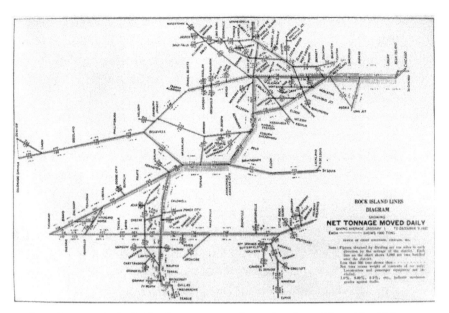

By the early 1930s, the Rock Island was encountering serious financial troubles. This 1932 traffic density chart suggests why. Although the initial core and the Golden State Route handled substantial tonnage, its maize of secondary and branch lines, especially in Iowa and Oklahoma, were not so busy.

Dan Sabin coll.

In January 1932 the Hoover administration, with congressional backing, grudgingly launched the Reconstruction Finance Corporation. Soon this pump-priming agency began to provide emergency loans to banks, farm mortgage associations, insurance companies, and railroads. Later in the year Congress provided an additional way to assist the railroad industry. Lawmakers added Section 77 to the Bankruptcy Act of 1898, streamlining railroad bankruptcy proceedings and giving the ICC enhanced powers to protect the public and investors. The commission would become involved much earlier in the bankruptcy process than it had in the past.[72]

The Rock Island leadership believed that aid from RFC loans would stave off bankruptcy. In May 1932 the company asked for and received a $10 million loan to meet pending bond maturities. Yet more money was needed. In early 1933 the RFC awarded the railroad an additional $1,181,872. That amount was quickly followed by a loan for $2,536,828, but this infusion consumed nearly all of the railroad's remaining collateral. The struggling Rock Island staggered. In May 1933 it asked this lender of last resort to borrow more, but a rejection followed.[73]

John W. Barriger III, who headed the Railroad Division of the RFC, explained why the Rock Island was turned down for a fourth loan. "The Rock

Island needed several million dollars to meet a July 1, 1933 interest payment and was without funds, unless provided by the RFC. It had little or no collateral to offer, all it had was pledged for $13 million outstanding RFC loans." RFC head Jesse Jones asked Barriger for his opinion about granting more funds to this needy railroad. "I stuck my neck far out and said that Rock Island was one of the most ineffectively managed railroads in the nation and that if it passed into bankruptcy it would be what I termed a 'triple bankruptcy' financial, physical and managerial." Barriger continued, "If it were well managed it would not need the loan or even be in debt to RFC. If good management could be supplied for it, a loan would be justified but not while run by the current team." Jones accepted Barriger's assessment.[74]

The financial future looked grim. To compound the company's current state, on March 1 and April 1, 1934, it faced, in addition to equipment trust payments, bond maturities of $144,003,700. Being realists, Brown, Hayden, Gorman, and other board members had no other choice in June 1933 but to file for voluntary court protection under the revised federal bankruptcy statute.[75]

No one knew when hard times would end. Although the coming of Franklin Roosevelt and the New Deal offered hope in spring 1933, when no fewer than sixteen major relief and recovery bills passed during the famed "first 100 days," railroad troubles seemed likely to continue. Net operating revenues for carriers had dropped steadily from 1930 through 1932. Although they rebounded modestly in 1933, they declined again in 1934, unnerving many in the industry.[76]

To make matters worse for the Rock Island and those who depended on its services, the railroad was in a state of rapid decline. Later a *Fortune* writer echoed Barriger's harsh assessment of the company's inherent weaknesses, calling them "a case of total bankruptcy—financial, physical, and managerial." The writer added this devastating commentary: "Little of the track could sustain top passenger speeds of more than sixty miles an hour, and to pay dividends the company had halved maintenance of way, exhausted surplus, and borrowed from the RFC. Furthermore, it was no temporary indigent seeking refuge in receivership to work off an indiscreet financial lag or a break of bad luck; it was a chronic offender with an unhappy heritage going back thirty-five years or more."[77]

FARRINGTON ERA

5

For the second time in fifteen years, the Chicago, Rock Island & Pacific Railway found itself in a federal district court. The company would not be alone. Approximately fifty railroads were in receivership. On June 7, 1933, Marcus Bell, vice president and general counsel, filed with the US District Court for the Northern District of Illinois in Chicago a petition for protection under Section 77 of the Federal Bankruptcy Act. That same day federal district judge James H. Wilkerson (1869–1948), who had been involved in the shopmen's strike of 1922 and who had later gained national attention for sentencing Al Capone to prison for income tax evasion, formally approved the request and ordered the "railway company to run, manage, maintain and operate its properties under conditions set out in the [bankruptcy] order." The next major action came when Judge Wilkerson appointed Joseph B. Fleming, James E. Gorman, and Frank O. Lowden to serve as trustees. With Interstate Commerce Commission (ICC) approval, they assumed their duties on December 1, 1933.[1]

The selection of the three trustees made sense, as they had complementary skills. As president, James Gorman knew the Rock Island, including its financial challenges. Being a crackerjack traffic man, he also understood prospects for the freight business. Joseph Fleming (1881–1970), who lacked railroad connections, had established himself as a prominent corporate attorney in Chicago, as a partner in the respected law firm of Kirkland, Fleming, Green, Martin & Ellis. *Fortune* described him as "one of Chicago's shrewdest lawyers." Frank O. Lowden (1861–1943), a lawyer like Fleming, was a political heavyweight, having been a Republican member of the US House of Representatives from 1906 to 1911, governor of Illinois from 1917 to 1921, and a leading contender for his party's presidential nomination in 1920. He also claimed railroad ties, having served on the Pullman Company board of directors and knowing a number of prominent railroad officials. Incidentally, Lowden was reluctant to serve. According to his biographer, he accepted because "he was more attracted by the challenge of the task and the opportunity to show how a leading railroad could be rehabilitated without the aid of Wall Street bankers than by the annual salary of $15,000 and other perquisites." These three men worked well together; they were "a congenial triumvirate."[2]

A railroad reorganization has always been a complicated process, and this would be true for the Rock Island. Thurman Arnold, the brilliant Washington, DC, lawyer who gained fame as the trust-busting assistant attorney general in the Franklin Roosevelt administration, said this about a reorganization: "A corporate reorganization is a combination of municipal election, a historical pageant, an antivice crusade, a graduate school seminar, a judicial proceeding, and a series of horse trades, all rolled into one—thoroughly buttered with learning and frosted with distinguished names." Arnold added, "Here the union of law and economics is celebrated by one of the wildest ideological orgies in intellectual history. Men work all night preparing endless documents in answer to other endless documents, which other men read in order to make solemn arguments. At the same time, practical politicians utilize every resource of patronage, demagoguery, and coercion beneath this solemn smoke-screen." Few would take exception with his colorful assessment.[3]

No one expected the Rock Island reorganization to take nearly a generation to complete, yet the foundations were quickly laid. Judge Wilkerson and the ICC did not act alone. The Rock Island board of directors needed to appoint reorganization managers, and it did so with dispatch. Not surprisingly, Hayden, Stone & Company, aligned with Charles Hayden, became one of the three firms chosen. It was joined by Dillon, Read & Company and Chase National Bank of New York.

Once the company entered bankruptcy, the reorganization wheels began to turn. Protective committees of bondholders of the Rock Island and its subsidiaries were created, and a consulting engineer was hired to study the system. That report recommended major line sales, including most of the Choctaw Route, and sizable abandonments, but it was rejected by the trustees. They wanted a reorganization plan that kept the system together. The trustees also expressed support for acquiring portions of the proposed dismemberment of the 1,628-mile Minneapolis & St. Louis Railroad, specifically the 92 miles of the former Fort Dodge & Des Moines Railroad between Des Moines and Gowrie and the 21 miles between Mason City and Northwood, Iowa, trackage that would be owned jointly with the Chicago & North Western (North Western). The trustees suggested to the ICC a money-saving unification of its eleven subsidiary properties. Such an arrangement would secure the parent road's bonds by direct liens upon these properties. On August 11, 1933, the ICC approved the concept, yet it added a deal-breaking condition. The commission wanted the Rock Island to acquire the hundred-mile Wichita Northwestern Railway. This financially distressed twilight-era shortline connected at Pratt, Kansas, with the Golden State Route and wandered off to the northwest through wheat country, terminating at Vaughn, Kansas, with a branch to Kinsley, Kansas. The trustees objected to taking over this bankrupt property with its considerable liabilities to bondholders and public authorities, but the ICC refused to relent. Merger of the Rock Island subsidiaries appeared unlikely.[4]

As the Rock Island soldiered on under court protection, the aging James Gorman had grown weary of his multiple responsibilities. A combination of protective committees, banking interests, and the Reconstruction Finance Corporation (RFC), headed by the powerful Jesse Jones, pressured the trustees to name replacement management. It did not take long before a capable railroader took charge; the chief executive officer would be Edward (Ned) Miail Durham Jr. (1875–1954). Gorman, however, remained president and a trustee.[5]

Ned Durham possessed an impressive résumé. At the time of his selection, he served as senior vice president of the Missouri Pacific Railroad (MOP). That company was also in receivership, and Durham understood the ramifications of court control. His professional career had not begun at the MOP, however. Born in 1875 in Memphis, Tennessee, Durham received solid academic training, being educated at the Memphis Military Academy and Lehigh University, where in 1898 he earned a civil engineering degree. After graduation he worked on hydrographic surveys for the US War Department and with the Deep Water Commission of the State of New York. In 1899 Durham entered railway service, first briefly with the North Western as a transit man and for the next two decades with the Southern Railway in various engineering capacities. Prior to World War I he served a two-year stint as the valuation engineer for the Atlanta, Birmingham & Atlantic Railroad before returning to the Southern. In 1919 Durham joined the US Railway Administration as manager of its Department of Ways and Structures, and he later directed its Division of Liquidation Claims. In 1927 he joined the MOP in an executive capacity. By this time Durham had become widely respected within the industry; in fact, when his Rock Island appointment was announced, rumors had circulated that he would become the next president of the New York, New Haven & Hartford Railroad.[6]

Ned Durham resembled his immediate predecessors as a hands-on executive, and at age sixty he remained "sharp and vigorous." Not long after he settled into the administrative suite at La Salle Street Station, he set out to inspect the far-flung Rock Island System, including its shops, yards, and other facilities. Durham talked with employees, including more than division superintendents, roadmasters, trainmasters, and dispatchers; lowly trackmen became part of his fact-gathering conversations. He did not ignore customers, many of whom suffered from hard times and widespread drought. Durham surely knew that painful adage: "When there's no rain on the plains, there's no grain in the trains." After all, the company's lines crisscrossed predominantly rural areas, and its greatest single source of net income came from the movement of wheat. For the Rock Island, "no grain in the trains" meant these startling statistics: in 1929 it handled 285,279 tons of grain, but in 1934 the amount stood at 7,487 tons, a drop of 97.4 percent. Grain revenues reflected that collapse, declining by 98.1 percent between 1929 and 1934.[7]

Durham realized that the financial conditions of the Rock Island were improving. New Deal relief and recovery programs were having a positive impact on the industrial, commercial, and agricultural sectors, and a sense of economic optimism was slowly returning to the nation. Company operating revenues for 1934 stood at $66,961,688, and the following year they had increased to $67,116,854. In 1936 the amount reached $78,066,854. Since bankruptcy had released the railroad from paying practically all interest on its debt and dividends on its stock, more money could be earmarked for needed improvements, including maintenance of way and structures. That figure stood at only $6,939,186 in 1933; reached $8,338,438 in 1935; and climbed to $11,084,438 in 1936. The railroad also took advantage of federal relief programs, not relying solely on the RFC. In 1934 the trustees borrowed low-interest money from the Public Works Administration to hire hundreds of poverty-stricken men in the Dust Bowl and employed them mostly for maintenance work.[8]

One of Durham's key decisions as chief executive officer involved replacing the often less than pleasant Louis Fritch, who headed operations, with a more cooperative person. He was not about to have members of top management quarreling, a problem that had persisted for years. Fritch was livid, and he sought unsuccessfully to keep his job, but Durham had the power to replace any executive.[9]

It did not take long for Ned Durham to find his operating man, John D. Farrington (1891–1961). Company historian William Edward Hayes, who adored Farrington, described him as "a 45-year-old dynamo with a big iron jaw, an inexhaustible drive, and a demonstrated ability to get the ultimate in service and performance for every buck in his budget." In the mid-1940s Gilbert Burck, senior staff writer for *Fortune*, gave this assessment: "Despite hard times, [Farrington] rose steadily because he was able to tell men what to do and get them to do it. He speaks with great deliberation, but what he says is rarely tentative. He settles arguments quickly, and can bawl out a man in fearful fashion. Yet in John Farrington the Rock Island seems to have more than a first-rate operating man of the old school." Railroaders and nonrailroaders alike would add to these positive descriptions, collectively praising Farrington as the "Savior of the Rock Island." Who was this remarkable individual?[10]

On January 27, 1891, John Dow Farrington was born to a railroad family in Saint Paul, Minnesota. His father, Robert I. Farrington, worked for the Great Northern Railway (GN) in various capacities, including as comptroller and financial vice president. Since the late 1880s when he joined GN predecessor St. Paul, Minneapolis & Manitoba, the senior Farrington had developed a close relationship with its founder, James J. Hill, an indication of his talent and loyalty. Like his father, the young Farrington did not attend college. Yet he received a good education at the all-boys Saint Paul Academy in Saint Paul.[11]

As a teenager John Farrington went railroading, working summers with Great Northern survey crews. In June 1909, at age eighteen, he officially began his career with the GN in its engineering department. Wanting to leave his father's company, he took a job with another Hill road, the Chicago, Burlington & Quincy (Burlington). His lowly position was that of timekeeper for a track maintenance gang. Being bright and energetic, he won rapid promotions: foreman, roadmaster, assistant trainmaster, and trainmaster. However, Farrington interrupted his railroad career in 1917 when he rallied to the colors during World War I. He was commissioned as a lieutenant in the US Army's Seventeenth Engineers, and when discharged he had obtained the rank of major. Following his service in France, Farrington returned to the Burlington as an assistant superintendent of its Ottumwa (Iowa) Division. In 1920 he technically ran his own railroad, the Quincy, Omaha & Kansas City Railroad, serving as superintendent of what can best be described as a lackluster Burlington-owned trans-Missouri carrier. Two years later Farrington assumed a more important position as superintendent of the Burlington's Saint Joseph Division. In 1923

John D. Farrington (*center*) projects a commanding presence. In the early 1940s he stands with Birchel R. Dew, Des Moines Division superintendent (*left*), and a retiring passenger conductor.

Don Sabin coll.

he climbed up the corporate ladder again when he received greater responsibility as superintendent of the Aurora (Illinois) Division. Farrington's career continued to advance. On January 1, 1930, he became general superintendent of the Missouri District, and in May the following year he became general superintendent of both the Missouri and Iowa districts.[12]

This maturing railroader gained industry recognition in November 1931 when he became general manager of the Texas-based 902-mile Fort Worth & Denver City Railway (FW&DC; *City* was dropped in 1951), controlled by Burlington affiliate Colorado & Southern Railway. For the next five years, he did much to strengthen the property, ranging from the rehabilitation of its core to construction of valuable feeder lines. Significantly, Farrington improved relations with shippers, regulators, and politicians.

As might be expected, John Farrington, who officially began his twenty-five-year career with the Rock Island on May 16, 1936, with an annual salary of $25,000, wasted no time in learning about the road. It would be a new day for him and for the company. Being an engaged railroader, Farrington carefully explored the property. "He spent six months riding up and down its

7,650 miles of track in an automobile equipped with railroad wheels to find out what was wrong," the *New York Times* reported. Farrington discovered a railroad that was in a sorry state. Physically there were worn-out rails, rotting ties, plenty of inferior or no ballast, bad-order equipment, and structures suffering from deferred maintenance. Heavy freight trains often had to be broken into two and run as separate sections, and locomotive engineers needed to ease trains over shaky bridges at ten miles an hour or less. He realized that employee morale was bad; there had been mostly demotions and only limited promotions. Farrington further found that the public image of the company, based largely on its often low-performing passenger service, was poor at best.[13]

After that close-up look at the Rock Island, Farrington sprang into action. One of his early acts was to sell thousands of tons of scrap metal. Obsolete rail, rolling stock, and other equipment that possessed cash value littered the property, and Farrington became "a master junk dealer." He was allegedly "the best-mannered, best-dressed junkman in the Country." The Farrington scrap drive, which netted $1,465,000 during the first year and ultimately raised more than $5 million from old rail alone, helped to feed company coffers. Yet it was no financial cure all.[14]

PLANNED PROGRESS

The phrase *planned progress*, which in essence meant modernization, became the hallmark of the Farrington era. All railroads benefit from a top-notch physical plant and good rolling stock, and the Rock Island was no exception. Since it depended heavily on connecting roads for a large portion of its freight traffic, it needed to provide superior service. While planned progress involved the sale of scrap, it covered much more. These two words would be used to describe improvements that lifted the company out of its second bankruptcy and made it a respectable and even admired railroad during the immediate post–World War II period.

To find "cash in the weeds," Farrington backed line abandonments. Most or all of these low-density lines may have made economic sense when constructed, but they had outlived their usefulness, becoming a financial burden by the 1930s. Motorized vehicles—automobiles, buses, and trucks—and better roads created practical alternatives to rail transport. Admittedly, the Durham-Farrington regime did not embark on a massive quest for line retirements; the process became more gradual. After all, there would be regulatory hurdles to overcome, and a strong uptick in the economy and local conditions might improve the traffic picture. Between 1937 and 1940, eighteen branches were abandoned, severely pruned, or sold. The largest to fall to scrappers were the thirty-three-mile Ingersoll, Oklahoma–Anthony, Kansas, branch in April 1937 and the eighty-four-mile Pittsburg, Oklahoma–Frisco Junction, Oklahoma, branch in January 1940. During the war years more lines were dismantled; the company focused on unprofitable ones in eastern Iowa. The company also desired to contribute to the national scrap metal drive. By the mid-1940s more than six hundred miles had been retired.[15]

As any thoughtful executive would do, John Farrington brought about administrative changes. He overhauled the operating organization and created the post of system engineer of maintenance of way. This job was designed to oversee the track and structures department through the new positions of district maintenance engineers. These individuals watched over roadmasters and track supervisors. Farrington also launched a capital-expenditures department to coordinate betterments.[16]

There were the expected administrative hires. Many of these railroaders came from the Burlington system; Farrington was familiar with their performance. He refrained from hiring men who had already attained high ranks since the company could not afford to pay them top salaries. Yet this did not mean diminished quality. "Fortunately railroad salaries were so low that good men could be had for very little, especially when there was a chance to get ahead."[17]

A notable sign-on was William "Bill" H. Hillis. Since 1906 this railroader had advanced through the ranks of the Burlington, mostly on its Illinois lines. In 1931, however, he assumed the role of superintendent of construction during the building of the 110-mile Childress-to-Pampa, Texas, line for the Fort Worth & Denver City, and it was here that Farrington recognized his talents. With Farrington's movement to the Rock Island, he hired Hillis to take charge of the railroad's maintenance-of-way activities. Somewhat later, Hillis rose to assistant chief operating officer with jurisdiction over the engineering, construction, and maintenance departments.[18]

With strong encouragement from Ned Durham and backing from the trustees and court, John Farrington launched a program to rehabilitate the Golden State line. The initial phase involved grade reductions between Herington, Kansas, and Dalhart, Texas, and included four major line changes or revisions. The goal was to reduce to 0.5 percent the eastbound ruling grade. (The westbound profile was less important because typically smaller amounts of tonnage moved in that direction.) This line, if refurbished, would be the most attractive of all West Coast routes from an operating standpoint because it skirted the Rocky Mountains.[19]

The largest of these early betterments on the Golden State trackage involved reducing grades, ironing out shape curves, and replacing a bridge over the treacherous Cimarron River thirteen miles northeast of Liberal, Kansas. Farrington, working with Hillis, concentrated on the Cimarron project, agreeing that this undertaking, estimated to cost about $1.5 million, was critical in achieving the goal of planned progress. Relying heavily on additional sales of scrap for financing, grading began in late 1938, and work on the bridge followed. The former involved an arrow-straight 7.88-mile line between Kismet, on the east, and Hayne, on the west, shortening the distance by 3.56 miles and eliminating 113 feet of rise and fall and 353 degrees of curvature. The high-level steel-and-concrete bridge, which measured 1,268 feet in length, increased speeds and the cost of repairing the line every time the Cimarron washed it out. What the Rock Island proudly called the "Samson of the Cimarron" opened on July 8, 1939, when a freight train extra steamed across the structure. The American Bridge Company, the principal supplier of materials, aptly described the span as being "simple" and having "functional lines emphasizing its sturdiness and utility." Collectively between 1936 and 1940, the Rock Island rebuilt or improved 141 bridges at a cost of nearly $1 million, and it is estimated that by running heavier trains, which was in part made possible by strong bridges, the company saved about $1.7 million annually.[20]

Rockets

Although the Cimarron River bridge became the signature structural betterment during the formative years of planned progress, the public was more aware of the appearance of diesel-powered *Rocket* streamliners. These stainless-steel works of art stabilized and then bolstered passenger revenues, improved employee morale, and helped to create the image that the Rock Island was a comeback railroad. "We had to re-establish our identify with the public," recalled John Farrington. "I was sure the new trains would do it and fairly sure of their earning capacity." He likewise sensed correctly that Americans quickly viewed these diesel-powered streamliners with their aerodynamic art deco and modern styling as synonymous with speed, comfort, and cleanliness.[21]

The Rock Island had been an early user of internal-combustion passenger equipment. Its acquisition of several McKeen gasoline motor cars prior to World War I attests to a willingness to accept replacement technologies. Even before the emerging diesel-locomotive revolution, the company embraced distillate (light fuel oil) engines. In 1927 workers at the Horton shops stripped

The "Old Man" in the fleet of Rock Island internal-combustion locomotives was No. 10000. By 1948, when this photograph was taken, this compact albeit powerful unit sported a modern diesel power plant and not its original battery with onboard diesel-charging system. Yet No. 10000 can be considered the Rock Island's first diesel-era locomotive.

Louis A. Marre coll.

two forty-foot steel mail cars and installed in each a pair of six-cylinder distillate engines that produced 550 horsepower. These strange contraptions could pull fifteen to twenty-five freight cars. Two years later the Horton facility rebuilt three more mail cars and added dual eight-cylinder 400-horsepower engines. When diesels burst onto the railroad scene, the Rock Island claimed to be a pioneer. In July 1930 it took delivery of an Alco/General Electric/Ingersoll-Rand diesel-battery switcher, No. 10000. This "bi-power" locomotive lacked a diesel-electric propulsion system; a diesel generator continually recharged the batteries. Upgraded over time, No. 10000 for years faithfully shunted cars in and out of La Salle Street Station and operated in local transfer service. Its reason for being came in response to Chicago's tough anti-smoke ordinance. Not until 1937 did the Rock Island acquire its first "true" diesel-electric switchers.[22]

In fall 1936, with corporate and court approval but without any marketing studies, the Rock Island placed an order for six diesel-powered streamliner train sets for service on its major passenger routes. The Electro-Motive Division of General Motors (EMD) built the 1,200 horsepower units (TA models and the only ones ever produced), and the E. G. Budd Company provided the twenty stainless-steel cars. Unlike other early streamliners, where power and cars were articulated, the Rock Island locomotives were not permanently attached to the cars. When the railroad took delivery of these air-conditioned units, they consisted of three- and four-car articulated cars, similar to the original Burlington *Zephyr*, which had made a sensational dawn-to-dusk run on May 26, 1934, from Denver to Chicago to celebrate the reopening of the Century of Progress Fair. This "speed king of the rails" impressed Americans, and they probably sensed that the streamliner era was imminent. The Rock Island contributed to that expectation.[23]

The Rock Island chose the appropriate name *Rocket* for its streamliner fleet. It provided a sense of history. A locomotive christened the *Rocket* had pulled the first Rock Island passenger train between Chicago and Joliet in 1852. Furthermore, the word *rocket* sounded good to the ear when linked to Rock Island, providing a pleasant alliteration. These streamliners, too, were scheduled to be fast—rocket-like if you will. The company added to the rocket feeling with a paint scheme of alternating streamlined bands of maroon and vermillion augmented by silver stripes.

With appropriate promotions, including well-attended public displays of its train sets in scattered Rock Island cities, on August 29, 1937, the Rock Island dispatched the first of its daytime fleet of *Rockets*. Operating between Fort Worth and Houston, the *Texas Rocket* claimed that honor. It offered companion service to the Burlington's *Sam Houston Zephyr* and ran over the jointly owned Burlington-Rock Island Railroad, successor in 1930 to the long-bankrupt Trinity & Brazos Valley Railway. In November 1938 management reassigned this *Rocket* to the Kansas City and Dallas route. Back in the heart of Rock Island country, the second streamliner, the *Peoria Rocket*, entered service on September 19, 1937, between Illinois's two largest cities, Chicago and Peoria. Like its Texas counterpart, it was hailed as "a bright and beautiful thing to behold." Soon other *Rocket* routes "soared into prominence overnight": Chicago–Des Moines (September 25, 1937), Minneapolis–Kansas City (September 29, 1937), and Kansas City–Denver (October 18, 1937), although in February 1938 this *Rocket* was moved to a Kansas City–El Reno–Oklahoma City run. The *Rocky Mountain Rocket*, which served Chicago, Colorado Springs, and Denver, did not enter service until November 12, 1939, and for the time being the *Golden State Limited* remained under steam.[24]

Rock Island officials believed that good trains deserved others, and the *Rocket* fleet was expanded. The new flagship train became the *Rocky Mountain Rocket*. Differing from its predecessors, this *Rocket* sported a two-thousand-horsepower diesel-electric locomotive (E3A model) that pulled

In 1937 the Rock Island dispatched its *Rocket* demonstration train throughout its system to announce a "new era of railroad transportation." (A) The shiny *Rocket* attracts a crowd at the La Salle, Illinois, station, and somewhat later (B) many gather at the El Dorado, Arkansas, station.

Dan Sabin coll.

RIDE THESE STREAMLINED
DIESEL-POWERED "NO EXTRA FARE"
TRAINS BETWEEN HOUSTON AND DALLAS-FORT WORTH

Burlington Route · Rock Island

One of the luxurious air-conditioned chair cars in service on both the Sam Houston Zephyr and the Texas Rocket

The dinette, where popular priced meals are served

The hostess makes the traveler's journey enjoyable

LAST TO LEAVE—FIRST TO ARRIVE

—NORTHBOUND—			—SOUTHBOUND—	
SAM HOUSTON ZEPHYR	TEXAS ROCKET	SCHEDULES	TEXAS ROCKET	SAM HOUSTON ZEPHYR
8:15 am	5:00 pm	Lv.....Houston...Ar.	12:15 pm	9:00 pm
12:20 pm	9:00 pm	Ar......Dallas.....Lv.	8:15 am	5:00 pm
12:25 pm	9:05 pm	Lv......Dallas.....Ar.	8:00 am	4:45 pm
1:10 pm	9:50 pm	Ar....Fort Worth...Lv.	7:15 am	4:00 pm

250 MILES IN 240 MINUTES

As the Great Depression lifted, the Burlington-Rock Island Railroad issued a combination public timetable and brochure that promoted the Burlington's *Sam Houston Zephyr* and the Rock Island's *Texas Rocket*. Not only did these trains offer the latest creature comforts, but the company emphasized their "Last to Leave—First to Arrive" convenience.

Author's coll.

In a November 1939 named-train folder, the Rock Island ballyhooed its latest streamliner, "the New Rocky Mountain Rocket." The inside copy in part read: "The Rockets have been built for speed, safety and comfort and serve a highly developed intermediate territory between Chicago and Colorado. They are roller bearing equipped and operate smoothly at a cruising speed in excess of 90 miles per hour." The company underscored this travel attraction: "The only route operating separate direct lines and independent through service to both Denver and Colorado Springs."

Author's coll.

seven nonarticulated Budd and Pullman-Standard-built streamlined cars. In the consist for its 1,073-mile overnight trip between Chicago and Denver were the company's first streamlined sleepers, including an observation-lounge car with five double bedrooms. Passengers appreciated the high standards that its predecessor *Rocky Mountain Limited* had established: "courteous attendants, competent chefs and waiters, and the 'best meals on wheels.'" There were also stewardess-nurses who catered to children and the elderly, specialized personnel that many major passenger carriers provided on their premier trains. Although the *Rocky Mountain Rocket* train sets were about three hours slower than competing streamliners operated by the Burlington and the Chicago & North Western-Union Pacific, its equipment and service rivaled the best.

Soon after the introduction of the *Rocky Mountain Rocket*, the company added another long-distance streamliner, the *Choctaw Rocket*. On November 17, 1940, this train made its debut, operating in two sets over the 761 miles between Memphis and Amarillo. While not a carbon copy of the *Rocky Mountain Rocket*, this daily air-conditioned *Rocket*, powered by an EMD E6 diesel-electric locomotive, featured equipment built by Pullman-Standard, including a chair car, a sleeping car, and an observation-parlor-dining car. Since this was the era of Jim Crow laws, the latest addition to the *Rocket* stable resembled other Rock Island passenger trains that operated in the region; it had assigned spaces for African Americans. Perhaps the *Choctaw Rocket* might have been named the *Capital Rocket* since its route served both Little Rock and Oklahoma City. With its introduction, the Rock Island and Pullman-Standard provided the public with considerable hype: "See how streamlined service steps up the tempo of travel! Only a few days ago the rail trip from Memphis, Tennessee, to Amarillo, Texas, and return, consumed 44 full hours. Now, thanks to the new *Choctaw Rocket*, that running time has been safely reduced by 10 hours and 40 minutes . . . more than 24%!" This print advertisement copy surely caught readers' attention.[25]

The last prewar addition to the *Rocket* fleet involved a joint streamliner with the Burlington. This was the *Zephyr Rocket*, which on January 7, 1941, began traveling the 583 miles between Minneapolis and Saint Louis, of which 365 miles were on the Rock Island. This train, which connected with the Burlington at Burlington, Iowa, included major stops at Cedar Rapids and Waterloo, Iowa, and Albert Lea, Minnesota, on the Rock Island, and at Fort Madison and Keokuk, Iowa, and Hannibal and West Quincy, Missouri, on the Burlington. "While the Zephyr-Rockets' overnight schedules are ideal for commercial travel," lauded a travel brochure, "they are likewise especially convenient for the summer vacationist en route to the Minnesota Lakes or Northwoods, or the winter traveler hurrying to the balmy Southland that lies beyond St. Louis." The two railroads pooled equipment, including heavyweight sleeping cars, for this fourteen-hour overnight trip. This interline service considerably reduced travel time over a route that had been popular since the late 1870s.[26]

The Rock Island made wise financial decisions with the purchase of its first and subsequent *Rockets*. Between 1937 and 1947, these trains generated $46 million, a 734 percent return on a $6.6 million investment. The initial train sets,

Toward the end of the 1930s, passengers on several long-distance trains found that the onboard staff included young, attractive stewardesses. These women worked on the *Californian*, jointly operated by the Rock Island and Southern Pacific between Chicago and Los Angeles.

Dan Sabin coll.

moreover, paid for themselves in less than two years. The *Des Moines Rocket*, which operated on a daily 358-mile run, proved the most profitable, producing during its first decade of operation $1.385 of revenue per mile but only $0.508 of expenses per mile. The reason for this stellar showing involved multiple factors: the Rock Island had the only direct line between Des Moines and Chicago; the Iowa capital had established strong business, consumer, and recreational ties to the Windy City; and institutions of higher learning, including

On the eve of World War II, the early-morning lineup of a trio of passenger trains appears at the Des Moines station. The diesel on the left powers No. 17, a southbound local headed for Kansas City; in the middle is No. 16, the northbound local with steam headed for the Twin Cities; on the right is No. 506, the *Rocket*, soon to depart for Chicago. The Rock Island dominated rail transportation in Iowa's largest city.

Don L. Hofsommer coll.

Augustana College, Grinnell College, and the University of Iowa, dotted the route. The Quad Cities likewise shared characteristics similar to Des Moines. Furthermore, the *Des Moines Rocket* offered on-time schedules that did not require overnight accommodations. While coach and parlor-lounge seats were reserved and individually assigned in advance, there were no extra fare charges. Riders also had access to a dinette coach for food and beverages.[27]

Yet in the years immediately before the outbreak of World War II, which stunned the world in September 1939, the Rock Island and comparable carriers did not see an uptick in passenger revenues. The "Roosevelt Recession" of 1937–1938 dampened ticket sales. After August 1937 the economy declined sharply, damaged by a falloff in industrial production, rising unemployment, and weak commodity prices. Rock Island passengers generated revenues of $7,307,758 in 1936; $8,182,732 in 1937; $7,766,848 in 1938; and $7,689,881 in 1939. Finally, in 1940 the amount surpassed the 1937 total, reaching $8,271,251. Later, during the war years, this income soared. Fortunately, the *Rocket* fleet stabilized passenger revenues. If these streamliners had not been in service, the yearly figures surely would have been worse.[28]

The Rock Island *Rockets* provided public relations benefits. The company, of course, wanted to meet its competition. Other granger roads were moving from steam and heavyweight equipment to diesel-powered streamliners for their flagship trains. The North Western created its fleet of *400s*, the Milwaukee Road introduced its *Hiawathas*, and the Burlington had its *Zephyrs*. Rock Island officials also believed in the marquee value of modern passenger trains. If satisfied riders had freight to ship, they would consider billing it over the Rock Island. The company's *Rockets*, furthermore, were reliable. Take the *Peoria Rocket*. As of September 19, 1943, it had completed six years of operation and had been out of service only ten out of 8,816 consecutive trips between Chicago and Peoria. The few missed runs were due mostly to high water and track conditions. *Rocket* streamliners undeniably enhanced the company's tarnished image.[29]

The Farrington team recognized that the Rock Island had been struggling with low employee morale. Along with other aspects of planned progress, the *Rockets* were just what could mitigate defeatist attitudes. "It was the first time in decades," observed *Railway Age*, "that employees had something really new to talk about." In his autobiography, historian Hugh Hawkins, whose father worked as a dispatcher in Goodland, Kansas, recalled how the coming of the Farrington era had made a positive impact. "Though the Rock Island was in bankruptcy protection, and Dad sounded unhappy when he mentioned it, he also spoke confidently of reorganization and of Farrington, the new man at the top." Hawkins continued, "Dad had met John D. Farrington and shared his optimistic view that the newly purchased diesel engines would help put the company back in the black. Even better news came when the Rock Island began to advertise itself as 'The Route of the Rockets.' The magazine pictures and the posters that displayed these beautiful, sleek streamliners were at least as alluring as the latest automobile ads." Hawkins could have added that during this time of high unemployment and destitution Americans loved anything that was new and exciting.[30]

John Farrington and his associates did not ignore the advantages of having diesel locomotives handling freight assignments. Obtaining them involved working with the American Locomotive Company (Alco). Since the Rock Island experienced good results with its Schenectady-built DL-103 passenger diesel from this EMD competitor, Farrington met with Alco representatives to discuss designing a special freight diesel. "During the meeting he sketched out his ideas regarding a combination locomotive that could work in the yard as well as on branch lines in low-speed passenger and freight service," related diesel historian J. Parker Lamb. He further explained: "Diesel locomotives up until this time had been developed in an industry that still carried a steam era mind-set. This meant that a different locomotive design was required for each type of service: freight, passenger, and yard. The recognition that a diesel-electric locomotive was not bound by these rigid service definitions represented a major conceptional breakthrough that would eventually reshape attitudes about motive power utilization within the entire railroad industry." The result of Farrington's request led to the first road switcher, the RS-1. By mid-1942 the Rock Island owned four of these versatile locomotives. Later there would be the rugged RS-2 and RS-3 types.[31]

Planned progress took other forms. The Farrington administration had great expectations with the anticipated growth of its Rock Island Motor Transit Company. After 1938 this rail-truck service, which was becoming popular with other carriers for the movement of less-than-carload (LCL) shipments, expanded rapidly. By the immediate post–World War II years, Rock Island trucks operated parallel to approximately five thousand miles of the system's rail lines. As the company told its security holders in 1948: "[Motor Transit] equipment comprises 509 pieces of modern highway trucks, tractors and trailers. It affords in 90 percent of the territory it serves first morning delivery from the point where transfer is made from rail cars to trucks." Better customer service remained a continuing goal of this revitalizing railroad.[32]

ONGOING REORGANIZATION

The designated court-appointed trustees faced a daunting task with their reorganization efforts. They needed to oversee the daily operations of a complex railroad system and to prepare a financial reorganization plan that all parties—including the federal court, ICC, and creditor groups—could accept. Although three men worked well together, James Gorman was in failing health and would die in 1942, the aging Frank Lowden experienced frequent bouts of illness after spring 1937, and Joseph Fleming faced other demands on his professional time. Yet the trustees soldiered on toward that goal of a court-free carrier that could achieve long-term profitability.

While the trustees sought to keep in the good graces of lenders, most of all the Reconstruction Finance Corporation, there were constant problems with the five protective committees. These feisty groups, which represented particular issues of Rock Island and Rock Island subsidiary company bonds, sought to make certain that their assets would be maximized at the termination of the receivership, considering "any new spending by the road as money diverted from their own pockets." They wanted to wait until economic conditions improved. They feared that if a reorganization plan appeared too early, they would sustain considerable losses.[33]

In order to support planned progress, the trustees needed to reassure the protective committees that the railroad was gaining financial strength with betterments, administrative changes, and other well-conceived responses to the challenges created by hard times. An important triumph involved the trustees negotiating compromise agreements with local, state, and federal authorities for property tax and corporation income tax obligations. By 1937 they had achieved full tax settlements for four previous years. This represented a significant victory, amounting to savings of approximately $2,250,000. Additionally, assessed valuations of company properties experienced an annual tax reduction of roughly $500,000. The trustees also realized a lowering of the interest rate from 6 to 4 percent on its $13,500,000 of RFC loans. There were other cost savings. One involved changes in the administration and organizational activities, such as the updating of the accounting system.[34]

The trustees carefully watched a plethora of financial reports. They understood that the Roosevelt Recession, modal competition, and other factors diminished operating revenues. But they felt optimistic. The total stood at $67,116,85 for 1935, climbed two years later to an encouraging $81,643,250, but fell to $77,777,807 in 1938. Fortunately an upturn followed: $78,467,818 in 1939 and $80,701,923 in 1940. There was the growing realization that America was on the verge of world war, and that would mean much more freight and passenger traffic for the nation's railroads.[35]

WORLD WAR II

Contemporaries and others later agreed that America's railroads experienced their finest hour during World War II. The statistics bear out such an assessment. Because federal authorities severely rationed gasoline, tires, replacement parts, and vehicle production, the airline, bus, and truck companies could not maintain their prewar levels of service, let alone expand. Further hindering highway movements was a national speed limit of thirty-five miles per hour. German U-boat attacks against American shipping during the early part of the conflict disrupted the flow of goods, especially petroleum, through the Panama Canal and from Gulf ports to the Eastern Seaboard. Consequently railroads became the only viable alternative to land and water transport. They responded to these transportation challenges, managing to carry 83 percent of the increase of *all* traffic between 1941 and 1944. Specifically, railroads moved 91 percent of military freight and 98 percent of military personnel. Freight traffic, measured in ton miles, climbed from 373 billion in 1940 to 737 billion in 1944, an amount that would not be equaled until 1966. Passenger volume, expressed in revenue passenger miles, soared from 23 billion in 1940 to 95 billion in 1944, a sum never again attained. No wonder passenger revenue miles in 1944 exceeded those of 1939 by 322 percent. All of these stunning figures came about through the cooperative efforts of the Office of Defense Transportation, led by former ICC commissioner Joseph B. Eastman, and not through federalization as had occurred during the Great War. Nevertheless, obstacles existed; the War Production Board, for example, severely limited requests for new locomotives, freight and passenger equipment, and steel rails.[36]

Rock Island management and employees responded to the challenges of war. "Keeping 'em rolling for Victory" became the determined slogan. In early 1941, before Pearl Harbor but when war seemed inevitable, the company created a special military department designed to work with the War Department, including such services as overseeing the movement of armed forces personnel. Once the conflict began, the Rock Island wholeheartedly embraced the war effort. Examples abound. When the government called for scrap drives for copper, brass, and other strategic metals, officials ordered that all ornate light fixtures in La Salle Street Station be removed. Workers salvaged more than a ton of metals; one unit alone weighed eight hundred pounds. And the company readily complied with federal commands. In a train order issued at the Topeka yard on June 15, 1942, the dispatcher sent out this message: "Practice Black Out 1030 pm to 1101 pm tonight Dickinson Wabaunsee and Riley Counties trains operating thru these counties at that time must dim head lights close cab curtains and prevent as far as possible any flashes of light Lights in passenger cars to be dimmed and curtains drawn and doors kept closed." When high water on the Arkansas River in spring 1943 caused a break in a vital oil pipeline, the company permitted engineers to install an emergency line across its bridge at Little Rock, and in less than a hundred hours, oil again flowed. A year later operating officials aided soldiers of the 743rd Railroad Operating Battalion, based at Camp Robinson, Arkansas, by allowing them to conduct training exercises along the Choctaw Route between Memphis and Little Rock. Throughout the conflict, management urged employees to buy war bonds, and most complied. More obvious to patrons were adjustments in train movements. Troop specials, known as "mains," received high priority, and the company did what it could to make these military trips pleasurable. Train escorts—Passenger Department representatives—needed to adhere to this company order: "When the wheels of the last troop train have stopped, and the last soldier has returned home, it is to them that we must turn; for

The pressing travel demands caused by World War II prompted cancellation of the joint Rock Island-Southern Pacific *Arizona Limited*. Trains No. 29 and 30, which linked Chicago with the Arizona cities of Tucson, Chandler, and Phoenix—"America's sunniest resort section"—provided wintertime service on "the Direct Low Altitude Route" between 1940 and 1941.

Author's coll.

their patronage will mean the difference between success and failure." Civilian passengers were respected, but they were encouraged to travel during nonpeak times and to expect inconveniences. A 1944 public timetable contained this message: "Trains are crowded—occasionally late. Yet the patience and cooperative attitude of civilian travelers have been very gratifying to us. Many patrons stand in line for a seat in the diner. This we regret, but new diners cannot be built as critical materials are more urgently needed elsewhere." This contrite yet forceful statement continued: "We are ever alert to reduce all the inconveniences to our patrons that we possibly can, but we earnestly request consideration of our problems, and acceptance of available accommodations." The Rock Island also needed to adjust its passenger service. The *Arizona Limited* is the premier example. This train, in conjunction with the Southern Pacific, entered service in 1940, but two years later it disappeared from the timetable. This deluxe, extra-fare heavyweight train, which required a six-dollar surcharge, had operated only during the winter months, serving such popular Grand Canyon State destinations as Tucson, Chandler, and Phoenix. Its primary raison d'être was to carry winter vacationers, largely from the Midwest, who sought sunny, warm weather. Yet near the end of the war, the company added the *Des Moines Limited*, a day train that operated between Chicago and the Iowa capital, and made other changes in anticipation of postwar travel needs.[37]

An important physical betterment that occurred during the war years involved a 15.1-mile line relocation in Mercer County, Missouri. The objective of this $2.019 million project was to reduce grades and curvatures, thus improving operating conditions for the heavy wartime traffic. This replacement trackage involved one of the company's most important stretches of line, which expedited freight and passenger trains between Chicago and California and Minneapolis and Texas and released locomotives that had been required for pusher service for use elsewhere.[38]

No different from other carriers, the Rock Island faced a labor shortage early on. Enlistments and the draft meant that hundreds of employees left their posts to don uniforms. The company responded by encouraging employees not to retire, and some retirees returned to their former posts. Women also joined the workforce, usually only "for the duration," being hired for clerical, agency, and tower positions. Some, including African Americans, also accepted manual labor jobs, often wiping locomotives, cleaning passenger cars, handling mail and express, and accepting unskilled or semiskilled shop assignments. Teenage boys between sixteen and draft eligibility at age eighteen took mostly unskilled positions. During the Great Depression the company had supported

A veteran crew member boards No. 2657—a Mikado-type (2-8-2) locomotive built by Alco in 1923—in El Reno, Oklahoma, to begin switching assignments. During World War II this freight yard became a vital point for heavy wartime traffic.

Keith L. Bryant Jr. coll.

the deportation of Mexican nationals, but as war developed it rescinded this policy. Hundreds of *traqueros* (track workers), with federal sanction, became engaged in maintenance-of-way jobs as they had in the past.[39]

Increased revenues reflected the surge in wartime business. Operating revenues skyrocketed from $78,467,818 in 1939 to $192,046,910 in 1945. Net operating income rose from $15,458,536 in 1939 to $74,923,371 in 1944 but fell to $55,962,109 in 1945. This decrease reflected the company's retirement of its RFC loans and reduction of other financial obligations.[40]

REORGANIZATION BATTLES

The dark cloud that hung over the Rock Island comprised not finances but rather the ongoing process of reorganization. The efforts to exit from bankruptcy came with delay after delay and seemed never ending. This course of events reminded some of *Jarndyce v. Jarndyce,* a legal case, described in the Charles Dickens novel *Bleak House,* that went on forever.

The reasons for not terminating the receivership in a reasonable length of time involved more than the wrangling among representatives of creditor and stockholder groups. The fault lay largely with Michael Igoe (1885–1967), the federal district judge who had replaced Judge James Wilkerson in 1941, and Aaron Colnon (1894–1950), whom Judge Igoe tapped in April 1943 to take the place of the late Frank Lowden as one of the two trustees. A month later ICC approved the Colnon selection.[41]

It would be Aaron Colnon, more than Judge Igoe, who often gave John Farrington and Joseph Fleming, the sole original trustee, acid stomachs and sleepless nights. Their nemesis was an individual who had neither a direct railroad connection nor a distinguished legal or political background. Rather Colnon, who held an undergraduate degree from Loyola University and a law degree from Northwestern University, initially worked in real estate and finance after serving as a junior officer in the US Army during World War I. In 1930 this man on the make became executive vice president of the Chicago Trust Company, and three years later he took charge of the Fort Dearborn Mortgage Company. As a businessman he possessed determination and arrogance, but he could be superficially charming when necessary.[42]

There is no reason to doubt William Edward Hayes, who knew intimate details of the reorganization struggle, or to challenge his conclusion that Colnon had a personal agenda. This new cotrustee wanted to oust John Farrington and assume the presidency and the financial advantages and other perks that went with it. Colnon believed that this was an achievable goal; he and Judge Igoe were friends, even allies. Colnon employed direct tactics. He let it be known to fellow trustee Joseph Fleming that he "was running the show." Later Colnon suggested to Fleming that if he cooperated with him, as the future president he could become the general counsel. Colnon also resorted "to invective and personal abuse" against Farrington, hoping that he would resign in frustration. He sought, too, to gain support from other important participants, employing charm and promises.[43]

Aaron Colnon was not going to steamroller his way to power. Fleming backed Farrington, and leaders of the protective committees expressed their support; after all, Farrington had done a remarkable job as the chief operating officer and after 1942 as chief executive officer. As for Farrington, he was not about to allow Colnon to seize power and to profit personally.

Not long after Colnon became cotrustee, the process of completing the reorganization pushed ahead. Judge Igoe largely approved the latest plan, which at its core sought a reduced capitalization of $368 million. Throughout this long and bitterly contentious case, he believed that a final plan should be modified as a result of the company's strong wartime earnings, permitting some compensation to owners of *all* classes of securities. Since the ICC needed to bestow its blessings, the judge requested certain changes, wanting authority to approve or reject the reorganization managers for the various creditor groups. Stockholders, represented by Edward Brown, chairman of the First National Bank of Chicago, liked the judge's thoughts about protecting their investments. They opposed the current plan, which called for the elimination of their equity investments, and so took that matter to court. Brown and the debtor company lost, and so in June 1944 Judge Igoe held what would be the final hearings on the reorganization. As it stood, he could reject any reorganization managers that the creditors suggested, but he could not name them.[44]

Aaron Colnon closely monitored these happenings. He hoped that by suggesting various individuals who would support him and be acceptable to the judge, he could increase his influence. Colnon also caused more mischief. One example involved canceling the insurance contract that the Rock Island had with a Baltimore agency—one awarded through competitive bidding—and unilaterally, with the judge's blessings, giving it to a Chicago firm. Colnon admitted that the head of the replacement provider was a close friend. His actions cost the railroad about $25,000 in additional insurance premiums in 1945.[45]

A new fly in the ointment appeared, and it involved veteran US senator Burton K. Wheeler, an ultraprogressive anticorporation Democrat from Montana who chaired the Senate's Interstate Commerce Committee. He argued that railroad reorganizations hurt small investors. This fiery lawmaker asked, "What do Senators believe the people of the country will think of Government agencies [ICC] which permit the wiping out of $2,500,000,000 of railroad stock, a considerable portion of which was owned by working men and women, by widows and orphans, while at the same time bonds which had been selling at $2.50 rose to par and over by reason of the fact that the guess made by the ICC resulted in wiping out the stocks?" Wheeler's plan of action? He proposed legislation that would grant debtor companies more time to reorganize and thus give "needy" investors the opportunity to protect their assets. When applied to the Rock Island, this argument made little sense. The Alleghany Corporation—which controlled the profitable coal-carrying Chesapeake & Ohio and several other railroads and was led by financier Robert R. Young, the "Populist of Wall Street"—had emerged as the largest Rock Island stockholder.[46]

The Wheeler proposal ultimately failed. Although the bill passed Congress, President Harry Truman pocket vetoed it. He proposed that the upcoming Eightieth Congress rework the measure, believing that the Wheeler legislation favored certain railroads. That new Congress, the most conservative since the 1920s, was not about to support what many members viewed as an antibusiness proposition.

The bouncing about of the reorganization Ping-Pong ball continued. Aaron Colnon pushed for his own plan to finalize the reorganization. He wanted to pay off the bondholders of the several subsidiary companies and to reduce the interest from 4 to 3 percent on the general mortgage bonds and from 4.5 to 3 percent on the secured 4.5 percent bonds. This proposal did not sit well with the New York–based life-insurance firms, especially Metropolitan Life Insurance Company, major holders of these investments. Judge Igoe, however, backed his friend's proposal, calling it "just and reasonable." Predictably, the bondholder committees sought relief in federal court.[47]

The bankruptcy would end in 1947. Yet before the new Chicago, Rock Island & Pacific *Railroad* Company could make its debut on January 1, 1948, debate over aspects of the reorganization package remained. By this time the Alleghany Corporation had joined forces with Colnon and Igoe. The Young company envisioned the Rock Island as an ideal link in assembling a coast-to-coast railroad system that would include the New York Central (NYC). An obvious advantage of having the Rock Island under its control would be that it and the NYC shared La Salle Street Station. By now the Alleghany Corporation had amassed a substantial amount of Rock Island securities. In February a federal circuit court ruled unanimously that the reorganization plan submitted to the Igoe court in 1943 must be implemented and remanded the case back to the ICC. This meant that the claims of senior creditors would win priority over all others and that equity holders would lose their investments. The decisions of Judge Igoe had not impressed the three appellate justices.

Legal fighting had not abated. But the railroad appeared to be on the verge of exiting bankruptcy on June 16 when Judge Evan Evans, a senior member of the circuit court of appeals, reaffirmed the plan. Junior creditors remained determined to protect their investments, and earlier their lawyers had filed a writ of certiorari with the US Supreme Court to reopen the case. In the process they won backing from the ICC. In October the high court denied this request, sustaining the lower court's decision. Yet another delay occurred when the Texas attorney general lodged a complaint about the reorganized railroad being incorporated in Delaware. In late December that matter was settled; Texas had no standing in the proceedings. On December 31, 1947, Judge Igoe signed "under protest" the final order that created the successor company, ending the fifteen years, six months, and twenty-three days in bankruptcy.[48]

The immediate post–World War II years were a time of optimism at the Rock Island. In 1948 a mighty Northern-type (4-8-4) locomotive, No. 2680, speeds a string of freight cars along the main line east of Des Moines.

George Niles photograph, author's coll.

The financial structure that took effect on January 1, 1948, lacked any unusual features in a modern railroad reorganization. The Chicago, Rock Island & Pacific Railroad saw its capitalization reduced significantly, dropping from $452,290,000 to $356,117,327, and it had its interest on the funded debut slashed from about $14.3 million to $1.7 million. The new preferred stock issue raised approximately $70.5 million, and the common generated about $141 million. Earlier preferred and common stockholders saw their investments evaporate. Those who held several issues of secured bonds received a variety of securities, including first and general mortgage bonds as well as preferred and common stock. There were cash payments, representing unpaid interest from July 1, 1933. In a formal announcement of the return of the Rock Island to corporate control, which appeared widely in newspaper advertisements on January 5, 1948, management lauded the reorganization as creating "a conservative financial structure and ample strength to meet the responsibilities of the future." It had reduced the funded debt from $279,649,720 as of July 1, 1933, to $100,853,150, exclusive of equipment trust obligations. The text listed the new members of the board of directors, mostly businessmen from the service area, and indicated that they "may be counted on to support Rock Island management in improvement in plant, continuous improvement in equipment and continuous improvement in service." At last John D. Farrington assumed the presidency. No longer would he need to worry about the actions or antics of Michael Igoe and Aaron Colnon. It is doubtful that Farrington attended Colnon's funeral mass, held in November 1950.[49]

MORE PROGRESS

While the public (and many employees) probably paid scant attention to the stormy reorganization proceedings, they likely noted a continually improved Rock Island. Planned progress experienced some of its finest days during the immediate years following the emergence of the bankrupt-free company. But headwinds existed. There was little likelihood that the Farrington railroad could become a Burlington or some other well-heeled carrier. Its critical grain carloadings depended heavily on the whims of Mother Nature and market conditions; it reached too many cities on trackage rights and therefore could not serve these urban customers, and it remained a bridge road for much of its non-agricultural traffic, requiring friendly connections and aggressive solicitations. Farrington did not publicly (or privately) address these systemic issues that ultimately wrecked the company. As he told stockholders in 1951, "High wages and prices for materials are the worst problems affecting the road today."[50]

Although the nation experienced a recession in 1949, Rock Island leaders had reason to feel optimistic, at least for the foreseeable future. Its financial footing appeared solid. Stockholders had approved a new first mortgage bond issue of $55 million, and these proceeds, together with funds on hand, retired the old outstanding first and general mortgage bonds. This refinancing left a manageable mortgage debt, exclusive of equipment obligations, and provided more money for betterments and other needs.

In an early postwar action, the Farrington administration decided to upgrade the *Golden State Limited*. In 1946 the Rock Island and Southern Pacific agreed to replace this historic luxury train with what would be called the *Golden Rocket*. A year later they placed a joint order with Pullman-Standard for two eleven-car train sets that "employed the latest postwar techniques in car architecture and engineering." These consists would feature a Mexican theme. "El Café," the coffee shop–lounge, for example, called for an interior red-and-yellow canopy, red leather upholstery, and hand-carved wooden trim. Once production had begun, both roads launched their own publicity campaigns. One version used by the Farrington road read: "ON THE WAY! Another magnificent Rock Island streamlined train—the 'Golden Rocket'— still faster, more beautiful and more comfortable—will offer 39¾-hour service between Chicago and Los Angeles. Be on the lookout!" A *Holiday* advertisement proclaimed: "Riding the Golden Rocket will be a thrilling adventure; its decorations capture the picturesque beauty of the Southwest—the grandeur of its mountains, deserts and canyons—the inspiring colors of its flowers, minerals and native costumes." All seemed to be on track for what would be one of America's finest long-distance trains. It would match the forty-hour schedules of the best runs operated by the Santa Fe and Union Pacific. Then came a surprise. The Southern Pacific got cold feet, and in late 1947 it canceled its share of the Pullman-Standard order. The Rock Island did not. By spring 1948 the company had taken possession of its rolling stock, allowing it to give the *Golden State* a facelift. Yet an attractive opportunity for passengers who patronized Golden State Route had been lost.[51]

The Farrington team had success with new *Rockets* along other main corridors. In 1945 it introduced the *Twin Star Rocket*, which operated over the 1,370 miles between Houston, Dallas, Kansas City, Des Moines, and Saint Paul/Minneapolis. This streamliner claimed to make the longest north-south run of any American passenger train on a single railroad. Two years later the *Corn Belt Rocket* was born. It ran from Chicago overnight to Omaha and returned with daytime service. Management wanted to compete directly with the Burlington's recently introduced *Nebraska Zephyr*, which linked Chicago, Omaha, and Lincoln. Improvements to passenger service continued. Additional replacement equipment appeared on the streamliner fleet. The *Twin Star Rocket* is representative; new all-room sleepers, diners, and observation parlor cars enhanced its consists.

Less snappy than the *Rockets* was the *Imperial*, a new Chicago-to-Los Angeles train that made its debut on October 6, 1946. It featured heavyweight equipment, although initially the Rock Island leg diesels, not steamers, provided the power. This long-distance named train received an upgrade in 1948 when its travel time was shortened to fifty-three hours, forty-five minutes westbound and fifty-one hours, forty-five minutes eastbound. Discontinuance of local trains along the Golden State Route in 1952 meant that the *Imperial* took over those assignments, albeit on a much slower schedule.[52]

In 1952 management still believed in the future of the railroad passenger business. "It does not lie in the direction of providing local services in thinly populated areas such as are served by the majority of our lines," opined Almond D. Martin, general passenger traffic manager. "It lies in the direction of fast, comfortable service between metropolitan centers which are far apart—too far for a comfortable automobile or bus ride."[53]

In 1951 the *Twin Star Rocket*, with a new E8A on the point, approaches Houston Junction, Texas, in all of its glory. Few if any contemporary observers would believe that thirty years later the Rock Island would be in liquidation.

George Werner photograph

That same year the *Twin Star Rocket* leaves the Mississippi River bridge near Inver Grove, Minnesota, on its southbound run.

Dan Sabin coll.

On October 14, 1951, railroad photographer Wallace Abbey captured Rock Island No. 405, an EMD-built FP7A diesel that the manufacturer had delivered two years earlier. This unit reveals the dazzle of locomotives in full *Rocket* dress. Taken at Joliet Union Station, this image might be titled "Santa Fe Meets Rock Island."

Wallace W. Abbey photograph, Center for Railroad Photography & Art coll., www.railphoto-art.org

The Rock Island gained local and industry recognition for introducing the nation's first streamlined suburban train. That event took place on November 17, 1949, when a diesel locomotive and its Pullman-Standard-built cars made their maiden run over the forty miles between Chicago and Joliet. The company proudly described the equipment: "Cars are made of light weight steel, equipped with coil spring trucks and shock absorbing devices for easy riding roller bearings, high speed electric brakes, and tight-lock couplers are other features." These twenty eighty-five-foot hundred-passenger capacity cars, eight of which were air-conditioned, were a popular improvement over the scores of Harriman coaches. These so-called "Capone Era" cars, with their rattan seats and open windows, had long outlived their usefulness. And the Rock Island became the first to dieselize

Following World War II, the Rock Island gussied up some of its major passenger stations, including La Salle Street Station. This photograph, which dates from the 1950s, shows the ticket counter that served Rock Island customers.

Dan Sabin coll.

During the waning years of the Farrington administration, some company passenger trains might be powered by a BL2, a diesel type frequently based in Cedar Rapids. This 1951 photograph shows No. 428, acquired in 1949, with its train waiting at the Waterloo, Iowa, station. The BL2 was an odd creature best described as an outlier locomotive.

Dan Sabin coll.

Branch lines often became the last stand for Rock Island steam. On November 24, 1949, No. 1952, a 2-8-0 locomotive, heads the northbound freight train No. 811 outside Oelwein, Iowa, on the Cedar Rapids-Decorah branch.

W. L. Heitter photograph, Ron Lundstrom coll.

completely its suburban service. Significantly, the number of steam passenger miles system-wide declined rapidly. In 1952 the only remaining passenger trains under steam were Nos. 6 and 9 between Chicago and Des Moines.[54]

The postwar years witnessed the triumph of diesel. By the end of 1952, the company had completely dieselized its operations, except during the following year for some seasonal freight traffic. The last steam locomotives in revenue service came in July 1953, and their final assignments occurred during the Des Moines River flood that struck the Iowa capital in April 1954. Although the company had had diesels for switching and passenger operations since the 1930s and had used twelve EMD four-unit FT units received in 1944 and 1945 to expedite its *Rocket* freights and twelve rare EMD F-2s acquired in 1946 to handle main-line freights, the process of retiring steam for freight operations accelerated in 1948. That year the company awarded EMD this impressive order: thirty F-7s, ten FP-7s, and three F-7s with steam boilers for passenger assignments. A year later EMD completed its delivery.[55]

Management loved dieselization. It realized that tremendous operating benefits could be achieved, saving roughly 25 percent on its investment when

Railroad enthusiasts loved to photograph No. 9014, an oddball Saint Louis Car Company–built 800 horsepower diesel. Photographed on July 28, 1948, this piece of motive power pulls a freight train through Oelwein, Iowa.

W. L. Heitter photograph, Ron Lundstrom coll.

freight diesels replaced 4-8-4s and other steamers. So the Rock Island pressed hard to acquire this power from various manufacturers and not just from EMD. But in the process the company, like many Class 1 roads, appeared to embrace the Noah's Ark practice of obtaining two from every manufacturer. This meant no standardization of parts and lash-ups of mismatched power. "The Rock Island got a lot of belated recognition by rail fans with its varied diesel fleet," commented locomotive historian Lloyd Stagner. "Although obvious problems arose over the economic validity of unstandardized dieselization, rail fans were not moved to question economics."[56]

The Farrington administration planned to work on additional line relocations, wishing to reduce grades and curvatures in order to accelerate freight and passenger schedules. Concentration centered on the Golden State Route. In addition to earlier relocations in Kansas and Missouri, the company tackled the hill and dale terrain of southern Iowa. In February 1946 it completed an 18.12-mile line from south of Centerville east to Paris, shortening that distance by nearly four miles and reducing the maximum grade from 1 to 0.5 percent and cutting maximum curvatures from four degrees to one. This betterment included a large steel bridge over the flood-prone Chariton River. Service to Unionville ended, but the company retained a small section of the original line to serve freight customers in Centerville and to interchange with the Burlington and the electric Southern Iowa Railway. As soon as this segment opened, another project continued eastward, stretching about seventeen miles from Paris to Floris. This line was completed on October 22, 1946. Finally, another seventeen-mile relocation, which started on May 20, 1946, focused on the troublesome line between Brighton and Ainsworth; it opened on August 15, 1947.[57]

In 1951 the Rock Island began work on the Atlantic Cutoff, "the largest rail relocation project ever attempted on the railroad." Just as southern Iowa contained hilly terrain, so too did the Chicago-Omaha artery in western Iowa. Already the Farrington administration had orchestrated 120 miles of line relocations, and this major Hawkeye State project involved 34 miles of construction west of Atlantic to a connection with the Chicago Great Western (CGW) at McClelland. The Rock Island also leased from the CGW about 11 miles of its Fort Dodge–Council Bluffs line beyond McClelland for rehabilitation. This $7 million project shortened the main stem by 10.2 miles and significantly reduced grades and curvatures. On September 15, 1953, the company inaugurated service over this impressive betterment. Cuts in some places measured sixty feet and featured one fill that contained about one million cubic feet of earth. The improved main line, which trimmed as much as half an hour from passenger schedules and one and a half hours from freight transit time, bypassed the communities of Shelby, Avoca, Walnut, and Marne, but for several years the company maintained "shuttle service over the old line to serve all of the these places except Marne." A year after completing the Atlantic Cutoff, the Rock Island opened six miles of reengineered line near Adair, east of Atlantic, and about the same time it finished a shorter relocation project outside Colfax, east of Des Moines.[58]

The postwar decade witnessed other aspects of the physical plant upgrades. The Rock Island completed several multimillion construction projects, including a passenger coach shop and yard at Forty-Seventh Street in Chicago and an electric shop at Silvis, Illinois, designed to service the expanding diesel locomotive fleet. In 1948 the Rock Island's first push-button hump-retarder yard took shape at Armourdale in Kansas City, Kansas, featuring forty-three classification tracks, floodlights, radio communications, and an icing dock. "This awe-inspiring facility is designed for speedy and efficient classification of freight cars." A year later a similar hump-retarder classification yard opened at Silvis. "The operation is directed by control operators stationed in three 30-foot towers," explained a railroad source. "The entire

The Farrington administration took pride in upgrades to its sprawling yards complex in Silvis, Illinois, and Armourdale, Kansas, during the immediate post–World War II days. Hump towers served as signature structures.

Dan Sabin coll.

area is illuminated by 100 foot flood light towers to permit 24-hour operation." Silvis was even busier than Armourdale. "It is the 'hub' of Rock Island
freight operation with 30 heavy trains entering and leaving the yards daily.
About 3,325 cars daily, inbound and outbound, are handled." The company
bragged about these two classification yards: "[They] provided the last word
for a more efficient operation of the system's fleet of Rocket Freights." The
Rock Island pushed ahead with installation of automatic block signals. In
1949, for example, workers placed these safety devices on sixty-three miles
of track between Brinkley and North Little Rock, Arkansas. That year the
final link of installing CTC equipment between Chicago and Kansas City
took place. By 1952 the company had installed an extensive radio network,
operating end-to-end service along approximately 2,500 miles of main line. "It
blankets terminals with swift, certain contact, joins way-side stations, moving trains and dispatchers' offices for the fullest use of every piece of rolling
stock," claimed the Communications and Electronics Division of Motorola.
The track structure was not ignored; hundreds of miles of heavier rail and tons
of rock ballast graced rights-of-way. Freight equipment orders included thousands of box, gondola, hopper, and covered hopper cars. Planned progress was
proudly symbolized with the 1945 opening of "the most completely equipped
laboratory in the railroad industry," located in Chicago at Forty-Seventh
Street and Wentworth Avenue. "The 16,275 square feet of floor area in the
building is functionally subdivided to meet the separate requirements of
analysis and research related to the study of materials and supplies used in
railroad operations," the company reported. This coverage ranged from elec-
trical and mechanical apparatus on the *Rocket* streamliners to the testing of
paint, fuel, and lubricants.[59]

To help celebrate its ongoing accomplishments, the Rock Island joined
with thirty-five railroads to participate in the Chicago Railroad Fair of 1948
and 1949. Conceived by the public relations department of the Chicago &
North Western, this event commemorated the centennial of the first railroad to
serve Chicago—North Western predecessor Galena & Chicago Union—and
spotlighted the post–World War II railroad industry by showcasing historic
and modern equipment, promoting passenger travel, and instilling the notion
of progress. On a mile-long strip abutting Lake Michigan south of the Loop,
the Rock Island created its "Rocket Village" in the middle of a fifty-acre site.
Centerpieces of the exhibit included a nineteenth-century wooden Rock
Island dining car and the stainless-steel El Café coffee shop-tavern car built
for the *Golden Rocket*. The fair exceeded all expectations. Between July 20 and
October 2, 1948, more than 2.5 million visitors paid a modest admission fee

to learn about railroading. This overwhelming public response led to a repeat performance; more than 2.7 million people attended the extravaganza during summer and early fall 1949. Farrington, who served on the fair's executive committee, wrote this copy for the company's 1949 fair brochure: "[Rocket Village provides] a 'taste' of the gay Fiesta atmosphere of the Southwest; a glimpse of the Colorado Rockies; a striking contrast of the old and new in Dining Cars; dancing, movies, entertainment, refreshments . . . at your service!" The Rock Island involvement at the Chicago fair far exceeded its modest centennial celebrations that occurred three years later, with theme "A marvel in 1852—even more so in 1952."[60]

The Rock Island could afford to participate in the Chicago Railroad Fair. The year 1948 saw its gross income establish a new high mark of $197,404,990, but a decline followed in 1949 and 1950. Why this downswing? The explanation lies with the slump in the national economy, coupled with two events that hurt earnings. Toward the end of World War II, a new era of rancor and strife appeared on the labor front. Most significantly for the Rock Island members of the feisty Switchmen's Union of North America ("Snakes"), who for some time had been negotiating for a national contract that called for a forty-hour week and an eighteen-cent pay raise, left their posts. On June 25, 1950, for the first time in company history, switchmen brought about a total operational shutdown. Finally, through the intervention of the Truman administration, business resumed on July 9. The Korean War had just broken out, and the US military would not tolerate a disruption of transcontinental traffic. The switchmen won. They got their original demands along with other concessions. Their victory contributed to soaring labor costs, which jumped from approximately $65 million annually in 1944 to nearly $80 million by 1948 and continued to increase into the 1950s. The year 1950 also saw a widespread drought on the southern and central Great Plains, which adversely affected grain production and hence decreased carloadings. Happily, 1951 set a landmark record in gross income of $198,549,699.[61]

The impressive gross revenues for 1951 would have been greater had the Rock Island not experienced the worst natural disaster in its ninety-nine-year history. In July repeated storms pounded the watersheds of the Kansas (Kaw) and Missouri Rivers in the greater Kansas City region. The recently opened Armourdale Yard, located near the confluence of these surging rivers, sustained the brunt of the flooding. On July 12 the first alarm sounded when the Rock Island bridge at Topeka went underwater, halting traffic between Kansas City and southwestern points. Soon thereafter, with little notice, floodwaters rose rapidly at the Armourdale complex. Employees succeeded in moving diesel locomotives to the top of the hump, but they could not rescue hundreds

Repeated rainstorms that struck parts of the Midwest during July 1951 caused havoc along hundreds of miles of Rock Island trackage. A freight train proceeds cautiously through a flooded section near Chesterfield, Missouri, on the Saint Louis line.

Dan Sabin Coll.

of freight cars. Water engulfed them, ruining the contents of scores of loaded cars. Sadly, workers who lived nearby lost their homes. But through herculean efforts operations were restored "in record time." The price tag for the physical damage neared $5.5 million, and the loss of traffic and cost of rerouting approached an estimated $9 million.[62]

One factor that contributed to the overall health of the Rock Island during the postwar era involved the growth of on-line industries. Historically, the company was limited in several urban centers, such as the Twin Cities, because it gained entrance through trackage rights. Even in the home terminal of Chicago, industrial trackage was woefully small. During this period the industrial department made some important gains. Acquisition of the Pullman Railroad Company, which officially took place on January 1, 1950, bolstered Windy City traffic and traffic potential. This nineteen-mile switching road, owned by the Pullman-Standard Car Manufacturing Company, also included 364 acres of prime industrial real estate that was close to the Calumet Harbor and a major highway entering South Chicago. "This property is well located and will enable us to provide locations for heavy industry in the City of Chicago," the company announced in 1949. About this time the Rock Island built a five-mile cutoff line in greater Denver, permitting freight trains to move directly from Sandown Junction east of the city on the Union Pacific's Kansas Pacific line to the new North Yard (the Denver origin and termination point of Rock Island freight trains), a joint venture with the Denver & Rio Grande Western. This well-placed trackage ended painfully slow journeys through Denver's congested freight yards, simplified the movement of transcontinental freight, and cut hours off the transit time through this gateway. For future development, the industrial department also acquired 355 acres in the Mile High City that led to a traffic-generating automobile transfer facility. The company made more land purchases designed to attract businesses, including seventy acres in Colorado Springs and eighty acres in Des Moines. During the ten years from 1943 to 1952, nearly three thousand new industries would be served, but most were only small to moderate rail users. Revenues generated from agriculture continued to dominate, constituting about a third of all income.[63]

AN ERA ENDS

As the decade of the 1950s progressed, optimism still reigned at the Rock Island. Until 1956 gross income remained relatively stable, helped by freight and passenger revenues generated by military traffic during the Korean War. Take comments made by John W. Barriger III, former head of the Railroad Division of the RFC and ex-president of the Monon Railroad who since mid-1953 had served as a Rock Island vice president. That November, in a presentation to the New York Society of Security Analysts, he offered this glowing, if not exaggerated, assessment: "The Rock Island is not only strong from the standpoint of property conditions, management and operations, but likewise has one of the most conservative capital structures in relation to its property value, revenues and earning power of any American Railway."[64]

Still, there were indications that the Rock Island was about to encounter serious challenges. Competition from automobiles and trucks steadily increased, accelerated by the rapid construction of multilane, controlled-access highways, most of all by federal interstates after 1956. Use of these high-speed arteries meant that more high-end goods and riders left the rails. Commercial aviation, too, drew away long-distance business travelers from the *Rockets* and the *Golden State*. Furthermore, virtually unregulated and untaxed barge lines increased their haulage of bulk commodities, principally aggregates, coal, grain, and petroleum. A veteran employee recalled that after 1952 the company installed less than a million crossties annually, an indication that track maintenance was experiencing cutbacks.[65]

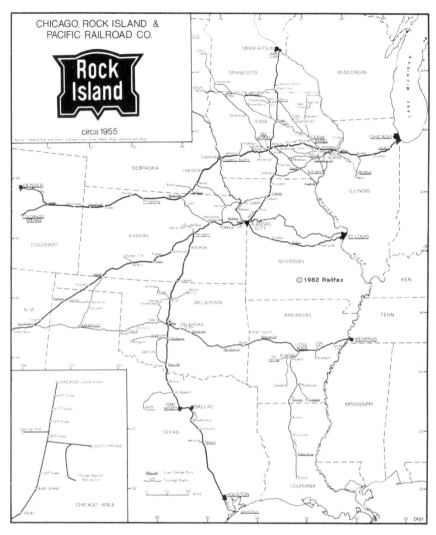

As the John D. Farrington era moved toward its close, the Rock Island continued to maintain a web of main and branch lines. In 1955 it operated a total of 7,923 miles.

Author's coll.

Although John D. Farrington had garnered widespread recognition for his "Rock Island miracle" and established himself as "Mr. Rock Island Railroad," he, like all presidents, had limitations, such as his frugality. If one were to visit his La Salle Street Station office, located in the executive suite on the tenth floor, it would reveal a Spartan appearance; no luxury furniture or expensive decorations adorned his work space. That might be considered an exemplary personal trait, but when it was applied to the railroad, John Barriger said it well: "Being a penny pincher [Farrington] limited his plans to the minimum necessities of the present rather than expanding them to the opportunities of the future."[66]

Yet that Farrington mind-set could pay dividends. In 1951 he fretted about mounting losses with dining-car operations. That year the Rock Island lost a reported million dollars, much of which was caused by food spoilage. The company was hardly unusual in the industry; diners were consistent financial losers. The Farrington response? He ordered executive assistant Merle Reynolds, who surprisingly lacked a background in restaurant operations, to explore the causes of red ink and to take corrective measures. This he did with vigor and success. In April 1952, the Rock Island introduced carefully studied precooked, frozen, and restored meals—or what railroad writer Lucius Beebe despairingly called "prefabricated dinners"—on most of its trains out of Chicago. These offerings were prepared at the Fifty-First Street commissary in Chicago and served from refitted onboard kitchens. Support commissaries also appeared in El Reno and Minneapolis as these menu items expanded to additional dining-car runs. Reynolds substituted paper mats and napkins, plastic dishes, and stainless-steel cutlery for the traditional table settings, although partial reintroduction of original items—for example, linen tablecloths—occurred. By 1953 the Rock Island claimed that Reynolds's innovations had trimmed monthly deficits by nearly 25 percent.[67]

Not only was there that modest dining-car victory, but Farrington sought to make the Rock Island less dependent upon agricultural traffic. Yet his administration failed to attract major on-line shippers. Furthermore, Farrington lacked an aggressiveness when it came to traffic solicitations; he lacked enthusiasm for traffic people and traffic associations. Farrington did make an effort to bring the company a committed traffic person when he hired John Barriger. But Barriger laughingly said that his boss "believes that traffic, like rain, falls on the just and the unjust alike." Naive thinking at best.[68]

John Barriger expressed additional concerns about John Farrington. As he explained in 1973, "Farrington failed to make this railroad the competitive force in its area that its fundamental advantages offered. His lack of vision and fiscal courage alienated Southern Pacific and led it to concentrate its interest for an eastern outlet in the Cotton Belt. There had been a time during the war years when SP stock was still selling at single digit prices and while Rock Island had sufficient cash to buy control of it but failed to do so although the opportunity was considered." This esteemed industry expert continued: "This led Cotton Belt to solicit non-perishable freight to and from SP points west of El Paso going through the St. Louis rather than via Rock Island and Kansas

City–Chicago gateways. This was a serious and lasting blow to CRI&P." Here's Barriger's final assessment of Farrington and the Rock Island: "While Farrington did develop RI temporarily into a moderately successful property throughout the period of his active association with that railroad, he would never approve of standards for its rehabilitation, maintenance and service to meet effectively the competition of his very strong surrounding rivals, Union Pacific, Santa Fe, Burlington and Missouri Pacific."[69]

After nearly three decades with the Rock Island, John Farrington was wearing out, and by 1956 he had reached the customary age for industry white-collar employees to retire. Then there was his domestic life; he felt the heartache of his wife's death in 1954, although he remarried the following year. Like other contemporary railroad executives, Farrington retained a presence at company headquarters, but the daily hands-on operations went to another railroader. "Farrington loved the Rock Island," opined one Rock Island employee. "He always wanted to make it better. He knew that he had made a real difference." The industry believed that Farrington had done much to uplift a listless, dilapidated, and debt-soaked railroad of the 1930s and accepted his own assessment that the Rock Island was the "hardest railroad in the U.S. to operate." Yes, John Farrington excelled, but he did so with limitations.[70]

SAVING THE ROCK

6

ALTHOUGH JOHN D. FARRINGTON REMAINED ACTIVELY INVOLVED IN the affairs of the Rock Island by chairing its board of directors, his successor as chief executive officer was Downing B. Jenks (1915–1996), whom Farrington had groomed for his job. Born in Portland, Oregon, Jenks showed a love of railroads early on. As a youngster he enjoyed playing with his model trains and spending time around the railroad corridor. Apparently this fascination was in his blood, as he had come from a distinguished railroad family. Jenks's paternal grandfather, Cyrus, had served as a superintendent for the Great Northern Railway (GN), and his father, Charles, served as general manager of the Spokane, Portland & Seattle Railway (SP&S) at the time of his birth and later became vice president of operations at GN. His maternal grandfather, W. O. Downing, claimed a railroad connection, working as an attorney in Missouri for several roads, including the Chicago, Burlington & Quincy (Burlington). "In Downing Jenks's mind it was not enough just to follow in these footsteps," concluded historian Craig Miner. "He wished to build upon the family tradition to influence rail history."[1]

The bright and determined Jenks received excellent preparations for his twenty-one-year career at the Rock Island. While an industrial engineering major at Yale University, he found summer employment as a chainman on the SP&S. After obtaining his bachelors of science in 1937, Jenks worked briefly in the engineering department of the Pennsylvania Railroad before he joined the GN as a roadmaster. During the course of nine years, he advanced to division engineer, trainmaster, and division superintendent. Like so many railroaders, Jenks interrupted his career during World War II, serving between 1942 and 1945 with the 704th Railway Grand Division in Africa and Europe. While in the army he rose in rank from first lieutenant to lieutenant colonel.[2]

Following his military service, Jenks resumed his railroading career. Initially he worked for the Great Northern, but in 1948 he accepted the position of general manager at the Chicago & Eastern Illinois Railroad (C&EI). The following year Jenks became vice president, but he stayed only briefly, joining the Rock Island in 1950 as assistant vice president. Soon he won elevation to vice president and general manager. Admired by Farrington and respected by other officials and employees, he soon became assistant vice president for operations and then vice president for operations. In 1953 Jenks advanced to executive vice president and joined the board of directors. Three years later he became the Rock Island president at the tender age of forty. Jenks's rapid ascendency was widely applauded. "Fortunately for this company, in its executive vice president, Downing B. Jenks, there was available within its own official family an executive of exceptional talent, capacity for leadership, and experience in railway administration," said John W. Barriger III, then a Rock Island vice president.[3]

As his military background might suggest, Jenks was a fastidious person and a no-nonsense railroader. "He brooked no moral compromise," noted Craig Miner, "and subscribed to a personal code much like that of the Boy Scouts, of which he served as national president." As the scouting head in 1977, Jenks glorified the values of "integrity, honesty, [and] acceptance of authority." This one-year term gave him opportunities to extol his favorite leisure pursuits of mountain hiking and other outdoor activities.[4]

When Downing Jenks took command, he demonstrated that he was a hands-on railroader. This energetic executive was not about to become bound to the office. "You've got to get out and see the property, see what's going on, talk to people." This had been Jenks's management style since his days as a division superintendent on the Great Northern, and it remained so at the Rock Island and eventually when he became head of the Missouri Pacific.[5]

What was Jenks's presidential vision? Not long before he assumed the job, he made it clear that the Rock Island faced serious challenges. These included increased modal competition, burdensome federal and state regulations, excessive taxation, rising labor costs, heavy dependence on agricultural traffic, and the constant need for multiple physical upgrades. In his mind, these challenges would be best met with opportunities found in modernization, innovation, and employee training.[6]

Jenks wholeheartedly endorsed the company's training program, which had been launched in 1951. It was much needed. "When we started our training program, we found that deans and instructors [at colleges and universities] were definitely not recommending to their students that they get into the railroad business," he recalled. "We were able to convince them of the fallacy of this thinking, and we are now [1954] getting very enthusiastic support from the schools." This proactive work paid dividends. A good example was the career of William "Bill" Hoenig, who became a top operating officer at the Rock Island and later a senior executive at the Southern Pacific. "When I was completing my degree in civil engineering at Iowa State College in 1956, Professor William Thompson told me that the Rock Island would be a good place to work and to find opportunities." Hoenig considered this "the best advice that I ever received at Iowa State."[7]

Surely Jenks's training at Yale and his earlier experiences at the GN, the C&EI, and more recently the Rock Island convinced him that modern technologies would do much to retain and attract customers and bolster revenues. Aspects of the past troubled Jenks. "We still dispatch trains to a large extent using Morse code. We still use some freight and passenger cars built back in 1910. Many of our operating and shop practices are definitely what were developed and in use during the last century." His solutions included improving communications, principally with radio and microwave equipment and even television cameras. Jenks showed interest in the potential of AC-powered diesel locomotives, advanced rolling stock designs, welded rail, and what might be called information processors. Resembling other industry thinkers—most notably John Barriger, whose well-received book, *Super Railroads for a Dynamic American Economy*, appeared in 1956—Jenks promoted grade and curvature reductions and expanded centralized traffic control (CTC). He especially applauded research conducted by individual carriers and railroad supply firms. "The only way the railroad industry can become decadent is through decadent thinking." Creative ideas and their implementation should guarantee a bright future, making for sustained resiliency. The company's current tag line, "Rock Island Lines—the railroad of planned progress . . . geared to the nation's future," could be achieved.[8]

Downing Jenks anticipated tough challenges. He knew that it would be a constant struggle to manage the repeated wage demands of organized labor. By 1957 wages and benefits had soared nearly 60 percent in a decade, and there appeared to be no end in sight. Since the progressive era there remained the seemingly perpetual need to seek regulatory and tax relief. Jenks was willing, even anxious, to negotiate and to explain Rock Island's case. Yet he realized that he could not move at warp speed to bring about change. Jenks and his administration were helpless to combat the inflation that affected the industry, from more expensive track materials to office supplies.

Neither the Rock Island nor Jenks had given up on certain long-distance passenger trains. During the twilight years of the Farrington administration, the company made adjustments on certain runs. Systemwide, the number of passengers had dropped from 11,713,373 in 1951 during the height of the Korean War to 10,601,100 in 1953. A leading example of the drop involved the Choctaw Route. By the early 1950s, ridership had fallen off considerably between Memphis and Amarillo, and no longer was there a need to offer a "complete travel service." Therefore, in February 1952 the *Choctaw Rocket* (in 1950 the *Rocket* name was dropped west of Oklahoma City) was replaced by local trains between Memphis and Oklahoma City. In August 1953 two Budd Company Rail Diesel Cars (RDC-3) entered service on the daily 355-mile Little Rock–Oklahoma City run. These self-propelled, stainless-steel units could pull, if needed, a lightweight coach. The primary purpose of this train was to handle the US mail and packages for the Railway Express Agency. Since the company anticipated a modest passenger load, it had no need for a baggage section, a standard RDC-3 feature, and so Budd extended space for mail handling, creating a thirty-foot Railway Post Office compartment. The two RDC-3s, initially named the *Choctaw* but later called the *Choctaw Rockette*, operated between Little Rock and Oklahoma City, but they were extended to Memphis in September 1953 and to Amarillo in July 1955. (The *Cherokee*, which in March 1949 replaced the *Memphis-Californian* between Memphis and Tucumcari, continued to serve the entire Choctaw Route until 1967.) The success of these two RDC-3s led to the purchase of three additional units. One Budd car arrived in 1955, and the others entered service the following year. Two operated between Kansas City and Fort Worth but for a portion of the trip became the rear car of the *Kansas City Rocket*, and another rolled over the seventy-three miles between Herington and Wichita.[9]

There would be much more buzz about the January 30, 1956, morning debut of the *Jet Rocket*, a futuristic train that offered the hope of making passenger operations financially sustainable. "This lightweight, low-center-of-gravity train," proclaimed *Modern Railroads*, "combines comfort, speed, and economy." Built at a cost of $600,000 by American Car & Foundry Company, the *Jet Rocket*, an adaptation of Spain's Talgo trains, consisted of three independent car units that provided seating for 304 passengers, and a lighter-weight EMD 1,200-horsepower locomotive provided the power. All went smoothly during the well-publicized inaugural trip from Chicago to Peoria. "It is our belief that with this train we will be able to re-educate the traveling public to the advantages of train travel," opined Jenks, "getting them off the jam-packed highways and into the worry-free relaxation of a train." Soon the public timetable dropped the *Peoria Rocket*. In its place the *Jet Rocket*, renamed the *Peorian*, made two daily 322-mile round trips between Illinois's two largest cities.[10]

The *Jet Rocket* attracts the curious on a chilly day in Des Moines. Shortly this futuristic train will enter regular service between Chicago and Peoria.

Dan Sabin Coll.

The experimental No. 1, the former *Jet Rocket*, which the Rock Island relegated quickly to Chicago suburban assignments, is outbound from La Salle Street Station on April 20, 1956. Soon it would be scrapped at the Silvis Shops. The company's three ultra-lightweight trains, according to Rock Island diesel authority Louis Marre, were "heartily detested by anyone who had to endure their noisy, rough-riding, bus-body coaches."

Jim Buckley photograph, Louis A. Marre coll.

However, enthusiasm for the *Jet Rocket* quickly turned to dross. The Rock Island, including Jenks, realized its purchase had been a mistake. The public agreed. The train experienced mechanical problems, especially with its braking system. Riders found it noisy and rough-riding, and they disapproved of its small seats, cramped toilets, and low ceilings. The novel closed-circuit television camera, mounted in the nose of the locomotive, proved disturbing. "The idea was to create some excitement by giving lounge passengers a simulated cab ride," explained one commentator. "However, after the paying customers got a look at the repeated near-misses with pedestrians, school buses, gasoline trucks and gravel haulers at grade crossings, excitement quickly gave way to sheer terror." After several months the *Peoria Rocket* returned, and the *Jet Rocket*, after a modest reconfiguration of interior spaces, entered commuter service between Chicago and Joliet. Because of high maintenance costs and the lack of a buyer, this experimental train eventually became so much junk.[11]

While modifications to passenger operations were ongoing, the Rock Island adjusted its mileage. During the 1950s, though, the abandonment of branches was relatively modest. The most notable involved trimming the Watertown line back from Watertown to Clear Lake, South Dakota, a distance of twenty-three miles, although the company sold about two miles in greater Watertown to the Minneapolis & St. Louis Railway. A similar mileage reduction came with the retirement of the Des Arc-to-Searcy, Arkansas, appendage. Several smaller removals also occurred, including the remainder of the Ardmore, Oklahoma, branch. Just as there were line construction projects associated with track relocations, a somewhat parallel event occurred in 1958 when eleven new miles opened between Winterset and Winear (Earlham), Iowa, and a connection with the east-west main line.[12] Although the company had served Winterset from Des Moines for more than eighty years, handling cars from a quarry near Winterset over the existing branch had two drawbacks. Since the rock was destined for a customer on the western side of the capital city, it had to travel a longer distance, and there was a wheel tax for switching on the Des Moines Union Railroad. The Winear addition allowed the Rock Island to retire twenty-five miles of the Winterset branch from Summerset Junction yet still maintain service to Indianola.[13]

Downing Jenks did his best to upgrade the physical plant and equipment, including motive power and specialized freight cars, and to attract trackside industries, but these were daunting tasks. One encouraging response involved embracing the piggyback revolution that had begun industry-wide during the mid-1950s and that included such carriers as the Missouri-Kansas-Texas, Chicago & North Western (North Western), and Pennsylvania. In 1954 the Interstate Commerce Commission (ICC), in a landmark case, had ruled that motor carriers could enter into through-route and joint-rate arrangements with railroads for piggyback, and railroads could transport freight for shippers and freight forwarders on open tariffs.[14] The Rock Island had experimented with the "truck ferry" concept before World War II, but because of disappointing financial returns and the anti-piggyback attitude of operating personnel, it did not reintroduce the service until 1958. The business appeared promising, although profit margins were tight. The company did benefit from having its Rock Island Motor Transport (RIMT) subsidiary as a participant. This attitude came to prevail: "Piggyback combines the absolute best features of rail and highway transportation."[15]

Even with the introduction of piggyback service, the overall financials did not look either good or encouraging. Operating revenues, which amounted to $213,9388,266 in 1952, dropped to $189,381,739 in 1955 but rose to $207,883,953 in 1958. During these years, net railway operating income generally sank: $25,339,376 in 1952 and just $13,188,857 in 1958. In 1959, there would be an uptick of $219,453,607 in operating revenues, but in 1960 they fell to $211,775,603. Yet net income plunged from $11,843,607 in 1959 to a distressing $8,341,221 the following year. Modal competition, increased operating expenses, a national business recession, and other factors were the culprits.[16]

Downing Jenks envisioned a way to remedy a deteriorating situation: corporate merger. After all, the late 1950s saw the start of railroad unifications that heightened into merger madness during the 1960s and 1970s. For the decade preceding 1966, the ICC received fifty merger applications from Class I roads. "Everyone, it seemed, was trying to find a dance partner," opined an industry executive. The result would be that by the early 1980s numerous "fallen flags" dotted the corporate graveyard, with parent companies adding subsidiaries or even forming wholly new units. These initial corporate marriages looked promising, specifically the Louisville & Nashville Railroad absorbing the Nashville, Chattanooga & St. Louis Railway and Norfolk & Western Railroad acquiring the Virginian Railway. The latter merger made two vibrant Pocahontas coal haulers into an immensely profitable one and helped to intensify unification talks. Some industry experts believed that a real threat of financial disaster existed for those carriers who failed to find one or more partners.

The Rock Island's first foray into merger discussions took place in 1959 and involved the North Western. These two sprawling granger roads largely complemented each other, with the 7,533-mile Rock Island having a strong presence in Missouri, Kansas, Oklahoma, Arkansas, and parts of Texas and the 10,729-mile North Western operating a web of lines in Nebraska, South Dakota, and Wisconsin. They were, of course, historic competitors between the Chicago and Omaha gateways. Both, too, had extensive trackage in Iowa and sections of Minnesota and Illinois. By the late 1950s, midwestern carriers had excess capacity, and unifications could streamline the railroad map and improve earnings. In fact, only 3 percent of the Rock Island's track miles, primarily between Chicago and Iowa, were considered "heavily used." Unlike the Downing road, the North Western enjoyed a stronger industrial base, although it also was a major hauler of agricultural traffic.[17]

The attempt to unite the Rock Island and the North Western, however logical, went nowhere. The principal sticking point involved the value of each company. Moreover, there were personalities differences. Apparently Downing Jenks did not get along with Henry Crown (1896–1990), the largest individual Rock Island investor and chair of its finance committee. Crown had arranged these meetings with Ben W. Heineman, the youthful, dynamic North Western board chairman. He admired Heineman, likely because Heineman thought big. As the North Western head admitted, "It's no secret that I favor the construction of a vast railroad system centered broadly in the west, consisting of *at least* [*sic*] the North Western, the Milwaukee, the Rock Island and the Chicago Great Western, but including such other smaller roads as might care to join with us as well."[18]

At first glance Henry Crown might be compared to former Rock Island cotrustee Aaron Colnon. Both men fiercely promoted their own agendas, yet there was a world of difference between them. Although each man was ambitious, hard driving, and intelligent, Crown was honorable—"His word was his bond"—and extremely wealthy. Furthermore, he demonstrated an acute memory, possessed an amazing grasp of detail, and always prepared before entering into a business commitment. "When [Crown] gets into a deal," remarked a Chicago real-estate executive, "he knows the size of your underwear."[19]

Much more so than Colnon, Crown was a true American success story. The son of poor, hardworking Russian-Jewish immigrants (née Krinsky) and one of seven children, he had limited formal education, having dropped out of school after the eighth grade. After various jobs, the young Crown joined his two brothers in the building-supply business, in 1919 launching the Sol R. Crown Company, predecessor of what became the Material Service Corporation, the largest building-supply concern in the world. In 1959 Crown merged Material Supply into his General Dynamics Corporation.[20]

Although Colonel Henry Crown (so called because of his rank in the US Army Corps of Engineers during World War II) led an active business life with the Material Service Corporation and other large-scale business investments, he became interested in Rock Island securities during its second bankruptcy. While recuperating from a horseback-riding accident in 1946, Crown scoured financial publications to relieve his boredom, and that is when the Rock Island caught his eye. He saw that its bonds were selling for as little as thirty cents on the dollar, and that intrigued him. Furthermore, these bonds traded for less than the cash the company had on hand. Crown started buying. His son Robert allegedly said, "Dad, another bushel basket of those damned bonds showed up today." Owning more than $4 million worth of these depressed securities at the time of the 1948 reorganization, Crown exchanged them for 100,000 shares of Rock Island preferred and common stock. The following year he and two Rock Island board associates, grain dealer James Norris and tractor manufacturer Charles Wiman, bought out the holdings of investor Robert Young, amounting to 250,000 shares.[21]

Not only did Crown have a large financial stake in the Rock Island (and other major roads), but the industry fascinated him. "There was a railroad team track not far from our house on Milwaukee Road," he once recalled.

"I would lie in bed awake, hearing the whistles and the bells of locomotives, and think how exciting it would be to drive them back and forth across the country." At least Jenks and Crown had something in common: love of the flanged wheel.[22]

Downing Jenks never abandoned his desire for a merger. In 1958 John Farrington had proposed corporate marriage with the 9,889-mile Chicago, Milwaukee, St. Paul & Pacific Railroad (Milwaukee Road), another struggling granger road. Historically, its midwestern lines were concentrated in Illinois, Iowa, Minnesota, Wisconsin, and South Dakota. In 1909, however, the Milwaukee Road broke out of its service territory when it opened its Pacific Coast Extension. This well-engineered albeit costly construction linked existing trackage in South Dakota with deep water in Washington State. Jenks liked this merger plan. Informal unification talks progressed to the point where the Rock Island and Milwaukee boards approved a $350,000 joint study by the respected consulting firm of Coverdale & Colpitts. Both Farrington and Jenks saw hope, but on November 19, 1960, the Rock Island board shelved the project. Henry Crown was the principal culprit, believing that combining two weak roads would create a larger weakling. At this point he appeared more favorably inclined to have the North Western as a merger partner. Henry Crown continued to disappoint Jenks. "Crown seemed to be in favor of all the merger proposals except the one we were working on," he said sardonically.[23]

Another possibility developed. Why not a Rock Island merger with the 8,732-mile fan-shaped Missouri Pacific Railroad (MOP)? Henry Crown suggested merger discussions with this Saint Louis–based carrier, which interchanged with Rock Island at such places as Saint Louis, Kansas City, Omaha, Little Rock, Wichita, and Dallas-Fort Worth. Crown recognized that the MOP enjoyed access to the chemical and refinery business on the Gulf coast of Texas and Louisiana and had other traffic attractions. In early November 1960, Jenks traveled to Saint Louis to discuss unification with MOP officials. While they expressed no interest in becoming corporately involved with the Rock Island, Jenks impressed them. Several weeks after Jenks's initial visit, he accepted an offer to become MOP president and board member. His decision to leave the Rock Island stemmed largely from his unhappiness with Crown. Jenks, too, was a realist, knowing that the Rock Island faced a multitude of systemic problems. At the MOP, "a railroad with a future," Jenks demonstrated his administrative skills, making it one of America's most respected carriers and after 1983 a productive part of the Union Pacific. One Rock Island official said, "Unfortunately Jenks used his greatest talents on the MOP!"[24]

The resignation of Downing Jenks created a leadership void. The board, however, quickly named board chair John Farrington as interim president. "I intend my tenure as president to be temporary," he told shareholders. "The management team taking over is experienced, aggressive and, I feel, capable of operating this profitably, even in times of reduced traffic volume, as has been done in the past."[25]

Farrington was correct; he remained in the presidential suite only briefly. However, his assessment that the next management team would be capable was mistaken. R. Ellis Johnson (1909–1974) became the next president. On February 1, 1961, he assumed the newly created position of executive vice president, and he subsequently became chief executive. This Osawatomie, Kansas, native, who came from a middle-class family, received a public school education in his hometown and at age sixteen launched his railroad career locally with the Missouri Pacific as an assistant file clerk. Johnson remained with the MOP in various office capacities until he joined the Rock Island in 1936 as secretary to the general manager in Kansas City. For the next seven years, he served as assistant trainmaster and as trainmaster in several locations before taking a two-year stint as superintendent of the Burlington-Rock Island Railroad in Houston. After World War II, Johnson held additional superintendent assignments, and in time he became general manager in Des Moines. Continuing to advance, Johnson won promotion in 1954 to vice president of operations. Farrington liked Johnson, believing him to be a good operating man and presidential material, and the board agreed.[26]

Ellis Johnson was no Downing Jenks. In reality he was "an old-time railroader who liked to cuss a lot," hardly a carbon copy of the talented Jenks. Johnson unfortunately lacked financial and leadership skills. He certainly was not the executive to navigate a successful merger, whether with the Southern Pacific, Union Pacific, or some other road. A Rock Island official explained, "He was a caretaker president."[27]

There is considerable evidence to support Johnson's depiction as manager of the status quo. Between 1961 and 1965, the Rock Island barely held on, "living on borrowed time." Operating revenues remained flat, at $203,332,262 in 1961; $200,926,687 in 1962; $202,407,391 in 1963; and $204,641,965 in 1964. Net income, though, dipped from $6,516,163 in 1961 to $3,844,785 in 1964. When it came to something as mundane as the volume of crossties installed, during the Johnson presidency the number was approximately 450,000 annually. This was at least half the number needed, but likely it should have been

The Rock Island attempted to manage declining passenger volume by using its small fleet of Budd-built Rail Diesel Cars (RDC). In July 1962 a few revenue patrons board northbound No. 28 in El Reno, Oklahoma. The power for this train does not come from RDC No. 9016 but rather from an A unit and a GP7. This surely was an unprofitable trip for the company.

George Werner photograph

a million or more, especially on deteriorating branch lines where slow orders were rampant. The movement of wheat, vital to the railroad's bottom line, also dipped, largely because of poor growing conditions. The company was negatively affected, too, by increased truck competition, expanding interstate highway construction, increasing labor costs, and detrimental federal and state regulations.

As president, Johnson still oversaw some needed improvements and growth. One example involved new suburban equipment. In 1964 the company took delivery of twenty Budd-built double-deck stainless-steel air-conditioned commuter coaches, an important component to upgrading its suburban fleet. Then there was an impressive rise in piggyback movements, with both truck trailers and auto-rack cars. Intermodal traffic (trailer-on-flat car, or TOFC) increased by more than 30 percent in 1962 and by another 40 percent in 1963. In 1963 the Rock Island joined Trailer-Train, launched in 1955 by the Pennsylvania and Norfolk & Western. This cooperatively owned company standardized TOFC practices and provided members with good equipment at reasonable costs. Involvement with Trailer-Train contributed to the Rock Island's solid growth.[28]

At times the Rock Island did not have the financial resources to construct state-of-the-art intermodal facilities, and so it made do with what it had. "They [Rock Island personnel] were good improvisors. In order to load trailers onto flat cars, for example, they simply took an old flat car, removed the trucks from one end in order to create a ramp up to the height they needed. It cost them $1,200," remarked a Union Pacific official. "In contrast, UP did the same thing in Denver with a $14,000 structure that was built so solidly you could load the Empire State Building right on top."[29]

LANGDON RENAISSANCE

By 1965 Colonel Henry Crown, the "Rock Island Lines potentate," and other company insiders wanted to change the corporate leadership. They agreed that Ellis Johnson was not the chief executive to foster growth in an increasingly challenging transportation environment. For some time Crown had in mind for the job a top-notch railroader: Jervis Langdon Jr. (1905–2004).

Who was this railroad executive? Unlike Ellis Johnson, this Elmira, New York, native came from a wealthy and distinguished family. Langdon was proud to claim Samuel Langhorne Clemens (Mark Twain) as his great uncle (by marriage). The future railroader had an excellent formal education, which included precollege years at the Hill School in Pennsylvania; Cornell University, following in the footsteps of his father; and somewhat later the Cornell University Law School. Like Downing Jenks, Langdon early on fell in love with railroads—a passion that his uncle Edward Loomis, a senior Lehigh Valley Railroad official, helped to cultivate. The young Langdon reveled in exploration of the Lehigh shops and yards in nearby Sayre, Pennsylvania. The gregarious and unassuming Langdon struck up friendships with employees, and they allowed him to "catch a ride [to and from Elmira] on a Lehigh train."[30]

In 1927 Jervis Langdon went railroading with the Lehigh. Although Uncle Edward had become president, Langdon started as an entry-level clerk in New York City. After all, railroaders, including college graduates, had a long-standing tradition of launching their careers on the bottom rung of the corporate ladder. Since Langdon did not want to be known as the president's pet, he accepted the advice of an acquaintance and entered law school. Yet he was not about to abandon the industry that he adored. With degree and bar admission in hand, he returned temporarily to the Lehigh but soon joined the New York Central's legal department. Starting in the summer of 1934, he worked on a succession of rate cases and other assignments. Although he liked the Central, he accepted an offer from the Chesapeake & Ohio (C&O) two years later to become an assistant general attorney at a salary that was three times what he had been earning. Like so many railroaders—whether white or blue collar—he would undergo a wartime interlude. Even though, because of his age, Langdon was not subject to the draft, he enlisted in the US Army Air Corps. Already a flying enthusiast, Langdon may have loved airplanes as much as he did trains. During the war he served as an aviator in the China-Burma-India Theater. Following the conflict, Langdon returned to the workplace, including stints with Capital-PCA Airlines, Southern Freight Association, Association of Southeastern Railroads, and starting in 1956 the Baltimore & Ohio (B&O).[31]

It was at the B&O that Jervis Langdon made his mark. He rose rapidly, becoming vice president and general counsel in two years and president in 1961. Being at the B&O throttle meant dealing with a host of challenges. The company was struggling financially; in fact, insolvency loomed. The B&O also felt threatened by the prospect of a merger between its major competitors.[32]

Langdon went to work. Deadwood employees were removed from administrative posts, and talented ones were promoted and encouraged to be creative. And the railroad was substantially modernized, with enhanced clearances through the Allegheny Mountains, "unitized" or unit coal trains, and a profitable piggyback operation. Langdon orchestrated an impressive turnaround; by 1963 the B&O was no longer experiencing financial chaos. In 1963 net income reached $5.5 million, and a year later it rose to $7.2 million. Freight revenues for 1964 climbed to $344.3 million, the best in five years, at $10.7 million more than during the previous year.[33]

The concept of railroad unification was not an anathema to Jervis Langdon; he believed that railroads must consolidate. Early in his presidency he made this statement before a US Senate antitrust subcommittee: "Instead of suppressing competition, railroad consolidations, including acquisitions or control, have the completely opposite effect of promoting competition by strengthening individual railroad competitors."[34]

With merger plans on the rise throughout the industry, the B&O was not immune; control of the B&O was in the works. In February 1963 the wealthy

Chesapeake & Ohio officially took over the railroad, forging a combined eleven-thousand-mile system claiming assets of $2.3 billion and operating revenues that exceeded $700 million. In reality this meant needed capital for the B&O and creative ideas for the C&O. Yet there was no official corporate merger; that formality did not take place until 1987. In the interim the B&O functioned as a subsidiary of the C&O, then Chessie, and later CSX.[35]

Langdon became unhappy with the B&O, growing bitter about C&O meddling. He did not care for important decision-making coming from C&O headquarters in Cleveland and despised the self-satisfied C&O corporate culture. While Langdon "had deep affection for the B&O" and was proud of his accomplishments, he resigned from the presidency in September 1964. Even though Langdon took early retirement, he would not remain retired. This committed railroader knew that he could land another executive position. The next step in his career would be chairman and chief operating officer of the Rock Island and shortly its president following the forced early retirement of Ellis Johnson.

Before Jervis Langdon arrived in Chicago, negotiations ensued with Henry Crown about salary. There was a sticking point. Langdon believed that high-ranking officers should not be paid excessively and objected to receiving more annual compensation than he had earned at the B&O. Langdon refused Crown's offer of considerably more than $100,000, but they finally settled on $90,000. Once that matter had been resolved, Langdon relocated his family to suburban Chicago and started work in the executive suite at La Salle Street Station. Company rank and file warmly greeted his presence. "When Langdon arrived at the Rock Island, he brought about a spirit of hope for an extremely troubled railroad," an employee remembered. "Morale had been so low that you could pick it up."[36]

Jervis Langdon hit the ground running. "Rock Island's problems cannot be postponed," he emphasized. "They are here now and must be dealt with." In his estimation, "the Rock Island was a very highly marginal operation." Langdon realized that he faced monster challenges. The overall condition of the property was sorry. "Physically it was a relatively slow railroad. With the exception of the line to Tucumcari, it was probably a 40-mile-an-hour railroad and in certain cases on the tangent track it was a 50-mile-an-hour railroad. But the line to Denver was marginal and relatively slow." Then there were those largely grain-gathering appendages. "The branch lines [which comprised about one-fifth of the trackage] were in marginal condition, so marginal that we had to use boxcars for the origination of grain and corn with most of the elevator operators and the big shippers all wanting the [heavier] covered

Billionaire businessman Henry Crown (*right*), the powerful voice on the Rock Island board of directors, convinced Jervis Langdon Jr. to take the throttle at the Rock Island. These two men worked well together. The locomotive idling behind Langdon and Crown is No. 326, a recently acquired Electro-Motive Division, General Motors Corporation GP35.

Author's coll.

The appointment of Jervis Langdon Jr. as company president lifted the spirits of Rock Island employees. He was gregarious and kind, and he tried to recognize workers' contributions. This 1965 photograph shows Langdon shaking hands with a locomotive engineer.

Author's coll.

hoppers." Notwithstanding the line relocations that took place during the Farrington era, bottlenecks remained on most of the road's main stems. Take the Chicago–Omaha artery. Its tracks meandered ten miles through the side streets and alleys of East Moline, Rock Island, and Davenport and seven miles through Des Moines. The railroad required continued track and line upgrades. The railroad also badly needed replacement rolling stock, most pressingly locomotives, and a larger freight car fleet, including specialized equipment. As for the former, scores of obsolete units had outlived their usefulness, and non-standardization continued to plague maintenance. "As late as 1965 the road stabled power by eight builders in more than 50 models." And for the latter, "freight sales personnel reported losses of traffic amounting to thousands of cars because of recurring car shortages." The company, moreover, "was unable to participate in pools of specialized equipment because of a lack of appropriate cars for such assignments." Communications and office equipment also needed upgrades, primarily the elimination of Morse circuits and procurement of adequate facilities for voice transmission, data processing, and train dispatching. As in the past, the Rock Island desperately required more large on-line customers. It continued to be plagued by having to compete for traffic with an average of 5.4 other roads at important terminals. Then there was the looming possibility of merger with the Union Pacific. In fact, on January 10, 1965, not long after Langdon took charge, stockholders voted overwhelming to approve such a unification. Langdon was delighted; he wanted to merge with a prosperous road. "Only massive infusions of cash which the Union Pacific stands committed to advance—*once merger is approved* [italics added]—will save the Rock Island and enable it to become a viable unit in a strong transportation system." He was not naive, knowing that the merger process would be complicated and lengthy. But it was a battle that must be won. Yet Langdon was hardly dismayed about his presidency. "The fun in this job," he told *Business Week*, "is to see the Rock Island getting up a head of steam over very difficult challenges."[37]

An early response in Langdon's quest to make the Rock Island an acceptable merger partner with the Union Pacific was to ensure that intelligent, creative, and dedicated senior executives would be part of his turnaround team. This had been a successful policy at the B&O. "Langdon took some time to assess the capabilities of people. There were no snap judgments." He discovered a paucity of talented officials at the Rock Island. "They didn't have anybody who was worth a damn except a few fellows in an intermediate state," he later reflected. "Top people were just no good at all." Retirements (and some early) helped to solve that problem, and there would be promotions and transfers. Langdon wisely sought talent from outside the ranks. In July 1965 he brought in the smart, hardworking William "Bill" Dixon from the B&O to serve as director of industrial engineering. Eventually Dixon became senior vice president and Langdon's replacement in the presidential suite. Langdon wanted to hire more B&O people, but he had agreed to limit any brain drain from the C&O-controlled company. A savvy non-B&O hire that did not please merger prospect Union Pacific was G. W. Kelly, who served as general manager of the Texas & New Orleans Railroad, a Southern Pacific (SP) affiliate. Already he knew the Rock Island, having earlier studied the Rock Island when Donald Russell, SP president, in 1962 expressed interest in acquiring the road. Luckily for Langdon, Kelly already had qualified for his SP pension and was not taking a risk when he accepted the Rock Island offer. He would serve as senior vice president of operations, directing system operations, including maintenance of the property and equipment. Kelly excelled at that job, becoming "the eyes and ears for Mr. Langdon." Following Kelly's fatal heart attack in October 1968, the board of directors did not exaggerate when it passed this resolution of condolence: "Mr. G. W. Kelly reorganized practically every phase of the Company's operations and property maintenance programs, introduced modern practices and procedures, including training of personnel, and raised the competitive standing of the Company to a high level." Later the Rock Island renamed Silvis Yard in his honor.[38]

In addition to personnel changes, the Langdon administration wasted no time in making structural adjustments. An important one involved the operating department, with the rationale "to give shippers better service and fully dependable schedules." Over the decades the Rock Island and other Class I carriers repeatedly revamped their divisional and operational units. June 1, 1965, saw the abolishment of the Western Division, which extended between Council Bluffs and Denver-Colorado Springs. This trackage came under the supervision of the Des Moines Division. The remaining six divisions included the Chicago, Rock Island, Des Moines, Missouri-Kansas, Southern, and Arkansas, with their headquarters in Chicago, Rock Island, Des Moines, Kansas City, El Reno, and Little Rock. This restructuring meant that Kansas City became the pivotal point as far as managerial jurisdictions for the six divisions. A general manager and a senior assistant general manager had their offices at Armourdale (Kansas City, Kansas). These two executives reported directly to G. W. Kelly.[39]

Having the "right people in place" and streamlining the division structure resulted in noticeable service improvements. The company enhanced freight-train schedules, terminal operations, interchange arrangements, locomotive distributions, and freight-car utilizations. The addition of seventeen

The TOFC or piggyback business became a bright spot on the revenue front during the Langdon presidency. Automobiles emerged as an important part of this sector.

Author's coll.

EMD SW-1200 switch engines and twenty 2,500-horsepower EMD GP-35 road units also made significant contributions. "Additional through scheduled freight trains were placed in service on several principal routes," Langton told shareholders. "Local freight service was increased from tri-weekly to daily on many parts of the railroad. A classification system was devised on many parts of the railroad. Freight train speeds have been increased over many parts of the railroad, and more yard engine assignments have been authorized to accommodate new traffic demands." The financial report for the first quarter of 1965 showed a $2,711,073 deficit, but a fourth quarter revealed a net income of $3,179,328. Smiles surely appeared on the faces of Rock Island personnel.[40]

A bright spot for the Rock Island involved the growth of its piggyback (TOFC) business. Under Langdon's tenure the intermodal operation was revamped and made more profitable. The company provided creative service plans, more dependable operations, and faster schedules, especially for eastbound movements. In 1965 TOFC revenues exceeded $13 million, an increase of 25.1 percent over the previous year. Then they took off: $15.2 million in 1966, $19.4 million in 1967, $27.5 million in 1968, and $31 million in 1969. During this time equipment upgrades occurred, including new TOFC facilities (Houston, for example); acquisition of 1,100 forty-foot refrigerated trailers for meat and other perishables; and expansion of the TOFC sales force. The pride and joy

A boost to the TOFC and the overall freight picture came with the acquisition of thirty-four GP35 locomotives, all of which were acquired in mid-1965. No. 331 pulls a freight train through Alexandria, Louisiana, and its several empty cars suggest that forest products were an important part of the traffic mix on the Little Rock Division. At the time of the shutdown, this locomotive was returned to lessor Greyhound Corporation.

Dan Sabin coll.

was the "completely modern" piggyback facility at Twelfth and Taylor Streets in Chicago. By 1969 it was capable of handling seventy rail flatcars and providing parking space for six hundred trailers, and it had a huge mobile crane for loading and unloading.[41]

Notwithstanding the profitable TOFC sector, by the close of the 1960s the Rock Island had hardly achieved financial bliss. Always the straight shooter, Jervis Langdon described its current status: "In 1969 our deficit was $9.3 million, or approximately $5 million greater than in 1968," hardly an encouraging state of affairs. He explained why: "Rock Island's operating plant is obsolete, with millions of dollars of deferred maintenance going back many years, and economical operations are not possible. In fact, the sharply increased freight business on the Rock Island has accentuated the disabilities of its physical plant and made mandatory a complete rehabilitation and modernization."[42]

MERGER MAGIC?

Shippers, investors, and employees, including Jervis Langdon, held out hope for the Rock Island. Their guarded optimism centered on completion of the merger process with the Union Pacific, a company that in early 1962 decided it wanted the road. Langdon knew that if the ICC approved, the Rock Island-UP unification would significantly alter the national railroad map. Such a union would give UP direct access to more gateways, most importantly Chicago and Saint Louis. The Windy City was especially attractive. If the UP reached this railroad mecca, it could connect with twenty major roads rather than seven at Council Bluffs. If this happened, there would be losers. A host of midwestern and western roads saw their balance sheet threatened, and for some it could become a matter of survival. "We had nearly every western railroad against us," noted Langdon. The Rock Island could count on support or neutrality only from the Burlington, Great Northern, and Northern Pacific railroads. These Northern lines were then in the process of forging the Burlington Northern, becoming a true megamerger in 1970. As a skilled lawyer who understood how the regulatory process functioned, Langdon believed that the best path to victory would be to have a broad settlement among the affected carriers *before* the ICC examiner held a pre-hearing conference. The North Western needed to be involved; it was the railroad that the merger would affect most adversely. This carrier, the eastern part of the Overland Route, depended heavily on interchange traffic with the UP at Fremont, Nebraska, where an estimated 150,000 to 175,000 freight cars annually exchanged hands. Under the leadership of Ben Heineman, the North Western was not about to let a Rock Island-UP union destroy its livelihood, and it quickly sought to line up antimerger partners.[43]

Prior to Langdon's active involvement in what would become the most protracted and tangled merger proceedings in American railroad history, important developments had occurred. In 1962, when the UP learned that the SP was seriously eyeing the Rock Island, these giants made a deal. Once the UP acquired the Rock Island, it would sell for $120 million what the SP wanted, specifically Rock Island trackage south and west of Kansas City, except for one branch. The crown jewel would be the Tucumcari–Kansas City line, which would shorten SP's transcontinental route by five hundred miles and make it more competitive with the Santa Fe, which had single-line control between Chicago and California. A bonus for the SP would be the Memphis–Tucumcari trackage, reducing by more than one hundred miles its existing Memphis–Los Angeles route. The UP would keep the remainder, including those coveted Chicago and Saint Louis lines. With this gentlemen's agreement in hand, the UP filed merger papers with the ICC in September 1964, and the SP submitted its paperwork the following April.[44]

It's all smiles in 1965 as the Rock Island contemplates a merger with the Union Pacific. On the left is Rock Island president R. Ellis Johnson, and behind him is Frank E. Barnett, Union Pacific vice president. On the right is Jervis Langdon Jr., Rock Island chairman and soon to be president.

Dan Cupper coll.

There was more. Once the North Western got wind of a possible Rock Island-Union Pacific marriage, it responded, offering Rock Island shareholders a package deal of trust bonds, common stock, and five dollars in cash for each Rock Island share. It was a reasonable proposal, but the Rock Island had already made a merger commitment to the UP. Henry Crown and his colleagues also may have had misgivings about the financial health of the North Western. This offer, however, was *not* a merger proposal; North Western sought only stock control. Heineman and associates anticipated a union between the North Western, Milwaukee Road, and Rock Island, or what they called the "Midwest Regional Railroad." Even though these peer roads had excess trackage, each one owned profitable core routes and feeder lines. The determination of the Heineman road to protect itself meant that the Rock Island and UP faced a serious adversary. Although the North Western had made some legal missteps with its quest for stock control, it remained active in what became a battle between David and Goliath.[45]

The Rock Island realized that it had more to worry about than Ben Heineman and the North Western. Jervis Langdon discovered that working with the powers at Union Pacific became an ongoing challenge; they expected to call the shots, setting the tone for merger proceedings. The fact that he wished to talk with other railroad leaders, including Heineman, annoyed UP officialdom. "We've got no intention of talking with those people," snarled UP general counsel Frank Barnett. There were other concerns, including Langdon's belief that UP must sell its stake in IC Industries, whose Illinois Central Railroad owned a competing line between the Chicago and Omaha gateways. Such a corporate involvement could cause opposition from the US Department of Justice and the ICC. Barnett summed up succinctly his company's attitude: "Leave it up to the lawyers," and it would do so with troubling results.[46]

May 4, 1966, became a red-letter day for the Rock Island-Union Pacific merger case and the North Western application for stock control. Joining ICC staff members were a gaggle of individuals who packed a large room at the Conrad Hilton Hotel in Chicago. There were lawyers from nineteen railroads, news media representatives, and North Western, Rock Island, and UP employees. Surely no one expected that formal hearings would stretch into 1969 with a process that would not end officially until 1974.[47]

The hearings did not go well for the Rock Island-Union Pacific merger. One disappointment was UP president Edd Bailey, who led off the witnesses. "He just showed that he didn't know really what it [merger] was all about," remembered Langdon. "He stumbled around, he didn't have his facts straight, he spoke very hesitatingly, and he was just a disaster as a witness."[48]

The opposition, led by the North Western, generally performed well. Ben Heineman wisely enlisted the support of the Santa Fe. This Southern Pacific rival tentatively agreed to purchase the Rock Island's southern lines and to lease trackage from Kansas City to Saint Louis, a gateway that it had longed to serve. The North Western did much more; it waged an aggressive public relations offensive that focused on the theme of "the Great Train Robbery," with the message that a merger would make the strong stronger and the weak weaker.[49]

Union Pacific did not ignore the North Western advertising campaign. With its deep pockets, it spent three times as much defending its proposed acquisition of the Rock Island. In January 1966 the railroads jointly launched a news organ, *Merger Messenger*, designed "to keep all employees and friends informed on progress of the Union Pacific-Rock Island merger." Its primary intent, of course, was to show the benefits of this corporate union.[50]

As the merger proceedings continued, the relationship between the two railroads became somewhat rocky. The UP did not care for the Rock Island's upgrades, arguing repeatedly before the ICC that it needed to rescue a faltering Rock Island. UP president Edd Bailey remained personally hostile to the merger. One of his reservations involved traffic interchange: "The Rock Island turned over only 6 per cent of our westbound traffic, compared to 22 percent on C&NW," he wrote in his autobiography. "We'd have to change a lot of shippers' minds who had become accustomed to our use of C&NW if we were to merge with Rock Island." Tensions increased when the UP fussed about a loan to allow the Rock Island to acquire badly needed covered hopper cars, and it rejected through freight rates via Denver, wanting for itself the long haul through the Council Bluffs gateway. When in 1967 the Rock Island faced a temporary cash-flow tightness, UP officials refused to extend a $2 million bridge loan. "They wouldn't have lost any money, and yet they turned us down flat," recalled Jervis Langdon. Fortunately, Henry Crown and Langdon got this financing from a Chicago bank.[51]

By early 1969 it had become clear that the ICC would not decide the UP-Rock Island merger and North Western stock control requests in a reasonable length of time. This should have surprised no one; the ICC had long moved at the pace of a snail in deciding requests for rate increases, passenger-train takeoffs, and line abandonments. By February these merger hearings had generated more than forty-three thousand pages of testimony, exhibits, and related documents. The bulk of this material dealt with threats of traffic diversion from railroads that would potentially be affected. Still there was that real possibility of merger. "The UP merger was the light at the end of the tunnel," opined a Rock Island official. "We had hope that there would be much better times. So people hung tight."[52]

IMPROVEMENTS AND ADJUSTMENTS

The Langdon administration remained determined to improve the Rock Island. It did not want the Union Pacific to acquire a poorly managed and ramshackle property. Such efforts, of course, had to be financially feasible. But *if* that merger did not occur, the Rock Island needed to handle that contingency. In a letter to Merle Miller, editor of the *Belleville* (Kansas) *Telescope*, Jervis Langdon stated the company position: "How long it will take to effect the Union Pacific merger is difficult to say, but, at best, it is a matter of years. This makes it mandatory that, in the interval, the management will run the Rock Island as if there were no merger in prospect and take every possible step to improve its competitive position and increase its earning power." The railroad subscribed to the notion that "when you're poor, you must live by your wits." In fact, the Rock Island came up with a new slogan: "Same Name—New Railroad."[53]

One Langdon administration response to enhance the bottom line involved strengthening marketing functions. The company named multiple specialized marketing managers. The one in Chicago focused on chemicals and petroleum, food products, and metals. The Detroit manager headed up the automotive and farm implements division. The Portland, Oregon, manager took care of forest products, and his Kansas City counterpart led grain and grain products.[54]

From his experiences with coal traffic at the B&O, Langdon knew the value of unit trains. On the Rock Island such a concept could potentially save on additional equipment, create less yard work, reduce labor costs, please customers, and generate profits. Although the company handled only a modest volume of coal, grain traffic, although mostly seasonal, was large and well suited for the unit-train concept. Plans developed quickly for these grain movements. "The plan we worked out," as Langdon told participants at a transportation conference in September 1966, "called for train consists of 100 jumbo covered hoppers, 100 ton capacity each, with terminal time, both at origins and destination, limited to 24 hours." If volume could be better distributed with a ten-thousand-ton grain train operating on a four-day turnaround, market research personnel reasoned, there would be a major improvement over the 1.2 loads per car per month that were then being obtained. Such a unit train could mean attractive freight rates for shippers over truckers, who enjoyed a growing business.[55]

Alas, the plan—utterly sound—failed to function as anticipated. "What these shippers really wanted, it soon developed, was a low rate but the unit train which they thought would make such a rate possible would only be operated whenever they were ready with 10,000 tons to move to the common destination," Langdon explained. "The shuttle concept the shippers flatly rejected as beyond their ability to handle."

Soon Rock Island marketers concocted an alternative grain-shipping scheme. In conjunction with the Frisco, it involved a combination of car reservations and incentive rates for export shipments of corn, milo, and wheat. "For the first time," the Rock Island pointed out, "the shipper will know when he will get his cars, how many he will get, and when his shipment can be expected at destination." Again the effort resulted in disappointment. Responding to conflicting interests in the grain business, the ICC refused to endorse the Rock Island-Frisco proposal. Once more, federal railroad regulation had its negative effect.

The revenue-hungry Rock Island never surrendered. In 1968 it finally achieved, with ICC sanction, much of its goal. This time a key provision involved a reduction of shipping rates that averaged 20 to 25 percent below the former tariffs. Monstrous but slow-moving Rock Island trains, one of which totaled 201 cars in a test run, now made nearly 5 trips monthly between such wheat centers as Enid and Texas ports, compared to the previous average of 1.3 trips every thirty days. Additional service improvements and competitive pricing helped to increase grain revenues from $3.2 million in 1967 to $10.3 million a year later.[56]

The Rock Island took pride in new service agreements with several inter-change partners. In August 1966, *Railway Age* gave the company and the New York Central (NYC) prominent coverage under this attention-grabbing headline: "Freight Trains Adopt the Space Age." The article described the debut of two trains—*Gemini I* and *Gemini II*—that operated as run-throughs between NYC's Elkhart, Indiana, yard and Rock Island's Silvis facilities, bypassing the congested Chicago terminal area. This "significant speedup" was facilitated by the two roads operating these trains on a pool basis, with locomotives and cabooses running between Elkhart and Silvis and pausing only at DePue, Illinois, to change crews. The Rock Island wisely assigned its new EMD GP35s and GE U25Bs ("U-boats"), the first modern power in years, to these hotshot trains. Somewhat later, the Rock Island further breached the east-west wall in Chicago by introducing a run-through with the Erie Lackawanna [EL]. This involved dispatching pre-blocked cars with pooled power and cabooses between Marion, Ohio, and Silvis, reducing transit time by twenty-four hours. More important than either the NYC or EL run-throughs was a similar one forged with the Southern Pacific via Tucumcari. The improved service involved the Rock Island's longest and most profitable haul. Memorable was a test run conducted in 1968 in which a train with "a lot of power and ten or twelve freight cars and several office cars and all green signals" beat the competing Santa Fe service by several hours in a run from Chicago to Los Angeles. But establishing competitive runs on a regular basis, although possible, would be difficult to achieve.[57]

Although improvements to freight operations became mandatory for sustaining the Rock Island, the company needed to end "substantial" passenger losses. Officials realized that this service was on a downward spiral nationwide and that their company was not immune. "Passenger train revenues continued their decline in 1965 and were responsible for holding Rock Island's overall revenue increase to 3 percent as compared with the 5 percent increase for freight," Langdon wrote in the company's 1965 annual report. "Rock Island must reduce the staggering deficits on the passenger side."[58]

Yet before the ax fell on several long-distance *Rockets*, management sought to mitigate the flow of red ink. In 1964 it introduced a coach-seat reservation plan on the most popular trains. The cost was fifty cents. Although the Rock Island indicated that it did this primarily to better determine equipment needs, especially during peak travel periods, the plan brought in a modest amount of additional revenue, averaging $22,000 a month. But this additional charge may have prompted short-distance travelers to seek alternative transportation. A more important cost-saving measure came a year later. As of July 1, 1965, the company stripped all of its intercity passenger trains (except the joint *Golden State*) of their dining cars, parlor cars, and sleepers. The explanation was straightforward: "The ever-increasing cost of providing this service, and the declining trend in patronage," commented Henry Koukal, general manager of passenger services, "coupled with our low financial position, left us no alternative." Yet passengers had access to food and drink; snack-beverage cars replaced money-losing diners. "Repeated surveys have indicated that Rock Island passengers want lower priced meals while on the train," said the company, "even if it means eliminating the atmosphere of the traditional, but costly-to-operate, dining car."[59]

Of course, the best way to reduce balance-sheet hemorrhaging caused by passenger-train losses involved takeoffs. This process required public hearings and related bureaucratic delays with the ICC for interstate runs and state public service commissions for intrastate ones. During the Langdon years, entries in the public timetable and official guide continually shrank. The year 1964 witnessed multiple discontinuances, including trains Nos. 27 and 28 between Herington and Wichita, Nos. 39 and 40 between Rock Island and Kansas City, Nos. 23 and 24 between Memphis and Amarillo, and Nos. 17 and 18 between Fort Worth and Houston. Two years later the death of the flagship *Rocky Mountain Rocket* occurred. Its discontinuance was not unexpected. The ICC hearing examiner reported how ridership had averaged per trip, dropping from 96 passengers in 1964 to 73.5 in 1965 and 51.5 during the first half of 1966. Furthermore, fifty-five crew members were needed to support this *Rocket* between terminals. Continued operations would produce an estimated annual loss of $488,000. Once it was withdrawn, the railroad retained the Chicago-to-Omaha segment, renaming that train the *Cornhusker*. Also in 1966, the *Twin Star Rocket* disappeared. Service ended between Fort Worth and Kansas City, but the Kansas City-to-Twin Cities leg remained. The train's new moniker became the *Plainsman*. The Rock Island sought to focus on midrange markets between a number of midwestern points, creating, in the words of Jervis Langdon, "a pattern of service specifically designed to serve

On June 20, 1967, not long before the last run of train No. 22, US mail is being worked at the Amarillo, Texas, station. The RPO is located in the front section of an attached RDC car. Soon No. 22 departs Amarillo with a sizable consist of mail and express.

Don L. Hofsommer photographs

those cities." However, the next year witnessed the discontinuance of the last passenger train between the Twin Cities and Saint Louis. Considerable opposition appeared, but the ICC ruled that other commercial transportation provided adequate service between these cities.[60]

A crushing blow to the remaining Rock Island passenger service came when the US Post Office removed Railway Post Office (RPO) cars from several runs effective May 1, 1967. Head-end business was critical for such operations, and this decision meant an annual loss of approximately $1 million. Cutbacks followed. On the Chicago–Omaha route, the only trains that remained were No. 7, no longer called the *Cornhusker*, and No. 10, no longer the *Corn Belt Rocket*. Soon Nos. 21 and 22 between Memphis and Tucumcari vanished.[61]

In 1968, the death of Nos. 3 and 4, the famed *Golden State*, saddened repeat long-distance railroad patrons and railroad enthusiasts alike. The commission granted the discontinuance following extensive public hearings in eleven cities in seven states. Although the service was still relatively well patronized, the ICC based its decision on the Rock Island's weakening financial condition. "The hard fact of the matter is that the Rock Island is in no shape to continue the service, and that fact is recognized even by some of those in outright opposition to the discontinuance." The final westbound run departed La Salle Street Station on the morning of February 19, and the last inbound train reached Chicago on the evening of February 21. The *Golden State* arrived on time, although only fifty-one passengers detrained, and only a handful from California. The Santa Fe, the principal competitor to the fallen *Golden State*, continued to provide attractive, on-time service between Chicago and Los Angeles.[62]

What remained? In 1968 the company operated skeletal service between Chicago, Peoria, Quad Cities, and Omaha and also between Kansas City and Twin Cities, but then the latter trains disappeared. In July 1969, Nos. 17 and 18 made their final runs. Shortly before their demise, a reporter for the *Des Moines Register* rode the train from Kansas City to Minneapolis. He made three conclusions: "(1) The service is not especially good, but probably the best that can be expected in the circumstances; (2) the trains are a convenience but not a necessity; (3) it would require more investment to make the railroad fully competitive than the probable results would justify." Not long after these north-south trains stopped, the Rock Island terminated Nos. 7 and 10 in Council Bluffs rather than having them cross the Missouri River into Omaha. The change likely was meant to discourage patronage. In fact, ridership had dwindled. "The trains have been averaging only a station [wagon] load

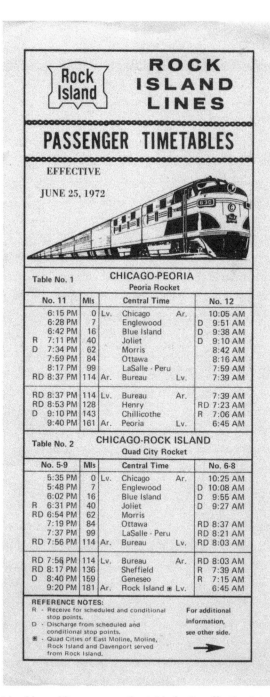

ROCK ISLAND LINES

Rock Island

PASSENGER TIMETABLES

EFFECTIVE
JUNE 25, 1972

Table No. 1 — CHICAGO-PEORIA
Peoria Rocket

No. 11	Mls		Central Time		No. 12
6:15 PM	0	Lv.	Chicago	Ar.	10:05 AM
6:28 PM	7		Englewood	D	9:51 AM
6:42 PM	16		Blue Island	D	9:38 AM
R 7:11 PM	40		Joliet	D	9:10 AM
D 7:34 PM	62		Morris		8:42 AM
7:59 PM	84		Ottawa		8:16 AM
8:17 PM	99		LaSalle - Peru		7:59 AM
RD 8:37 PM	114	Ar.	Bureau	Lv.	7:39 AM
RD 8:37 PM	114	Lv.	Bureau	Ar.	7:39 AM
RD 8:53 PM	128		Henry		RD 7:23 AM
D 9:10 PM	143		Chillicothe		R 7:06 AM
9:40 PM	161	Ar.	Peoria	Lv.	6:45 AM

Table No. 2 — CHICAGO-ROCK ISLAND
Quad City Rocket

No. 5-9	Mls		Central Time		No. 6-8
5:35 PM	0	Lv.	Chicago	Ar.	10:25 AM
5:48 PM	7		Englewood	D	10:08 AM
6:02 PM	16		Blue Island	D	9:55 AM
R 6:31 PM	40		Joliet	D	9:27 AM
RD 6:54 PM	62		Morris		
7:19 PM	84		Ottawa		RD 8:37 AM
7:37 PM	99		LaSalle - Peru		RD 8:21 AM
RD 7:56 PM	114	Ar.	Bureau	Lv.	RD 8:03 AM
RD 7:56 PM	114	Lv.	Bureau	Ar.	RD 8:03 AM
RD 8:17 PM	136		Sheffield		R 7:39 AM
D 8:40 PM	159		Geneseo		R 7:15 AM
9:20 PM	181	Ar.	Rock Island ▣ Lv.		6:45 AM

REFERENCE NOTES:
R - Receive for scheduled and conditional stop points.
D - Discharge from scheduled and conditional stop points.
▣ - Quad Cities of East Moline, Moline, Rock Island and Davenport served from Rock Island.

For additional information, see other side.

➡

When the Rock Island issued its passenger timetable for the effective date of June 25, 1972, this double-sided card listed only skeletal service, showing the remaining trains on its historic lines between Chicago and Rock Island and Bureau and Peoria.

Author's coll.

(nine passengers) eastward from Des Moines," the *Des Moines Register* observed, "and a motorcycle load (one or two passengers) westbound." On May 31, 1970, these two trans–Hawkeye State trains made their farewell trips.

Nevertheless, strong opposition erupted before the end of Nos. 7 and 10. The Iowa Commerce Commission, for one, did not care for either the Rock Island or the ICC pro-abandonment actions. "There is nothing reasonable about this carrier's outrageous performance, and it should not be permitted to benefit from its failure to provide reasonable service." Iowa regulators continued, arguing that "the Rock Island did little or nothing to encourage the public to ride its trains and that, in fact, passengers were deliberately and systematically driven off. The passenger trains were operated in a manner reminiscent of the Toonerville Trolley." Operational costs spelled the doom of Nos. 7 and 10, with the company annually losing an estimated $1.3 million. The commission employed a procedural issue to keep the trains running, but on October 1, 1970, the ICC ruled that they could end permanently.[63]

As the 1970s began, the Rock Island still remained an intercity passenger carrier. It operated two daily trains between Chicago and Rock Island and four dailies between Chicago and Peoria. The company did not join the National Railroad Passenger Corporation (Amtrak), launched on May 1, 1971. This quasi-public corporation assumed control of all intercity passenger trains except those on four railroads: Denver & Rio Grande Western, Georgia Railroad (part of the Family Lines), Rock Island, and Southern. The Rock Island's reasoning was simple: it could not afford the entry price. This meant that it must run these trains until March 1, 1973, at which time it could reconsider joining Amtrak. If the company did not, operations would need to continue until January 1, 1975, with no assurance that a discontinuance would follow. The Rock Island, though, would remain in the passenger business until December 31, 1978, aided by Illinois Commerce Commission–approved fare hikes and supported by grants from the Illinois Department of Transportation. Perhaps surprising to some, these trains for a time lacked the shabbiness that might be expected during the final years of a privately run passenger operation. Each consist offered a club-lounge car in addition to comfortable air-conditioned coaches. As track conditions and car maintenance deteriorated, speeds declined, riding roughness increased, and multiple equipment failures occurred. As a result, many patrons sought alternative transportation.[64]

The Rock Island, however, retained its role as an important commuter road in greater Chicago. As of January 1969, the company dispatched thirty-eight inbound and thirty-nine outbound weekday commuter trains. Approximately

Sporting the Ingram-inspired replacement R shield and *Independence* to honor America's bicentennial, No. 652, an E8A delivered from EMD in 1952, awaits with the two-car *Quad City Rocket* in La Salle Street Station on June 6, 1976.

Henry Posner III photograph

fourteen thousand riders made these in and out trips. The railroad categorized its runs as either "main line" or "suburban." The former operated the forty miles between La Salle Street Station and Joliet, with stops at intermediate stations. South of Blue Island, the commuter territory included the communities of Robbins, Midlothian, Oak Forest, Tinley Park, Mokena, and New Lenox. The latter category operated between the Chicago station and Gresham tower on the main line at Eighty-Seventh Street and then turned westward over the sixteen-mile "suburban branch," terminating at Vermont Street in Blue Island. Stations on this line were closely spaced and "bore more resemblance to a streetcar line than a line-haul railroad."[65]

Largely for financial reasons, the Rock Island had been slow to upgrade its equipment and to convert to more efficient and economical push-pull operations. "With push-pull trains, we can cut the turn-around time at either end of the line to a minimum," explained passenger executive Henry Koukal, "and thus get maximum utilization of the equipment." The push-pull concept, pioneered by the North Western, featured a diesel locomotive that always remained at the same end of the train, pushing the coaches inbound and pulling them outbound. The last car of each train had an engineer's control cab.

On July 26, 1976, a battered E6A diesel locomotive heads an afternoon rush-hour train with its bi-level consist at Joliet. No. 630 arrived from EMD in 1964.

Henry Posner III photograph

Whether in the steam or diesel era, the Rock Island battled snow throughout much of its far-flung system. In February 1969, a locomotive pushes a plow through drifts outside the Freeborn County, Minnesota, village of Clarks Grove near the Iowa border.

Don L. Hofsommer photograph

In 1965 the Rock Island received its first push-pull equipment, specifically twenty bi-level coaches from the Budd Company, of which five had control cabs. In 1970 the company took possession of ten bi-level Pullman-Standard cars, greatly enhancing the quality of service.[66]

Perhaps a historic event overlooked by most residents along the Rock Island occurred in 1966, when regulators allowed the Rock Island to terminate its less-than-carload (LCL) business. By doing so it eliminated "a large deficit." The company was not alone; most railroads during this time exited from the labor-intensive and costly service. Once, though, LCL had been a thriving dimension of the freight sector, bringing customers an array of items, ranging from stoves to furniture.[67]

NEW LEADERSHIP

On July 1, 1970, Jervis Langdon left the Rock Island. He had reached that bewitching age of sixty-five and concluded that his tenure should end. Langdon's decision involved more than his milestone birthday on January 28, 1970. What seemed to trouble him the most was the unwillingness of the Union Pacific to negotiate with other railroads, especially the North Western. "You've got to persuade the Union Pacific to sit down and talk about a compromise here," he told Henry Crown, "because otherwise I am sure that the conditions the commissioners are going to impose in their decision, even if they vote in favor of the merger, will be so onerous on the Union Pacific that they're going to reject it." Langdon, Crown, and a UP director did discuss the situation. Langdon, in fact, urged the UP to buy the North Western. The UP reacted negatively: "We couldn't do that. Don't have enough money and so forth and so on and all kinds of phoney excuses." UP was not about to alter its position. Much later in his life, Langdon believed that "so far as I know, to the bitter end of the proceedings, no effort was ever made to reach an understanding with *any* of the opposing roads." It was no surprise that Rock Island employees expressed nearly universal sadness about Langdon's departure. "Langdon was thought of as a savior up to the last day," a long-time employee reflected. Perhaps he was.[68]

Who should take charge? Jervis Langdon and the directors decided that Langdon protégé Bill Dixon and lawyer Theodore "Ted" E. Desch should run the Rock Island. Dixon became president, and Desch assumed the position of chief operating officer and vice chairman of the board. Henry Crown wanted Alfred Perlman of the Penn Central, formerly the dynamic head of the New York Central, to take the presidency, but other directors, including

Bruce Norris, who led the Norris Grain Company, did not share his enthusiasm. The appointment of Desch was something of surprise, even to company employees.[69]

Who were Dixon and Desch? Bill Dixon (1918–2014), the anointed president, possessed strong credentials. Born into a middle-class family in Pittsburgh, Pennsylvania, he attended the hometown Carnegie Institute of Technology, graduating in 1940 with a degree in chemical engineering. The following year Dixon completed a special transportation program at Yale University. With the outbreak of World War II, he enlisted and became attached to the US Army Military Railway Service. Dixon was delighted; he had loved trains since childhood, and that passion never faded. Commissioned as an officer in the 711th Railway Operating Battalion, he participated in the construction of the Claiborne-Polk Military Railroad in Louisiana and spent time overseas with the Trans-Iranian Railroad. After the war, Dixon aided South Korea in rebuilding its railroad infrastructure following the Japanese occupation. Subsequently he served briefly as a transportation inspector for the New Haven Railroad before joining the B&O in 1948. During the Korean War, Dixon, a captain in the Army Reserves, interrupted his domestic railroad employment to serve for several years with the US Army's Transportation and Development Station.[70]

At the B&O Dixon did not initially have star status. "Bill was not an impressive guy. He didn't talk much and was shy and never developed much self-confidence," recalled an associate. Nevertheless, Dixon was bright, well trained, experienced, and dedicated. Fortunately Jervis Langdon recognized his talents and plucked him out of the ranks to take charge of the industrial engineering group, a company think tank. This group of imaginative, mostly young railroaders did much to make the railroad more efficient and prosperous. No wonder Langdon demanded that Dixon join him at the Rock Island. During Langdon's tenure, he rose from an assistant to the president to become the senior vice president.[71]

Ted Desch (1931–2017) was much younger than Bill Dixon (38 vs. 51), and he had followed a different educational path. This Chicago native grew up near the Rock Island tracks in its southside Beverly Hills neighborhood. Following graduation from high school, he entered the University of Illinois. Desch earned his bachelor's degree in 1952 and a law degree two years later. After a stint as a junior officer in the US Army between 1954 and 1956, he joined the Rock Island as an assistant general attorney, and by 1965 he had become general counsel. In 1968 he took the post of vice president and general counsel. A gregarious, hardworking railroader with a dry wit, Desch worked on various legal matters, ranging from real estate transactions to the merger application with the Union Pacific.[72]

When Dixon and Desch became leaders of the Rock Island, they realized that their tasks would not be easy. Although the Langdon years had seen important operational and physical improvements, the railroad, in the words of one high-ranking employee, "was really starting to sink." He added, "Only the UP could save us." In their first report to shareholders, both executives understood the challenges the company faced. "Yet there is a level below which Rock Island cannot reduce its expenses without seriously impairing its competitive capabilities," wrote Dixon. "Merger with the Union Pacific is so vital not only to Rock Island but to the shippers and the communities dependent upon it." Desch explained: "The marginal character of Rock Island's earning power, so often stressed in the Company's case for merger with Union Pacific, was dramatically illustrated by the $16.7 million loss resulting from 1970's operations." He added, "Caught in the throes of a growing softness in the economy, yet faced with the necessity to pay substantial wage increases as part of the national labor settlement, the Company was unable to produce net income despite two freight rate increases granted during the year by the Interstate Commerce Commission and despite the tightest control of operating expenses." The Rock Island was not the only railroad in trouble. There were many. In 1970 Penn Central—the 1968 union of the New York Central, Pennsylvania, and New Haven Railroads—sought court protection. This corporate failure badly damaged the image of the industry and had a direct effect on the Rock Island. The company needed to write off doubtful accounts receivable from the failed road, and there were other negative ramifications.[73]

While the Dixon-Desch administration continued to wait on the ICC to make a final decision on the merger with the Union Pacific, it forged ahead. There were bright spots. During the next several years, some shippers employing the line either were new or had expanded their rail operations, and these customers included such firms as John Deere, Goodyear Tire & Rubber, and Union Carbide. An uptick in automobile and automotive-parts traffic and grain shipments occurred. The latter grew in June 1971 when the company started to move corn and soybeans in fifty-four jumbo-car trains from northwest Iowa elevators to Gulf ports, aided by the inauguration of competitive rates with competing transportation. About the same time, there was a welcomed movement over Rock Island rails. Five or six times a month, the company received trains of coiled steel from the Southern Pacific at Tucumcari and hauled them over the Golden State Route to Kansas City, where they were interchanged with the Milwaukee Road. The origin was Fontana, California, and the destination was Hennepin, Illinois. The intermodal business also climbed upward; the number of trailers handled in 1972 totaled 141,715, a gratifying increase of 10 percent more than the previous year. The Rock Island continued to reduce its workforce, which dropped from 12,091 in 1970 to 11,241 in 1973, down from 14,354 in 1964. The company also won regulatory permission to reduce money-losing branch line mileage, having retired nearly 650 miles since 1960. In 1972 it added to that total an additional 210 miles of unwanted trackage. Abandonments in that year involved the sale of 120 miles to newly launched shortline railroads in Iowa and Texas and the future fate of many more miles of Rock Island lines. By 1973 mileage stood at 6,255.[74]

An impact of the leadership of Bill Dixon, an early enthusiast for computers during his years at the B&O, involved the Rock Island's great strides with this beneficial technology. Although the company already had entered the computer age, major upgrades occurred in 1973. Two IBM System/370 Model 145 computers replaced smaller capacity units, improving efficiency and reducing costs.[75]

Despite the efforts made by the Dixon-Desch administration, the Rock Island continued to lose money. While operating revenues increased from $273,464,000 in 1970 to $329,001,000 in 1973, net railway operating income during this period stood at a *negative* $14,358,810 and dropped to a negative $18,185,556. By 1975 the company had lost in excess of $100 million during the previous decade. The financial picture looked grim, even desperate. A contributing factor, beyond company control, was the increasing inflation, affected by the federal government's decision to wage the Vietnam War without a tax hike and the increased petroleum costs triggered by the Arab oil embargo that began in October 1973. A month later Desch told the board that without an infusion of funds, the railroad would likely run out of cash by the end of January 1974. Bankruptcy loomed.[76]

CONTINUING MERGER SAGA

A merger with the Union Pacific was the enduring hope that could save the Rock Island. On July 8, 1970, the decision-making process of ICC examiner (later renamed administrative law judge) Nathan Klitenic began to unfold. In a brief "digest," Klitenic denied both the North Western's control application and the Santa Fe's bid to acquire the Rock Island's southern lines. The merger would be approved. Rock Island executives, board members, and others associated with the company took heart from this document. But the merger meant that it would be subject to certain undisclosed conditions. That left affected railroads in limbo about their fate. Soon Klitenic became ill, forcing the ICC to move the case to another unit. Merger opponents objected, but on April 6, 1971, the ICC reassigned responsibilities to Klitenic, who had regained his health.[77]

While the Rock Island family clung to the possibility of a merger, much remained to be determined. On September 1, 1971, volume 1 of the Klitenic report became public. It dealt extensively with the descriptions and positions of the various parties, and it reaffirmed Klitenic's conclusion that a Rock Island-UP merger should be approved. Ted Desch explained another pertinent aspect: "The subject of protective conditions and various applications of other railroads for inclusion in a Rock Island-Union Pacific merged system was largely left for development in subsequent volumes." When would the process end?[78]

More would come from the ICC. On March 21, 1972, Klitenic released volume 2. This second report failed to offer much insight. It provided some detail as to what specific conditions would be imposed in the event of the Rock Island-UP merger. The rationale for those conditions, however, was largely deferred to a volume 3. Finally, on February 15, 1973, nearly three and a half years after the digest appeared, volume 3, or the Klitenic plan, became known. Klitenic again endorsed the merger, but there were conditions. An important one said that the North Western must be included in the UP as a condition for approval. The most sweeping element of the Klitenic plan, however, involved placement of all trans-Chicago West railroads into four dominant systems: Burlington Northern, Santa Fe, Southern Pacific, and Union Pacific. This "messianic restructuring" rivaled plans for the creation of supersystems that dated back to the 1920s and early 1930s. "In sum a wholly unreasonable set of conditions was engrafted on the examiner's approval of the Rock Island-Union Pacific merger," remarked Desch. The affected parties not surprisingly filed a petition with the ICC to ask for dismissal of the entire proceeding. The ICC rejected this request, and subsequently the grieved parties submitted briefs and argued the case before the full commission. The last important event came on December 4, 1974. In this 305-page formal decision, the ICC still supported the central argument that merger would allow the financially strong UP to save the deteriorating Rock Island. But it imposed a set of conditions that generally differed from those recommended by Judge Klitenic. The ICC once more denied the quest by the North Western for the Rock Island. If the UP took control of the Rock Island, it must sell the Omaha-to-Denver trackage to the Denver & Rio Grande Western, the Memphis-to-Amarillo segment to the Santa Fe, and the Golden State line from Kansas City to Tucumcari to the Southern Pacific. In addition to these stipulations, the Santa Fe must acquire the struggling Missouri-Kansas-Texas, which would give it access to Saint Louis (Santa Fe would not obtain trackage rights over the Rock Island between Kansas City and Saint Louis), and for five years after consummation of the merger, UP was not to divert to Rock Island tracks any freight UP had previously interchanged at the Omaha gateway with either the North Western or the Milwaukee Road. The involved parties had ninety days to respond. The burning question was how the Union Pacific would react. The answer soon became known; UP would *not* seek acquisition of the Rock Island.[79]

By the time the final report appeared for this drawn-out affair, which officially approved the Rock Island–Union Pacific merger, the proceedings had produced more than 150,000 pages of testimony and exhibits, briefs, petitions, and replies, which Ted Desch flippantly remarked had a "cumulative weight that could be measured in tons." It had been a field day for lawyers: "112 of them for the quarreling railroads and 57 for other interests." The entire merger experience hardly spoke well for the industry or certainly for the ICC. Desch concluded, "I hold the view that the ICC had the power and the Congressional mandate to knock heads together and force the warring railroads to try the case expeditiously and to *order* [sic] the hearing examiner to issue a rational report within a reasonable period of time. The failure of the ICC to bring this pressure to bear on the parties and the examiner ultimately destroyed the Rock Island." The excessive length of time it took to conclude the merger case, railroad scholar Richard Saunders Jr. observed, "would haunt the ICC and be one of the nails in its eventual coffin." Jim Farrell, a UP official, expressed a similar view: "The futility of that merger process review was a 'brick' in building toward the forthcoming reformation of ICC regulatory practices that would substantially benefit the railroad industry later when it escaped successfully from many of the monopolistic laws and rules imposed on them decades earlier."[80]

FINAL BANKRUPTCY

By 1974 the Rock Island showed evidence of becoming a transportation slum. At this time approximately two thousand miles of main-line tracks had slow orders, meaning that trains needed to creep along at twenty miles per hour or so. Some observers, including employees, referred to the railroad as the "Rickety Rock." A Burlington Northern worker said, "At the time, the Rock Island was the ugly stepsister of Western railroads. Granted, bad track, ramshackle depots, and rundown locomotives were common to many U.S. railroads in the days before 1980's deregulation, but in my opinion, the Rock Island was in a corner of the basement by itself." The company suffered a plethora of problems, ranging from obsolete rolling stock to structures in poor repair. Even its diesels often suggested poverty. Since hood doors were interchangeable, especially on early General Electric models, shop workers at El Reno and Silvis selected whatever doors were handy, and so the spelling of *ROCK ISLAND* on various units looked strange, creating a mismatch of lower- and uppercase letters and misplaced letters as well. Moreover, the company often did not repaint the used units it acquired from other railroads. "Rock Island was surely the king of different paint schemes," opined J. David Ingles of *Trains*, "as well as the misspelling champion." Since board members had expected the merger with the Union Pacific to solve the railroad's financial problems and provide investors with a good stock exchange ratio for dividend-paying UP shares, they, especially Henry Crown, were not anxious to invest in the property, even for basic maintenance.[81]

Anxiety about the future of the Rock Island spread among those associated with the railroad. Board members expressed concern about the effectiveness of the leadership provided by Bill Dixon and Ted Desch. There was a feeling that these executives had not been aggressive enough during the protracted merger negotiations. John W. Barriger III, one of the nation's most respected railroad executives, did not mince words about the four successors to Downing Jenks: Ellis Johnson, Jervis Langdon, Bill Dixon, and Ted Desch. In an April 1974 memorandum, "Current Situation of the Milwaukee and Rock Island Railroads," he called these men the "four horsemen of the apocalypse, blindly taking that once fine railroad to the brink of disaster over which it will plunge this year unless either or both the Union Pacific and USRA [US Railway Association]–FRA [Federal Railroad Administration] come to its rescue."[82]

Anxiety was not limited to the top echelon. Blue-collar workers felt disheartened by the failed merger with the Union Pacific and worried about their future. So many had held out hope that the UP would save their employer. Manly, Iowa, agent Delos Werle caught the feelings of colleagues when he said, "And then we were so sure we were gonna merge with that Union Pacific. This would have been a *real* railroad with that UP, boy. Let me tell you from what I've seen of that UP, oh! That's a railroad and a half." He added, "But there was too much red tape, and pretty soon the Rock Island's gone downhill and the UP—when they could've had us—they said, 'Sorry, can't afford the repairs.'" Leon Willingham, superintendent of operations at the El Reno car shops, commented at the time of liquidation, "Most of these guys don't know if they'll have a job or not next month." He believed that if the railroad or his section of the railroad were to be acquired by another Class I, the new owner probably would not need another shops facility. If someone else did, they would likely pay a lower wage.[83]

A leadership change was in the air. And it was largely triggered by the failure of the Rock Island to obtain desperately needed financial assistance from the United States Railway Association (USRA), a nonprofit federal corporation (1974–1986). Bill Dixon, Ted Desch, their associates, and others believed that federal loan money was essential if bankruptcy were to be averted. The USRA would be their last best hope.

The "Great Railway Crisis" was at hand. The United States Railway Association had come about as the result of the Penn Central Railroad bankruptcy, the failure of other carriers in the Northeast, and the problems facing additional roads that teetered on financial collapse. The demise of the nineteen-thousand-mile Penn Central after only 872 days between merger and bankruptcy seemed to share the same relationship to railroads as did the RMS *Titanic* to ships or the *Hindenburg* to aviation. It appeared that a breakdown of the national economy would follow if Penn Central, most of all, shut down. Rail-dependent businesses were at risk of closing, and Congress was not about to let that happen. In January 1974 lawmakers responded with the Regional Rail Reorganization (3R) Act, a measure designed to launch the planning-reorganization process that would create the Consolidated Rail Corporation (Conrail) in 1976. This quasi-public road would take control of the key trackage of the bankrupted railroads. Formation of the USRA was a critical part of the legislation. This agency, under section 211 of the 3R Act, had the power to make loans and loan guarantees to any railroad that connected with one in reorganization and required financial assistance to prevent bankruptcy. There was the growing belief that a deadly malaise was spreading west of Chicago and Saint Louis. The Rock Island best represented that likelihood.

Rock Island officialdom understood that the USRA could become that all-important financial lifeline. It would be absolutely essential if the merger with the Union Pacific was never consummated. Management came to Washington to seek a $100 million loan. These dollars would be earmarked largely for track rehabilitation. But the USRA board rejected that request. The official response was that "there is no reasonable prospect that the loan could be repaid or that [federal funds] could prevent the Rock Island from going bankrupt."[84]

The failure to obtain that massive infusion of federal dollars altered the course of Rock Island history. "The loan application helped seal the fate of the

Rock Island-Union Pacific merger," concluded historian Gregory Schneider. It was at this point in the later part of 1974 that the UP terminated its quest for the Rock Island; the struggling railroad would have to fend for itself. It had been an incredibly long merger process, taking a dozen years before the ICC rendered a decision. There had been 274 days of public hearings, twice as many as were held during the Penn Central merger proceedings, and they had generated tens of thousands of pages of testimony and support documentation. "In the end, the Rock Island was derailed not in Enid, Oklahoma, or Chicago, but in Washington, D.C.," wrote Robert Bleiberg in *Barron's*. "And the villain of the piece is inevitably the Interstate Commerce Commission, which has done perhaps more damage to the nation's railroads than the marauding Confederate and Union armies combined." Bleiberg continued his castigation of the ICC: "In particular, by stalling the merger for a dozen years, during which officialdom leisurely indulged its propensity to redraw the U.S. railroad map, the ICC did the company and its shareholders irreparable harm." Death by regulation was not farfetched.[85]

Rock Island leadership was about to change. At the October 10, 1974, meeting of the board of directors, Bill Dixon and Ted Desch resigned, and a new president and chief executive officer was named. He was John W. Ingram (1929–2008). The railroad's last president possessed an extensive résumé. Although born in Cleveland, Ohio, Ingram grew up on Long Island. After high school he attended Pratt Institute as an engineering student but transferred to Syracuse University, where in 1952 he received a business degree. Three years later he earned a master's degree in transportation economics from the Graduate School of Business at Columbia University. Ingram began his railroad career while in high school, working summers as a brakeman on Long Island Railroad passenger trains. With his second degree in hand, he joined the New York Central Railroad, where he assisted president Alfred Perlman and by 1961 had become director of profit analysis. For the next five years, Ingram took a similar job at the Southern Railway. In 1966 he again changed employers, joining the William Johnson administration at the Illinois Central Railroad (IC) as assistant vice president of marketing, and two years later he became vice president of marketing. In 1971 Ingram left the private sector for the public one. He accepted the appointment from President Richard Nixon to become administrator of the Federal Railroad Administration. This agency, launched in 1967 as part of the US Department of Transportation, focused on policy and research matters, railroad assistance programs, and safety regulation.[86]

It was at the Illinois Central that John Ingram gained recognition for marketing and innovation. He originated two imaginative revenue-making concepts, Rent-a-Train and Mini-Train. The former, launched in 1967, allowed major grain shippers to rent an eighty-six-car train for an annual fee of $700,000 plus 1.5 mills per ton mile. "Once in operation, Rent-a-Train could move corn from central Illinois to the Gulf for 7 cents a bushel," wrote IC historian John Stover, adding, "the conventional rate from Iowa to the Gulf was about three times as much." Next came Mini-Train. Although no revenue triumph, it revealed creative thinking. Introduced in 1969, this plan offered rapid, dependable service in central Illinois for soybeans shipped from country elevators to a Swift & Company processing facility in Champaign. During their two-week life span, these trains made twenty short trips and hauled more than ten thousand tons of beans. While the trips were operationally successful, there was a fatal shortcoming; restrictive union agreements meant high labor costs.[87]

The imaginative Ingram had an obvious flaw: his personality. Colleagues and others found him to be "abrasive, acerbic, and arrogant," an overall "difficult guy." "Ingram was often blunt and really turned people off, telling them that they were jerks." Some disliked Ingram's "out-of-control professional ambitions." Ingram enjoyed having had that presidential appointment, and he wanted a Class I railroad presidency.[88]

How did John Ingram appear on the radar of the Rock Island board of directors? Ingram offered this explanation: "While I was at the FRA John Barriger decided I should work for the Rock Island. And he went and talked to a bunch of people on the Rock Island and a bunch of people on the Union Pacific . . . and got approvals here and there and everyplace." He continued, "What do you know somebody asked me if I would like to come and work for us. The Rock Island not being my idea of a dream railroad. But anyway, I finally said yes." This account may or may not have been wholly accurate, but the *New York Times* and other sources indicated that Barriger, who at the time worked for the FRA, had been the instigator. Board members realized that Ingram understood the federal bureaucracy, and he could be the person who somehow might tap federal dollars. There was also his record for imaginative railroading, although he lacked much experience with operations.[89]

John Ingram understood the inherent weaknesses of the Rock Island. "Its traffic consists primarily of agricultural products, both primary and secondary, as well as agricultural machinery, fertilizers and other such materials. It is over 7000 miles long, but of those miles only about 200, the trackage within Chicago and the Quad Cities-Muscatine Illinois/Iowa industrial area, are really heavily used." He added "The Rock has one of the lowest average traffic densities in the railroad industry." Ingram later said the obvious: "Turning

Rock Island around won't be done overnight." In 1976 a colleague described Ingram's situation this way: "From the first day he assumed leadership of the railroad, he has been pulling a solid trainload of problems with a bad order locomotive."[90]

Immediately Ingram tried to bolster the railroad. This energetic executive, for one thing, sought to alter its badly tarnished image through cosmetic changes. By early 1975 locomotives and rolling stock sported a different livery; train watchers saw white and light blue—or what officials called "New Image Blue"—replacing crimson and yellow. Since the company had failed to keep its equipment clean, locomotives, cars, and cabooses soon looked poorly kept—even ugly. "The new paint scheme was dubbed 'bankruptcy blue' within the first few months of its appearance," wrote Gregory Schneider. More striking to some was the disappearance of the company's venerable shield emblem; its replacement was the capital letter R. "Symbolic of the Rock Island's desire to 'rise again' are the bold new 'R' trademark and designation 'THE ROCK' [reporting marks ROCK] now being applied to locomotives undergoing rebuilding, boxcars, and the first of 150 leased jumbo covered hopper cars," the 1974 annual report explained. Most observers were not impressed. "By not completely enclosing the colored area, the color appears about to drain out, and the slanted leg of the R makes it look as if it were pushing against the vertical line in an attempt to topple it over," commented historian James Ward. "The result is a static design with some faint circular symbolism but little else save instant recognition." British graphic designer Ian Logan bluntly said, "The herald was replaced by an insipid 'updated' version." The company argued in its defense that these changes were designed "to change the railroad's basic 'look,' to a more distinct, more contemporary look, and one that would be less expensive, too. Accordingly we retired the old colors and symbol, honorable though they were, and symbolically announced a New Rock Island."[91]

There would be no "New Rock Island." On March 17, 1975, five months into the Ingram presidency, the Rock Island threw in the towel and sought bankruptcy protection in federal court. But before that pivotal event took place, the Ingram team made a last-ditch effort to get financial help. The Rock Island had not given up on Washington. In late 1974, the application, which was made during the waning months of the Dixon-Desch administration, was updated and revised. The Ingram team hoped that federal dollars would be spent on rehabilitating principal arteries rather than patching up the entire system. On February 4, 1975, the USRA announced tentative approval of a $9.1 million loan for working capital to prevent the Rock Island from going bankrupt. When the company officially wired its acceptance ten days later, it said, "If there is something we can do that we are not doing [to obtain the loan] tell us what we need to do. We have reduced employment about eight percent, train-miles 20.9 percent, and engine hours 10 percent. We are trimming expenses and eliminating non-essential programs everywhere—but we are close to the bottom of the barrel." Then bad news came on February 25 when the USRA announced that it was "unable to complete arrangements" for this $9.1 million infusion. Why the sudden turnabout? The government argued that the decline in carloadings had not been included in the Rock Island's financial projections. Unquestionably, recession-level carloadings had damaged revenues. "In other words, the railroad had been unsuccessful in predicting the depth of the 1974–1975 recession," snapped a disgusted Ingram. "Since railroads are a derived demand industry, to forecast railroad prospects accurately requires accurate predictions of the future of the industries served. A perhaps impossible precognition was required by our government for approving loans to the Rock Island."[92]

Yet there was another plausible explanation for the denial. "Ingram was the wrong man for the [presidential] job. He was a disaster," opined D. F. Brosnan, manager of marketing research and a former USRA staff member. "The real reason why the Rock Island had trouble with the FRA was that FRA employees hated Ingram. They wanted revenge. That agency was a personnel snake pit. So the Rock Island lost out and in the process the North Western became the darling of the FRA." (The USRA worked in cooperation with the FRA.)[93]

Not to be overlooked was the feeling among the FRA staff that there existed too much trackage in the country, especially in the Midwest. As Brosnan suggested, the North Western prospered to the detriment of the Rock Island. Simply stated, there had to be winners and losers. The Rock Island would be the sacrificial lamb.[94]

The process of seeking federal aid had been emotionally draining. "We have been to Washington so many times, that one of our staff members decided to keep his house there and use it rather than a hotel," observed a Rock Island official in October 1975. "One can easily get a persecution complex in this industry."[95]

Bankruptcy became the prudent course of action. On one fateful day in March 1975, the *daily* cash forecast sheet revealed a negative balance. Perhaps that was no surprise. The Rock Island's financial condition had generally been in a downward trajectory for years, having operated at a net loss since 1965 and suffering a negative cash flow since 1973. In 1974 the railroad lost more than $23 million, and expenses, particularly for fuel, were rapidly increasing. Federal District Judge Frank J. McGarr (1921–2012) of the Northern Illinois District

Court in Chicago, who had been on the bench since September 1970, went to work and quickly named his former law partner William "Bill" M. Gibbons (1919–1990) as the sole trustee. The judge explained why he had not named multiple trustees, including one or two experienced railroaders: "You can't run some complicated operation with a committee." Although neither man had railroading experience, Gibbons knew corporate bankruptcy and real-estate law. Fortunately, both judge and trustee were hardworking and ethical.[96]

Although the Rock Island had begun to slash its operating costs in December 1974, it continued the process after entering court protection. By the close of 1975, about 40 percent of management and about a third of total employment had been cut. The Ingram team restructured the operating divisions; the railroad now had only four. A redundant piggyback department was also abolished. "Without these cost reductions," noted Ingram, "the Rock Island would not have survived the cost inflation experienced by the industry." This was the time of unprecedented "stagflation," characterized by high inflation, rising unemployment, soaring interest rates, and sluggish economic growth.[97]

During the initial months under court control, there was uncertainty about whether the Rock Island would be reorganized or liquidated. In April 1975, Judge McGarr opted for the former course of action: "It is not my intention to order the cessation of railroad operations at any time in the foreseeable future." He believed that a successful reorganization was possible. Gibbons's assignment was return the railroad to profitability.[98]

There never was any question about the fate of Rock Island commuter service. On any given workday by the mid-1970s, twelve thousand or more passengers used its sixty or so trains. A few runs, most notably the Joliet–Chicago *Bankers*, handled as many as a thousand inbound rush-hour riders. The La Salle Street Station remained an attractive Loop location; many patrons walked to their places of employment. During the early phase of the bankruptcy, these loyal passengers, however, continued to endure museum pieces of rolling stock. While some modern bi-level and single-level coaches made up the commuter fleet, several dozen open-vestibule, non-air-conditioned ones, dating from the 1920s, remained in service. Some commuters jokingly called them "Jesse James" cars and "swore that there were holes in them from bullets and arrows."[99]

As the Rock Island struggled, its track structure in greater Chicago deteriorated. The public probably sensed this only if they rode commuter trains or knew people who did. Speeds continued to drop. "By the spring of 1976 the increasing number of slow orders was making a mockery of the timetable," remembered Anthony Haswell, who in June 1975 became managing director of passenger service. Operations started to improve once the Regional Transportation Authority (RTA), a multi-county public body created in 1973, entered the picture, agreeing in October 1976 to a purchase-of-service agreement. At first, capital expenditures from RTA went for locomotives, including cab-control cars, and bi-level coaches, but later dollars were earmarked for desperately needed track rehabilitation.[100]

The public sector also brought assistance for track improvements beyond Chicagoland. During the immediate years prior to bankruptcy, the Rock Island had tried to maintain its principal arteries. Where welded rail existed on main lines, it helped to sustain the track structure, even though it might be spiked to rotting ties. Branch lines, though, had often declined to dangerous levels where spikes failed to hold jointed rails evenly because of bad ties, and the track was losing gauge. The result was that way freights needed to crawl along at ten miles per hour or less. There were a few bright spots. The Iowa Department of Transportation (IDOT) stands out. In 1974 lawmakers created the Rail Assistance Program, which aided several troubled Hawkeye State railroads to rehabilitate hundreds of miles of grain lines. During 1975 this agency joined forces with a shippers' group, the Audubon-Atlantic Branch Line Improvement Association, to upgrade the twenty-five-mile Audubon branch. IDOT spent $740,000, and the shippers contributed $260,000. Although these expenditures permitted safe transportation of heavier cars at a maximum speed of twenty-five miles per hour, the number of carloadings fell short of expectations. The goal was 1,000 carloads annually, but in 1977 only 327 cars were handled.[101]

Whether successful or not, the Audubon restoration pleased Rock Island officials. This example of state support prompted economist and executive vice president Dr. Paul Banner to comment, "The state transportation agencies may give us a real pain, but at the same time, they seem to be more responsive to the needs of the area and the railroads, and certainly, we have had an extremely good relationship with the states in our area." He went on to note, "I would say that one of our greatest supporters has been the state of Iowa."[102]

Even on substandard branches, the Rock Island, under John Ingram's guidance, sought ways to generate traffic. Prior to the bankruptcy, management had quoted incentive ten- and twenty-car rates. Elevator owners in southeastern Iowa, for example, could attract new business and receive better prices when their grain went over Rock Island rails to Mississippi River barges in Keokuk. Grain was often trucked to these loading facilities from nearby locations to take advantage of this financially attractive service. But a widely watched trial took place in 1978 with the introduction of turnaround

"MiniTrains," which handled corn, soybeans, wheat, rice, pulpwood, coke, stone, and scrap metal. This experiment paralleled a concept that Ingram had introduced at the IC. Under the MiniTrain agreement with the operating unions, the Rock Island could use a three-man crew on as many as five shorter-haul trains, but only on an *experimental* basis. Movements could handle just a single commodity that moved less than one hundred miles. Between March 8 and March 28, 1978, a MiniTrain shuttled corn and soybeans from the Continental Grain Company elevator in Keota, Iowa, located on the Washington-Oskaloosa branch, to its facility in Muscatine, a distance of fifty-two miles. The experiment worked, even though the track between Washington and Keota had a five-mile-per-hour speed restriction. Management hoped that MiniTrains could become commonplace. Yet that would not happen, largely because of work-rule restraints. In 1992 John Baskin Harper, who between 1976 and 1978 served as manager, operations research, and advocate of the MiniTrain, offered these thoughts: "The Rock Island's short-haul trains were, in effect, a *no-cost* [sic] solution to many of the preceding century's accumulation of *artificial* [sic] and unnecessary regulatory and work-rule restrictions, artificial restrictions that unfortunately in many cases became and remain imbedded in the thinking of railroad customers, management, employees, and regulators alike."[103]

If there was a good year for the bankrupt Rock Island, it came during the national bicentennial year of 1976. The company showed modest vitality, in part because court protection meant that it did not face property tax obligations. Operating revenues rose from $321,571,000 in 1975 to $341,320,000 in 1976. But sluggish grain carloadings the following year meant that revenues dropped precipitously to $295,089,000. Once again heavy dependence on cyclical, low-rated agricultural commodities came into play.[104]

Notwithstanding the Union Pacific merger debacle, some at the Rock Island did not abandon the hope for a corporate merger or some means of uniting with one or more carriers. Shortly after assuming his position as trustee, Gibbons wanted to participate in a major mid-continent merger involving the Missouri Pacific in its quest to bring into its corporate fold two affiliated roads, Chicago & Eastern Illinois and Texas & Pacific. The MOP had acquired financial control of the former in 1923 and the latter in 1967, and on November 1, 1974, it sought regulatory approval for this structural simplification. But the Rock Island sought inclusion. "A Rock Island-Missouri Pacific merger would create a strong regional system for the middle third of the continent," said Gibbons. "I think it would also satisfy the creditors, the stockholders and I think it would make a fine railroad." His objective failed. The ICC quickly concluded that such a unification would not be in the public interest. On May 4, 1976, it approved the expanded fourteen-thousand-mile MOP system. This decision did not upset Rock Island powerhouse Henry Crown. He wanted the company out of the railroad business and its assets sold. Funds should not be spent on developing it. Crown continued to say that the railroad was patently not reorganizable.[105]

While it was not a merger proposal, John Ingram in early 1978 suggested an imaginative way for several railroads to reduce costs and to improve service. It involved formation of a consortium of multiple midwestern carriers: Illinois Central Gulf, Kansas City Southern (KCS), Katy, Milwaukee Road, and Rock Island. Ingram had in mind what he called "Farm Rail," seeking to "combine some of the trackage where [these roads] operate; consolidate freight yards in some major transportation centers; pool equipment; combine some sales offices; centralize their computerized payroll functions; and perhaps even pool revenues." As he told a US House of Representatives subcommittee, this "experiment" was "a matter of hanging together or hanging separately." In mid-1976 a first step had already occurred when the financially strapped Milwaukee Road began to use a portion of the Rock Island's Kansas City line, specifically the 243 miles between Muscatine, Iowa, and Polo, Missouri. Since the Rock Island had a better-engineered route and good signaling and had not decayed too badly, the Milwaukee could increase train speeds and avoid a monstrous grade outside Muscatine. There was also the likelihood that it could abandon part of its Kansas City trackage. Farm Rail, however, went nowhere. "It didn't get out of the barnyard," wrote David P. Morgan of *Trains*. The other railroads, with the possible exception of the Milwaukee, which filed for bankruptcy on December 19, 1977, had no desire to help the bankrupt Rock Island. KCS management, for one, had its eyes on acquiring Rock Island trackage, namely from Kansas City to Chicago. Corporate opponents regarded the Ingram plan as a delaying tactic to prevent dismemberment.[106]

Ingram and staffers came up with additional ways to bolster traffic and revenues. Late in 1977 they orchestrated a "sales blitz campaign." These blitzes were held in Little Rock, Oklahoma City, and the Quad Cities and were conducted by representatives from marketing, operations, pricing, and sales and coordinated by newspaper and television advertising and special shipper dinners. Success followed. "For the first eight months of 1978 new business directly attributable to the blitzes totaled 2,278 cars and 1,017 TOFC trailers which produced Rock Revenue of $1,228,000." In the latter part of 1978, Ingram and others launched, with special permission from the ICC, a "freight sale." During the period between Thanksgiving and New Year's Eve, the company offered a

The Ingram crusade to bolster the company coffers involved a creative short-term piggyback freight sale. This advertisement appeared in the *Denver Post*.

Author's coll.

20 percent discount for TOFC shipments from Denver to points on the system and, in combination with other TOFC rates, for shipments destined beyond its rails. It wanted to reduce the number of empty backhaul trailers out of the Mile High City; westbound traffic was acceptable, but eastbound movements were not. In a media advertising campaign, the Rock Island boasted that it was the "Creator of America's First Freight Sale." The copy read in part: "We've stopped operating in the old-fashioned, traditional way. To be competitive, we've challenged the *status quo* and responded to nationwide shipping needs with innovative and unique service." The sale meant substantial savings for shippers. Western Forge Corporation in Colorado Springs, for example, could send a shipment of hand tools to Kansas City for $385, compared to the regular rate of $488. It is doubtful whether much additional revenues filled company coffers, but there was industry buzz about this novel freight sale.[107]

Notwithstanding efforts to enhance revenues and to cut costs, the process of liquidation of major assets began. By the time the Rock Island entered bankruptcy, the Tucumcari line required extensive rehabilitation. Gibbons understood this and instigated discussion with Ben Biaggini, the Southern Pacific head, for a possible sale. Although discussions also included the Saint Louis line, the focus centered on the trackage between Santa Rosa, New Mexico, and Kansas City, including the Dodge City branch. (The SP had long leased the Santa Rosa-to-Tucumcari segment.) Earlier the Rock Island had expected the SP to pay $98 million for the southern half of its system, but because of escalating costs for upgrades, the final price for the Tucumcari portion was set at $57 million. With this agreement, in April 1978, the SP filed the appropriate papers with the ICC. SP affiliate St. Louis Southwestern would hold title to the trackage since it was free from existing SP gateway traffic agreements. While money was desperately needed for a Rock Island reorganization, the loss of the Tucumcari line would likely damage any realistic hope that it could occur. Yet Gibbons believed that a core network of lines might produce a successful income-based reorganization.[108]

About the time the Rock Island and Southern Pacific reached a sales agreement, at least two other railroads were eyeing Rock Island trackage. The Santa Fe showed interest in the Amarillo–Memphis line, and the Denver & Rio Grande Western considered the Denver–Kansas City/Omaha routes. The major stumbling block was that neither the Santa Fe nor the Rio Grande wanted to pay Gibbons's prices. Yet the Rock Island seemingly favored a partnership arrangement with the Rio Grande, allowing for joint usage of this trackage.[109]

At a glance, this Rock Island freight train in March 1977 appears to be contributing to a financially healthy railroad, and its well-maintained power suggests the same. The place is Wildorado, Oldham County, Texas, established in 1908 as rails reached this Panhandle village.

Don L. Hofsommer photograph

During the bankruptcy, the public sector provided some critical financial aid. In July 1976 Judge McGarr approved a $1.8 million emergency grant from the Regional Transportation Authority to offset part of the Rock Island's loss from its commuter operations. These dollars fell short of covering about $1.6 million in annual red ink. More assistance came in April 1978, when the FRA approved $31.2 million in loan guarantees and gave its conditional promise for an additional $50 million. More requests followed. Eagle-eyed government accountants, however, were not impressed with the actual numbers in these loan applications. Federal statutes required a reasonable expectation that Washington would recover its investments. The Rock Island did what it could to receive funding; the company maintained an aggressive lobbying presence in Washington. Antagonism by FRA personnel toward John Ingram had apparently lessened.[110]

Although the Ingram administration attempted to paint an optimistic picture for the Rock Island, conditions worsened. The punishing winter of 1977–1978 forced increased expenditures and caused lost business. Moreover, rival North Western benefited from federal rehabilitation dollars, spending these funds to upgrade its Chicago-Omaha-Fremont main stem (a route of

Even in the twilight of the Rock Island, TOFC traffic continued to be important to the bankrupt company's faltering bottom line. The location is Tucumcari, New Mexico (looking east), and the date is February 1977. On the right, a freight train arrives from Amarillo.

Don L. Hofsommer photograph

undisputed national importance) and the freight line between Proviso Yard (Chicago) and Milwaukee. The North Western wanted the Rock Island to collapse and realized that its nemesis was deteriorating rapidly. Not to be overlooked was Henry Crown's desire for liquidation. At the time, "he stated with certainty" that this would happen.[111]

As the decade neared a close, chances of a Rock Island salvation greatly diminished. Soon it became evident that the railroad was on the path to corporate failure. The Ingram administration tactic of exuding progress went nowhere. Its approach, although flawed, made sense; the company wanted to retain shipper loyalty and convince government officials that a successful reorganization was possible. Furthermore, Trustee Gibbons had not produced a final plan for reorganization for Judge McGarr to consider. But two unrelated outside events and a protracted labor dispute sealed the fate of the railroad. A "perfect storm" was about to strike.

Mother Nature cruelly attacked the Rock Island heartland. Winters during the late 1970s were severe, but the one of 1978–1979 was brutal. As the new year arrived, a series of blizzards pounded the Great Plains, and weather records between November and March recorded the worst winter of the

If one were to explore the Rock Island in the late 1970s, one would find poorly maintained track, even on main lines. Weeds often grew between the rails, and roadbed soft spots became commonplace. In May 1979 several pieces of Rock Island power, including two units with the Ingram-inspired color scheme, stand in Shawnee, Oklahoma.

Henry Frick photograph

twentieth century in much of the Midwest. Between January 12 and January 14, Chicago, for one, received a record sixteen inches of snow, which blanketed seven earlier inches. And frigid temperatures repeatedly gripped the region. The impact on railroads, whether rich or poor, was devastating, resulting in increased costs of operation and reduced traffic. For the battered Rock Island, extreme winter conditions during the first four months of 1979 meant a loss of $36.7 million. When snows finally melted, the extreme weather also worsened track conditions.[112]

Not only did the Rock Island encounter awful weather, but it faced a fuel crisis. Prices for petroleum products had been soaring since the 1973 Arab oil boycott, triggered by American support for Israel during the Yom Kippur War with Egypt and Syria. Then a 1979 oil shock, caused by a widespread panic due to greatly decreased Middle Eastern oil production in the wake of the Iranian Revolution, worsened the situation. In fact, petroleum prices peaked that year. "The company had been a relatively heavy buyer of oil on the spot market, a practice which had in years past reduced fuel costs but which backfired when OPEC increases hit hardest on the spot market," explained John Ingram. "There was no way, in the short run, that the resource-poor Rock

Island could absorb the increased costs." Ongoing annual inflation of 10 to 12 percent exacerbated the situation. The ICC did grant a Rock Island request for a $50-per-car surcharge on all railroad-owned covered hopper car loadings and a 4-plus percent increase in charges on all freight originating or terminating on the railroad. But the ICC hardly solved the fuel-cost problem. Then, during the summer of 1979, financially strapped independent truckers disrupted oil distribution as diesel prices soared. On July 3 the Rock Island had only a seven-day supply of fuel, forcing it to slash service, especially on branch lines.[113]

If weather and fuel problems were not enough, a labor crisis produced the crushing blow. In an era of strong and at times militant railroad unionism, the Rock Island and other carriers had modest or limited powers to combat wage demands, end obsolete work rules, and instigate other reforms. There was a notable exception, involving the Florida East Coast Railway (FEC). In January 1963 this small albeit strategic Class I road, which had recently emerged from bankruptcy, refused to accept a pay increase that nonoperating employees had negotiated at the national bargaining table. These disgruntled workers struck, and operating workers honored their pickets. Soon supervisory personnel took over train operations, an action that triggered union violence, including gunshots at locomotives, rail removals, and switch tampering. FEC management doggedly persisted. Not until 1971 did the nonoperating unions settle, but the operating ones held out five years longer. During and after the strike, the company successfully used two-man nonunion crews and operated cabooseless. The FEC became an impressive moneymaker, and its anti-union stance later helped to change the industry. The Ingram administration was well aware of what had occurred on the FEC. Could it become a model for the Rock Island?[114]

Labor troubles erupted on August 28, 1979. Two powerful unions, the Brotherhood of Railway and Airline Clerks (BRAC) and the United Transportation Union (UTU), which represented brakemen, conductors, firemen, and switchmen, went on strike. First it was BRAC, and two days later the UTU honored BRAC picket lines.[115]

Prior to the Rock Island strike, the BRAC membership had grown increasingly alarmed about automation and computerization. The computer age had arrived in railroading; the traditional importance of carbon paper, pencils, and tariff cases had faded or vanished. The union's new president, Fred J. Kroll, a former Pennsylvania Railroad accounting clerk, argued that clerks must negotiate with the railroads on job stabilization because of the rapid spread of "electronic equipment." BRAC sought five years of protection for members laid off because of replacement technologies. On July 10, 1978, its first major job action took place on the Norfolk & Western Railway (N&W). The issue involved more than changes in technology; the N&W wanted to reclassify about a thousand clerks as supervisory personnel, making them ineligible for BRAC membership. For eighty-two days management operated the railroad, and it did so with surprising success. An industry strike fund also aided the N&W, giving it a daily infusion of $800,000.[116]

BRAC decided to expand its work stoppage. Having failed to shut down the N&W, BRAC turned its wrath on the more than forty railroads that had contributed to the strike fund. The Rock Island was one of these carriers. A national crisis was brewing, and it did not take long for Washington to intervene. Using powers outlined in the Railway Labor Act, President Jimmy Carter called for a sixty-day cooling-off period. BRAC members returned to their jobs, and a week later their strike against the N&W officially ended. Yet workplace tensions continued.[117]

Although the Rock Island historically experienced reasonably good labor-management relations, a crisis would erupt. On December 31, 1977, the current three-year national wage agreement with railway unions was set to expire, and bargaining for a replacement contract would become ongoing. Even though the Rock Island did not participate in these negotiations, it planned to accept the final agreement. "The railroad agreed from the outset to be bound by national wage rates and saw no reason why its employees should not be paid at the same rate as others in the industry," recalled John Ingram. The fourteen labor unions that were involved represented approximately seven thousand Rock Island operating and craft employees. There was a critical stipulation. "At the outset the company stated that it could not be expected to provide any retroactive pay if bargaining did not produce a contract by the end of 1977," explained Ingram. Railroad leaders urged negotiators to produce work-rule changes, designed to benefit all carriers but especially those in distress. Being labor intensive, and given industry-wide bargaining, a company could win only by having reasonable labor costs.[118]

Then off came the wheels. All but two of the Rock Island unions reached agreements about salary and more acceptable work rules. But no such settlement included BRAC and UTU. The stumbling point was retroactive pay for the railroad's 1,800 BRAC and 2,500 UTU members. "It was impossible for the Rock Island to make retroactive wage payments," Ingram reiterated. "When the unions were encouraged to audit the books to make clear the facts relating to money available, they refused."

Negotiations occurred throughout 1977 and during most of the following year, but to no avail. During the early part of 1979, the situation had not markedly improved. The National Mediation Board and an internal special board of inquiry could not resolve the retroactive pay dispute. When the Rock Island refused to accept binding arbitration because of the costs involved, estimated in the millions of dollars, BRAC leadership announced that the railroad would be struck without advance notice. "This union didn't give a damn about the future of the Rock Island," explained a Rock Island official. "It didn't realize that its members could be giving up good paying jobs if the Rock sank." Both BRAC and UTU expected that the court would never allow the railroad to die and that eventually their members would receive their back and vacation pay. They were badly mistaken.[119]

As the strike commenced, management contemplated a last-ditch plan for reorganization. It involved creating a Rock Island with significantly less mileage that would resemble what the Milwaukee Road would become in the early 1980s when it launched Milwaukee II. This radically restructured property became a shadow of its former self, comprising 3,269 miles rather than the 10,074 miles that were operational in the late 1970s. As for "Rock Island II," it would be a 2,200-mile core road, linking Minnesota with the Gulf of Mexico and Chicago with Omaha. Also to be included were several Iowa grain-carrying appendages and the Peoria branch. It was well recognized that the company had the longest through route of about any railroad in the country, from Minneapolis to Galveston. Much of the remainder of the system would be sold to Class I's, upstart carriers, or public entities. Scrappers would take up the remaining track. In reality the Rock Island would increase its dependence on agricultural traffic. There was, of course, a grain-generating base; approximately 1,700 elevators remained captive to its rails. Somewhat earlier, a ranking official had commented: "It helps an awful lot to be a north-south railroad through America's breadbasket, where we follow the [wheat] combines north from Texas right on up to Minnesota during the various harvests and, as a result, manage to keep our equipment busier longer." This contemplated structure would serve a smattering of major on-line industries, including John Deere and Maytag, strung largely along sections of its historic artery between Chicago and Des Moines and also in greater Peoria.[120]

Rock Island II would be managed largely from recently rented office space at 322 South Michigan Avenue rather than from La Salle Street Station. The latter had become an uncomfortable work environment. Not only was a roach infestation an ongoing problem, but the absence of storm windows made for cold winter drafts and prevented the heating system from functioning properly. The new facility had no bugs and provided good climate control. Although the Rock Island was slipping into liquidation, employees assigned to the South Michigan Avenue address experienced a morale boost.[121]

Shortly after Christmas 1979, Trustee Bill Gibbons submitted his reorganization plan to Judge McGarr. Reflecting the earlier concept of a scaled-down Rock Island, this proposal called for a greatly reduced footprint. The new company would operate only between Chicago and Omaha and from Saint Paul to Kansas City, as well as along the Peoria line and several grain-carrying Iowa branches. The remainder of the railroad would be sold off or abandoned, and proceeds from these non-core assets would go to creditors. A skeleton workforce would operate the railroad. "[The plan] showed gross ton-miles growing significantly on each segment of the core, without any substantiation of how this was to be done considering the loss of traffic that affected the railroad in 1979," observed Gregory Schneider. "It also projected a total of $119 million for rehabilitating track through the five-year assessment of operations [1980–1985]." Optimistic yes, realistic no. The Gibbons team might have created a viable railroad in the post–Staggers Act era of partial deregulation, but this version of a Rock Island II was of dubious strength. Even John Ingram was concerned. "I remember John saying," a Rock Island official recalled, "'But I don't want to be president of a small railroad.'"[122]

The knockout punch came with a January 1980 report from the respected accounting firm of Peat Marwick Mitchell. It concluded that the Gibbons reorganization plan was not economically feasible; it could never deliver on its financial promises. On January 25, 1980, Judge McGarr held the "most consequential hearing in the Rock Island case." He announced that a cash-based reorganization was *impossible* and that the railroad should be liquidated. This decision was hardly unfounded; carloadings had declined from 760,000 in 1975 to only 332,000 in 1979, and red ink continued to mount, totaling $111 million from 1975 through 1978. Judge McGarr told Trustee Gibbons not to file his plan with the ICC but to prepare for liquidation. Advocates of a leaner Rock Island were not pleased, but the die had been cast.[123]

LIQUIDATION AND LEGACY

7

The Chicago, Rock Island & Pacific Railroad gained a unique distinction in American railroad history: it was the largest Class I road to be liquidated. Other important carriers have been abandoned totally or in part. The first one of note was the 338-mile Colorado Midland in 1918. Twenty-one years later, the 250-mile Fort Smith & Western folded, and in 1957 the 541-mile New York, Ontario & Western gave up the ghost. When the Central Railroad of New Jersey (Jersey Central), Erie Lackawanna, Lehigh Valley, and Reading Railroads joined the Consolidated Rail Corporation (Conrail) in 1976, their lines that were not conveyed to Conrail became part of individual corporate estates. This trackage was either sold off or abandoned. In the case of the Rock Island, the operating company and the financial structure disappeared, but only a portion of the physical plant was lost. The majority of customers continued to have rail access, provided by new owners, whether Class I roads or existing or start-up regional and short-line carriers. In some instances public agencies acquired ownership, and with two exceptions, they leased trackage rights to designated operators.[1]

Before the active process of liquidation commenced, US secretary of transportation Neil Goldschmidt instructed the Interstate Commerce Commission (ICC) to issue a directed-service order. Prior to the federal court–ordered dismemberment, the ICC on September 26, 1979, commanded that Kansas City Terminal Railroad (KCT), a switching company owned by multiple railroads and joined by the Denver & Rio Grande Western, St. Louis Southwestern (Cotton Belt), and Southern Pacific, to operate sections of the Rock Island and to pay the disputed wages to members of the Brotherhood of Railway and Airline Clerks (BRAC) and the United Transportation Union (UTU).

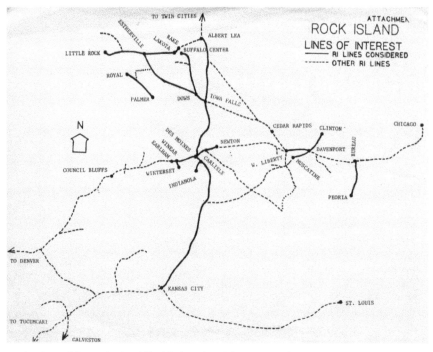

At the time of the Rock Island liquidation, the Chicago & North Western revealed to the trustee what lines it wanted to operate. Later the company purchased only the Spine Line and branches in northwestern Iowa.

Author's coll.

Washington financed these start-up freight operations by giving participating roads a contract for cost plus 6 percent profit. This arrangement initially expired on December 5, 1979, but ultimately was extended through March 31, 1980. Before that expiration date, freight traffic was embargoed. The ICC mandated that inbound shipments stop on February 15 and that outbound and local carloadings end on March 2. The commission also approved bids that granted railroads temporary operating rights through May 31, 1980, but later these arrangements continued until August 31, 1980. At the time KCT relinquished operations, which most observers agreed had been successful, twenty-one railroads had provided service over an estimated three thousand miles of the Rock Island.[2]

One railroad that wanted pieces of the Rock Island was the Chicago & North Western (North Western). It took over about eight hundred miles, including the Twin Cities–Des Moines–Kansas City or "Spine Line" and several branches in Iowa. Management considered the Spine Line a prize because it was much shorter and better engineered than North Western's ownership of the former Chicago Great Western trackage between these three cities. The Hawkeye State appendages served several large grain elevators, including ones in Dows, Klemme, Superior, and West Bend, and they were suited for handling unit trains of corn and soybeans. The railroad additionally sought to lock up agricultural traffic in its home territory. The North Western paid the trustee about $5 million annually for usage rights and became the first to reach such a lease agreement. It also leased 4,100 Rock Island freight cars at $13 million annually from the North American Car Corporation, which had signed an exclusive contract with the trustee for most of the Rock Island rolling stock. The North Western assigned this equipment principally to serve former Rock Island customers.[3]

The process of liquidation was not without problems. A thorny issue involved labor protection for about five thousand former Rock Island workers. Early on, these individuals (and their union representatives) believed that Washington would protect them, creating perhaps a federally organized Midwest Conrail. "There is a need for legislation to provide assistance to Rock Island employees who are not offered employment by interim operators and acquiring carriers," argued Secretary Goldschmidt. A legal debate erupted, involving federal legislation. On May 31, 1980, President Jimmy Carter signed the Rock Island Railroad Transition and Northeast Corridor Improvement Act (Rock Island Transition Act), a measure sponsored by Senator Nancy Kassebaum of Kansas. This Republican lawmaker sought to protect out-of-work Rock Island employees in her state. The national economy was in recession, and high unemployment was widespread. There were more than humanitarian motivations; there were political considerations. President Carter, for one, faced a tough reelection bid in 1980 and did not want to alienate railroad labor. Although the act contained a large appropriation for upgrading the Northeast Corridor, which Amtrak had acquired when Conrail emerged, it provided $75 million in loan guarantees to cover labor-protection expenses. Washington, though, would have a priority lien on revenues the trustee received from liquidation sales. This provision did not sit well with the court, creditors, and bondholders. Bankruptcy Judge Frank McGarr responded this way: "That Congress believes it can legislate a $75 million labor protection burden on the assets of the Rock Island comes to me as a startling concept."[4]

The judge and attorneys representing the estate (bondholders) questioned the constitutionality of the Rock Island Transition Act. They argued that it violated the takings clause of the Fifth Amendment to the US Constitution. Once the court ordered liquidation, the company no longer had common carrier status, and its public interest requirements had ceased; any labor-protection requirements were unconstitutional. The case of *Railway Labor Executives'*

Association v. Gibbons made its way to the US Supreme Court, and in March 1982 the justices ruled unanimously in favor of the estate. There would be no $75 million administrative claim.[5]

With the matter of the Rock Island Transition Act settled, Judge McGarr and trustee William "Bill" Gibbons focused on disposing assets, most importantly hundreds of miles of track, major facilities, and real estate. The top objective was to work out short-term trackage leases while likely protracted sale negotiations proceeded. This strategy made sense. Richard Lane, who served as director of rail assets disposition for Gibbons, explained: "The reasons for this decision were threefold: to preserve rail service to the fullest extent possible, to have the property to some extent maintained and protected, and to provide income to cover the ongoing costs of the liquidation." By mid-1982 lease revenues had reached approximately $1.5 million per month. "Rock Island's liquidation proved what many suspected since the restructure of the Northeast railroads," opined Henri Rush, general counsel for the Surface Transportation Board (successor to the ICC) in the 1990s, "a railroad is worth more—considerably more—broken up and sold in pieces than if it is put on the market as a single going concern." That had been Henry Crown's longtime belief and desire.[6]

Trustee Gibbons revealed that he was an astute and relentless negotiator. He held to this philosophy: "The only successful negotiation was one in which final agreement leaves both parties feeling slightly dissatisfied." Gibbons repeatedly cut good deals. But he did not act alone; a competent staff assisted him. When it came to line sales, associates prepared detailed evaluations that included the net liquidation value of the property and its likely value as an ongoing concern to a prospective purchaser. Armed with this information, Gibbons was prepared to deal with potential buyers, and he encouraged competition as he carved up the system. One lucrative result involved the contest for ownership of the Spine Line and Iowa grain branches. The initial purchase offer made by the North Western, the lease holder, amounted to about $55 million, but the Soo Line Railroad (Soo) decided that it wanted this trackage, most of all to gain access to Kansas City. But before the final document was finalized, Gibson and the North Western agreed to a purchase price of $76.35 million. Then a bidding war erupted. The Soo offered $81 million for most of the same trackage, and the North Western countered with a $85.35 million bid. Soon the Soo raised its offer to $88.5 million. At last the North Western won out, paying $93 million, even though the Soo had increased its offer to $100 million. The court, though, worried that the Soo's financing would fall through. And there was a remarkably profitable sale involving a miniscule piece of the Rock Island, namely 0.2 miles in El Dorado, Arkansas. This trackage provided a critical interchange between the El Dorado & Wesson Railway—a 5.5-mile shortline that served chemical, lumber, and poultry customers—and the Missouri Pacific. The price was $200,000. Overall, line sales generated an impressive $335 million.[7]

Not all trackage was sold. Although a section of the Chicago–Omaha main line was acquired by the Chicago Regional Transportation Authority and another part was leased to the recently launched Iowa Interstate Railroad, successor to the failed Iowa Railroad, no immediate buyer appeared for the line through the industrial upper Illinois River valley between Joliet and Bureau or the one from Bureau to Henry on the Peoria branch. The Grand Trunk Western looked at this property, but the line's "wretched physical condition" and the high asking price led its planning team to reject a purchase offer. Yet Gibbons worked out a fifty-year lease with the Chessie System, generating annual rental income of more than $2 million. This was the only long-term lease agreement that he consummated.[8]

There were non-rail assets to liquidate, primarily real estate. Signs quickly sprang up systemwide: "FOR SALE. THE ROCK. CALL 312/435–7758." A major sale involved the sprawling shops in Silvis, Illinois. The Chrome Crankshaft company, a locomotive rebuilder, purchased the complex but later sold it to the National Railway Equipment Company. Such transactions collectively produced more than $75 million. Then there was everything else, including remaining rolling stock, office equipment, and even historical artifacts, best represented by early twentieth-century inlaid mother-of-pearl framed pictures of a Rock Island passenger train that once graced company offices and stations. Easements for fiber optic, pipe, and power lines generated another $10 million. "There was plenty of meat on that caucus," recalled a former Rock Island employee. No one disagreed. The total for all sales from the court-ordered liquidation amounted to $471 million.[9]

The final financial transactions followed two avenues. Within two years of the launch of liquidation, sufficient funds had been generated to pay off creditors, including taxing authorities. In November 1982 Judge McGarr sanctioned dispersals but without interest. Such dispersals appealed to those parties who did not want to wait to learn if and when the court would approve interest awards; they received cash payouts of approximately $155 million. Perhaps they should have waited. At the time of the final reorganization on April 19, 1984, remaining creditors got checks that included interest payments of 7 percent.[10]

Now it was the investors' turn to take their slice of this money pie. The reorganized Chicago Pacific Corporation (CPC), which made its debut on

As liquidation began, bankruptcy signs sprouted systemwide. This one appeared on October 9, 1981, in Sibley, Iowa, a Rock Island junction point.

Author's photograph

June 1, 1984, and was tied closely to Crown family interests, had assets of $290 million. These owners received stock in CPC, which they could either keep or sell in over-the-counter trading. More money became available, mostly from trackage sales to the Iowa Interstate Railroad ($31.5 million), disposal of the Chessie lease ($18 million), and other sources, including continuing sales of real estate, mineral rights, and rolling stock. Not to be overlooked were valuable tax-loss carry-forwards that CPC enjoyed. Soon this cash-rich, non-transportation company acquired several firms, notably the Hoover Corporation, based in North Canton, Ohio. In October 1988, however, CPC disappeared, purchased in a friendly takeover by the Maytag Company, based in Newton, Iowa. Its manufacturing plant had long been served by the Rock Island and what became the Iowa Interstate Railroad. This was an ironic turn of fate for both company and railroad.[11]

LEGACY

If Americans lack familiarity with the Rock Island Railroad, they may recognize "The Rock Island Line," the folk song made famous in the 1940s by singer and musician Huddie "Lead Belly" Ledbetter (1888–1949). "Huddie knew a good song when he heard it, and quickly appropriated it," noted his biographers Charles Wolfe and Kip Lornell. Ledbetter was not alone in recording this high-energy piece. Others, including Harry Belafonte, Johnny Cash, Lonnie Donegan, Johnny Horton, and the Weavers, helped to put the song on the record charts during the 1950s and 1960s. When the urban folk-music revival of the middle and late 1950s was in full swing, "The Rock Island Line" became popular on both sides of the Atlantic. And it continues to be sung, whether onstage, in schools, or around campfires. Although multiple versions of "The Rock Island Line" exist, this is a common one:

> Well, the Rock Island Line is a mighty good road.
> I say the Rock Island Line is a road to ride.
> I said the Rock Island Line is mighty good road.
> If you want to ride, you got to ride it like you're flyin'
> Well, buy your ticket at the station at the Rock Island Line.
> Well, the train left Memphis just on time,
> Well, it made it back to Little Rock at eight-forty-nine.
> We have engineer men, brakemen too,
> Lord, Pullman porters and brakemen, too.[12]

The "The Rock Island Line" dates from the 1930s. During this time John Avery Lomax, a white southerner and collector of folk songs, including those sung by African Americans, served as an agent for the Library of Congress. This institutional connection gave him access to the best field-recording equipment and resulted in numerous contributions to the library's audio archive. When Lomax discovered the Rock Island song, he was not working alone. Lomax was joined by Ledbetter, who had recently been released from a Louisiana prison. In fall 1934 the two men traveled to Arkansas to record black musicians at the state prison in Little Rock and elsewhere. It would be at the Cummins prison farm located near Varner in Lincoln County (site of today's high-security state penitentiary) that Lomax and Ledbetter first heard "The Rock Island Line." It is not known who wrote the basic version, but Robert Brady Cochran, professor of English at the University of Arkansas, believes that Kelly Pace, a Cummins inmate, was the originator.[13]

Legacy involves still another art form: film. In anticipation of the Rock Island centennial, the company backed production of a Hollywood motion picture about the early years of the railroad. Filmed in Oklahoma and released on May 18, 1950, by Republic Pictures in TruColor, the action-packed ninety-minute *Rock Island Trail*, which stars Forrest Tucker, Adele Mara, Adrian Booth, and Bruce Cabot, features a stagecoach-train race between Joliet and Ottawa, the burning of the Mississippi River bridge, and a Sioux attack near Davenport. James Edward Grant, the screenwriter, took considerable liberties with historical facts, even though William Edward Hayes, the Rock Island public relations officer and historian, served as technical adviser. The film also had its own musical score.[14]

Although "The Rock Island Line" is widely recognized, and so perhaps is *Rock Island Trail* by movie buffs, a significant event in the company's history is less well remembered. This event involves a civil rights case, and like the folk song, it had a direct connection to Arkansas. The Rock Island gained national attention in the late 1930s and early 1940s because of an act of racial discrimination against a black US congressman, Arthur Wergs Mitchell (1883–1968), a lawyer and New Deal Democrat from Chicago.[15]

On April 20, 1937, Congressman Mitchell purchased a Pullman ticket from the Windy City to Hot Springs, Arkansas. All went well during the first leg of his overnight journey on the Illinois Central to Memphis. In Memphis Mitchell's Pullman car was transferred to Rock Island train No. 45, which departed Memphis at 8:30 a.m. and arrived in Hot Springs at 1:05 p.m. Soon after Mitchell had boarded, conductor A.W. Jones told him that the Arkansas segregation law required that he move to the Jim Crow coach. The congressman objected. His argument was straightforward: his first-class ticket entitled him to the Pullman car, and there was ample room to accommodate him. Even telling the conductor that he was a member of Congress made no positive impression. Mitchell recounted, "[He] said it don't make a damn bit of difference who you are as long as I was nigger you can't ride in this car. You will have to ride in the 'second- class' car and no other place on the train." Fearing arrest in a racially hostile state, Mitchell reluctantly vacated his Pullman seat and walked to the segregated coach. He described it as "poorly ventilated, filthy, filled with stench and odors emanating from the toilet and other filth, which is indescribable." Conductor Jones permitted his baggage to remain in the Pullman, and he returned a portion of the ticket that allowed Mitchell to receive a refund of $3.14 on the basis of the coach fare.[16]

Congressman Mitchell would not be a passive, disabused passenger. Three weeks later he launched formal protests, first in an Illinois court against the Rock Island and then with the Interstate Commerce Commission (ICC), the more important case. Mitchell and his lawyer argued that what had happened in Arkansas violated the nondiscrimination clause of the Interstate Commerce Commission Act, forbidding interstate railroads from subjecting anyone "to any undue or unreasonable prejudice or disadvantage whatsoever." They wanted the ICC to order an end to the practice of denying blacks equal first-class accommodations. At a March 1938 hearing, Conductor Jones explained the Rock Island's policy, testifying that it permitted blacks in Pullman cars but only in compartments or drawing rooms where they would be separated from white passengers. He also contended that the Jim Crow car was not substandard; it was new, it was air-conditioned, and it had flush toilets. That streamlined coach, however, did not enter service until August. In a decision rendered in November 1938, a majority of commissioners admitted that discrimination had occurred but "accepted it on the basis of limited black demand for Pullman facilities."[17]

Although the ICC dismissed the complaint, Mitchell did not abandon his quest for racial justice. He appealed to a federal court in Chicago, but in June 1940, a three-judge panel upheld the ICC's verdict. Next the congressman turned to the US Supreme Court.[18]

It would be in the nation's highest tribunal that Arthur Mitchell achieved a degree of satisfaction. On April 28, 1941, Chief Justice Charles Evans Hughes announced the unanimous decision by the justices in the case of *Mitchell v. United States*. The essence of this opinion was that Arkansas law (and hence the Rock Island) violated the Fourteenth Amendment by denying Mitchell equal rail accommodations. The inequality experienced by this first-class black passenger had not been remedied. The court did not rule that segregation was illegal; instead it decided that the failure of the Rock Island to offer identical accommodations to both races was illegal. "Although the Court had not voided Jim Crow, Mitchell was elated by the decision in his suit," concluded civil rights historian Catherine Barnes. "The ruling, he asserted, was 'the first real progress made during my lifetime in breaking down the vicious system of segregation which has enveloped Negroes in the South.'" *Mitchell v. United States* helped to lay the groundwork for future favorable legal precedents that paved the way for the Civil Rights Act of 1964. This landmark measure outlawed discrimination based on race, color, religion, sex, or national origin. Mitchell experienced additional satisfaction. The Rock Island settled Mitchell's suit by paying him $1,250, and in February 1951 it ended segregation on *all* of its passenger trains and in *all* facilities.[19]

While the Rock Island's musical, movie, and legal legacies are notable, there are other types of remembrances. For general readers there are articles and books that reference the railroad. A notable one is *My Island Home: An Autobiography*. The author, James Norman Hall (1887–1951), achieved recognition through his writings, such as his greatly admired book *Mutiny on the Bounty*. A native of Colfax, Iowa, located on the Omaha main line east of Des

Moines, Hall relates the excitement that he and his boyhood friends found in illegally riding the Rock Island:

> Number Six was due at Colfax at 10:45 P.M., but a good five minutes before that time it appeared around the curve westward, at the top of the Mitchellville grade, six miles away. The headlight proclaimed the glory of its coming, and the first faraway whistle was like a call to adventure in the summer night, sending shivers of delight up and down the spines of three of us more than ready to respond to it—Buller Sharpe, "Preacher" Stahl, son of the Methodist minister, and myself. Number Six took water at Colfax, and we waited beneath the water tank about fifty yards past the east end of the station. We would hear the fireman climb onto the tender and pull down the iron spout with the canvas nozzle attached; then in silence, save for the plash of water pouring in and the gentle yet powerful breathing of the engine. Presently up went the spout, spilling water remaining in it onto the ground just beyond where we were concealed. Then came the "high-ball"—that most stirring of signals—two short blasts of the whistle. Peering out from behind the post supporting the water tank we would see the conductor swinging his lantern from the station platform. The fireman gave a pull at the bell rope; the great wheels began to move, and at that the mighty "hough!" of the engine we skipped out, leaped on the pilot—and vanished into the pool of darkness just beneath the headlight.[20]

Usually Hall and his chums rode to Grinnell, thirty-two miles to the east. There they hopped a freight for their return home. Additional ticketless trips took place. Rock Island personnel finally discovered their illicit and dangerous activities and notified the Colfax mayor and the boys' parents. Hall reluctantly ceased his Rock Island adventures.[21]

Strong railfan interest in the Rock Island had led to a variety of heavily illustrated books. The most academic of this genre is Bill Marvel's *The Rock Island Line* (2013). The vast majority, however, focus on rolling stock and specific portions of the system. Representative works are Steve Allen Goen's *Down South on the Rock Island: A Color Pictorial, 1940–1969* (2002); Michael E. Hibblen's *Images of the Rail: Rock Island Railroad in Arkansas* (2017); John Kelly's *Rock Island Railroad: Travel on the Rockets* (2010); Thomas R. Lee's *Rock Island Westward* in three volumes (1992, 1998, 2016); Daryl McGeem's *Trackside on the Rock Island in Oklahoma with Frank Tribbey* (2012); Robert P. Olmsted's *Rock Island Recollections* (1982); Greg Stout's *Route of the Rockets: Rock Island in the Streamlined Era* (1997); Stephen M. Timko's *Rock Island Locomotive Portfolio, 1950–1980* (2018); Robert Yanosey's *Rock Island Power in Color* in two volumes (2014); and Louis A. Marre's *Rock Island Color Pictorial*, published in three volumes between 1990 and 1996, and also his *Rock Island Diesel Locomotives, 1930–1980* (1982).

Rock Island enthusiasts did more than produce books; they formed their own organization, the Rock Island Technical Society (RITS). It came into being in 1972 when a contributor to *Model Railroader* asked about the existence of a Rock Island–specific railfan group. Another enthusiast, David Engle, wrote back: "LET'S START ONE!" Shortly thereafter the society was incorporated by Engle, his wife, and a friend. Eventually RITS disintegrated because of infighting, lack of leadership, and allegations that a former officer embezzled society funds. In 2006 *Remember the Rock* began as an unaffiliated commercial entity, and it continues as an eighty-page semiannual publication. And the *Rock Island Reporter*, launched in 2013, provides a free fan-oriented e-newsletter.[22]

Much remains of the physical Rock Island. Not only do large segments of the right-of-way continue to support rock ballast, treated ties, and steel rails, but pieces of abandoned lines have been turned into recreational corridors. A prominent example is the Rock Island Trail State Park, opened in 1989 as part of the national Rails-to-Trails movement. The Illinois communities of Alta and Toulon are endpoints on this 28.5-mile crushed-stone walking and biking path, which once was part of the 85-mile Peoria Junction-to-Milan/Rock Island branch.[23]

Throughout the former Rock Island System, some support structures, often depots, remain in use by operating railroads, perhaps for track and signal maintainers, or have been adapted for nonrailroad purposes, including businesses, public agencies, and community organizations. One architectural gem created by the Warren Purdy administration, which dates from 1898, involved the Atlantic, Iowa, depot. In 2002 the Atlantic Rock Island Society Enterprise (ARISE), which acquired ownership, brought about an extensive restoration of what had become a structure in disrepair. This listing on the National Register of Historic Places houses the Atlantic Area Chamber of Commerce and contains a public conference center. The Renaissance revival–style multicolored brick building remains a focal point in this western Iowa county seat and trading center.[24]

Pieces of rolling stock exist, and some, nearly always locomotives and cabooses, are on public display. The most popular are former Rock Island steamers, such as No. 887, a 4-6-2 American Locomotive Company (Alco) product. Originally donated to the City of Peoria, it is presently part of the Wheels o' Time Museum in Dunlap, Illinois. Another Alco 4-6-2, No. 905, serves as the core attraction of the Rock Island 905 Railroad Museum located in Duncan, Oklahoma. A third Alco 4-6-2, No. 938, which for years rested on

In what at first glance appears to be a photograph from the Rock Island past, a modern Iowa Interstate Railroad (IAIS) diesel locomotive (ES44AC), with a westbound Bureau switcher and a Rock Island paint scheme, passes the Rock Island Depot Museum in Chillicothe, Illinois, midway on the Peoria line, on December 31, 2012. Henry Posner III, railroad enthusiast and principal owner of the IAIS, acquired the rights to this historic Rock Island beaver-pelt-inspired shield.

Eric Rasmussen photograph

the grounds of the Enid State School in Enid, Oklahoma, resides at the Illinois Railway Museum in Union.[25]

As with railroads in general, there are thousands of model railroaders, and the Rock Island is popular with these hobbyists. Commercial companies continue to produce models, usually in HO and O scale, of Rock Island locomotives, freight and passenger cars, and cabooses. A few individuals have built from scratch pieces of Rock Island equipment, stations, and the like. One gifted modeler, Gale Gish, went beyond the usual, constructing an amusement-park-size model of Rock Island gas-electric car No. 9014 for his backyard railroad.[26]

Mostly, one can find forgotten or unrecognized pieces of the Rock Island legacy. An example is Farrington Park in the western Missouri town of Windsor. Named in honor of longtime president John D. Farrington, this municipal park had its origins when the company completed its trans-Missouri line in 1904. Part of that construction involved building a reservoir to supply water for locomotives. Early on, the Rock Island allowed the town to take charge of "Rock Island Lake" and the surrounding grounds, resulting in a small urban

The municipal park in Windsor, Missouri, situated on the mostly abandoned Saint Louis–Kansas City line, is a present-day reminder of the Rock Island. Rather than being named for the railroad, it honors John D. Farrington. It was during the Farrington presidency that the company gave the town the land and a small lake.

Windsor Area Chamber of Commerce

park. On July 25, 1954, the company, no longer in need of boiler water, officially turned the park over to Windsor. Vice President John W. Barriger III, a man with a flair for public relations events, represented the railroad in the land-transfer ceremony. Immediately the property became "Farrington Park," a name that remains.[27]

Not to be overlooked is the human legacy. Former employees and their families continue to recall the good and the bad about their Rock Island experiences. The same can be said about others who have had contact with the railroad, most of all shippers. But over time individuals' memories fade and death takes its toll. Some remembrances, though, have become part of family oral traditions.

The liquidated Chicago, Rock Island & Pacific Railroad remains as "mighty fine roads." By the beginning of the second decade of the twenty-first century, about three-fourths of the trackage continued in service. Ownership belongs to five Class I roads, twenty-two regionals and shortlines, two commuter railroads, and one tourist hauler. Since the early 1980s, some segments have been abandoned, including shortlines Keota Washington Transportation Company and North Central Oklahoma Railroad. Much of the existing

The Iowa Interstate Railroad (IAIS) owns and has trackage rights over much of the historic Rock Island trans-Illinois and Iowa main line, but it uses only a single track. Remnants of the double track are revealed on May 26, 2011, as a westbound IAIS manifest crosses the Green River east of Colona, Illinois.

Eric Rasmussen photograph

trackage is in better shape today than when the Rock Island shut down in 1980. The Southern Pacific response stands out. When that company took possession of a major portion of the Golden State Route, it launched a multimillion-dollar rehabilitation. In 1981, for example, crews dumped a trainload of ballast somewhere between Topeka and Tucumcari on an almost daily basis. No more slow orders for this strategic line. When the Union Pacific acquired the Southern Pacific in 1996, it continued to make improvements. Currently the UP operates more than twenty trains daily on the Golden State Line. Before the demise of the Rock Island, six to eight trains made for a "busy" day.[28]

The fate of the Rock Island lines underscores the argument that its building, including that burst of construction during the 1880s, was hardly a mistake. The transportation picture, of course, has changed dramatically since that web of lines appeared during the railway age. For decades, Americans, especially agriculturalists, relied heavily on the iron horse; slow-moving, animal-powered vehicles traveling over poor and at times impassable roads offered little or no competition to flanged-wheel transport. Considering present traffic volumes on former Rock Island lines, which the Staggers

IOWA NORTHERN RAILWAY COMPANY

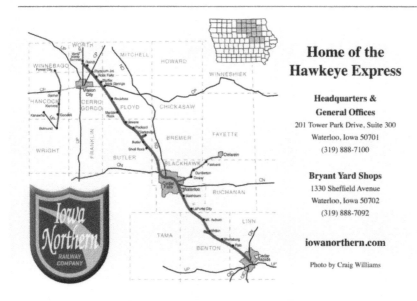

**Home of the
Hawkeye Express**

**Headquarters &
General Offices**
201 Tower Park Drive, Suite 300
Waterloo, Iowa 50701
(319) 888-7100

Bryant Yard Shops
1330 Sheffield Avenue
Waterloo, Iowa 50702
(319) 888-7092

iowanorthern.com

Photo by Craig Williams

One dynamic offshoot of the Rock Island is the Iowa Northern Railway, headquartered in Waterloo. This shortline transports grain, ethanol, and other commodities over slightly more than two hundred miles of rail. Most of its lines once belonged to the Rock Island.

Courtesy of Dan Sabin

Act in 1980 aided with partial deregulation, one cannot conclude that large chunks of its system were an unnecessary redundancy, notwithstanding experts who have contended that the nation's midsection had inordinate rail capacity.

The Rock Island saga has affected the railroad industry, past and present. It gave rise to multiple regional and short-line railroads. The Iowa Interstate Railroad and Northern Iowa Railway are examples of successful carriers. In time the Interstate Commerce Commission sped up the merger process; vivid memories of the Rock Island-Union Pacific merger debacle remained. When Burlington Northern and Santa Fe sought corporate marriage in the mid-1990s, new guidelines gave the ICC only sixteen months to approve or disapprove of what resulted in a successful application. Even the outcome of the BRAC-UTU strike, which sent shock waves through organized labor, had both short-term and lasting impact. "With the memory of the Rock Island fresh in everyone's mind, rail labor and commuter authorities [at a troubled Conrail] came to the bargaining table and made meaningful concessions,"

Not all pieces of the Rock Island survived, including former main lines. In the early 1980s, the abandoned remnants of a section of the "Mighty Fine Road" are seen west of Brinkley, Arkansas, along the Choctaw Route.

Dan Sabin coll.

opined railroad executive Jim McClellan. "In a few years, Conrail returned to profitability. So perhaps the Rock did not die in vain." Two-person crews on present-day freight trains are arguably partly a Rock Island legacy.[29]

Various individuals have assessed the Rock Island legacy, and two are representative. Late in his long life, Jervis Langdon Jr. offered his thoughts: "The Rock Island's storied past had more than its share of ups and downs, but it steadily provided long-term transportation to the public. I'm happy that much of its lines have survived and most are doing well." In a 2011 *Trains* essay, industry writer Fred W. Frailey remarked, "The fact that the Rock Island was dissolved by a bankruptcy judge but flourishes today under a bevy of different owners suggests it wasn't so redundant after all." Perhaps Ransom Cable and other builders of the Rock Island Lines might take pride in what ultimately happened to their railroad.[30]

NOTES

1. Pioneer Railroad

1. Brian McGinty, *Lincoln's Greatest Case: The River, the Bridge, and the Making of America* (New York: W. W. Norton, 2015), 159.

2. Michael P. Conzen and Kay J. Carr, eds., *The Illinois & Michigan Canal National Heritage Corridor: A Guide to Its History and Sources* (DeKalb: Northern Illinois University Press, 1988), xvii, 3–12; Ronald E. Shaw, *Canals for a Nation: The Canal Era in the United States, 1790–1860* (Lexington: University Press of Kentucky, 1990), 143; John Henry Krenkel, *Illinois Internal Improvements, 1818–1848* (Cedar Rapids, IA: Torch Press, 1958), 26–46.

3. Roger Biles, *Illinois: A History of the Land and Its People* (DeKalb: Northern Illinois University Press, 2005), 72; *Illinois Bounty Land Register* (Quincy, IL), 1835; *Chicago Weekly Journal*, April 17, 1848; James Davis, *Frontier Illinois* (Bloomington: Indiana University Press, 1998), 229–230; Louis P. Cain, "William Dean's Theory of Urban Growth: Chicago's Commerce and Industry, 1854–1871," *Journal of Economic History* 45 (June 1985): 246; *Statement of the Condition and Prospects of the Chicago & Rock Island Railroad Company* (New York: William C. Bryant, 1852), 9.

4. H. Roger Grant, *The North Western: A History of the Chicago & North Western Railway System* (DeKalb: Northern Illinois University Press), 6–11.

5. H. Roger Grant, *"Follow the Flag": A History of the Wabash Railroad Company* (DeKalb: Northern Illinois University Press, 2004), 3–8.

6. Roy P. Basler, ed., *Collected Works of Abraham Lincoln* (New Brunswick, NJ: Rutgers University Press, 1953–1955), 1:5–6.

During Abraham Lincoln's four terms in the Illinois General Assembly, from 1834 to 1842, he devoted considerable energy to promoting government funding for canals and railroads in a quest for a stronger Illinois economy.

7. "Source Material of Iowa History: The Davenport & Iowa City Rail Road," *Iowa Journal of History* 49 (July 1951): 264; *History of Scott County, Iowa* (Chicago: Inter-State Publishing, 1882), 318, 321–329.

8. John L. Scripps, *Rock Island and Its Surroundings in 1853* (Chicago, 1854), 4; Florence L. Dorsey, *Master of the Mississippi: Henry Shreve and the Conquest of the Mississippi* (Boston: Houghton Mifflin, 1941), 189–190; *Statement of the Condition and Prospects of the Chicago & Rock Island Railroad Company*, 4.

9. *Davenport (IA) Gazette*, January 7, February 4, 1847; Dwight L. Agnew, "Beginnings of the Rock Island Lines," *Journal of the Illinois State Historical Society* 45 (Winter 1953): 409; A. T. Andreas, *History of Chicago from the Earliest Period to the Present Time* (Chicago: A. T. Andreas, 1885), 2:148.

10. Agnew, "Beginnings of the Rock Island Lines," 409–410.

11. Alvin F. Harlow, "Farnam Built the Rock Island," *Trains* 9 (December 1948): 42; Shaw, *Canals for a Nation*, 53–54; Frederick C. Gamst, ed., *Early American Railroads: Franz Anton Ritter von Gerstner's Die innern Communicationen (1842–1843)* (Stanford, CA: Stanford University Press, 1997), 295, 362–363.

12. Harlow, "Farnam Built the Rock Island," 42–43; *New York Tribune*, October 5, 1883.

13. Harlow, "Farnam Built the Rock Island," 43–44; Dumas Malone, ed., *Dictionary*

of *American Biography* (New York: Charles Scribner's Sons, 1935), 9:58–59; Henry W. Farnam, *Henry Farnam* (New Haven, CT: Morehouse & Taylor, 1889), 32.

14. Farnam, *Henry Farnam*, 21; George Rogers Taylor, *The Transportation Revolution, 1815–1860* (New York: Holt, Rinehart & Winston, 1951), 38; Harlow, "Farnam Built the Rock Island," 44.

15. Harlow, "Farnam Built the Rock Island," 44–45; Farnam, *Henry Farnam*, 23–24.

16. Harlow, "Farnam Built the Rock Island," 45; Farnam, *Henry Farnam*, 24–25.

17. Farnam, *Henry Farnam*, 35–36.

18. F. Daniel Larkin, *John B. Jervis: An American Engineering Pioneer* (Ames: Iowa State University Press, 1990), 121–122; Farnam, *Henry Farnam*, 38.

19. The Michigan Southern & Northern Indiana Railroad might be referred to by its formal name or called the Michigan Southern or Indiana Railroad. Michigan Southern is more descriptive. The Indiana Railroad dates to 1852, and the MS&NI, organized in April 1855, became part of the Lake Shore & Michigan Southern in May 1869.

20. Harlow, "Farnam Built the Rock Island," 47; Larkin, *John B. Jervis*, 122.

21. Farnam, *Henry Farnam*, 39.

22. The location of the Chicago & Rock Island was hardly surprising. An early railroad advocate was William Redfield, a New Yorker who in 1829 disseminated a pamphlet that he revised the following year: *A Sketch of the Geographical Route of a Great Railway by Which It Is Proposed to Connect the Canals and Navigable Waters of New-York, Pennsylvania, Ohio, Indiana, Illinois, Michigan, and the Adjacent States and Territories.* Redfield's projection of a rail line across Illinois roughly followed what later occurred. Even before construction took place, this comment appeared in a Chicago & Rock Island prospectus: "Col. Morgan, who surveyed the line of a railroad from La Salle to Rock Island in 1850, in alluding to the great Western Railway proposed by Mr. Redfield, says—'He designated precisely the route which is now recommended, as part of that important line.' Col. Morgan also says that the route of the Rock Island and La Salle Railroad, 'is the best location for the proposed National thoroughfare across the great continent, which can be found between Lake Michigan and the Mississippi, *or anywhere else* [italics in original].'" *Statement of the Condition and*

Prospects of the Chicago & Rock Island Railroad Company, 16.

23. William Edward Hayes, *Iron Road to Empire: The History of 100 Years of the Progress and Achievements of the Rock Island Lines* (New York: Simmons-Boardman, 1953), 15; Agnew, "Beginnings of the Rock Island Lines," 441; Farnam, *Henry Farnam*, 40.

Although William Edward Hayes wrote an entertaining centennial account of the Rock Island, he lacked training as a historian. This Muncie, Indiana, native, who received a public-school education, went "railroadin'" after high school. His first job was with the New York Central, and he later joined the Rock Island and Northern Pacific. His job positions were varied, ranging from per diem clerk to train dispatcher. In 1922, at age twenty-five, Hayes joined the fourth estate, taking a position with the *New York Evening Journal*. In 1929, however, he renewed his tie to railroading when he helped to revive *Railroad Magazine*, a publication of the Frank A. Muncy Company. Throughout much of the 1930s, Hayes was engaged in writing, and his works include more than 250 short stories, novelettes, and fact articles for a variety of publishers. Most contained railroad-related content. During World War II he worked for the Office of Defense Transportation, and in 1947 he returned to the Rock Island, becoming an executive assistant to President John Dow Farrington by the time he prepared the company history. Hayes continued to work for the railroad until his retirement.

24. Agnew, "Beginnings of the Rock Island Lines," 412; Farnam, *Henry Farnam*, 40–41.

25. Agnew, "Beginnings of the Rock Island Lines," 412–413; Hayes, *Iron Road to Empire*, 16–17.

26. Larkin, *John B. Jervis*, 126; *Joliet* (IL) *Signal*, June 17, 1851.

27. *Statement of the Condition and Prospects of the Chicago & Rock Island Railroad*, 6; *The Chicago, Rock Island & Pacific Railway System and Representative Employees* (Chicago: Biographical Company, 1900), 75; Harlow, "Farnam Built the Rock Island," 47–48.

28. Hayes, *Iron Road to Empire*, 18; F. David Larkin, "John B. Jervis," in *Railroads in the Nineteenth Century*, ed. Robert L. Frey (New York: Facts-on-File, 1988), 202, 206; Agnew, "Beginnings of the Rock Island Lines," 415.

29. "Statement of Conditions and Prospects of the Chicago and Rock Island Railroad," September 1852, quoted in Agnew, "Beginnings of the Rock Island Lines," 423.

30. *Chicago Daily Democrat*, October 13, 1852; *Rock Island Lines News Digest* 11 (October 1952): 15.

31. William J. Petersen, "Railroads Come to Iowa," *Palimpsest* 41 (April 1960): 186; Harlow, "Farnam Built the Rock Island," 48–49.

32. *Annual Report of the President and Directors to the Stockholders of the Chicago and Rock Island Rail Road Company, July 1, 1859* (New York: Chicago and Rock Island Rail Road, 1859), 7.

33. *Chicago Press*, n.d., quoted in Franc B. Wilkie, *Davenport Past and Present: Including the Early History, and Personal and Anecdotal Reminiscences of Davenport* (Davenport, IA: Publishing House of Luse, Lane & Co., 1858), 114–116; Harlow, "Farnam Built the Rock Island," 49; *American Railroad Journal* 10 (June 24, 1854): 398.

34. William J. Petersen, "The Rock Island Railroad Excursion of 1854," *Minnesota History* 15 (December 1934): 405–420; Catherine M. Sedgwick, "The Great Excursion to the Falls of St. Anthony," *Putnam's Monthly* (September 1854): 320–323.

35. Harlow, "Farnam Built the Rock Island," 49–50; F. Wesley Krambeck, William D. Edson, and Jack W. Farrell, *Rock Island Steam Power* (Potomac, MD: Edson, 2002), 7.

36. Wilkie, *Davenport Past and Present*, 111; Alec Kirby, "Thomas C. Durant," in *Railroads in the Nineteenth Century*, ed. Robert L. Frey (New York: Facts-on-File, 1988), 111; Levi O. Leonard and Jack T. Johnson, *A Railroad to the Sea* (Iowa City: Midland House, 1939), 24; Farnam, *Henry Farnam*, 44; Stephen P. Hirshson, *Grenville M. Dodge: Soldier, Politician, Railroad Pioneer* (Bloomington: Indiana University Press, 1967), 12; *Manual of the Railroads of the United States* (New York: H. V. & H. W. Poor, 1868), 217; Harlow, "Farnam Built the Rock Island," 50; *Decisions of the Interstate Commerce Commission of the United States*, vol. 24, Valuation Reports (Washington, DC: US Government Printing Office, 1929), 845; Paul Wallace Gates, *The Illinois Central and Its Colonization Work* (Cambridge, MA: Harvard University Press, 1934), 19, 86.

37. *New York Times*, April 23, 1853; J. M. D. Burrows, *Fifty Years in Iowa: Being the Personal Reminiscences of J. M. D. Burrows* (Davenport, IA: Glass, 1888), 270; *Chicago, Rock Island & Pacific Railway System and Representative Employees*, 78.

38. *Report of the President and Directors of the Mississippi & Missouri Railroad Company to the Stockholders, 31st May, 1857* (New York: Wm. C. Bryant, 1857), iii; Petersen, "Railroads Come to Iowa," 184; Dwight L. Agnew, "Iowa's First Railroad," *Iowa Journal of History* 48 (January 1950): 2–3; Wilkie, *Davenport Past and Present*, 109–110.

John Adams Dix's son, Morgan, who assembled his father's memoirs, remembered, "On withdrawing from politics he accepted an invitation to become President of the Chicago and Rock Island Railroad, a post which brought much hard work, with small pecuniary return." He added, "It gave him, however, what he most desired, constant occupation, and filled his active mind with larger and important subjects." See Morgan Dix, compiler, *Memoirs of John Adams Dix* (New York: Harper & Brothers, 1883), 1:302.

39. Grenville M. Dodge, "Surveying the M. & M.," *Palimpsest* 18 (September 1937): 305, 307, 309; Genevieve P. Mauck, "Kanesville," *Palimpsest* 42 (September 1961): 385–398; Genevieve P. Mauck, "Council Bluffs Emerges," *Palimpsest* 42 (September 1961): 399; Agnew, "Iowa's First Railroad," 3, 5; Mildred J. Sharp, "The M. & M. Railroad," *Palimpsest* 3 (January 1922): 3; "The Pioneer Railroad of Iowa," *Iowa Historical Record* 8 (July 1897): 123–124; *History of Johnson County, Iowa, Containing a History of the County, and Its Townships, Cities and Villages from 1836 to 1882* (Iowa City: 1883), 263.

40. Wilkie, *Davenport Past and Present*, 110–112; "History of Scott County, Continued," *Annals of the State Historical Society of Iowa* (July 1863): 119; Hayes, *Iron Road to Empire*, 36; Sharp, "M. & M. Railroad," 6.

41. David Hudson, Marvin Bergman, and Loren Horton, eds., *The Biographical Dictionary of Iowa* (Iowa City: University of Iowa Press, 2008), 125–126, 132; Jack T. Johnson, *Peter Anthony Dey: Integrity in Public Service* (Iowa City: State Historical Society of Iowa, 1939), 45; Dodge, "Surveying the M. & M.," 303; Don L. Hofsommer, *Steel Trails of Hawkeyeland: Iowa's Railroad Experience* (Bloomington: Indiana University Press, 2005), 8.

42. Hirshson, *Grenville M. Dodge*, 26–27.

43. *American Railroad Journal* 12 (October 11, 1856): 645; Ruth Irish Preston, "The Lyons and Iowa Central Railroad," *Annals of Iowa* 9 (1910): 284–301.

44. Agnew, "Iowa's First Railroad," 14–15.

45. Agnew, "Iowa's First Railroad," 15.

46. Agnew, "Iowa's First Railroad," 16, 17; H. Roger Grant, ed., *Iowa Railroads: The Essays of Frank P. Donovan, Jr.* (Iowa City: University of Iowa Press, 2000), 170.

The Mississippi & Missouri could not claim to have operated the first steam locomotive west of the Mississippi River. That honor goes to the *Pacific*, which appeared on the Pacific Railroad, a Missouri Pacific predecessor, at Saint Louis on December 2, 1852. See Hubert H. Hoeltje, "The 'First' Locomotive," *Palimpsest* 12 (1931): 64–69.

47. Mildred Throne, "Streamliners in Iowa," *Palimpsest* 32 (June 1951): 229.

48. *Muscatine Daily Journal*, November 23, 1855; Hofsommer, *Steel Trails of Hawkeyeland*, 8.

49. *History of Johnson County, Iowa*, 238; Hirshson, *Grenville M. Dodge*, 13; Hayes, *Iron Road to Empire*, 39–43; Agnew, "Iowa's First Railroad," 23; Grant, *Iowa Railroads*, 170–171; *Speech of Gen. John A. Dix, President of the Mississippi and Missouri Railroad Company at the Celebration at Iowa City, Capital of the State of Iowa, on the Completion of the Road to the Latter Point* (New York: Wm. C. Bryant, 1856).

50. Dodge, "Surveying the M. & M.," 310; Johnson Brigham, *Des Moines Together with the History of Polk County, Iowa* (Chicago: S. J. Clarke, 1911), 1:111; Roscoe L. Lokken, *Iowa Public Land Disposal* (Iowa City: State Historical Society of Iowa, 1942), 164, 244–246; *History of Polk County, Iowa, Containing a History of the County, Its Cities, Towns* (Des Moines: Union Historical Company, 1880), 173.

51. *Annual Report of the President and Directors to the Stockholders of the Chicago and Rock Island Railroad Company, July 1st, 1860* (New York, 1860), 7; George W. Van Vleck, *The Panic of 1857, an Analytical Study* (New York: Columbia University Press, 1943), 72; James L. Huston, *The Panic of 1857 and the Coming of the Civil War* (Baton Rouge: Louisiana State University Press, 1987), 32.

52. Edward Hungerford, *The Story of the Baltimore & Ohio Railroad* (New York: G. P. Putnam's Sons, 1928), 1:316; Farnam, *Henry Farnam*, 55–56.

53. "Source Material of Iowa History," 261.

54. *Private Laws of the State of Illinois Passed at the First Session of the Eighteenth General Assembly, Begun and Held at the City of Springfield, January 7, 1853* (Springfield, IL: State Printer, 1853), 329; Benedict K. Zobrist, "Steamboat Men versus Railroad Men: The First Bridging of the Mississippi River," *Missouri Historical Review* 59 (January 1965): 160.

55. Bernie Babcock, "Lincoln and the First Mississippi Bridge," *Railroad Man's Magazine* 4 (February 1931): 328; David A. Pfeiffer, "Lincoln for the Defense: Railroads, Steamboats and the Rock Island Bridge," *Railroad History* 200 (Spring–Summer 2009): 49; Zobrist, "Steamboat Men versus Railroad Men," 162; McGinty, *Lincoln's Greatest Case*, 66.

56. River interests did not show any strong negativity toward the proposed bridging of the Mississippi River near Lyons City, Iowa, for the Lyons & Iowa Central Air Line Rail Road. Backers of that stillborn project planned to construct a suspension bridge at the narrows of the river by taking advantage of the Fulton Bluff on the Illinois side and the Long Grave Bluff on the Iowa side. This structure presumably would not impede steamboat traffic. See Preston, "Lyons and Iowa Central Railroad," 292, 296.

57. McGinty, *Lincoln's Greatest Case*, 69; *Western Journal* 2 (1849): 1–2.

During the 1850s, steamboat activity on the Mississippi River reached its peak and then declined. Although the Civil War caused major traffic disruptions, the steadily growing network of railroads was the principal cause of decline.

58. Dwight L. Agnew, "Jefferson Davis and the Rock Island Bridge," *Iowa Journal of History* 47 (January 1949): 4–5.

59. Daniel Webster Flagler, *A History of the Rock Island Arsenal* (Washington, DC: US Government Printing Office, 1877), 60; Pfeiffer, "Lincoln for the Defense," 51; John C. Parish, "The First Mississippi Bridge," *Palimpsest* 3 (May 1922): 136.

60. McGinty, *Lincoln's Greatest Case*, 66–67; Hayes, *Iron Road to Empire*, 44; Agnew, "Jefferson Davis and the Rock Island Bridge," 13; Dee Brown, *Hear That Lonesome Whistle Blow: The Epic Story of the Transcontinental Railroads* (New York: Henry Holt, 1977), 9.

61. Elwin L. Page, "The *Effie Afton* Case," *Lincoln Herald* 58 (Fall 1954): 3–4; Pfeiffer, "Lincoln for the Defense," 51–52.

62. Pfeiffer, "Lincoln for the Defense," 52.

63. McGinty, *Lincoln's Greatest Case*, 131–161; John William Starr, *Lincoln & the Railroads: A Biographical Study* (New York: Dodd, Mead & Company, 1927), 104–105; Zobrist, "Steamboat Men versus Railroad Men," 168.

64. McGinty, *Lincoln's Greatest Case*, 171.

65. Parish, "First Mississippi Bridge," 138–140; Pfeiffer, "Lincoln for the Defense," 53–54; *The American Law Register* 16 (May 1868): 409–411.

66. *Chicago, Rock Island & Pacific Railway System and Representative Employees*, 96; McGinty, *Lincoln's Greatest Case*, 2, 150, 186–187.

67. Frank J. Nevins, "The La Salle Street Station, Chicago, Illinois," *Railway and Locomotive Historical Society Bulletin* 50 (October 1939):84–87; *Chicago Herald*, October 21, 1855.

68. D. C. Brooks, "Chicago and Its Railways," (October 1872): 278, article in possession of author; Edward J. Wojtas, "The Fading Grandeur of La Salle Street Station," *Railroad* 86 (October 1970): 24; Andreas, *History of Chicago*, 3:189.

Line construction and betterments to Chicago financed by the Rock Island and other railroads reveal that the private sector made the Lakeside City a railroad mecca. In her 1937 *A History of Chicago, 1848–1871*, Bessie Pierce wrote, "Chicago as a city had made no railroad investments, and Chicagoans as a whole had not unduly loosened their purse strings to finance railway construction."

69. William Cronon, *Nature's Metropolis: Chicago and the Great West* (New York: W. W. Norton, 1991), 148.

70. William S. Greever, *Bonanza West: The Story of Western Mining Rushes, 1848–1900* (Moscow: University of Idaho Press, 1963), 157–168; "Railroad Carried Gold Seekers," *Rock Island Lines News Digest* 11 (October 1952): 18.

71. *Manual of the Railroads of the United States for 1868–69* (New York: H. V. & H. W. Poor, 1868), 212, 215–217.

72. *Annual Report of the President and Directors to the Stockholders of the Chicago and Rock Island Railroad Company, April 1st, 1866* (New York: L. H. Biglow, 1866), 7; Hayes, *Iron Road to Empire*, 51–53.

73. Brigham, *Des Moines*, 243, 251; Hayes, *Iron Road to Empire*, 54–55; Grant, *Iowa Railroads*, 175; Barbara Beving Long, *Des Moines and Polk County: Flag on the Prairie* (Northridge, CA: Windsor, 1988), 25; Tacitus Hussey, "How Des Moines Valley Railroad Came to Des Moines," *Annals of Iowa* 8 (1907): 132; *Decisions of the Interstate Commerce Commission*, 814.

Henry Farnum, so long associated with the gestating Rock Island, apparently became tired of active railroad building, and

so he devoted his time "to finance and musing." See Leonard and Johnson, *Railroad to the Sea*, 33.

74. *Poor's Manual of Railroads, 1868*, 212.

75. *Travelers Official Railway Guide of the United States and Canada, June 1868* (New York: National Railway Publication Company, 1968 rept.), 177.

76. Robert E. Stewart Jr., "History of the Suburban Service of the Rock Island Railroad in the Chicago Area, Part I," *Railway and Locomotive Historical Society Bulletin* 77 (July 1949): 35–39; *Railroad Gazette* 14 (April 2, 1870): 3.

77. *Poor's Manual of Railroads, 1868*, 212.

78. Chicago, Rock Island & Pacific Railroad public timetable, ca. 1871; Allan Bogue, *From Prairie to Corn Belt: Farming on the Illinois and Iowa Prairies in the Nineteenth Century* (Chicago: Quadrangle Books, 1968), 180–181.

79. *Poor's Manual of Railroads, 1868*, 215; John H. Vogel, *Great Lakes Lumber on the Great Plains: The Laird, Norton Lumber Company of South Dakota* (Iowa City: University of Iowa Press, 1992), 11.

80. *Poor's Manual of Railroads, 1868*, 217.

2. Expansion

1. *Annual Report of the President and Directors to the Stockholders of the Chicago, Rock Island and Pacific Railroad Company, April 1, 1869* (New York: L. H. Biglow, 1869); William Edward Hayes, *Iron Road to Empire: The History of 100 Years of Progress and Achievements of the Rock Island Lines* (New York: Simmons-Boardman, 1953), 56; H. Roger Grant, *North Western: A History of the Chicago & North Western System* (DeKalb: Northern Illinois University Press, 1996), 30; *History of Pottawattamie County, Iowa* (Chicago: O. L. Baskin, 1883), 188–189; Frank P. Donovan Jr., "The North Western in Iowa," *Palimpsest* 43 (December 1962): 556.

2. *History of Pottawattamie County*, 201; Homer H. Field and Joseph H. Reed, *History of Pottawattamie County, Iowa from the Earliest Historic Times to 1907* (Chicago: S. J. Clarke, 1907), 1:57; Hayes, *Iron Road to Empire*, 57; John H. White Jr., "Grant's Silver Locomotive," *Railway & Locomotive Historical Society Bulletin* 104 (April 1961): 55.

3. White, "Grant's Silver Locomotive," 55.

4. "The Silver Engine," *Rock Island Magazine* 17 (October 1922): 24; White, "Grant's Silver Locomotive," 58; Hayes, *Iron Road to Empire*, 57.

5. Edward Hungerford, *Men of Erie: A Story of Human Effort* (New York: Random House, 1946), 165.

6. Richard C. Overton, *Burlington Route: A History of the Burlington Lines* (New York: Alfred A. Knopf, 1965), 96.

The Burlington & Missouri River Railroad did not technically reach Council Bluffs on its own rails. Rather its Burlington, Iowa-East Plattsmouth, Iowa, main line connected at Pacific Junction, Iowa, with its affiliated St. Joseph & Council Bluffs Rail Road. This permitted Burlington trains to enter the Bluffs over that firm's trackage. Service between Saint Joseph, Missouri, and Council Bluffs had begun in August 1868.

7. Julius Grodinsky, *Iowa Pool: A Study in Railroad Competition, 1870–84* (Chicago: University of Chicago Press, 1950), 15–18; Overton, *Burlington Route*, 108–109.

8. Grant, *North Western*, 35.

9. Grant, *North Western*, 35; Overton, *Burlington Route*, 118–119.

10. Grodinsky, *Iowa Pool*, 75–76; Hayes, *Iron Road to Empire*, 76.

11. Hayes, *Iron Road to Empire*, 73–74; *Annual Report of the President and Directors to the Stockholders of the Chicago, Rock Island and Pacific Railroad Company, April 1, 1870* (New York: L. H. Biglow, 1870), 8.

12. *The Chicago, Rock Island & Pacific Railway System and Representative Employees* (Chicago: Biographical Company, 1900), 103–104; *Annual Report of the Directors to the Stockholders of the Chicago, Rock Island & Pacific Railroad Company, April 1, 1878* (Chicago: Cameron, Amberg & Co., 1878), 8–10.

13. Hayes, *Iron Road to Empire*, 78–79; *Chicago Daily Tribune*, September 29, 1871.

14. *Rock Island Magazine*, October 1922, 25; *Chicago Daily Tribune*, September 29, 1871.

15. Stuart Daggett, *Railroad Reorganization* (Cambridge, MA: Harvard University Press, 1908), 311.

16. H. Roger Grant, "Railroaders and Reformers: The Chicago & North Western Encounters Grangers and Progressives," *Annals of Iowa* 50 (Winter 1991): 772–786; Mildred Throne, *Cyrus Clay Carpenter and Iowa Politics, 1854–1898* (Iowa City: State Historical Society of Iowa, 1974), 180–183; *Annual Report to the President, Directors, and Stockholders of the Chicago, Rock Island & Pacific Railroad Company, April 1, 1875* (Chicago: Rand, McNally & Co., 1875), 9.

17. Daggett, *Railroad Reorganization*, 312.

18. Hayes, *Iron Road to Empire*, 80.

19. H. Roger Grant, ed., *Iowa Railroads: The Essays of Frank P. Donovan, Jr.* (Iowa City: University of Iowa Press, 2000), 177; Johnson Brigham, *Des Moines Together with the History of Polk County, Iowa* (Chicago: S. J. Clarke, 1911), 1:606–607; Hayes, *Iron Road to Empire*, 90; Joseph W. Walt, *Beneath the Whispering Maples: The History of Simpson College* (Indianola, IA: Simpson College, 1995), 58; *Rock Island Magazine*, October 1922, 26; *Decisions of the Interstate Commerce Commission of the United States*, vol. 24, Valuation Reports (Washington, DC: US Government Printing Office, 1929), 852.

20. *Annual Report to the President, Directors and Stockholders of the Chicago, Rock Island and Pacific Railroad Company, April 1, 1876* (Chicago: Rand, McNally & Co., 1876), 14; Overton, *Burlington Route*, 164–165.

21. Donovan L. Hofsommer, "A Chronology of Iowa Railroads," *Railroad History* 132 (Spring 1975): 74–75; John W. Wright, *History of Marion County, Iowa, and Its People* (Chicago: S. J. Clarke, 1915), 236–237; *History of Mahaska County, Iowa, Containing a History of the County, Its Cities, Towns, &c.* (Des Moines, IA: Union Historical, 1878), 348, 350.

22. *Rock Island Magazine*, October 1922, 25; Grant, *Iowa Railroads*, 177–178; Ray L. Bryant, *A Preliminary Guide to Iowa Railroads* (n.p.: privately printed, 1984).

23. Hayes, *Iron Road to Empire*, 91; *Annual Report 1878*, 7–8.

24. *Chicago, Rock Island & Pacific Railway System and Representative Employees*, 110; *Manual of the Railroads of the United States for 1885* (New York: Poor's Railroad Manual, 1885), 664–665; Daggett, *Railroad Reorganization*, 312–313.

25. Grant, *Iowa Railroads*, 178; Hayes, *Iron Road to Empire*, 87–89.

26. T. J. Stiles, *Jesse James: Last Rebel of the Civil War* (New York: Alfred A. Knopf, 2002), 233–234; William A. Settle Jr., *Jesse James Was His Name* (Columbia: University of Missouri Press, 1966), 48.

27. Stiles, *Jesse James*, 230–233; Ronald H. Beights, *Jesse James and the First Missouri Train Robbery* (Gretna, LA: Pelican, 2002), 19, 156; Settle, *Jesse James Was His Name*, 108; B. A. Botkin and Alvin F. Harlow, eds., *A Treasury of Railroad Folklore: The Stories, Tall Tales, Traditions, Ballads and Songs of the American Railroad Man* (New York: Crown, 1953), 194–197.

28. The James gang did not invent the peacetime train robbery. Immediately after the Civil War, the Reno gang, or Reno brothers gang, of Indiana likely first perpetrated this crime. See Robert W. Shields, *Seymour Indiana and the Famous Story of the Reno Gang Who Terrorized America with the First Train Robberies in World History* (Seymour, IN: privately printed, 1935); Botkin and Harlow, *Treasury of Railroad Folklore*, 187–192.

29. Grant, *Iowa Railroads*, 178.

30. Hayes, *Iron Road to Empire*, 90.

31. *Chicago, Rock Island & Pacific Railway System and Representative Employees*, 179–180; Edward Harold Mott, *Between the Ocean and the Lakes: The Story of the Erie* (New York: J. S. Collins, 1901), 493.

32. Grant, *Iowa Railroads*, 179; *Decisions of the Interstate Commerce Commission*, 814–815; *Thirteenth Annual Report of the Directors to the Stockholders of the Chicago, Rock Island and Pacific Railroad Company, April 1, 1879* (Chicago: Cameron, Amberg & Co., 1879), 10; George W. Hilton, *American Narrow Gauge Railroads* (Stanford, CA: Stanford University Press, 1990), 398–399.

33. Hofsommer, "Chronology of Iowa Railroads," 76; *Fourteenth Annual Report of the Directors to the Stockholders of the Chicago, Rock Island & Pacific Railroad Company, April 1, 1880* (Chicago: Cameron, Amberg & Co., 1880), 9.

34. *Chicago, Rock Island & Pacific Railway System and Representative Employees*, 111–112; Overton, *Burlington Route*, 173; Charles N. Glaab, *Kansas City and the Railroads: Community Policy in the Growth of a Regional Metropolis* (Madison: State Historical Society of Wisconsin, 1962), 175, 177; August Derleth, *The Milwaukee Road: Its First Hundred Years* (New York: Creative, 1948), 134.

35. *Poor's Manual of Railroads, 1885*, 666.

36. Chicago, Rock Island & Pacific Railroad public timetable, December 1878; Hayes, *Iron Road to Empire*, 91–92; *History of Pottawattamie County*, 251.

37. *Rock Island Magazine*, October 1922, 78; *American Railway Times*, July 7, 1877.

38. *Rock Island Magazine*, October 1922, 78; Hayes, *Iron Road to Empire*, 92.

39. Chicago, Rock Island & Pacific Railroad public timetable, December 1878; *Rock Island Magazine*, October 1922, 73–74, 80; John H. White Jr., *The American Railroad Passenger Car* (Baltimore, MD: Johns Hopkins University Press, 1978), 259.

40. Robert E. Stewart Jr., "A History of the Suburban Service of the Rock Island Railroad in the Chicago Area," *Railway & Locomotive Historical Society Bulletin* 77 (July 1949): 41–42.

41. "Ransom R. Cable," *Railway Age Gazette* 47 (November 26, 1909): 1013.

42. "Ransom R. Cable," 1013; Wade A. Calvert, *The Rock Island & Peoria Railway: The Peoria Route* (Port Byron, IL: Calvert Systems, 2006), 122–124; *Poor's Manual of Railroads, 1885*, 688; *Chicago, Rock Island & Pacific Railway System and Representative Employees*, 167; Hayes, *Iron Road to Empire*, 104–105.

43. Hayes, *Iron Road to Empire*, 109; Maury Klein, *Union Pacific: The Birth of a Railroad, 1862–1893* (Garden City, NY: Doubleday, 1987), 471–472; *New York Times*, July 8, 1884.

44. Grant, *Iowa Railroads*, 182.

45. Don L. Hofsommer, *The Iowa Route: A History of the Burlington, Cedar Rapids & Northern Railway* (Bloomington: Indiana University Press, 2015), 33–34.

46. *Poor's Manual of Railroads, 1885*, 730–731.

47. *Poor's Manual of Railroads, 1885*, 731.

48. Hofsommer, *Iowa Route*, 68–70; Overton, *Burlington Route*, 174.

49. Hofsommer, *Iowa Route*, 116; *Decisions of the Interstate Commerce Commission*, 929; Grant, *Iowa Railroads*, 186.

50. Hofsommer, "Chronology of Iowa Railroads," 77; *Decisions of the Interstate Commerce Commission*, 930; Grant, *Iowa Railroads*, 186–187.

51. *Decisions of the Interstate Commerce Commission*, 930.

52. Grant, *Iowa Railroads*, 181.

53. *Poor's Manual of Railroads, 1885*, 716; Don L. Hofsommer, *The Tootin' Louie: A History of the Minneapolis & St. Louis Railway* (Minneapolis: University of Minnesota Press, 2005), 17–19; Frank P. Donovan Jr., *Mileposts on the Prairie: The Story of the Minneapolis & St. Louis Railway* (New York: Simmons-Boardman, 1950), 64.

54. *Poor's Manual of Railroads, 1885*, 717.

55. Donovan, *Mileposts on the Prairie*, 79–80; Hofsommer, *Tootin' Louie*, 42; H. Roger Grant, *The Corn Belt Route: A History of the Chicago Great Western Railroad Company* (DeKalb: Northern Illinois University Press, 1984), 50–51.

Ransom Cable had made a good choice when he selected William H. Truesdale at both the M&StL and Rock Island.

When Truesdale left the Rock Island in 1899, he became the head of the Delaware, Lackawanna & Western, making it one of America's best and most profitable railroads. Robert J. Casey and W. A. S. Douglas, *The Lackawanna Story: The First Hundred Years of the Delaware, Lackawanna and Western Railroad* (New York: McGraw-Hill, 1951), 103–107.

56. *Manual of the Railroads of the United States for 1894* (New York: H. V. & H. W. Poor, 1894), 417; Hayes, *Iron Road to Empire*, 112–113; *Decisions of the Interstate Commerce Commission*, 927; *Manual of the Railroads of the United States for 1887* (New York: H. V. and H. W. Poor, 1887), 997; *Eighth Annual Report of the Directors to the Stockholders of the Chicago, Rock Island & Pacific Railway Company, April 1, 1888*, 10–11.

57. *Eighth Annual Report of the Board of Railroad Commissioners for the Year Ending December 1, 1890* (Topeka: Kansas Publishing House, 1890), xv.

58. S. F. Van Oss, *American Railroads as Investments: A Handbook for Investors in American Railroad Securities* (New York: G. P. Putnam's Sons, 1893), 523.

59. *Decisions of the Interstate Commerce Commission*, 923; Hayes, *Iron Road to Empire*, 113–115.

60. Leonard Wilson Thompson, "The History of Railway Development in Kansas" (PhD diss., State University of Iowa, 1942), 206; Hayes, *Iron Road to Empire*, 115–117; *Rock Island Magazine*, October 1922, 71; I. E. Quastler, *Prairie Railroad Town: The Rock Island Railroad Shops at Horton, Kansas, 1887–1946* (David City, NE: South Platte, 2003), 17.

61. Quastler, *Prairie Railroad Town*, 15, 17.

62. Hayes, *Iron Road to Empire*, 119–120; *Tenth Annual Report of the Directors to the Stockholders of the Chicago, Rock Island & Pacific Railway Company, April 1, 1890*, 14; Nancy Hope Self, "The Building of the Railroads in the Cherokee Nation," *Chronicles of Oklahoma* 49 (Summer 1971): 200, 204; Thompson, "History of Railway Development in Kansas," 210; *Seventh Annual Report of the Board of Railroad Commissioners for the Year Ending December 1, 1889* (Topeka: Kansas Publishing House, 1889), 277; *Topeka (Kansas) Capital*, January 1, 1888.

63. Frank E. Wolf, "Railway Development in Kansas" (MA thesis, University of Kansas, 1917), 55; Clarence L. Petrowsky, "The Influence of Railway Building on the Development of Southwest Kansas"

(MA thesis, University of Oklahoma, 1949), v, 29–30; Golda Mildred Crawford, "Railroads of Kansas: A Study in Local Aid" (DSS diss., Syracuse University, 1963), 26.

64. R. Alton Lee, *T-Town on the Plains* (Manhattan, KS: Sunflower University Press, 1999), 32–34.

65. Lee, *T-Town on the Plains*, 34.

66. In August 1888 Mark Low indicated that "except for purpose of receiving cattle in the Public Land Strip," the CK&N did not operate its line beyond Liberal. As he further explained, "The road was extended south from Liberal into the Public Land Strip solely for the purpose of enabling the company to transport Texas cattle, which could not be driven into the State of Kansas [because of the Texas Fever act]." *Sixth Annual Report of the Board of Railroad Commissioners for the Year Ending December 1, 1888* (Topeka: Kansas Publishing House, 1888), 129–130.

A small settlement quickly appeared at the end of the tracks. "They built the railroad, as I remember in August, 1888, shot it right on the southwest some seven or eight miles and stopped just over the Kansas line in No Man's Land," an area rancher remembered. "Here they built a big stock yard and a little town sprang up almost over night consisting principally of gamblers, girls and saloons." George Rainey, *No Man's Land: The Historic Story of a Landed Orphan* (Enid, OK: privately printed, 1937), 108.

67. Lee, *T-Town on the Plains*, 33; Hayes, *Iron Road to Empire*, 117–119.

68. Thompson, "History of Railway Development in Kansas," 208–209; *Decisions of the Interstate Commerce Commission*, 924; *Dodge City and Ford County, Kansas, 1870–1920* (Dodge City, KS: Ford County Historical Society, 1966), 29.

69. Crawford, "Railroads of Kansas," 78–81; *Sixth Annual Report of the Board of Railroad Commissioners*, 3; *Seventh Annual Report of the Board of Railroad Commissioners*, 292.

70. Wolf, "Railway Development in Kansas," 75; *Sixth Annual Report of the Board of Railroad Commissioners*, 3–4.

71. *Fifth Annual Report of the Board of Railroad of Railroad Commissioners for the Year Ending December 1, 1887* (Topeka: State Printer, 1887), 6–7; Frank S. Sullivan, *A History of Meade County, Kansas* (Topeka, KS: Crane, 1916), 32–33; Carl Van Doren, *An Illinois Boyhood* (New York: Viking, 1939), 25–26.

72. Marion Tuttle Rock, *Illustrated History of Oklahoma* (Topeka, KS: C. B. Hamilton & Son, 1890), 200–201.

73. Hayes, *Iron Road to Empire*, 120; *Decisions of the Interstate Commerce Commission*, 1001, 1003; *Chicago, Rock Island & Pacific Railway System and Representative Employees*, 118; Robert G. Athearn, *The Denver and Rio Grande Western Railroad: Rebel of the Rockies* (New Haven, CT: Yale University Press, 1962), 169; Hilton, *American Narrow Gauge Railroads*, 348; Thomas R. Lee, *Rock Island Westward: Rails to the Rockies* (Clay Center, KS: T. Lee, 1998), 2:13–14.

74. *Railroad Gazette*, January 17, 1890, 49.

75. Hayes, *Iron Road to Empire*, 127–130; Klein, *Union Pacific*, 577–578; *New York Times*, July 28, 1891.

76. *Railway Age Gazette* 47 (November 26, 1909): 103.

77. Berlin B. Chapman, "The Founding of El Reno," *Chronicles of Oklahoma* 34 (Spring 1956): 79, 81, 83.

78. Hayes, *Iron Road to Empire*, 125–126; *Decisions of the Interstate Commerce Commission*, 923, 934; *New York Times*, March 13, 1891; *Twelfth Annual Report of the Directors to the Stockholders of the Chicago, Rock Island & Pacific Railway Company, April 1, 1892*, 13.

79. Hayes, *Iron Road to Empire*, 143; *Decisions of the Interstate Commerce Commission*, 1066; *Manual of the Railroads of the United States for 1894* (New York: H. V. & H. W. Poor, 1894), 418; *Fourteenth Annual Report of the Directors to the Stockholders of the Chicago, Rock Island & Pacific Railway Company, April 1, 1894*, 11; Charles S. Potts, *Railroad Transportation in Texas* (Austin: Bulletin of the University of Texas, March 1909), 68–69; *Fort Worth Gazette*, August 20, 1893.

80. Jean C. Lough, "Gateway to the Promised Land: The Role Played by the Southern Kansas Towns in the Opening of the Cherokee Strip to Settlement," *Kansas Historical Quarterly* 25 (Spring 1959): 17–31; L. R. Elliott, "The Greatest Race of the Century," *Kansas Historical Quarterly* 23 (Summer 1957): 207.

The count of thirty-five cars may be incorrect. Another source indicated that there were fifty-six cars. See Caldwell Messenger, *The History of Sumner County, Kansas* (Dallas, TX: Curtis Media, 1987), 268.

81. *Chicago, Rock Island & Pacific Railway System and Representative Employees*, 120, 157–158; H. Roger Grant, *Kansas Depots* (Topeka: Kansas State Historical Society, 1990), 72–84;

Janet Greenstein Potter, *Great American Railroad Stations* (New York: John Wiley & Sons, 1996), 328.

82. *Travelers' Official Railway Guide for the United States and Canada* (New York: National Railway Publication Company, June 1892), 514–516; *Travelers' Official Guide of the Railway and Steam Navigation Lines in the United States and Canada* (New York: National Railway Publication Company, July 1895), 544; *Journal of Education* 41 (June 20, 1895): 425.

83. Bessie Louise Pierce, *A History of Chicago: The Rise of a Modern City, 1871–1893* (Chicago: University of Chicago Press, 1957), 522, 524; Kingfisher Study Club, compiler, *Echoes of Eighty-Nine* (Kingfisher, OK: Kingfisher Times and Free Press, 1939), 123; *Rock Island Magazine*, October 1922, 74.

84. Laura Solze Claggett, *History of Lincoln County, Colorado* (Dallas, TX: Curtis Media, 1987), 1:2, 4, 8; Rock, *Illustrated History of Oklahoma*, 200.

85. *The Free Press* (Kingfisher, OK), April 17, 1939; Ed H. Williams, "Reminiscences of Pioneer Days in Garfield County," *Chronicles of Oklahoma* 35 (Summer 1957): 163–168.

86. Hayes, *Iron Road to Empire*, 137–138.

87. Guy P. Webb, *History of Grant County, Oklahoma* (Medford, OK: Grant County Historical Society, 1971), 66; Berlin Chapman, "The Enid 'Railroad War': An Archival Study," *Chronicles of Oklahoma* 43 (Spring 1965): 150, 167–168; Danney Goble, *Progressive Oklahoma: The Making of a New Kind of State* (Norman: University of Oklahoma Press, 1990), 35–38.

88. Webb, *History of Grant County*, 66–67.

89. *Rock Island Magazine*, October 1922, 81; Webb, *History of Grant County*, 69.

90. Chapman, "Enid 'Railroad War,'" 176–191.

91. Hayes, *Iron Road to Empire*, 144; Franklin B. Locke, "Railway Crossings in Europe and America," *Century Magazine* 34 (May 1898): 91–107; David M. Young, *The Iron Horse and the Windy City: How Railroads Shaped Chicago* (DeKalb: Northern Illinois University Press, 2005), 161; *Eighteenth Annual Report of the Directors to the Stockholders of the Chicago, Rock Island & Pacific Railway Company, April 1, 1898*, 10; *Twentieth Annual Report of the Directors to the Stockholders of the Chicago, Rock Island & Pacific Railroad Company, April 1, 1900*, 11.

92. William "Bill" J. Dixon, interview, February 25, 2006.

93. Overton, *Burlington Route*, 206–214; Donald L. McMurry, *The Great Burlington Strike of 1888: A Case History in Labor Relations* (Cambridge, MA: Harvard University Press, 1956), vii, 38, 111.

94. Ray Ginger, *The Bending Cross: A Biography of Eugene V. Debs* (New Brunswick, NJ: Rutgers University Press, 1949), 92–96; Nick Salvatore, *Eugene V. Debs: Citizen and Socialist* (Urbana: University of Illinois Press, 1982), 115–118; Jack Kelly, *The Edge of Anarchy: The Railroad Barons, the Gilded Age, and the Greatest Labor Uprising in America* (New York: St. Martin's, 2018), 112.

95. Harry Jebsen Jr., "The Role of Blue Island in the Pullman Strike of 1894," *Journal of the Illinois State Historical Society* 67 (June 1974): 283.

96. Almont Lindsey, *The Pullman Strike: The Story of a Unique Experiment and of a Great Labor Upheaval* (Chicago: University of Chicago Press, 1942), 135.

97. *New York Times*, August 24, 1894; Jebsen, "Role of Blue Island in the Pullman Strike of 1894," 288.

98. Jebsen, "Role of Blue Island in the Pullman Strike of 1894," 286–293.

99. Lindsey, *Pullman Strike*, 336–338; Botkin and Harlow, *Treasury of Railroad Folklore*, 166–169.

100. Hayes, *Iron Road to Empire*, 145–146; *Poor's Manual of the Railroads of the United States* (New York: H. V. & H. W. Poor, 1898), 402.

3. Robber Barons

1. *The Chicago, Rock Island & Pacific Railway System and Representative Employees* (Chicago: Biographical Company, 1900), 173; T. Addison Busbey, ed., *The Biographical Directory of the Railway Officials of America* (Chicago: Railway Age, 1906), 487; *New York Times*, June 2, 1898, October 14, 1910.

2. William Edward Hayes, *Iron Road to Empire: The History of 100 Years of Progress and Achievements of the Rock Island Lines* (New York: Simmons-Boardman, 1953), 146–147.

3. Oliver Philip Byers, "Early History of the El Paso Line of the Chicago, Rock Island & Pacific Railway," in *Collections of the Kansas State Historical Society, 1919–1922*, ed. William E. Connelley (Topeka: B. P. Walker State Printer, 1923), 574.

4. Hayes, *Iron Road to Empire*, 151; David F. Myrick, *New Mexico's Railroads: A Historical Survey* (Albuquerque: University of New Mexico Press, 1970), 73–74, 86; *Poor's Manual of the Railroads of the United States* (New York: H. V. & H. W. Poor, 1902), 490, 493, 629; Don L. Hofsommer, *The Southern Pacific, 1901–1985* (College Station: Texas A&M University Press, 1986), 99–100.

5. Byers, "Early History of the El Paso Line of the Chicago, Rock Island & Pacific Railway," 576–577.

6. Rock Island System public timetable, August 1902; Myrick, *New Mexico's Railroads*, 78–79.

Alamogordo, New Mexico Territory, a recently established town, served as headquarters for the EP&NE and the location of its shops and other support facilities.

7. *Poor's Manual of Railroads, 1902*, 629–630; Hayes, *Iron Road to Empire*, 150; *Twenty-Second Annual Report of the Directors to the Stockholders of the Chicago, Rock Island & Pacific Railway Company, April 1, 1902*, 12.

8. Charles S. Potts, *Railroad Transportation in Texas* (Austin: University of Texas, 1909), 68.

9. Hayes, *Iron Road to Empire*, 152; Frederick A. Cleveland and Fred Wilbur Powell, *Railroad Finance* (New York: D. Appleton, 1912), 301; Don L. Hofsommer, *The Tootin' Louie: A History of the Minneapolis & St. Louis Railway* (Minneapolis: University of Minnesota Press, 2005), 76.

10. *Peoria (IL) Herald-Transcript*, March 31, 1900.

11. During World War I, American Express and the three other major private express firms were consolidated by the federal government to form American Railway Express, and in 1929 this company became the Railway Express Agency, owned by eighty-six railroads, including the Rock Island.

12. "Rock Island," typed historical document in John W. Barriger III papers, John W. Barriger III National Railroad Library, Saint Louis, MO; Alvin F. Harlow, *Old Way Bills: The Romance of the Express Companies* (New York: D. Appleton-Century, 1934), 473–478; *Poor's Manual of Railroads, 1902*, 631; S. F. Van Oss, *American Railroads as Investments* (New York: G. P. Putnam's Sons, 1893), 524; C. M. Keys, "The Newest Railroad Power," *World's Work* 10 (May–October 1905): 6306; "William Henry Moore," in *Dictionary of American Biography*, ed. Dumas Malone, (New York: Charles Scribner's Sons, 1934), 7:144; Albert W. Atwood, "Upsetting an Inverted

Pyramid," *Harper's Weekly*, March 28, 1914, 29.

13. "William Henry Moore," 7:143.

14. *The National Cyclopaedia of Biography* (New York: James T. White, 1917), 14:65; Will Payne, "The Imperturbable Moores: Extraordinary Financial Achievements of Two Chicago Lawyers," *Everybody's Magazine* 8 (June 1903): 578; *New York Times*, July 19, 1916.

15. Keys, "Newest Railroad Power," 6307; Payne, "Imperturbable Moores," 577.

16. *National Cyclopaedia of Biography*, 65; Keys, "Newest Railroad Power," 6307; Payne, "Imperturbable Moores," 579; "The Seven Railway Kings of America," *Current Literature* 42 (April 1907): 391.

17. Payne, "Imperturbable Moores," 580; "William Henry Moore," 7:143; "Seven Railway Kings of America," 391.

18. *National Cyclopaedia of Biography*, 65.

19. *New York Times*, February 26, 1915; Herbert N. Casson, *The Romance of Steel: The Story of a Thousand Millionaires* (New York: A. S. Barnes, 1907), 235.

20. Casson, *Romance of Steel*, 235; *New York Times*, February 26, 1915.

21. Frederick Lewis Allen, *The Great Pierpont Morgan* (New York: Harper & Row, 1948), 135; Charles R. Morris, *The Tycoons* (New York: Henry Holt, 2005), 210–211, 215; David Nasaw, *Andrew Carnegie* (New York: Penguin Books, 2006), 561–562; Joseph Frazier Wall, *Andrew Carnegie* (New York: Oxford University Press, 1970), 728–732.

22. Jean Strouse, *Morgan: American Financier* (New York: Perennial, 1999), 407; Payne, "Imperturbable Moores," 581; Casson, *Romance of Steel*, 236; Atwood, "Upsetting an Inverted Pyramid," 29; "William Henry Moore," 7:144.

23. *New York Times*, February 26, 1915; Payne, "Imperturbable Moores," 581; Albro Martin, *Enterprise Denied: Origins of the Decline of American Railroads, 1897–1917* (New York: Columbia University Press, 1971), 19.

24. Hayes, *Iron Road to Empire*, 151–153; "In Re Financial Transactions, History, and Operation of the Chicago, Rock Island & Pacific Railway Company," in *Interstate Commerce Commission Reports: Reports and Decisions of the United States* (Washington, DC: Interstate Commerce Commission, 1916), 36:44, 47, 49.

25. Stuart Daggett, *Railroad Reorganization* (Cambridge, MA: Harvard University Press, 1908), 318–319.

26. Stephen E. Wood, "The Development of Arkansas Railroads: Early Interest and Activities, Part I," *Arkansas Historical Quarterly* 7 (Summer 1948): 116–118; Dallas M. Herndon, "History of the Little Rock and Memphis Railroad Co.," *Rock Island Magazine* 17 (October 1922): 87; *Poor's Manual of Railroads of the United States* (New York: H. V. and H. W. Poor, 1900), 466–668; *Poor's Manual of Railroads, 1902*, 634–635.

27. Hayes, *Iron Road to Empire*, 159; Daggett, *Railroad Reorganization*, 320.

28. Hayes, *Iron Road to Empire*, 162–163, 174; *Poor's Manual of the Railroads of the United States, 1899* (New York: H. V. & H. W. Poor, 1899), 609; *The Official Guide of the Railways and Steam Navigation Lines of the United States, Porto Rico, Canada, Mexico and Cuba* (New York: National Railway Publication Company, June 1904), 687.

29. Hayes, *Iron Road to Empire*, 164; Don L. Hofsommer, *The Iowa Route: A History of the Burlington, Cedar Rapids & Northern Railway* (Bloomington: Indiana University Press, 2015), 225–227.

30. Daggett, *Railroad Reorganization*, 321; Atwood, "Upsetting an Inverted Pyramid," 29; "William Henry Moore," 7:144.

Never missing a beat as promoters, the Reid-Moore syndicate dressed up the Rock Island annual reports. They appeared in a larger format and on expensive paper stock. Some issues contained color maps. Poole Brothers of Chicago served as the printer, a firm known for its high-quality public timetables and named-train folders.

31. Hayes, *Iron Road to Empire*, 165–166; Daggett, *Railroad Reorganization*, 321–323; *New York Times*, August 1, 1902.

32. Daggett, *Railroad Reorganization*, 322, 326.

33. Atwood, "Upsetting an Inverted Pyramid," 30; *New York Times*, July 25, 1902; Hayes, *Iron Road to Empire*, 167. See, for example, Lewis C. Van Riper, *The Ins and Outs of Wall Street* (New York: L. C. Riper, 1898), 11.

34. Hayes, *Iron Road to Empire*, 165; "William Henry Moore," 7:144; Atwood, "Upsetting an Inverted Pyramid," 30.

35. *Poor's Manual of the Railroads of the United States, 1902*, 752; Keys, "Newest Railroad Power," 6310.

36. *New York Times*, May 12, 1903; John Moody, ed., *Moody's Manual of Corporate Securities* (New York: Moody, 1904), 533.

37. Daggett, *Railroad Reorganization*, 328–329; *New York Times*, May 26, 1903.

38. Hayes, *Iron Road to Empire*, 169.

39. Busbey, *Biographical Dictionary of the Railway Officials of America*, 676; Edwin Markam, "Where the Railroad Presidents Come From," *System: The Magazine of Business* 30 (July 1916): 181; J. L. Allhands, *Boll Weevil: Recollections of the Trinity & Brazos Valley Railway* (Houston, TX: Anson Jones, 1946), 11–12; Don L. Hofsommer, "Benjamin Franklin Yoakum," in *Railroads in the Age of Regulation, 1900–1980*, ed. Keith L. Bryant Jr. (New York: Facts On File, 1988), 491; *World's Work* (September 1912): 518.

40. Hayes, *Iron Road to Empire*, 168, 175–176.

41. "Benjamin L. Winchell," *Railroad Age Gazette* 47 (December 10, 1909): 1137; Busbey, *Biographical Directory of the Railway Officials of America, 1906*, 665; Hayes; *Iron Road to Empire*, 168; "Benjamin L. Winchell," *The World To-Day* 6 (May 1904): 688; Frank H. Spearman, *The Strategy of Great Railroads* (New York: Charles Scribner's Sons, 1906), 142.

Benjamin Winchell found employment with future components of major railroads. The Kansas City, Fort Scott & Gulf joined the Frisco; Kansas City, Lawrence & Southern Kansas the Santa Fe; Union Pacific, Denver & Gulf the Union Pacific; the Denver, Leadville & Gunnison the Colorado & Southern.

42. Hayes, *Iron Road to Empire*, 170–171; *Twenty-Sixth Annual Report of the Directors to the Stockholders of the Chicago, Rock Island & Pacific Railway Company, June 30, 1906*, 10.

43. Will H. Lyford, *History of the Chicago and Eastern Illinois Railroad Company* (Chicago: Gunthrop-Warren, 1913), 1–78.

44. *Poor's Manual of the Railroads of the United States, 1906* (New York: Poor's Manual, 1906), 410; *Decisions of the Interstate Commerce Commission of the United States* (Washington, DC: US Government Printing Office, 1929), 24:930; Clifton E. Hull, *Shortline Railroads of Arkansas* (Norman: University of Oklahoma Press, 1969), 120–121.

45. George W. Hilton, *American Narrow Gauge Railroads* (Stanford, CA: Stanford University Press, 1990), 314; Hayes, *Iron Road to Empire*, 173–174; *Twenty-Ninth Annual Report of the Chicago, Rock Island and Pacific Railway Company, Fiscal Year Ended June 30, 1909*, 9.

46. *Decisions of the Interstate Commerce Commission of the United States*, 1034; George Hosking, ed., *Moody's Manual of Railroads and Corporation Securities* (New York: Moody, 1911), 21.

47. Juanita Whitaker Green, *The History of Union County, Arkansas* (n.p.: privately printed, 1954), 48.

48. Gene V. Glendinning, *The Chicago & Alton Railroad: The Only Way* (DeKalb: Northern Illinois University Press, 2002), 150.

49. *Interstate Commerce Commission Reports*, 51; Maury Klein, *The Life & Legend of E. H. Harriman* (Chapel Hill: University of North Carolina Press, 2000), 172; Hofsommer, *Tootin' Louie*, 76; Don L. Hofsommer, "Edwin Hawley," in *Railroads in the Age of Regulation*, ed. Keith L. Bryant Jr. (New York: Facts On File, 1988), 190–191; "William H. Moore," in *Railroads in the Age of Regulation*, ed. Keith L. Bryant Jr. (New York: Facts On File, 1988), 311.

50. *Interstate Commerce Commission Reports*, 991; Taylor Hampton, *The Nickel Plate Road: The History of a Great Railroad* (Cleveland, OH: World Publishing Corporation, 1947), 230–256; *Twenty-Eighth Annual Report of the Directors to the Stockholders of the Chicago, Rock Island & Pacific Railway Company, June 30, 1908*, 10.

51. Hofsommer, *Tootin' Louie*, 76; Hayes, *Iron Road to Empire*, 175.

52. Richard C. Overton, *Burlington Route: A History of the Burlington Lines* (New York: Alfred A. Knopf, 1965), 272–273; Allhands, *Boll Weevil*, 39, 183.

53. *Interstate Commerce Commission Reports*, 52–53; *Poor's Manual of the Railroads of the United States* (New York: Poor's Manual, 1911), 931, 1067, 1189; Allhands, *Boll Weevil*, 194–196; George H. Drury, compiler, *Historical Guide to North American Railroads* (Milwaukee, WI: Kalmbach, 1985), 46.

54. Hayes, *Iron Route to Empire*, 171, 181–182; *Thirtieth Annual Report of the Chicago, Rock Island and Pacific Railway Company for Fiscal Year Ended June 30, 1910*; *Interstate Commerce Commission Reports*, 832.

55. Prior to 1910 the Rock Island altered schedules and made routing changes for the *Golden State Limited*. Between May 1903 and December 1904, the company suspended operations, and from 1905 to 1906 the train traveled over the Chicago & Alton between Joliet and Kansas City.

56. Rock Island System public timetable, May 14, 1905; Arthur D. Dubin, *More Classic Trains* (Glendale, CA: Interurban, 1974), 368.

57. Rock Island System public timetable, May 14, 1905; *Literary Digest*, February 21, 1903.

58. II. Roger Grant, "The Green Mountain Train Wreck: An Iowa Railroad Tragedy," *Palimpsest* 65 (July–August 1984): 135–145; Robert B. Shaw, *A History of Railroad Accidents, Safety Precautions and Operating Practices* (n.p.: privately printed, 1978), appendix.

59. John H. White Jr., *The American Railroad Passenger Car* (Baltimore, MD: Johns Hopkins University Press, 1975), 587.

60. Edward J. Wojtas, "Rock Island Doodlebugs," *Railroad Magazine* 78 (April 1966), 17–18; James R. Fair Jr., *The North Arkansas Line: The Story of the Missouri & North Arkansas Railroad* (San Diego, CA: Howell-North Books, 1969), 95.

61. Maury Klein, *Union Pacific: The Rebirth, 1894–1969* (New York: Doubleday, 1989), 296–298; *Electric Railway Journal* 39 (June 3, 1911): 94; Wojtas, "Rock Island Doodlebugs," 18–19, 22.

62. White, *American Railroad Passenger Car*, 588; Wojtas, "Rock Island Doodlebugs," 19.

63. *Railroad Gazette*, February 14, 1902; *Chicago Tribune*, July 11, 1903; Christopher Brown, *Still Standing: A Century of Urban Train Station Design* (Bloomington: Indiana University Press, 2005), 2.

It would be in July 1904 that passenger trains of the Chicago & Eastern Illinois Railway, which belonged to the Rock Island-Frisco-C&EI combine, operated into La Salle Street Station. In July 1913 this tenancy ended.

64. *Chicago Tribune*, July 11, 1903.

65. For decades the Rock Island and other carriers were plagued with the loss of depots because of fire and storm. Scores of frame buildings burned. The most unlucky place on the system was Lafayette, Illinois, located on the Peoria-to-Rock Island branch. Around the turn of the twentieth century, five depots fell victim to flames.

66. Rock Island System public timetable, May 14, 1905.

67. Earle D. Ross, *Iowa Agriculture: An Historical Survey* (Iowa City: State Historical Society of Iowa, 1951), 125; Roy V. Scott, "Railroads and Farmers: Educational Trains in Missouri, 1902–1914," *Agricultural History* 36 (January 1962): 4, 12.

By 1910 the Rock Island enthusiastically preached the practice of dry farming in semiarid regions. "Wheat six feet in length is exhibited by [the Rock Island] in its offices throughout the East as sample of what the farmers in its territory do, under its help and supervision," railroad writer Edward Hungerford observed in 1911. "That sort of thing silently makes traffic every day in the year. It is worth a dozen times what it costs the railroad." Edward Hungerford, *The Modern Railroad* (Chicago: A. C. McClurg, 1911), 364.

68. Wilma Rugh Taylor, *Gospel Tracks through Texas: The Mission of Chapel Car Good Will* (College Station: Texas A&M University Press, 2005), ix, 151–152.

69. *Poor's Manual of the Railroads of the United States, 1909* (New York: Poor's Railroad Manual, 1909), 423.

70. Hayes, *Iron Road to Empire*, 178; *Interstate Commerce Commission Reports*, 51; *New York Times*, January 10, 1909.

71. *Chicago Evening Post*, December 1, 1909; Keith L, Bryant Jr., "A Horatio Alger Story: Henry U. Mudge," *Railroad History* 182 (Spring 2000): 14.

72. James B. Herald to Keith L. Bryant Jr., February 7, 1999, in possession of author; Bryant, "Horatio Alger Story," 10–14; *Biographical Directory of the Railway Official of America, 1906*, 433.

73. Murray Webb Latimer, *Industrial Pension Systems in the United States and Canada* (New York: Industrial Relations Counselors, 1932), 24–25; *Thirtieth Annual Report of the Chicago, Rock Island and Pacific Railway Company for Fiscal Year Ended June 30, 1910*, n.p.; *Thirty-Fifth Annual Report of the Chicago, Rock Island and Pacific Railway Company and Proprietary Companies Fiscal Year Ended June 30, 1915*, 13.

74. Bryant, "Horatio Alger Story," 17; *Biographical Directory of the Railway Officials of America*, 8th ed. (New York: Simmons-Boardman, 1922), 243.

75. Hayes, *Iron Road to Empire*, 183–184; "An Operating Study of the Rock Island," *Railway Age Gazette* 60 (May 19, 1916): 1069.

76. "Operating Study of the Rock Island," 1066–1067; William Z. Ripley, *Railroads: Finance and Organization* (New York: Longmans, Green, 1915), 84–85, 152–154, 236, 378, 393, 398; William Z. Ripley, "Railroad Over-Capitalization," *Quarterly Journal of Economics* 24 (August 1914): 604.

77. K. Austin Kerr, *American Railroad Politics, 1914–1920* (Pittsburgh: University of Pittsburgh Press, 1968), 16–17; Martin, *Enterprise Denied*, 127.

78. Interstate Commerce Commission, *Decisions of the Interstate Commerce Commission*

of the United States, July, 1915, to December, 1915, (Washington, DC: Government Printing Office, 1916), 26:57.

79. Interstate Commerce Commission, *Decisions of the Interstate Commerce Commission*, 26:57; Hayes, *Iron Road to Empire*, 185.

80. Interstate Commerce Commission, *Decisions of the Interstate Commerce Commission*, 26:58–59.

81. Interstate Commerce Commission, *Decisions of the Interstate Commerce Commission*, 26:60; Hayes, *Iron Road to Empire*, 189; *New York Times*, October 12, 1917.

82. John L. Weller, *The New Haven Railroad: Its Rise and Fall* (New York: Hastings House, 1969), 161–195; Ernest Ritson Dewsnup, "Recent Financial Investigations by the Interstate Commerce Commission," *Annals of the American Academy of Political and Social Science* 63 (January 1916): 199–205.

83. Interstate Commerce Commission, *Decisions of the Interstate Commerce Commission*, 26:43, 47.

84. Interstate Commerce Commission, *Decisions of the Interstate Commerce Commission*, 26:50.

85. Interstate Commerce Commission, *Decisions of the Interstate Commerce Commission*, 26:55–57, 61.

86. William Z. Ripley, *Railroads: Finance & Organization* (New York: Longmans, Green, and Co., 1915), 525.

87. What happened to the four members of the Reid-Moore syndicate? In 1908 William Leeds died in Paris, France, of a chronic heart condition, resulting in part from "added work imposed on Mr. Leeds during the recent financial troubles." He did not die in poverty, leaving an estate estimated at $40 million. The next to pass was James Moore, who succumbed at his home in Lake Geneva, Wisconsin, in 1916, also of heart disease. At the time of his death, his estate was believed to be worth $20 million. Judge Moore outlived the Rock Island bankruptcy, dying from a heart attack in his New York City mansion in 1923. He enjoyed his twilight years as a horseman, building a stable "which was regarded as the equal of any in the turf world, and he had the best string of hackneys in the country." Judge Moore's wealth likely far exceeded that of his late brother. The passing of the last syndicate member, Daniel Reid, occurred in New York City in 1925. His mental and physical health had declined rapidly after 1919. Pneumonia

was listed as the official cause of death. Reid lost part of his once great wealth in two highly publicized divorce settlements. Before his death he also had made sizable donations to various institutions and causes. The Reid estate amounted to only $4.7 million, still an impressive amount for the time.

4. Rough Tracks

1. *New York Times*, April 21, 1915; *Thirty-Fifth Annual Report of the Chicago, Rock Island and Pacific Railway Company and Proprietary Companies, Fiscal Year Ended June 30, 1915*, 9.

2. *The National Cyclopaedia of American Biography* (New York: James T. White, 1917), 14:410–411; Allen Johnson and Dumas Malone, eds., *Dictionary of American Biography* (New York: Charles Scribner's Sons, 1931), 3:298–299; *New York Times*, December 14, 1928.

3. *Thirty-Fifth Annual Report, 1915*, 12.

4. Keith L. Bryant Jr., "A Horatio Alger Story: Henry U. Mudge," *Railroad History* 182 (April 2000): 18; *New York Times*, January 31, 1920; *Denver Post*, November 15, 1915; Robert G. Athearn, *The Denver and Rio Grande Western Railroad: Rebel of the Rockies* (New Haven, CT: Yale University Press, 1962), 236.

5. "An Operating Study of the Rock Island," *Railway Age Gazette* 60 (May 19, 1916): 1066; James N. Rosenberg, "Phipps v. Chicago, Rock Island & Pacific Ry. Co.," *Columbia Law Review* 24 (March 1914): 267; William Edward Hayes, *Iron Road to Empire: The History of 100 Years of Progress and Achievement of the Rock Island Lines* (New York: Simmons-Boardman, 1953), 198–199; *Poor's Manual of Railroads* (New York: Poor's Manual Company, 1918), 777.

6. Johnson and Malone, eds., *Dictionary of American Biography*, 3:299.

7. "Rock Island," in John W. Barriger III papers, John W. Barriger III National Railroad Library, Saint Louis, MO, hereafter cited as Barriger papers.

8. Stuart Daggett, "Recent Railroad Failures and Reorganizations," *Quarterly Journal of Economics* 32 (May 1918): 454.

9. Hayes, *Iron Road to Empire*, 199.

10. *Who's Who in Railroading: United States–Canada–Mexico–Cuba* (New York: Simmons-Boardman, 1930), 197; *New York Times*, March 26, 1942.

11. "James E. Gorman Passes On," *Railway Age* 112 (April 4, 1942): 693; Hayes, *Iron*

Road to Empire, 199–200; *Financial World* 38 (September 23, 1922): 402; *Who's Who in Railroading*, 1930, 181.

12. K. Austin Kerr, *American Railroad Politics, 1914–1920* (Pittsburgh, PA: University of Pittsburgh Press, 1968), 72–91; John F. Stover, *The Life and Decline of the American Railroad* (New York: Oxford University Press, 1970), 161; Aaron A. Godfrey, *Government Operation of the Railroads, Its Necessity, Success, and Consequences, 1918–1920* (Austin, TX: San Felipe, 1974).

13. *Poor's Manual of Railroads* (New York: Poor's Manual Company, 1918), 779; Walker D. Hines, *War History of the American Railroads* (New Haven, CT: Yale University Press, 1928), 253, 255; Hayes, *Iron Road to Empire*, 200.

14. *Lincoln (NE) Journal Star*, November 27, 2011; *Thirty-Ninth Annual Report of the Chicago, Rock Island and Pacific Railway Company and Proprietary Companies, Fiscal Year Ended December 31, 1918*, 9; Hayes, *Iron Road to Empire*, 202–203.

15. *Thirty-Ninth Annual Report of the Chicago, Rock Island and Pacific Railway Company*, 7; Hayes, *Iron Road to Empire*, 201–202; James E. Lane, "USRA Freight Cars: An Experiment in Standardization," *Railroad History* 128 (Spring 1973): 28.

16. *New York Times*, April 23, 1930; Hayes, *Iron Road to Empire*, 204.

17. William Norris Leonard, *Railroad Consolidation under the Transportation Act of 1920* (New York: Columbia University Press, 1946), 57–63; Richard Saunders Jr., *Merging Lines: American Railroads, 1900–1970* (DeKalb: Northern Illinois University Press, 2001), 45–46.

18. J. W. Barriger, "Comments on Rock Island-Frisco Consolidation," memorandum to D. B. Jenks, March 2, 1956, Barriger papers; Leonard, *Railroad Consolidation under the Transportation Act of 1920*, 66–67, 134.

19. John F. Stover, *American Railroads*, 2nd ed. (Chicago: University of Chicago Press, 1997), 180.

20. Leonard, *Railroad Consolidation under the Transportation Act of 1920*, 299–310.

21. Leonard, *Railroad Consolidation under the Transportation Act of 1920*, 308–309.

22. Leonard, *Railroad Consolidation under the Transportation Act of 1920*, 311–336.

In the early 1920s, the ICC approved an expanded Nickel Plate Road. Its owners, the Van Sweringen brothers of Cleveland, also used the holding-company stratagem to circumvent the commission in order to gain financial control over several important railroads, including the Chesapeake & Ohio, Erie, Missouri Pacific, and Pere Marquette. The "Vans" employed tactics similar to those of the Reid-Moore syndicate.

23. Leonard, *Railroad Consolidation under the Transportation Act of 1920*, 335–336.

24. See James Grant, *The Forgotten Depression: 1921: The Crash That Cured Itself* (New York: Simon & Schuster, 2014).

25. Colin J. Davis, *Power at Odds: The 1922 National Railroad Shopmen's Strike* (Urbana: University of Illinois Press, 1997), 30–39; Leonard, *Railroad Consolidation under the Transportation Act of 1920*, 53–54.

26. Davis, *Power at Odds*, 57–62.

27. *Rock Island (IL) Argus and Daily Union*, July 3, 1922; *Annual Report of the Delaware, Lackawanna and Western Railroad Company* (New York: Delaware, Lackawanna & Western Railroad, 1923), 6.

28. "Bombing Features Western Strike Developments," *Railway Age* 73 (August 26, 1922): 370; "Strike Conditions in Western Territory Show Continued Improvement," *Railway Age* 73 (September 2, 1922): 422; "Lull in Violence One of Week's Developments," *Railway Age* 73 (September 16, 1922): 504.

29. *Financial World*, September 23, 1922, 392; *Rock Island (IL) Argus and Daily Union*, September 19, 1922.

30. William E. Hooper, "General Atterbury's Attitude toward Labor," *World's Work* 44 (September 1922): 507.

31. Michael M. Bartels, *Rock Island Town* (David City, NE: South Platte, 1999), 35; *Forty-Third Annual Report of the Chicago, Rock Island and Pacific Railway Company and Subsidiary Companies, Fiscal Year Ended December 31, 1922*, 8; "Rioting and Intimidations at Various Points," *Railway Age* 73 (August 5, 1922): 283–284.

32. I. E. Quastler, *Prairie Railroad Town: The Rock Island Railroad Shops at Horton, Kansas, 1887–1946* (David City, NE: South Platte, 2003), 83. See, for example, Herbert G. Gutman, "Two Lockouts in Pennsylvania, 1873–1874," *Pennsylvania Magazine of History and Biography* 83 (July 1959): 307–326 and "An Iron Workers' Strike in the Ohio Valley, 1873–1874," *Ohio Historical Quarterly* 68 (1959): 373–370.

33. Quastler, *Prairie Railroad Town*, 83, 87.

34. Quastler, *Prairie Railroad Town*, 87.

35. Quastler, *Prairie Railroad Town*, 87.

36. James N. Giglio, *H. M. Daugherty and the Politics of Expediency* (Kent, OH: Kent State University Press, 1978), 146–150.

37. Quastler, *Prairie Railroad Town*, 90; Davis, *Power at Odds*, 157.

38. *Railway Age* 73 (August 12, 1922): 319; H. Roger Grant, "Celebrating a Century," *Classic Trains* 2 (Fall 2001): 68–72; Hayes, *Iron Road to Empire*, 205; J. E. Gorman, "Our Policy," *Rock Island Magazine* 17 (October 1922).

There was one celebration that vaguely resembled what Rock Island officialdom did in 1922, and it involved the Missouri-Kansas-Texas Railway (Katy). Its president, John W. Barriger III, the consummate cheerleader and publicity hound, liked commemorative events. In 1947, as head of the Monon, he had orchestrated its well-received centennial. But as Katy's chief executive, he was too late for a centennial. What to do? Barriger honored the sixtieth anniversary of the founding of the oil boomtown of Burkburnett, Texas. On June 15, 1967, he orchestrated a special train and large community observance that included a mock train robbery, a rodeo, a barbecue, and multiple speeches.

39. W. E. Babb, "Our Septuagenary," *Rock Island Magazine* 17 (October 1922): 7.

40. Babb, "Our Septuagenary," 7–8.

41. Babb, "Our Septuagenary," 8.

42. Babb, "Our Septuagenary," 8–11; "Des Moines Meeting Was Among Most Important," *Rock Island Magazine* 17 (October 1922): 32.

43. "The Rock Island Tournament," unidentified clipping in possession of author.

44. "Rock Island Celebrates Seventieth Anniversary," *Railway Age* 73 (October 21, 1922): 737–738.

45. *Railway Age* 75 (October 27, 1923): 786; "Rock Island to Hold Tournament," *Railway Age* 77 (August 2, 1924): 209; "Rock Island Teaches Citizenship," *Railway Age* 78 (January 31, 1925): 322; J. E. Gorman, *On the Human Side of Railroading* (Chicago: Chicago, Rock Island & Pacific Railway, 1929).

46. *Poor's Manual of Railroads* (New York: Poor's Publishing, 1922), 350; Robert Lee Wyatt III, *Grandfield: The Hub of the Big Pasture* (Marceline, MO: Walsworth, 1974), 1:141–158, 167–168; *Railway Age* 68 (June 11, 1920): 1696; US Department of the Interior, National Register of Historic Places Continuation Sheet, Rock Island Depot, Tillman County, OK, 12–13.

47. "Southwestern Roads Vie for New Lines in Texas Panhandle," *Railway Age* 87 (September 7, 1929): 597–599.

48. Stephen Bogener, "The Varied Economy of West Texas," in *West Texas: A History of the Giant Side of the State*, ed. Paul H. Carlson and Bruce H. Glasrud (Norman: University of Oklahoma Press, 2014), 190; Bobby D. Weaver, ed., *Panhandle Petroleum* (Amarillo, TX: Panhandle-Plains Historical Society, 1982), 43–45, 50–51.

49. *Rock Island Magazine* 24 (July 1929): 6; Dennis Opferman, "The Big Hill," *Remember the Rock Magazine* 6 (2010): 12–15.

50. "Rock Island Builds Line in Texas," *Railway Age* (April 20, 1929): 897; Opferman, "Big Hill," 4–5.

51. Francis Stanley, *The Stinnett, Texas Story* (Nazareth, TX: privately printed, 1974), 2–3, 5–6, 12.

52. Don L. Hofsommer, *The Quanah Route: A History of the Quanah, Acme & Pacific Railway* (College Station: Texas A&M University Press, 1991), 66–67; S. G. Reed, *A History of the Texas Railroads* (Houston: St. Clair, 1941), 400–401.

53. Hayes, *Iron Road to Empire*, 207–208.

54. Alfred W. Bruce, *The Steam Locomotive in America: Its Development in the Twentieth Century* (New York: W. W. Norton, 1952), 89–90; "Rock Island Buys 4-8-4 Type Locomotives," *Railway Age* 87 (December 7, 1929): 1325–1326; E. Wesley Krambeck, William D. Edson, and Jack W. Farrell, *Rock Island Steam Power* (n.p.: Edson, 2002), 109.

55. Lloyd E. Stagner, *Rock Island Motive Power, 1933–1955* (Boulder, CO: Pruett, 1980), 1.

56. Hayes, *Iron Road to Empire*, 208; "New Kansas City Line Opened to Freight Traffic," *Rock Island Magazine*, August 1931, 9–10; "Rock Island Feted in Opening New Missouri Line," n.d., Barriger papers.

57. Richard C. Overton, *Burlington Route: A History of the Burlington Lines* (New York: Alfred A. Knopf, 1965), 337–359; John S. Porter, ed., *Moody's Manual of Investments: Steam Railroads* (New York: Moody's Investors Service, 1926), 1123; "Chicago, Rock Island & Pacific," *Standard Service on Railroads*, November 1, 1928.

58. "La Salle Street Station," unidentified newspaper clipping from Jervis Langdon Jr. papers in possession of author.

59. Lucius Beebe and Charles Clegg, *The Trains We Rode: Northern Pacific-Wabash* (Berkeley, CA: Howell-North Books, 1966), 2:696–706.

60. *The Official Guide of the Railways* (New York: National Railway Publication Company, February 1928), 936; Arthur D. Dubin, *More Classic Trains* (Glendale, CA: Interurban, 1974), 371.

61. *Official Guide of the Railways*, 936.

62. *Official Guide of the Railways*, 936.

63. Will C. Hollister, *Dinner in the Diner* (Corona del Mar, CA: Trans-Anglo Books, 1965), 51.

64. Mildred Middleton, interview, August 23, 2012.

During the 1920s the Guthrie Center branch was located on the Iowa Division, one of thirteen divisions and terminals. They included the Chicago Terminal, Illinois Division, Iowa Division, Missouri Division, Cedar Rapids-Minnesota Division, Dakota Division, Nebraska-Colorado Division, Saint Louis-Kansas City Terminal Division, Kansas Division, El Paso Division, Arkansas-Louisiana Division, Pan Handle Division, and Oklahoma-Southern Division.

65. *New York Times*, May 3, 1956; *Who's Who in Railroading*, 1930, 63.

66. Hayes, *Iron Road to Empire*, 210–211; *New York Times*, June 29, 1935.

67. Hayes, *Iron Road to Empire*, 211–213.

68. J. W. Barriger, "Comments on Rock Island-Frisco Consolidation," memorandum to D. B. Jenks, March 2, 1956, Barriger papers.

69. Hayes, *Iron Road to Empire*, 217.

70. John Sherman Porter, ed., *Moody's Manual of Investments: American and Foreign* (New York: Moody's Investors Service, 1935), 374; "The Spectacular 'Rockets,'" *Railway Age* 133 (October 13, 1952): 112.

71. Hayes, *Iron Road to Empire*, 219; William Pollard to author, June 20, 2018.

72. Ari and Olive Hoogenboom, *A History of the ICC: From Panacea to Palliative* (New York: W. W. Norton, 1976), 123; William D. Middleton, George M. Smerk, and Roberta L. Diehl, eds., *Encyclopedia of North American Railroads* (Bloomington: Indiana University Press, 2007), 929–930; John Will Chapman, *Railroad Mergers* (New York: Simmons-Boardman, 1939), 113–122.

73. *New York Times*, May 7, 1932.

74. "Rock Island," memorandum dated August 10, 1973, Barriger papers.

75. *New York Times*, June 8, 1933.

76. *Yearbook of Railroad Information* (New York: Committee on Public Relations of the Eastern Railroads, 1936), 39.

77. "Rock Island Revived," *Fortune* 30 (December 1944): 140.

5. Farrington Era

1. Lloyd K. Garrison, "Reorganization of Railroads under the Bankruptcy Act," *University of Chicago Law Review* 1 (May 1933): 72; *New York Times*, June 8, 1933; John Sherman Porter, ed., *Moody's Manual of Investments: American and Foreign* (New York: Moody's Investors Service, 1935), 366.

Although the Missouri Pacific Railroad could claim to have been the first railroad to file under Section 77 of the Bankruptcy Act and in 1956 the last one to be reorganized, the Rock Island would be under court protection for nearly as long.

2. *Who's Who in America* (Chicago: A. N. Marquis, 1942), 818; "Rock Island Revived," *Fortune* 30 (December 1944): 141; William T. Hutchinson, *Lowden of Illinois: The Life of Frank O. Lowden* (Chicago: University of Chicago Press, 1957), 2:712.

3. Thurman W. Arnold, *Folklore of Capitalism* (New Haven, CT: Yale University Press, 1937), 230.

4. *Moody's Manual of Investments, 1935*, 366; Don L. Hofsommer, *The Tootin' Louie: A History of the Minneapolis & St. Louis Railway* (Minneapolis: University of Minnesota Press, 2005), 181; William Edward Hayes, *Iron Road to Empire: The History of 100 Years of Progress and Achievements of the Rock Island Lines* (New York: Simmons-Boardman, 1953), 228–229; *New York Times*, August 18, 1933; *Poor's Manual of Railroads, 1924* (New York: Poor's Publishing, 1924), 1830–1831.

The struggling Wichita Northwestern Railway barely survived the Great Depression, being abandoned in March 1941.

5. *New York Times*, November 27, 1935.

6. *Who's Who in Railroading: United States–Canada–Mexico–Cuba* (New York: Simmons-Boardman, 1930), 147; Hayes, *Iron Road to Empire*, 229–230; *New York Times*, November 8, 1935, November 27, 1935.

7. "Freight Traffic," in John W. Barriger III papers, John W. Barriger III National Railroad Library, Saint Louis, MO, hereafter cited as Barriger papers.

8. John Sherman Porter, ed., *Moody's Manual of Investments: American and Foreign*

(New York: Moody's Investors Service, 1938), 371.

9. Hayes, *Iron Road to Empire*, 233–234.

10. Hayes, *Iron Road to Empire*, 233; "Rock Island Revived," 144.

11. T. Addison Busbey, ed., *The Biographical Directory of the Railway Officials of America* (Chicago: Railway Age, 1906), 193; Dan Butler, "John D. Farrington," in *Railroads in the Age of Regulation, 1900–1980*, ed. Keith L. Bryant Jr. (New York: Facts On File, 1988), 140.

12. Butler, "John D. Farrington," 140; *New York Times*, October 14, 1961.

13. *New York Times*, October 14, 1961; "John D. Farrington Dies," *Rocket 20* (November–December 1961): 2.

14. Hayes, *Iron Road to Empire*, 238; S. Kip Farrington Jr., *Railroads of Today* (New York: Coward-McCann, 1949), 94.

15. "Rock Island Lines Removed or Sold Since January 1, 1936," ca. 1955 map in possession of author.

16. "Rock Island Revived," 141.

17. "Rock Island Revived," 141.

18. *Who's Who in Railroading in North America* (New York: Simmons-Boardman, 1946), 325; "William H. Hillis," *Railway Age* 107 (October 7, 1939): 543.

19. In comparison to competitors Chicago & North Western-Union Pacific and Atchison, Topeka & Santa Fe, the differences in distances between Chicago and Los Angeles were minimal. Mileage for the Santa Fe totaled 2,226; Rock Island-Southern Pacific (after initial betterments) stood at 2,272; and C&NW-UP had 2,299.

20. "Rock Island Completes 'Samson of the Cimarron,'" *Railway Age* 107 (July 15, 1939): 122; "Rock Island Revived," 146; Wallace W. Abbey, "Samson of the Cimarron," *Trains and Travel* 13 (February 1953): 48–49.

21. "Rock Island Revived," 147.

22. David P. Morgan, "M-300 to M-10000: The Formative Years," *Trains* 24 (November 1963): 43; Louie A. Marre, *Rock Island Diesel Locomotives, 1930–1980* (Cincinnati, OH: Railfax, 1982), 15, 19; Jeffrey W. Schramm, *Out of Steam: Dieselization and American Railroads, 1920–1960* (Bethlehem, PA: Lehigh University Press, 2010), 127; J. Parker Lamb, *Evolution of the American Diesel Locomotive* (Bloomington: Indiana University Press, 2007), 30.

In early 1930 the Illinois Central and the Rock Island briefly tested a Baldwin-built oil-electric switching locomotive, No. 61000, in greater Chicago.

23. The EMD diesels were called TAs—the T stood for *twelve* since they were rated for 1,200 horsepower. The A referred to the first and only unit. These locomotives featured V-16 engines, forerunners of Electro-Motive's famous F-unit series, which appeared in 1939, and ones that could effectively replace steam locomotives in main-line freight service.

24. Hayes, *Iron Road to Empire*, 240; Peter Hansen, "The Rock's Camelot," in *Great Trains Heartland: The Golden Age of Midwestern Rail Travel*, ed. Robert S. McGonigal (Waukesha, WI: Kalmbach, 2017), 75–76; Burlington-Rock Island Railroad public timetable, October 10, 1939; "Streamliners Roll up a Record," *Business Week*, February 10, 1947, 49; Paul C. Nelson, "Rise and Decline of the Rock Island Passenger Train in the 20th Century," *Annals of Iowa* 41 (Summer 1971): 663.

In conjunction with the introduction of *Rocket* streamliners, the Farrington administration gussied up some of its passenger depots. Take Des Moines. The company wanted to update this late-Victorian structure. So in 1937 Raymond Loewy, the famed industrial designer, worked his magic by creating an art deco modern look for the building's public spaces, the ticket office and waiting areas.

25. Pullman-Standard Company advertisement, n.d., Barriger papers.

26. Hansen, "Rock's Camelot," 79; *Zephyr Rockets New Service between St. Louis–St. Paul–Minneapolis* (n.p.: Burlington Route-Rock Island Lines, 1941).

27. "Streamliners Roll up a Record," 16; Farrington, *Railroads of Today*, 245.

28. John Sherman Porter, ed., *Moody's Manual of Investments: Railroad Securities* (New York: Moody's Investors Service, 1942), 1553.

29. "Peoria Rocket Misses Only 10 Trips out of 8,816," *Railway Age* 115 (October 16, 1943): 622.

30. "The Spectacular 'Rockets,'" *Railway Age* 133 (October 13, 1952): 111; Hugh Hawkins, *Railwayman's Son: A Plains Family Memoir* (Lubbock: Texas Tech University Press, 2006), 71; "John D. Farrington Dies," *Rocket 20* (November–December 1961), 2.

31. Lamb, *Evolution of the American Diesel Locomotive*, 61, 63.

In the early 1980s, a locomotive engineer on the Southern Division said this about the Alco RS-type diesels: "Oh, they were good engines! Rugged. You could walk away with the whole yard with an Alco. They weren't as slippery as these Geeps we're using now; they could *pull!*" Paul Schneider, "In the Violet Hour," *Trains* 43 (March 1983): 29.

32. *Report to the Security Holders of the Chicago, Rock Island & Pacific Railroad, July 1, 1948*, 9.

33. Hutchinson, *Lowden of Illinois*, 713–714.

34. Hutchinson, *Lowden of Illinois*, 715.

35. Porter, *Moody's Manual of Investments*, 1942, 1553.

36. Office of War Information, *Right-of-Way*, (Washington, DC: National Archives, 1943), 16-mm film; *Historical Statistics of the United States: Colonial Times to 1957* (Washington, DC: US Department of Commerce, 1960), 427, 430–31.

37. Edward J. Wojtas, "The Fading Grandeur of La Salle Street Station," *Railroad Magazine* 86 (October 1970): 28; Rock Island Lines, Train Order No. 516, June 15, 1942, in possession of author; S. Kip Farrington Jr., *Railroads at War* (New York: Samuel Curl, 1944), 193, 196; Chicago, Rock Island & Pacific Railway Company public timetable, June 1944; "Rock Island Adjusts Schedules to Improve Troop Service," *Railway Age* 115 (September 11, 1943): 429; "Rock Island Is Training Railway Soldiers," *Railway Age* 116 (April 29, 1944): 824; Lucius Beebe and Charles Clegg, *The Trains We Rode* (Berkeley, CA: Howell-North Books, 1966), 2:716–717; "Des Moines Day Train in Operation, Aug. 5," *Rock Island Lines News Digest* 4 (July 1945): 7.

38. "Line Relocation on Rock Island Speeds War Traffic," *Railway Age* 145 (October 23, 1943): 633.

39. Nathaniel Otjen, "Creating a Barrio in Iowa City, 1916–1936: Mexican Section Laborers and the Chicago, Rock Island and Pacific Railroad Company," *Annals of Iowa* 76 (Fall 2017): 406–432.

40. "1942 Income Largest for Rock Island," *Railway Age* 114 (May 22, 1943): 1071; John Sherman Porter, ed., *Moody's Manual of Investments: Railroad Securities* (New York: Moody's Investors Service, 1946), 384–385.

41. *Chicago Tribune*, August 22, 1967; Hayes, *Iron Road to Empire*, 253.

While the railroad world knew Judge Igoe for his role in the Rock Island reorganization, he likely gained greater public recognition as the federal judge who oversaw the bankruptcy of the Tucker Corporation, the controversial automobile company of Preston Tucker.

42. *Who's Who in Railroading in North America*, 1946, 133; *Who Was Who in America* (Chicago: A. N. Marquis, 1960), 174; Hayes, *Iron Road to Empire*, 253.

43. Hayes, *Iron Road to Empire*, 254, 257–258.

44. *New York Times*, June 29, 1946.

45. Hayes, *Iron Road to Empire*, 261.

46. *New York Times*, June 29, 1946; Gregory L. Schneider, *Rock Island Requiem: The Collapse of a Mighty Fine Line* (Lawrence: University Press of Kansas, 2013), 19–20; Hayes, *Iron Road to Empire*, 263–265.

47. *New York Times*, November 23, 1946.

48. "Senator Reed Defers I.C.C. Investigation," *Railway Age* 123 (October 18, 1947): 666–667.

49. *Journal of Commerce*, January 6, 1948; "Bankruptcy Ends for Rock Island," *Railway Age* 124 (January 10, 1948): 128.

50. *New York Times*, April 20, 1951.

51. Arthur D. Dubin, *Some Classic Trains* (Milwaukee, WI: Kalmbach, 1964), 220–222.

52. Lloyd E. Stagner, *Rock Island Motive Power, 1933–1955* (Boulder, CO: Pruett, 1980), 190–191.

53. "The Spectacular 'Rockets,'" *Railway Age*, October 13, 1952, 113.

54. Farrington, *Railroads of Today*, 246; *Chicago, Rock Island and Pacific Railroad Company Annual Report for the Year Ending December 31, 1949*, 10; Hayes, *Iron Road to Empire*, 286; *Des Moines (IA) Register*, March 19, 1952.

55. Stagner, *Rock Island Motive Power*, 155–156.

56. Stagner, *Rock Island Motive Power*, 157.

57. Willard V. Anderson, "Rebirth of a Railroad," *Trains* 8 (December 1947): 24.

58. *Atlantic (IA) News-Telegraph*, September 14, 1953; *Wall Street Journal*, April 20, 1953; H. Roger Grant, ed., *Iowa Railroads: The Essays of Frank P. Donovan, Jr.* (Iowa City: University of Iowa Press, 2000), 196.

59. *Report to the Security Holders, July 1, 1948*, 6; *Manual of Information for Use of Guests on Investors' Special, Chicago-Dallas and Return, March 16, 17 and 18, 1955*, 13, 162; *Rock Island Lines News Digest* 11 (October 1952): 15; "How Motorola 2-Way Radio Blankets the Rock Island," *Railway Age*, October 13, 1952, 26–27; *Chicago, Rock Island and Pacific Railroad Company, 1949 Annual Report*, 3, 9–10.

With its sprawling system, the Rock Island maintained a variety of freight-car repair tracks and shops. Minor repairs could be made at thirty locations, scattered from Amarillo, Texas, to Manly, Iowa. All of these facilities were outdoors except the one at El Dorado, Arkansas, which was protected by an unenclosed roof. General or heavy repairs took place at Biddle (Little Rock), Arkansas; Blue Island, Illinois; El Reno, Oklahoma; and Kansas City, Kansas. While Blue Island workers benefited from an enclosed work space, the other three had only roof protection from the elements. During the 1950s other peer roads had similar facilities.

60. H. Roger Grant, *The North Western: A History of the Chicago & North Western Railway System* (DeKalb: Northern Illinois University Press, 1996), 177–178; "Plans for the 'Greatest Railroad Show' Well Laid," *Railway Age* 124 (1948): 853; *Seeing Rock Island at the Chicago Railroad Fair, 1949* (Chicago: Chicago, Rock Island & Pacific Railroad, 1949).

61. Hayes, *Iron Road to Empire*, 287–288; *New York Times*, July 9, 1950.

62. Hayes, *Iron Road to Empire*, 290; *New York Times*, July 14, July 16, 1951.

63. *Chicago, Rock Island and Pacific Railroad Company, 1949 Annual Report*; *Moody's Manual of Investments American and Foreign: Transportation* (New York: Moody's Investors Service, 1953), 193.

64. H. Roger Grant, *John W. Barriger III: Railroad Legend* (Bloomington: Indiana University Press, 2018), 115.

65. Interview with George Durbala, September 29, 2005, hereafter cited as Durbala interview.

66. Grant, *John W. Barriger III*, 114.

67. Nancy Ford, "He Didn't Know It Couldn't Be Done," *Trains & Travel* 13 (February 1953): 18–21; "Frozen Foods," *Railway Age*, October 13, 1952, 159–160; Beebe and Clegg, *Trains We Rode*, 696.

68. Grant, *John W. Barriger III*, 114.

69. John W. Barriger, "Rock Island," August 10, 1973, in Barriger papers.

70. Butler, "John D. Farrington," 142; Durbala interview.

6. Saving the Rock

1. *St. Louis Post-Dispatch*, October 27, 1996; H. Craig Miner, "Downing B. Jenks," in *Railroads in the Age of Regulation, 1900–1980*, ed. Keith L. Bryant Jr. (New York: Facts On File, 1988), 235–236; H. Craig Miner, *The Rebirth of the Missouri Pacific, 1956–1983* (College

Station: Texas A&M University Press, 1983), 45–46.

2. Russell F. Moore, ed., *Who's Who in Railroading in North America* (New York: Simmons-Boardman, 1964), 266; Miner, *Rebirth of the Missouri Pacific*, 46.

3. Miner, "Downing B. Jenks," 235; H. Roger Grant, *Visionary Railroader: Jervis Langdon, Jr. and the Transportation Revolution* (Bloomington: Indiana University Press, 2008), 123.

4. Miner, "Downing B. Jenks," 237; Miner, *Rebirth of the Missouri Pacific*, 49; "New BSA President," *Scouting* 65 (September 1977): 6.

5. Miner, *Rebirth of the Missouri Pacific*, 47.

6. "Sky Is the Limit as Executive Views Future of Rock Island Lines and Railroad Industry," *Rock Island News Digest* (November 1954): 13–16.

7. William C. Hoenig, interview, May 30, 2018, hereafter cited as Hoenig interview.

8. "Sky Is the Limit," 14–16; H. Roger Grant, "John W. Barriger's Super Railroads," *Classic Trains* 20 (Summer 2019): 46–53.

9. John Sherman Porter, ed., *Moody's Transportation Manual* (New York: Moody's Investors Service, 1959), 701; Donald Duke and Edmund Keilty, *RDC: The Budd Rail Diesel Car* (San Marino, CA: Golden West Books, 1990), 217–220; Steve Allen Goen, *"Down South" on the Rock Island: A Color Pictorial* (La Mirada, CA: Four Way West, 2002), 6.

During the 1950s the Rock Island continued its post–World War II quest to end money-losing passenger trains. One contentious cutback took place on the Arkansas Division and involved a feud between the railroad and the Louisiana Public Service Commission (LPSC). Management sought to terminate the daily motor train between Little Rock and Winnfield, Louisiana. Initially it won permission from the Arkansas Public Service Commission for abandonment of the Arkansas segment, and on November 11, 1954, service ended between Little Rock, Fordyce, and El Dorado. Regulators in Baton Rouge assumed that the company planned to continue the train between Winnfield and El Dorado, allowing passengers to connect with the Missouri Pacific for Little Rock. They were mistaken. In an act of spite, the Rock Island terminated its Louisiana service "in the middle of nowhere" at Junction City, Louisiana, sixteen miles south of El Dorado, adhering to the LPSC's refusal to grant an abandonment. A new wye permitted the turning of its motor trains at this remote location. Amazingly, ridership did not evaporate, largely because the train connected with the Illinois Central at Ruston and the Kansas City Southern at Winnfield. Finally the LPSC permitted the takeoff, and the last run of what railfans dubbed the "*Louisiana Rocket*" occurred on February 28, 1958. See Goen, "*Down South" on the Rock Island*, 6, 16.

10. *The Rocket* (February 1956): 10–11; "What's New about the Jet Rocket," *Modern Railroads* 11 (April 1956): 150–151, 153, 155–156, 158.

11. Bill Marvel, *The Rock Island Line* (Bloomington: Indiana University Press, 2013), 126–127; H. Roger Grant, *Railroads and the American People* (Bloomington: Indiana University Press, 2012), 90; Tom Brugman to author, January 8, 2019.

The Rock Island acquired a set of experimental Aerotrains built in 1955 by EMD at La Grange, IL, for main-line service on the New York Central, Pennsylvania, and Union Pacific Railroads. But their poor riding qualities and high interior noise levels prompted their withdrawal. In November 1958 Aerotrains became part of the Rock Island's suburban fleet, joining that futuristic-looking *Jet Rocket*. These new acquisitions performed adequately in the short-distance suburban territory, where relatively low speeds dominated. After the company received twenty double-deck, push-pull commuter cars, the Aerotrains were retired in April 1965. The following year the Rock Island donated a train (locomotive and two coaches) each to the National Railroad Museum in Green Bay, WI, and the National Museum of Transportation in Saint Louis, MO. *The Rocket* 25 (November–December 1966): 5.

12. The Rock Island coined the Winear name, a combination of *Win* for Winterset and *ear* for Earlham. The place was merely a junction point, but the name appeared in Des Moines Division operating timetables.

13. "Rock Island Lines Removed or Sold since January 1, 1936," January 1, 1974 map in possession of author; *Moody's Transportation Manual*, 1959, 699.

14. A through-route is one over which a shipment can move on one bill of lading at a single rate over two or more carriers. An open tariff is one on file with the ICC that can be used by any shipper, including common carrier trucking firms.

15. John S. Gallagher Jr., "Even Highway Trailers Are Going by Rail," *Trains and Travel* 12 (August 1951): 24–27; David J. De Boer, *Piggyback and Containers: A History of Rail Intermodal on America's Steel Highway* (San Marino, CA: Golden West Books, 1992), 23; Hoenig interview.

For several decades RIMT also operated two bus routes. One provided connections between Peoria and Bureau, Illinois, for passengers using the *Golden State Limited*. The other provided feeder service between the Rock Island station at Owatonna and Rochester, Minnesota. This allowed the railroad to serve the famed Mayo Clinic in Rochester.

16. *Moody's Transportation Manual, 1959*, 706; John Sherman Porter, ed., *Moody's Transportation Manual* (New York: Moody's Investors Service, 1961), 1012.

17. Theodore Desch, interview, October 9, 2006, hereafter cited as Desch interview.

18. Gregory L. Schneider, *Rock Island Requiem: The Collapse of a Mighty Fine Line* (Lawrence: University Press of Kansas, 2013), 34; "Ben Heineman's Shrewd Poker Game," *Forbes* 94 (September 1, 1964): 20.

19. Dan Rottenberg, "The Last Run of the Rock Island Line," *Chicago Magazine*, September 1984, 197; *New York Times*, August 16, 1990; Harry M. Petrakis and David B. Weber, *Henry Crown: The Life and Times of the Colonel, Book One* (Chicago: Henry Crown, 1998), 39.

20. See Petrakis and Weber, *Henry Crown, Book One*.

21. Rottenberg, "Last Run of the Rock Island Line," 197; Schneider, *Rock Island Requiem*, 27; *New York Times*, August 16, 1990.

22. Petrakis and Weber, *Henry Crown, Book Two*, 28.

23. Schneider, *Rock Island Requiem*, 34–35; Miner, *Rebirth of the Missouri Pacific*, 47–49.

24. Miner, *Rebirth of the Missouri Pacific*, 48–49; Hoenig interview.

25. *Rock Island Lines Annual Report 1960*, 6, 11.

26. Russell F. Moore, ed., *Who's Who in Railroading in North America* (New York: Simmons-Boardman, 1959), 330–331; *Arizona Republic* (Phoenix), June 14, 1974; Schneider, *Rock Island Requiem*, 40; *Railway Age* 150 (January 23, 1961): 33.

27. Desch interview.

28. De Boer, *Piggyback and Containers*, 67–71.

29. Edd H. Bailey, *A Life with the Union Pacific: The Autobiography of Edd H. Bailey* (Saint Johnsbury, VT: Saltillo, 1989), 129–130.

30. Grant, *Visionary Railroader*, chap. 1.

31. Grant, *Visionary Railroader*, chap. 2.

32. Grant, *Visionary Railroader*, 59–62, 70.

33. Grant, *Visionary Railroader*, 71–106.

34. Grant, *Visionary Railroader*, 103.

35. Grant, *Visionary Railroader*, 103–105.

36. George H. Durbala, interview, September 29, 2005, hereafter cited as Durbala interview.

37. *Rock Island Lines News*, August 22, 1966; Grant, *Visionary Railroader*, 130.

38. Grant, *Visionary Railroader*, 133–135; *Rocket* 24 (March–April 1965): 9; Board of Directors' minutes, Chicago, Rock Island & Pacific Railroad Collections, University of Oklahoma Libraries, Western History Collections, box 64.

Two top officials whom Langdon pushed out before they had reached retirement age were Oscar Limestall, vice president of operations, and Eldon Tharp, vice president of traffic.

39. "Operating Department Reorganized," *Rocket* 24 (May–June 1965): 11.

40. Durbala interview; "New GP-35 Diesels Arrive," *Rocket* 24 (May–June 1965): 16; *Rocket* 24 (November–December 1965): 16; *Chicago, Rock Island and Pacific Railroad Company, 1965 Annual Report*, 4, 11–12.

41. "TOFC: Rock Island Aims at a 100% Increase," *Railway Age* 159 (October 25, 1965): 36–37; *Annual Report Rock Island Lines, 1969*, 7–8; "From Chicago to Des Moines to Kansas City on the Rock Island Lines, 1-26-69," in possession of author.

42. *Annual Report Rock Island Lines, 1969*, 4.

43. "Jervis Langdon Remarks about the CRIP-UP Merger Attempt in Conversation with TED [Theodore Edward Desch]," July 10, 1998, in possession of author; Frank Koval, interview, September 9, 1988.

44. Richard Saunders Jr., *Merging Lines: American Railroads, 1900–1970* (DeKalb: Northern Illinois University Press, 2001), 329; Don L. Hofsommer, *The Southern Pacific, 1901–1985* (College Station: Texas A&M University Press, 1986), 266–268; Gus Welty, ed., *Era of the Giants: The New Railroad Merger Movement* (Omaha, NE: Simmons-Boardman, 1982), 90–91.

45. Thomas H. Ploss, *The Nation Pays Again: The Demise of the Milwaukee Road, 1928–1986* (n.p.: privately printed, 1986), 123.

46. Grant, *Visionary Railroader*, 155.

47. Dan Cordtz, "The Fight for the Rock Island," *Fortune* 73 (June 1966): 141.

48. Grant, *Visionary Railroader*, 156.

49. H. Roger Grant, *The North Western: A History of the Chicago & North Western System* (DeKalb: Northern Illinois University Press, 1996), 213–214; Cordtz, "Fight for the Rock Island," 141.

50. Grant, *Visionary Railroader*, 158; *Merger Messenger*, February 1, 1966.

51. Grant, *Visionary Railroader*, 158–159; Bailey, *Life with the Union Pacific*, 129.

52. Hoenig interview.

53. Jervis Langdon Jr. to Merle M. Miller, January 10, 1966, Chicago, Rock Island & Pacific Railroad Collections, University of Oklahoma Libraries, Western History Collections, box 94.

54. "Rock Island Lines: Where the Action Is," n.d., in possession of author.

55. "RSMA Seminar, Knickerbocker Hotel, Chicago, Ill.," September 1966, in possession of author.

56. Grant, *Visionary Railroader*, 149–150.

57. "Freight Trains Adopt the Space Age," *Railway Age* 161 (August 8–August 15, 1966): 11; "Joint Operation Set Up by RI, EL," *Railway Age* 164 (April 22, 1968): 12; William J. Dixon, interview, February 25, 2006, hereafter cited as Dixon interview.

58. *Rock Island Lines 1965 Annual Report*, 5.

59. *Chicago, Rock Island and Pacific Railroad Company 1964 Annual Report*, 8; "Sleepers Discontinued," *Rocket* 24 (July–August 1965): 14; "Snack-Beverage Cars Put on Trains," *Rocket* 24 (July–August 1965): 14.

60. *Chicago, Rock Island and Pacific Railroad Company 1964 Annual Report*, 8; "RI Plans Revision of Passenger Operations," *Railway Age* 160 (April 4, 1966): 7; *Wall Street Journal*, October 12, 1966; *Des Moines Register*, March 31, 1967, April 10, 1967.

61. Paul C. Nelson, "Rise and Decline of the Rock Island Passenger Train in the 20th Century," *Annals of Iowa* 41 (Fall 1971): 739–740.

62. "Golden State Makes Final Run," *Rocket* 27 (March–April, 1968): 12–13.

63. Nelson, "Rise and Decline of the Rock Island Passenger Train in the 20th Century," 751–53; *Des Moines Register*, June 25, 1969; "Train Run Ends," *Rocket* 30 (November–December 1970): 15.

64. Marvel, *Rock Island Line*, 131; *Rock Island Lines Annual Report, 1971*, 11; Richard Saunders Jr., *Main Lines: Rebirth of the North American Railroads, 1970–2002* (DeKalb: Northern Illinois University Press, 2003), 56; "Harold

Krewer on the Last Days of the Quad Cities and Peoria Rockets," *Rock Island Reporter* 21 (January 2019): 12–13.

65. "From Chicago to Des Moines to Kansas City on the Rock Island Lines, 1-26-69"; Anthony Haswell, "My Ride on the Rock," *Trains* 43 (March 1983): 39.

66. "Suburban Service Upgraded," *Rocket* 24 (May–June 1965): 12; Grant, *North Western*, 203; Robert P. Olmsted and Joe McMillan, *The 5:10 to Suburbia: Chicago's Suburban Railroads, 1960–1975* (n.p.: privately printed, 1975), 79.

67. *Rock Island Lines Annual Report, 1966,* 5.

68. Grant, *Visionary Railroader*, 164.

69. *New York Times*, September 15, 1970.

70. Dixon interview; Moore, *Who's Who in Railroading in North America, 1964,* 136; "W. J. Dixon Appointed Industrial Engineer," *B&O Magazine* 48 (October 1963): 3.

71. E. Ray Lickty, interview, October 21, 2005; Grant, *Visionary Railroader*, 82–89.

72. Frederick C. Osthoff, ed., *Who's Who in Railroading in North America* (New York: Simmons-Boardman, 1968), 131; Schneider, *Rock Island Requiem*, 98.

73. Hoenig interview; *Rock Island Lines Annual Report, 1970,* 4.

74. *Rock Island Lines Annual Report, 1970,* 13; *Rock Island Lines Annual Report, 1971,* 8; *Rock Island Lines Annual Report, 1972,* 7; *Rock Island Annual Report 1973,* 9.

75. *Rock Island Lines Annual Report 1973,* 9; Desch interview.

76. *Moody's Transportation Manual* (New York: Moody's Investors Service, 1974), 814–815; Neil E. Harl, *The Farm Debt Crisis of the 1980s* (Ames: Iowa State University Press, 1990), 13; Schneider, *Rock Island Requiem*, 130–131.

77. Theodore E. Desch, "The Rock Island Merger Case: A Bureaucratic Debacle," Rock Island Technical Society, Naperville, Illinois, April 29, 1987, in possession of author; Schneider, *Rock Island Requiem*, 97.

78. Desch, "Rock Island Merger Case."

79. Desch, "Rock Island Merger Case"; Frank N. Wilner, *Railroad Mergers: History, Analysis, Insight* (Omaha, NE: Simmons-Boardman Books, 1997), 206–208; Saunders, *Main Lines*, 19; Schneider, *Rock Island Requiem*, 142–143.

80. Desch, "Rock Island Merger Case"; Saunders, *Main Lines*, 19; Jim Farrell to author, January 9, 2019.

81. Thomas G. Hoback to author, June 6, 2018; Hoenig interview; Paul D. Schneider,

"The Rock," *Trains* 65 (March 2005): 34; J. David Ingles, "How Many Ways Can You Spell Rock Island?" *Classic Trains* 19 (Winter 2018): 58–61.

82. Hoenig interview; H. Roger Grant, *John W. Barriger III: Railroad Legend* (Bloomington: Indiana University Press, 2018), 182.

83. Paul Schneider, "In the Violet Hour," *Trains* 42 (March 1983): 23, 28.

84. *The Great Railway Crisis: An Administrative History of the United States Railway Association* (Washington, DC: National Academy of Public Administration, 1978), 391; *Wall Street Journal*, February 5, 1975.

Money demands made to the USRA by financially troubled railroads led Congress to pass the Railroad Revitalization and Regulatory Reform Act, or 4R Act, in 1976. This measure provided emergency aid, and it supported an assessment of the long-term needs of the industry so that federal funds could be spent wisely. This congressional action did much to stabilize the industry.

85. Schneider, *Rock Island Requiem*, 135–136; Robert M. Bleiberg, "Over the Long Haul: A Chronicle of Railroad Ups and Downs," *Barron's*, October 22, 1979, 7.

86. *Who's Who in Railroading and Rail Transit* (New York: Simmons-Boardman, 1977), 192; Schneider, *Rock Island Requiem*, 140; John F. Stover, *History of the Illinois Central Railroad* (New York: Macmillan, 1975), 487.

87. Stover, *History of the Illinois Central Railroad*, 492–493.

88. Schneider, *Rock Island Requiem*, 139; David J. DeBoer, interview, June 27, 2016; D. F. Brosnan, interview, November 16, 2018, hereafter cited as Brosnan interview.

89. "An interview with John Ingram," February 7, 2004, Railroad Executive Oral History Program, John W. Barriger III National Railroad Library, Saint Louis, MO; *New York Times*, April 27, 1974.

90. John W. Ingram, "Government and the Midwest Railroads: Notes on the Demise of the Chicago, Rock Island and Pacific Railroad Company," 19 (Spring 1980): 29; Don L. Hofsommer, *Steel Trails of Hawkeyeland: Iowa's Railroad Experience* (Bloomington: Indiana University Press, 2005), 228; Dr. Paul H. Banner, untitled speech, Chicago, IL, September 24, 1976, in possession of author, hereafter cited as Banner untitled speech, September 24, 1976.

91. *A Report to the Stockholders of the Chicago, Rock Island and Pacific Railroad Company,*

1974 and the Quarter Ended March 31, 1976;
Schneider, *Rock Island Requiem*, 141–142;
James A. Ward, "On the Mark: The History
and Symbolism of Railroad Emblems,"
Railroad History 153 (Autumn 1985): 70.

92. Ingram, "Government and the
Midwest Railroads," 30–31.

93. Brosnan interview.

94. Brosnan interview.

95. Dr. Paul H. Banner, speech before the
American Paper Institute, October 24, 1975,
in possession of author.

96. *Chicago Tribune*, January 10, 2012,
November 1, 1990; Schneider, *Rock Island
Requiem*, 155.

97. Ingram, "Government and the
Midwest Railroads," 31.

98. Schneider, *Rock Island Requiem*,
158–159.

99. Haswell, "My Ride on the Rock," 39;
E. W. King Jr., "Disaster du Jour, and Other
Stories," *Trains* 46 (June 1986): 32.

100. Haswell, "My Ride on the Rock," 10.

101. Schneider, *Rock Island Requiem*, 133;
Gregory L. Schneider, "Saving a Piece of the
Rock: The State of Iowa and the Railroad
Problem, 1972–1974," *Annals of Iowa* 73 (Fall
2014): 353, 359.

102. Dr. Paul H. Banner, undated and
unidentified speech, in possession of author.

103. *Annual Report, 1974, and the Quarter
Ended March 31, 1976*, 3; John Baskin Harper,
"Rock Island Short-Haul Minitrain Experi-
ment," *Rock Island Digest* 9 (1989): 1–19.

About the time that the Rock Island
was in its death throes, railroad executives
contemplated the economic value of short,
fast, and frequent freight trains. They might
provide a way to compete successfully with
trucks on short-haul routes. In 1974 Illinois
Central Gulf started "Slingshot" service
between Chicago and Saint Louis, and five
years later the Milwaukee Road tried its
"Sprint" trains between Chicago and the
Twin Cities.

104. *Moody's Transportation Manual* (New
York: Moody's Investors Service, 1977), 142.

105. *Traffic World*, November 3, 1975; *New
York Times*, September 19, 1975; Gus Welty,
ed., *Era of the Giants: The New Railroad Merger
Movement* (Omaha, NE: Simmons-Boardman,
1982), 93; Schneider, *Rock Island Requiem*, 165.

The most profitable of these
short-haul experimental trains involved
wheat movements from several stations in
Kansas to Hutchinson, producing operating

revenues of $560,694, and the next most
profitable involved hauling stone from Perch
Hill, Texas, to Dallas and yielded $137,560.

106. Schneider, *Rock Island Requiem*, 202;
David P. Morgan, "FarmRail Flak," *Trains* 38
(April 1978): 9–10.

107. Schneider, *Rock Island Requiem*, 211;
Dennis Opherman to author, November 23,
2018; *Gazette-Telegraph* (Colorado Springs,
CO), November 29, 1978.

In its 1979 annual report, the Southern Pacific made this statement: "Performance measures based on profitability
of new business, an improved system for
serving large national accounts, special
incentives and promotions such as the
successful 'Backhaul Bonanza' campaign,
and a more integrated approach to marketing, rail, truck and intermodal services
are among the main features of the new
program."

108. Schneider, *Rock Island Requiem*, 173–
174; Hofsommer, *Southern Pacific*, 282–283.

109. John W. Barriger IV, interview, June 19,
2018.

110. *Moody's Transportation Manual* (New
York: Moody's Investors Service, 1979), 131.

111. Grant, *North Western*, 223; Thomas
Koglin to author, October 23, 2018.

112. Schneider, *Rock Island Requiem*, 217.

113. Ingram, "Government and the Midwest Railroads," 35–36.

114. Seth H. Bramson, *Speedway to Sunshine:
The Story of the Florida East Coast Railway* (Buf-
falo, NY: Boston Mills, 2010), 149–153, 165;
Saunders, *Main Lines*, 135.

115. Schneider, *Rock Island Requiem*, 227.

116. *New York Times*, November 1, 1976;
Robert E. Bedingfield, *The Norfolk and Western
Strike of 1978* (Roanoke, VA: Norfolk & West-
ern Railway, 1979), 1–27.

117. Saunders, *Main Lines*, 136–137.

118. Ingram, "Government and the Midwest Railroads," 35.

119. Brosnan interview.

120. William D. Middleton, George M.
Smerk, and Roberta L. Diehl, eds. *Encyclope-
dia of North American Railroads* (Bloomington:
Indiana University Press, 2007), 226–227;
Banner, untitled speech, September 24, 1976.

121. Brosnan interview.

The Rock Island also maintained
offices about two blocks from La Salle Street
Station. The Information Systems Department occupied space in this building. These
employees did not need to relocate.

122. Schneider, *Rock Island Requiem*, 245; Judith Anderson to author, November 26, 2018.

123. Schneider, *Rock Island Requiem*, 245–249.

7. Liquidation and Legacy

1. George H. Drury, compiler, *The Historical Guide to North American Railroads* (Milwaukee, WI: Kalmbach Books, 1985), 139–140, 187, 229–231.

2. Richard Saunders Jr., *Main Lines: Rebirth of the North American Railroads, 1970–2002* (DeKalb: Northern Illinois University, 2003), 179; Gregory L. Schneider, *Rock Island Requiem: The Collapse of a Mighty Fine Line* (Lawrence: University Press of Kansas, 2013), 238–244, 254; "Rock Island Gets Nod to Abandon System except Saleable Lines," *Traffic World*, June 9, 1980, 23.

Early in October, bankruptcy judge Frank McGarr ordered Trustee William Gibbons to terminate top management officials, including John Ingram.

3. H. Roger Grant, *The North Western: A History of the Chicago & North Western Railway System* (DeKalb: Northern Illinois University Press, 1996), 232–233.

4. *New York Times*, May 23, 1980.

5. Schneider, *Rock Island Requiem*, 260–264, 277–280.

6. Richard J. Lane, "Liquidating the Rock," *Railroad History* 181 (Autumn 1999): 106–107; Frank N. Wilner, *Railroad Mergers: History, Analysis, Insight* (Omaha, NE: Simmons-Boardman Books, 1997), 210.

Sale of the Tucumcari line between Saint Louis and Santa Rosa, New Mexico, had been negotiated and approved by Judge McGarr prior to his liquidation order.

7. Lane, "Liquidating the Rock," 109–110.

8. Lane, "Liquidating the Rock," 109; Don L. Hofsommer, *Grand Trunk Corporation: Canadian National Railways in the United States, 1971–1992* (East Lansing: Michigan State University Press, 1995), 96.

9. Lane, "Liquidating the Rock," 111; George H. Durbala, interview, September 29, 2005.

10. Lane, "Liquidating the Rock," 111; Schneider, *Rock Island Requiem*, 289.

11. Lane, "Liquidating the Rock," 111; Schneider, *Rock Island Requiem*, 287–292; *Wall Street Journal*, October 34, 1984; *Washington Post*, October 24, 1988; *New York Times*, April 21, 1984, October 16, 1985, October 25, 1988.

The Whirlpool Corporation ultimately acquired Maytag. That transaction took place in 2006, resulting in the closing of the Maytag plant in Newton, Iowa.

12. Charles Wolfe and Kip Lornell, *The Life and Legend of Leadbelly* (New York: Harper Perennial, 1992), 126, 258; Robert Cochran, "Ride It Like You're Flyin': 'The Rock Island Line,'" *Arkansas Historical Quarterly* 56 (Summer 1997): 202, 224, 226.

Lonnie Donegan, the popular British skiffle music artist of the 1950s and 1960s, used a version of "The Rock Island Line" that had little to do with the actual Rock Island Railroad.

13. Cochran, "Ride It Like You're Flyin'," 201–202, 229; Nolan Porterfield, *Last Cavalier: The Life and Times of John A. Lomax, 1867–1948* (Urbana: University of Illinois Press, 1996), 333–334.

In a study of the musical group the Weavers, it is suggested that Clarence Wilson, a member of Rock Island Colored Booster Quartet, which consisted of shop workers in Little Rock, originated the Rock Island Line song. See Jesse Jarnow, *Wasn't That a Time: The Weavers, the Blacklist, and the Battle for the Soul of America* (New York: Da Capo, 2018), 162.

14. *Rock Island Trail*, Republic Production, 1950.

15. *New York Times*, May 19, 1968.

Congressman Mitchell represented the portion of Chicago that contained La Salle Street Station and other Rock Island Railroad facilities.

16. Dennis S. Nordin, *The New Deal's Black Congressman: A Life of Arthur Wergs Mitchell* (Columbia: University of Missouri Press, 1997), 249–250, 254–255; Catherine A. Barnes, *Journey from Jim Crow: The Desegregation of Southern Transit* (New York: Columbia University Press, 1983), 1; *Mitchell v. United States et al.*, 313, 577, 89.

17. Barnes, *Journey from Jim Crow*, 21–24; Nordin, *New Deal's Black Congressman*, 257.

18. Barnes, *Journey from Jim Crow*, 24.

19. *Mitchell v. United States et al.*; *Washington Post*, March 14, 1941; *New York Times*, April 29, 1941; Barnes, *Journey from Jim Crow*, 29–31.

20. James Norman Hall, *My Island Home: An Autobiography* (New York: Little, Brown and Company, 1952), 7–8.

21. Hall, *My Island Home*, 9, 17–18.

22. Tom Brugman to author, January 14, 2019; David Engle to author, February 13, 2019.

23. See Jim David, *The Rock Island Trail: Echoes of the Past* (Pekin, IL: Robin Thompson Charm School, 2007).

24. "Rock Island Depot in Atlantic, Iowa," National Register of Historic Places Registration Form, January 1994.

Hundreds of former Rock Island depots have been destroyed. The list of casualties includes the iconic La Salle Street Station. It was last used for railroad purposes, namely for commuters, in 1981, and soon thereafter it was demolished. A modest depot south of the razed terminal continues to serve commuter runs on Metra's Rock Island District to Joliet. Area redevelopment has led to the construction of a high-end commercial complex on the former station site, and additional structures have appeared on the adjoining land between Congress Parkway and Roosevelt Road.

25. Greg Smith and Karen-Lee Ryan, compilers, *700 Great Rail-Trails: A National Directory* (Washington, DC: Rails-to-Trails Conservancy, 1995), 27; J. David Conrad, compiler, *The Steam Locomotive Directory of North America, Volume One: Eastern United States and Canada* (Polo, IL: Transportation Trails, 1988), 50, 291; Bob Lipka to author, October 17, 2018.

Railroad donations to public bodies can become complicated. The story of No. 886, née No. 887, is a case in point:

> The story is told from the late 50's or early sixties that the City of Peoria, Illinois requested Rock Island's 886 as it was the last passenger steam engine out of Peoria. Unfortunately by the time the request got to the proper authorities at the railroad 886 had been scrapped. 887 was given a cleanup and fresh paint as well as new number boards. 887 from then on would be known as 886. After leaving the engine shop in Peoria looking all shiny and new, the engine was moved up the Peoria to Rock Island branch and resided in Lower Glen Oak Park on Perry Street. As the neighborhood deteriorated over the years vandals started taking small parts. The Peoria Park District moved 886 to Detweiler Golf Course within a few yards of the Peoria to Chicago line where it resided for years fenced. Finally the Park District lost interest in maintaining the steamer. Eventually Wheels O' Time museum acquired the steamer and took it up the river bluff on the back of a flatbed. It is within a couple miles of the old Peoria to Rock Island branch. (Bob Lipka to author, October 17, 2018)

26. *Rock Island Reporter* 21 (January 2019): 63–64, 70–72.

27. John W. Barriger III photo scrapbook, John W. Barriger III National Railroad Library, Saint Louis, MO.

Farrington Park can be reached by a recent rails-to-trails pathway, Rock Island Spur Trail. This linear parkway connects with the Katy Trail, a mostly trans-Missouri corridor, using the abandoned Saint Louis line of the Missouri-Kansas-Texas Railroad.

28. Bill Metzger and Matt Van Hattem, "What Ever Happened to the Rock Island?" *Trains* 69 (March 2009): 50–51; Fred W. Frailey, *Southern Pacific's Blue Streak Merchandise: Six Decades of the Great American Freight Train* (Waukesha, WI: Kalmbach Books, 1991), 114–115; Dan Sabin to author, March 1, 2019.

Since 1982 the number of operators of former Rock Island lines has declined, the result of corporate mergers and failed shortlines and other abandonments. Some trackage, too, is out of service. Initially there were thirty-nine entities involved in the Rock Island carve-up.

29. Jim McClellan, *My Life with Trains: Memoir of a Railroader* (Bloomington: Indiana University Press, 2007), 70.

30. Kent Shoemaker, interview, November 4, 2005; Fred W. Frailey, "Behold the Life after Death of the Rock Island Lines," *Trains* 71 (February 2011): 15.

INDEX

H. ROGER GRANT is Kathryn and Calhoun Lemon Professor of History at Clemson University. He is author of numerous books, including *Visionary Railroader, John W. Barriger III, Railroaders without Borders, Railroads and the American People*, and *Transportation and the American People*.

Milton Keynes UK
Ingram Content Group UK Ltd.
UKHW050844300723
425972UK00002B/42